Bread Machine Cookbook

Discover 650 + Tasty and No-Fuss Recipes To Have Everyday Homemade Fresh Bread For You And Your Family. Mastering All Baking Secrets With This Essential Guide For Beginners

By

Natalie Allen

Table of Contents

Gluten-Free Bread**Errore. Il segnalibro non è definito.**

Classic and Whole-Wheat Breads _____ 201

Introduction

*B*read is a food that is consumed every day. Of course, you can find bread in every grocery store but lately that bread is not as healthy as it was a few years ago. That is the main reason why you need to start preparing your bread at home!

This bread machine and the instructions present in this book are everything that you need to learn how to prepare something so healthy and delicious. The recipes that will be cooked in here are also healthy, easy to follow, and do not spike your sugar levels or assist you gain weight. On the contrary, this homemade bread recipes will help you lose weight while being completely healthy and surfeit.

The instructions in this book will guide you as well. I know that it is not easy to start learning something new, especially when this is a relatively new machine. The technology is advancing as days pass and you need to take the first step. Gladly, this book will assist you and help you learn how to make the best options.

The Infamous Bread Machine – Everything that you need to know

Bread is one of our staple foods and is eaten almost all the time. We rely on the supermarket or the bakery to make purchases - but the trend is increasingly towards self-baking.

The quality of bread plays an important role for many: It should be as fresh as possible, free from additives and it should taste good.

While I like the concept of making bread entirely from scratch, the lag time between realizing that warm carbs are what's missing in my life and actually holding a freshly-baked brioche can be significant. Many recipes involving yeast require kneading, refrigerating, or babysitting, making spur-of-the-moment bread out of the question. That is, unless, you have a bread machine.

Most bread machines require about 10 minutes of prep time, which is mostly spent measuring ingredients and putting them into a pan. After that's done, you pick a setting, turn on the machine, and three or four hours later you (ideally) have a warm, golden-brown loaf. But with so many bread machines on the market, how do you choose the right one? Well, my friend, you have made the right choice and finally you have chosen the right one – our bread machine!

Is this bread machine worth it?

This depends on a number of factors, including how much bread you eat, how much time you want to spend making bread, and what kind of bread you're looking to get.

If you're looking for a good crusty loaf of rustic-style bread—something thick and hearty—a bread machine may is not your best bet. Countertop machines won't get as hot as your oven will, so most machines tend to make something closer to your standard sandwich bread. However, if you find yourself buying several loaves a week from the store, and would love to spend less money, or have fresher bread without the hassle and time involved in baking, a bread machine, even a relatively nice one, can end up paying for itself in a short time.

The advantages

Using a bread machine has a number of advantages over bread that is bought or baked in the oven:

- *The bread is always fresh*

- *The bread only contains the ingredients that you put in yourself*

- *There are no additives or baking additives*

- *The bread can be made according to individual taste*

The bread machine won't heat up your kitchen

When summer comes and the weather turns sweltering, your bread machine helps keep your kitchen comfortable. Completely self-enclosed, it stays cool to the touch, even when baking. So, go ahead, simmer up some soup. Bake a fresh-fruit dessert; peach cobbler is always welcome. Give your regular oven a vacation this summer – and keep your cool!

The bread machine simmers and stirs and finishes dishes all by itself

The machine's jam cycle does a great job with things like hot artichoke dip (above). Put the ingredients into the pan; press start; come back an hour later to creamy, simmering dip, ready to serve to your arriving guests. And how about a main course? Try sloppy joes or chili.

If You Are New to Bread Baking

If you have no experience and don't have the time to learn but you still want freshly baked bread, then this is it! The bread machine will make you into a baker quickly. You can, save money, save time, be in control of your diet (you know what you are putting into your body) and enjoy fresh bread it's plain and simple.

Clean, Tidy and Easy to Operate

*B*aking bread is an ancient craft thousands of years old and requires us and our kitchen to devote ourselves to the crafts. When we finish working on the dough, instead of resting and patiently waiting for the bread to come out of the oven, we find ourselves cleaning up the kitchen, flour and bits of dough off the counter, dishes in the sink and all that jazz.

The bread machine makes the whole process so much easier.

All you have to do is put the ingredients in the bread machine, press a button, adjust the timer and that's it. The kitchen stays clean and all that's left to do is wait for the bread to be ready. hallelujah!

If you make bread on a daily basis and considering the intense Schedule that most of us maintain and know too well, this factor becomes very significant.

Timing – unlike a mixer, a bread machine will have built-in periods to stop mixing, allow for a rise, punch down the bread, and so on. Machines can also bake the bread mixers can't.

It teaches you how to make bread without it (although you won't want to do that at all, the machine is perfect)

If you have no experience and don't have the time to learn but you still want freshly baked bread, then this is it! The bread machine will make you into a baker quickly. You can, save money, save time, be in control of your diet (you know what you are putting into your body) and enjoy fresh bread it's plain and simple.

The Healthy Choice

Like anyone who makes bread own his own, making bread at home is a much healthier option than buying bread at a supermarket or even certain bakeries, where most bread is made with some degree of baking enhancements. When deciding what ingredients to put in your bread you can choose healthier ingredients, whether it's organic flour, whole wheat, gluten-free bread or whatever your diet restriction or preferences.

There is a great selection of cookbooks on the market designed especially for bread machines to help you achieve your bread golds.

The costs

In the case of the bread maker, the purchase costs are initially taken into account, but afterwards the operating costs are low.

You have the choice of either using ready-made bread mixes or mixing the ingredients yourself. The costs are then around 0.60 - 1.00 EUR for one bread, depending on how big the bread is to be and whether you use ready-made mixes or your ingredients.

The electricity consumption is extremely low, in most cases, the cost of the electricity required will be around 7-10 cents for the entire baking process.

The purchase of the bread maker is also financially worthwhile, depending on the price of the bread maker, the purchase will pay for itself after a short time.

Additional Uses for Bread Machine

This bread machine can allow additional uses beyond making bread from start to finish.

It can be used for the dough kneading, the dough can be made into rolls or buns and other uses that can surprise you such as making jam, rice dishes, yogurt, cake, sauces, soup and even scrambled eggs. Not that I necessarily recommend this route, but if for any reason your stove is out of order- it could be a valid alternative.

What you need to pay attention to leaning When you should clean it?

Ideally, you should clean it after every use. This means cleaning it after you've taken the loaf out. The bread maker must be cleaned after you've cooked something insufficiently. For example, under-cooked dough that contains eggs and butter will turn your machine into a bacteria factory if you don't clean it immediately.

You should clean the bread maker after you take it out of storage. After all, any dirt, grime, and debris on it will otherwise get into your food. Always clean a used bread maker after you buy it. Just because they sold it in the box doesn't mean they didn't touch it or try to make something in it.

Here are the steps for cleaning:

Step 1:

First, put the bread maker on its side. Sweep out the crumbs with a basting brush or paintbrush. Make no attempt to rinse the interior with water. You will destroy electrical components.. Don't try to brush them out with your hand, since it may be hot enough to burn you.

Use a clean paintbrush and sweep the flour residue and crumbs out of the unit. What if there is still moist dough? Don't try to scrape it out. You could damage the machine by doing that. Let it dry. Then remove it.

If there is liquid in the unit, such as when your dough was too watery or you spilled liquid egg whites, use a clean cloth to wipe it up. Note that this cloth shouldn't be used to clean the rest of the machine. Throw it in the washing machine.

Step 2:

The next step is cleaning the heating elements. Many people forget the need to do this, though flour and other grime on the heating elements are fire hazards. Others are afraid to clean the heating elements, since they're the most sensitive part of the bread maker. You can clean them.

- *Wipe them down with a moist cloth.*

- *Do not spray it with water, because you could short something out. It may require repeated passes to get clean.*

- *Don't push down or scrub hard on the heating elements. You could bend or detach them, though the heating elements are hard to replace or fix. That's why many people are afraid to clean them.*

- *This can be a good time to clean the outside of the unit. If you spilled baking mix on the outside of the unit, you could wipe it down with cleaning wipes.*

- *Don't spritz it with water or cleaning solutions. You probably want to wipe down the buttons with cleaning wipes. This will kill any germs left by your dirty hands as you pushed the buttons.*

Step 3:

The next step is cleaning the heating elements. Many people forget the need to do this, though flour and other grime on the heating elements are fire hazards. Others are afraid to clean the heating elements, since they're the most sensitive part of the bread maker. You can clean them. *Wipe them down with a moist cloth.*

Do not spray it with water, because you could short something out. It may require repeated passes to get clean.
Don't push down or scrub hard on the heating elements. You could bend or detach them, though the heating elements are hard to replace or fix. That's why many people are afraid to clean them.

This can be a good time to clean the outside of the unit. If you spilled baking mix on the outside of the unit, you can wipe it down with cleaning wipes.
Don't spritz it with water or cleaning solutions. You probably want to wipe down the buttons with cleaning wipes. This will kill any germs left by your dirty hands as you pushed the buttons.

Step 4:
 Clean the Bread Pan
The third step is cleaning the bread pan. This is the easiest part, and it is the step most people do regularly on their own. In some cases, you can clean it by running it through the dishwasher. However, not all bread pans are dishwasher safe.

- *Use a warm soapy rag and rinse it. Rinse it in clean water to wash away the soap residue.*

- *If the bread pan is not non-stick or the food sticks, anyway, use a sponge with a scrubber surface.*

- *Do not use a steel scrubbing sponge or stiff bristle brush that could scratch up the surface, giving food residue a place to hide and breed bacteria.*

- *Read the manual. This will tell you how to remove the mixing paddles and properly clean them. These may or may not be dishwasher safe, but they need to be cleaned.*

- *When you wash the mixing paddles, dough hook and other attachments, give them time to dry before you reassemble them.*

- *Ideally, they should be left to dry in an upright position. Letting everything dry helps prevent rust from forming inside your bread maker. And know that there isn't anything you can do once it starts to rust, though that makes it harder to scrub away food residue over time.*

Step 5:

Let everything dry before you put it back in the machine. This cleans away the food residue without creating a breeding ground for mold. However, you don't want to use harsh chemicals like bleach inside the bread machine or baking span. The most obvious reason is that this leaves toxic chemicals on a surface you use to make food. The other reason is that it will destroy the finish inside the bread machine that allows you to easily remove the loaf and evenly bake the bread. Spraying harsh chemicals inside the bread machine could short things out, too, just like a jet of water would.

Measurement Conversions

US STANDARD	US STANDARD (OUNCES)	METRIC (APPROXIMATE)
2 tablespoons	1 fl. oz.	30 mL
¼ cup	2 fl. oz.	60 mL
½ cup	4 fl. oz.	120 mL
1 cup	8 fl. oz.	240 mL
1½ cups	12 fl. oz.	355 mL
2 cups or 1 pint	16 fl. oz.	475 mL
4 cups or 1 quart	32 fl. oz.	1 L
1 gallon	128 fl. oz.	4 L

Volume Equivalent (Dry)

US STANDARD	METRIC (APPROXIMATE)
⅛ teaspoon	0.5 mL
¼ teaspoon	1 mL
½ teaspoon	2 mL
¾ teaspoon	4 mL
1 teaspoon	5 mL
1 tablespoon	15 mL
¼ cup	59 mL
⅓ cup	79 mL
½ cup	118 mL
⅔ cup	156 mL
¾ cup	177 mL
1 cup	235 mL
2 cups or 1 pint	475 mL
3 cups	700 mL
4 cups or 1 quart	1 L
½ gallon	2 L
1 gallon	4 L

Oven Temperatures

FAHRENHEIT (F)	CELSIUS (C) (APPROXIMATE)
250°F	120°C
300°F	150°C
325°F	165°C
350°F	180°C
375°F	190°C
400°F	200°C
425°F	220°C
450°F	230°C

Cheese & Italian Styled Breads

1) Italian Bread

Ingredients:

- Water - ⅔ cup
- Olive oil - 1 tbsp.
- Sugar - 1 tbsp.
- Salt - ¾ tsp.
- White bread flour - 2 cups
- Bread machine or instant yeast - 1 tsp.

Direction: PREP: 10 MINUTES OR LESS/MAKES 1 LOAF

- ✓ Preparing the Ingredients Add everything in the bread machine according to instructions.
- ✓ Select the Bake Cycle Select Basic/White bread and Light or Medium crust.
- ✓ Press Start. When done, remove the bread. Cool, slice, and serve.

2) Close-Grained Cheddar Cheese Bread

Ingredients: 1 POUND LOAF

- Lukewarm milk ½ cup
- Plain bread flour 1 ½ cups
- Salt ⅔ tsp
- Sugar ½ tbsp
- Extra-sharp cheddar, grated ½ cup
- Parmesan cheese, grated 6 tsp
- Instant yeast ¾ tsp

Direction: 3 hours and 40 minutes / Prep 5 minutes / Cook 3 hours 35 minutes

- ✓ Fill your bread maker with all of the ingredients in the precise sequence provided.
- ✓ Select the basic cycle setting and the soft crust function.
- ✓ When the bread is finished, turn it out onto a drying rack to cool before serving.
- ✓ Tip(s): After your bread machine has kneaded the dough for 10 minutes, quickly examine its consistency.
- ✓ If all is well, your dough should be mostly smooth, but slightly sticky.
- ✓ Add flour if it's too sticky, or milk if it's too chunky. If you wish to add a little extra bite to your bread, you can literally spice things up by adding between ½ to 1 tsp of tabasco sauce.
- ✓ This should be added last, after the yeast, but before you begin kneading.
- ✓ This bread goes especially well with rosemary.
- ✓ Feel free to season your fresh loaf with some while it is cooling down, or add it later as part of a sandwich.

3) Olive Bread

Ingredients: 1 POUND LOAF

- Lukewarm water ½ cup
- Extra-virgin olive oil ½ tbsp
- Plain bread flour 2 cups
- Salt 1 pinch
- Sugar 1 ¼ tbsp
- Bread machine yeast ¾ tbsp
- Pitted black olives, finely diced ½ cup

Direction: 2 hours and 10 minutes / Prep Time: 10 minutes / Cook Time: 2 hours

- ✓ Add the ingredients to the bread machine in the sequence stated above or as directed in the instruction manual for your bread maker.
- ✓ Do not add the olives in yet.
- ✓ Select the basic setting or wheat function, and the medium crust function.
- ✓ Add the diced olives when the machine signals that mix-in ingredients may be included.
- ✓ If your machine lacks this feature, add the olives following the first kneading cycle.
- ✓ When the bread is finished, flip it out onto a drying rack and allow it to cool slightly before serving.
- ✓ TIP(S): If your olives are in brine, be sure to pat them dry before dicing them and adding them into your bread mixture.

4) Traditional Italian Bread

Ingredients:

- 12 slice bread (1½ pounds)
- 1 cup water, at 80°F to 90°F
- 1½ tablespoons olive oil
- 1½ tablespoons sugar
- 1⅛ teaspoons salt
- 3 cups white bread flour
- 2⅔ cups white bread flour
- 1½ teaspoons bread machine or instant yeast

Direction: PREP: 10 MINUTES /MAKES 1 LOAF

- ✓ Preparing the Ingredients. Put the ingredients in your bread maker according to the manufacturer's instructions.
- ✓ Select the Bake Cycle Close the lid, Turn on the bread maker.
- ✓ Select the White / Basic setting, then select the dough size, select light or medium crust.
- ✓ Press start to start the cycle.
- ✓ When this is done, and the bread is baked, remove the pan from the machine.
- ✓ Let stand a few minutes.
- ✓ Remove the bread from the skillet and leave it on a wire rack to cool for at least 10 minutes.
- ✓ Slice and serve.
- ✓

5) Zesty Cheddar Bread

Ingredients:

- 12 slice bread (1½ pounds)
- 1 cup buttermilk
- ⅓ cup butter, melted
- 1 tablespoon sugar
- 2 tablespoons finely chopped chipotle chiles in adobo sauce (from 7-oz can)
- 2 eggs 2 cups all-purpose flour
- 1 cup shredded Cheddar cheese (4 oz)

- 2 teaspoons baking powder
- 1 teaspoon baking soda
- ½ teaspoon salt
  Direction: PREP: 10 MINUTES /MAKES 1 LOAF

- ✓ Preparing the Ingredients. Choose the size of loaf of your preference and then measure the ingredients.
- ✓ Add all of the ingredients mentioned previously in the list.
- ✓ Close the lid after placing the pan in the bread machine.
- ✓ Select the Bake Cycle Turn on the bread machine.
- ✓ Select the White/Basic setting, select the loaf size, and the crust color.
- ✓ Press start. When the breadmaker cycle is complete, carefully remove the pan from the machine and allow it to cool before serving.
- ✓ Remove the bread from the pan, put in a wire rack to Cool about 5 minutes.
- ✓ Serve warm

6) French Cheese Bread

Ingredients:

- 1 tsp sugar
- 2¼ tsp yeast
- 1¼ cup water
- 3 cups bread flour
- 2 tbsp. parmesan cheese
- 1 tsp garlic powder
- 1½ tsp salt
  Direction: PREP: 10 MINUTES /MAKES 14 SLICES

- ✓ Preparing the Ingredients In the order and at the temperature specified by the maker of your bread machine, add each ingredient to the bread machine.
- ✓ Select the Bake Cycle Close the lid, select the basic bread, medium crust setting on your bread machine, and press start.
- ✓ Take out the baked bread from the bread machine and allow it to cool on a cooling rack.
- ✓
- ✓

7) Romano Oregano Bread

Ingredients:

- 12 slice bread (1½ pounds)
- 1 cup lukewarm water
- 3 tablespoons sugar
- 1½ tablespoons olive oil
- 1 teaspoon table salt
- 1 tablespoon dried leaf oregano
- ½ cup cheese (Romano or Parmesan), freshly grated
- 3 cups white bread flour
- 2 teaspoons bread machine yeast
  Direction: PREP: 10 MINUTES /MAKES 1 LOAF

- ✓ Preparing the Ingredients. Choose the size of loaf of your preference and then measure the ingredients.
- ✓ Add all of the ingredients mentioned previously in the

list.
- ✓ Close the lid after placing the pan in the bread machine.
- ✓ Select the Bake Cycle Turn on the bread machine.
- ✓ Select the White/Basic setting, select the loaf size, and the crust color.
- ✓ Press start.
- ✓ When the breadmaker cycle is complete, carefully remove the pan from the machine and allow it to cool before serving.
- ✓ Remove the bread from the pan, put in a wire rack to Cool about 5 minutes.
- ✓ Slice

8) Jalapeno Cheese Bread

Ingredients:

- 3 cups bread flour
- 1½ tsp active dry yeast
- 1 cup water
- 2 tbsp. sugar
- 1 tsp salt
- ½ cup shredded cheddar cheese
- ¼ cup diced jalapeno peppers
  Direction: PREP: 10 MINUTES /MAKES 14 SLICES

- ✓ Preparing the Ingredients. In the order and at the temperature specified by the maker of your bread machine, add each ingredient to the bread machine.
- ✓ Select the Bake Cycle Close the lid, select the basic bread, medium crust setting on your bread machine, and press start.
- ✓ Take out the baked bread from the bread machine and allow it to cool on a cooling rack.
- ✓

9) Cheesy Chipotle Bread

Ingredients:

- 8 slice bread (1 pounds)
- ⅔ cup water, at 80°F to 90°F
- 1½ tablespoons sugar
- 1½ tablespoons powdered skim milk
- ¾ teaspoon salt
- ½ teaspoon chipotle chili powder
- 2 cups white bread flour
- ½ cup (2 ounces) shredded sharp Cheddar cheese
- ¾ teaspoon bread machine or instant yeast
  Direction: PREP: 10 MINUTES /MAKES 1 LOAF

- ✓ Preparing the Ingredients. Choose the size of loaf of your preference and then measure the ingredients.
- ✓ Add all of the ingredients mentioned previously in the list.
- ✓ Close the lid after placing the pan in the bread machine.
- ✓ Select the Bake Cycle Turn on the bread machine. Select the White/Basic setting, select the loaf size, and the crust color.
- ✓ Press start.
- ✓ When the breadmaker cycle is complete, carefully

- remove the pan from the machine and allow it to cool before serving.
- ✓ Remove the bread from the pan, put in a wire rack to Cool about 5 minutes.
- ✓ Slice

10) **Cheddar Cheese Bread**
Ingredients:

- 1 cup lukewarm milk
- 3 cups all-purpose flour
- 1¼ tsp salt
- 1 tsp tabasco sauce, optional
- ¼ cup Vermont cheese powder
- 1 tbsp. sugar
- 1 cup grated cheddar cheese, firmly packed
- 1½ tsp instant yeast

Direction: PREP: 10 MINUTES /MAKES 1 LOAF

- ✓ Preparing the Ingredients In the order and at the temperature specified by the maker of your bread machine, add each ingredient to the bread machine.
- ✓ Select the Bake Cycle Close the lid, select the basic bread, medium crust setting on your bread machine, and press start.
- ✓ Take out the baked bread from the bread machine and allow it to cool on a cooling rack.

11) **Apricot–Cream Cheese Ring**
Ingredients:

- 1/3 cup water
- 2 tablespoons butter, softened
- 1 egg
- 2 cups bread flour
- 2 tablespoons sugar
- ½ teaspoon salt
- 1¾ teaspoons bread machine or fast-acting dry yeast filling
- 1 package (3 oz) cream cheese, softened
- 1½ tablespoons bread flour
- ¼ cup apricot preserves
- 1 egg, beaten
- 2 tablespoons sliced almonds

Direction: PREP: 10 MINUTES / MAKES 10 SERVINGS

- ✓ Preparing the Ingredients. Measure carefully, placing all bread dough ingredients in bread machine pan in the order recommended by the manufacturer.
- ✓ Dough/Manual cycle should be selected. The delay cycle should not be used.
- ✓ Using lightly greased hands, gently remove dough from pan.
- ✓ Cover and set aside on a lightly floured surface for 10 minutes to rest.
- ✓ In small bowl, mix cream cheese and 1½ tablespoons flour. 4 Grease 9-inch round pan with shortening.
- ✓ Roll dough into 15-inch round.

- ✓ Place in pan, letting side of dough hang over edge of pan.
- ✓ Spread cream cheese mixture over dough in pan; spoon apricot preserves onto cream cheese mixture.
- ✓ Select the Bake Cycle Make cuts along edge of dough at 1-inch intervals to about ½ inch above cream cheese mixture.
- ✓ Twist pairs of dough strips and fold over cream cheese mixture.
- ✓ Cover and let rise in warm place 40 to 50 minutes or until almost double.
- ✓ 5 Heat oven to 375°F. Brush beaten egg over dough. Sprinkle with almonds.
- ✓ Bake 30 to 35 minutes or until golden brown.
- ✓ Cool at least 30 minutes before cutting.

12) **Cottage Cheese and Chive Bread**
Ingredients:

- ⅜ cup water
- 1 cup cottage cheese
- 1 large egg
- 2 Tbsp butter
- 1½ tsp salt
- 3¾ cups white bread flour
- 3 Tbsp dried chives
- 2½ Tbsp granulated sugar
- 2¼ tsp active dry yeast

Direction: PREP: 10 MINUTES /MAKES 14 SERVINGS

- ✓ Preparing the Ingredients In the order and at the temperature specified by the maker of your bread machine, add each ingredient to the bread machine.
- ✓ Select the Bake Cycle Close the lid, select the basic bread, medium crust setting on your bread machine, and press start.
- ✓ Take out the baked bread from the bread machine and allow it to cool on a cooling rack.

13) **Mexican Style Jalapeno Cheese Bread**
Ingredients:

- 12 slice bread (1½ pounds)
- 1 small jalapeno pepper, seeded and minced
- ¾ cup lukewarm water
- 2 tablespoons nonfat dry milk powder
- 1 tablespoon unsalted butter, melted
- 1 tablespoon sugar
- 1 teaspoon salt
- 3 tablespoons finely shredded cheese (Mexican blend or Monterrey Jack)
- 2 cups white bread flour
- 1½ teaspoons bread machine yeast

Direction: PREP: 10 MINUTES /MAKES 1 LOAF

- ✓ Preparing the Ingredients. Choose the size of loaf of your preference and then measure the ingredients.
- ✓ Add all of the ingredients mentioned previously in the list.

- ✓ Close the lid after placing the pan in the bread machine.
- ✓ Select the Bake Cycle Turn on the bread machine. Select the White/Basic setting, select the loaf size, and the crust color.
- ✓ Press start.
- ✓ When the breadmaker cycle is complete, carefully remove the pan from the machine and allow it to cool before serving.
- ✓ Remove the bread from the pan, put in a wire rack to Cool about 5 minutes. Slice

14) **Ricotta Bread**

Ingredients:

- 3 Tbsp skim milk
- ⅔ cup ricotta cheese
- 4 tsp unsalted butter, softened to room temperature
- 1 large egg
  2 tbsp. granulated sugar
- ½ tsp salt
- 1½ cups bread flour, + more flour, as needed 1
- tsp active dry yeast

Direction: PREP: 10 MINUTES /MAKES 14 SLICES

- ✓ Preparing the Ingredients In the order and at the temperature specified by the maker of your bread machine, add each ingredient to the bread machine..
- ✓ Select the Bake Cycle Close the lid, select the basic bread, medium crust setting on your bread machine, and press start.
  Take out the baked bread from the bread machine and allow it to cool on a cooling rack.

15) **Roasted Garlic Asiago Bread**

Ingredients:

- 12 slice bread (1½ pounds)
- ¾ cup plus 1 tablespoon milk, at 70°F to 80°F
- ¼ cup melted butter, cooled
- 1 teaspoon minced garlic
- 2 tablespoons sugar
- 1 teaspoon salt
- ½ cup (2 ounces) grated Asiago cheese
- 2¾ cups white bread flour
- 1½ teaspoons bread machine or instant yeast
- ½ cup mashed roasted garlic

Direction: PREP: 10 MINUTES /MAKES 1 LOAF

- ✓ Preparing the Ingredients. Choose the size of loaf of your preference and then measure the ingredients.
- ✓ Add all of the ingredients mentioned previously in the list.
- ✓ Close the lid after placing the pan in the bread machine.
- ✓ Select the Bake Cycle Turn on the bread machine. Select the White/Basic setting, select the loaf size, and the crust color.
- ✓ Press start.
- ✓ When the breadmaker cycle is complete, carefully

remove the pan from the machine and allow it to cool before serving.
- ✓ Remove the bread from the pan, put in a wire rack to Cool about 5 minutes.
- ✓ Slice

16) **Jalapeno Cheddar Bread**

Ingredients:

- 12 slice bread (1½ pounds)
- 1 cup lukewarm buttermilk
- ¼ cup unsalted butter, melted
- 2 eggs, at room temperature
- ½ teaspoon table salt
- 1 jalapeno pepper, chopped
- ½ cup Cheddar cheese, shredded
- ¼ cup sugar
- 1⅓ cups all-purpose flour
- 1 cup cornmeal
- 1 tablespoon baking powder

Direction: PREP: 10 MINUTES /MAKES 1 LOAF

- ✓ Preparing the Ingredients. Choose the size of loaf of your preference and then measure the ingredients.
- ✓ Add all of the ingredients mentioned previously in the list.
- ✓ Close the lid after placing the pan in the bread machine.
- ✓ Select the Bake Cycle Turn on the bread machine.
- ✓ Select the Rapid/Quick setting, select the loaf size, and the crust color.
- ✓ Press start.
- ✓ When the breadmaker cycle is complete, carefully remove the pan from the machine and allow it to cool before serving.
- ✓ Remove the bread from the pan, put in a wire rack to Cool about 5 minutes.
- ✓ Slice

17) **Oregano Cheese Bread**

Ingredients:

- 3 cups bread flour
- 1 cup water
- ½ cup freshly grated parmesan cheese
- 3 tbsp. sugar
- 1 tbsp. dried leaf oregano
- 1½ tbsp. olive oil
- 1 tsp salt
- 2 tsp active dry yeast

Direction: PREP: 10 MINUTES /MAKES 1 LOAF

- ✓ Preparing the Ingredients In the order and at the temperature specified by the maker of your bread machine, add each ingredient to the bread machine.
- ✓ Select the Bake Cycle Close the lid, select the basic bread, medium crust setting on your bread machine, and press start.
- ✓ Take out the baked bread from the bread machine

and allow it to cool on a cooling rack.

✓

18) Cheddar Cheese Basil Bread
Ingredients:

- 12 slice bread (1½ pounds)
- 1 cup milk, at 80°F to 90°F
- 1 tablespoon melted butter, cooled
- 1 tablespoon sugar
- 1 teaspoon dried basil
- ¾ cup (3 ounces) shredded sharp Cheddar cheese
- ¾ teaspoon salt
- 3 cups white bread flour
- 1½ teaspoons bread machine or active dry yeast.

Direction: PREP: 10 MINUTES /MAKES 1 LOAF

✓ Preparing the Ingredients. Choose the size of loaf of your preference and then measure the ingredients.
✓ Add all of the ingredients mentioned previously in the list.
✓ Close the lid after placing the pan in the bread machine.
✓ Select the Bake Cycle Turn on the bread machine. Select the White/Basic setting, select the loaf size, and the crust color.
✓ Press start.
✓ When the breadmaker cycle is complete, carefully remove the pan from the machine and allow it to cool before serving.
✓ Remove the bread from the pan, put in a wire rack to Cool about 5 minutes.
✓ Slice

19) Spinach and Feta Bread
Ingredients:

- 1 cup water
- 2 tsp butter
- 3 cups flour
- 1 tsp sugar
- 2 tsp instant minced onion
- 1 tsp salt
- 1¼ tsp instant yeast
- 1 cup crumbled feta
- 1 cup chopped fresh spinach leaves

Direction: PREP: 10 MINUTES /MAKES 14 SLICES

✓ Preparing the Ingredients Add each ingredient except the cheese and spinach to the bread machine in the order and at the temperature recommended by your bread machine manufacturer.
✓ Select the Bake Cycle Close the lid, select the basic bread, medium crust setting on your bread machine, and press start.
✓ When only 10 minutes are left in the last kneading cycle add the spinach and cheese.
✓ Take out the baked bread from the bread machine and allow it to cool on a cooling rack.
✓

20) Blue Cheese Bread
Ingredients:

- 3/4 cup warm water
- 1 large egg
- 1 teaspoon salt
- 3 cups bread flour
- 1 cup blue cheese, crumbled
- 2 tablespoons nonfat dry milk
- 2 tablespoons sugar
- 1 teaspoon bread machine yeast

Direction: PREP: 10 MINUTES /MAKES 12 SLICES

✓ Preparing the Ingredients Add the ingredients to bread machine pan in the order listed above, (except yeast); be sure to add the cheese with the flour.
✓ Form a well in the flour and add the yeast.
✓ Select the Bake Cycle Select Basic bread cycle, medium crust color, and press Start.
✓ When finished, transfer to a cooling rack for 10 minutes and serve warm.

21) Parsley Garlic Bread
Ingredients:

- 12 slice bread (1½ pounds)
- 1 cup lukewarm milk
- 1½ tablespoons unsalted butter, melted
- 1 tablespoon sugar
- 1½ teaspoons table salt
- 2 teaspoons garlic powder
- 2 teaspoons fresh parsley, chopped
- 3 cups white bread flour
- 1¾ teaspoons bread machine yeast

Direction: PREP: 10 MINUTES /MAKES 1 LOAF

✓ Preparing the Ingredients. Choose the size of loaf of your preference and then measure the ingredients.
✓ Add all of the ingredients mentioned previously in the list.
✓ Close the lid after placing the pan in the bread machine.
✓ Select the Bake Cycle Turn on the bread machine.
✓ Select the White/Basic setting, select the loaf size, and the crust color.
✓ Press start.
✓ When the breadmaker cycle is complete, carefully remove the pan from the machine and allow it to cool before serving. Remove the bread from the pan, put in a wire rack to Cool about 10 minutes.
✓ Slice

22) Prosciutto Parmesan Breadsticks
Ingredients:

- 1 1/3 cups warm water
- 1 tablespoon butter
- 1 1/2 tablespoons sugar
- 1 1/2 teaspoons salt

- 4 cups bread flour
- 2 teaspoons yeast

For the topping:

- 1/2-pound prosciutto, sliced very thin
- 1/2 cup of grated parmesan cheese
- 1 egg yolk
- 1 tablespoon of water

Direction: PREP: 10 MINUTES /MAKES 12

- ✓ Preparing the Ingredients In the order indicated, place the first batch of dough ingredients (excluding yeast) in the bread pan.
- ✓ No topping ingredients should be added at this point.
- ✓ To the dry ingredients, create a well in the center and add the yeast.
- ✓ Sélectionnez le cycle de pâtisserie. On the bread machine's cycle menu, select Dough.
- ✓ Once done, transfer the dough to a lightly floured board.
- ✓ Roll the dough out flat to a thickness of approximately 1/4 inch, or half a centimeter.
- ✓ Wrap the dough in plastic wrap and set aside for 20–30 minutes to rise.
- ✓ Sprinkle dough evenly with parmesan and carefully lay the prosciutto slices on the surface of the dough to cover as much of it as possible.
- ✓ Preheat an oven to 400°F.
- ✓ Cut the dough into 12 long strips, about one inch wide.
- ✓ Twist each end in opposite directions, twisting the toppings into the bread stick.
- ✓ Place the breadsticks onto a lightly greased baking sheet.
- ✓ Whisk the egg yolk and water together in a small mixing bowl and lightly baste each breadstick.
- ✓ Bake for 8 to 10 minutes or until golden brown.
- ✓ Remove from oven and serve warm.

23) **Jalapeño Corn Bread**

Ingredients:

- 12 to 16 slices bread (1½ to 2 pounds)
- 1 cup buttermilk, at 80°F to 90°F
- ¼ cup melted butter, cooled
- 2 eggs, at room temperature
- 1 jalapeño pepper, chopped
- 1⅓ cups all-purpose flour
- 1 cup cornmeal
- ½ cup (2 ounces) shredded Cheddar cheese
- ¼ cup sugar
- 1 tablespoon baking powder
- ½ teaspoon salt

Direction: PREP: 10 MINUTES /MAKES 1 LOAF

- ✓ Preparing the Ingredients. Choose the size of loaf of your preference and then measure the ingredients.
- ✓ Add all of the ingredients mentioned previously in the list.

- ✓ Close the lid after placing the pan in the bread machine. Select the Bake Cycle Turn on the bread machine.
- ✓ Select the Quick/Rapid setting, select the loaf size, and the crust color.
- ✓ Press start.
- ✓ When the breadmaker cycle is complete, carefully remove the pan from the machine and allow it to cool before serving.
- ✓ Remove the bread from the pan, put in a wire rack to Cool about 5 minutes.
- ✓ Slice

24) **Cheddar Bacon Bread**

Ingredients:

- 12 slice bread (1½ pounds)
- ½ cup lukewarm milk
- 1½ teaspoons unsalted butter, melted
- 1½ tablespoons honey
- 1½ teaspoons table salt
- ½ cup green chilies, chopped
- ½ cup grated Cheddar cheese
- ½ cup cooked bacon, chopped
- 3 cups white bread flour
- 2 teaspoons bread machine yeast

Direction: PREP: 10 MINUTES /MAKES 1 LOAF

- ✓ Preparing the Ingredients. Choose the size of loaf of your preference and then measure the ingredients.
- ✓ Add all of the ingredients mentioned previously in the list.
- ✓ Close the lid after placing the pan in the bread machine.
- ✓ Select the Bake Cycle Turn on the bread machine.
- ✓ Select the White/Basic setting, select the loaf size, and the crust color.
- ✓ Press start.
- ✓ When the breadmaker cycle is complete, carefully remove the pan from the machine and allow it to cool before serving.
- ✓ Remove the bread from the pan, put in a wire rack to Cool about 5 minutes.
- ✓ Slice.

25) **Italian Cheese Bread**

Ingredients:

- 1¼ cups water
- 3 cups bread flour
- ½ shredded pepper jack cheese
- 2 tsp Italian seasoning
- 2 Tbsp brown sugar
- 1½ tsp salt
- 2 tsp active dry yeast

Direction: PREP: 10 MINUTES /MAKES 14 SLICES

- ✓ Preparing the Ingredients. In the order and at the temperature specified by the maker of your bread machine, add each ingredient to the bread machine.

✓ Select the Bake Cycle Close the lid, select the basic bread, medium crust setting on your bread machine, and press start.

✓ Take out the baked bread from the bread machine and allow it to cool on a cooling rack.

✓

✓

26) **Olive Cheese Bread**

Ingredients:

- 12 slice bread (1½ pounds)
- 1 cup milk, at 80°F to 90°F
- 1½ tablespoons melted butter, cooled
- 1 teaspoon minced garlic
- 1½ tablespoons sugar
- 1 teaspoon salt
- 3 cups white bread flour
- ¾ cup (3 ounces) shredded Swiss cheese
- 1 teaspoon bread machine or instant yeast
- ⅓ cup chopped black olives
  Direction: PREP: 10 MINUTES /MAKES 1 LOAF

✓ Preparing the Ingredients. Place the ingredients in your bread machine as recommended by the manufacturer, tossing the flour with the cheese first.

✓ Choose the Bake Cycle Set the machine to Basic/White bread, choose between light or medium crust, then push Start.

✓ When the breadmaker cycle is complete, carefully remove the pan from the machine and allow it to cool before serving.

✓ Remove the bread from the pan, put in a wire rack to Cool about 10 minutes.

✓ Slice

✓

27) **Cheesy Sausage Loaf**

Ingredients:

- 1 cup warm water
- 4 teaspoons butter, softened
- 1 1/4 teaspoons salt
- 1 teaspoon sugar
- 3 cups bread flour
- 2 1/4 teaspoons active dry yeast
- 1-pound pork sausage roll, cooked and drained
- 1 1/2 cups Italian cheese, shredded
- 1/4 teaspoon garlic powder
- Pinch of black pepper
- 1 egg, lightly beaten
- Flour, for surface
  Direction: PREP: 10 MINUTES /MAKES 1 LOAF

✓ Preparing the Ingredients Add the first five ingredients to the bread maker pan in order listed above.

✓ Make a well in the flour; pour the yeast into the hole. Select the Bake Cycle Select Dough cycle and press Start.

✓ Turn kneaded dough onto a lightly floured surface and roll into a 16-by-10-inch rectangle.

✓ Cover with plastic wrap and let rest for 10 minutes Combine sausage, cheese, garlic powder and pepper in a mixing bowl.

✓ Spread sausage mixture evenly over the dough to within one 1/2 inch of edges.

✓ Start with a long side and roll up like a jelly roll, pinch seams to seal, and tuck ends under.

✓ Place the loaf seam-side down on a greased baking sheet.

✓ Cover and let rise in a warm place for 30 minutes.

✓ Preheat an oven to 350°F and bake 20 minutes.

✓ Brush with egg and bake an additional 15 to 20 minutes until golden brown.

✓ Remove to a cooling rack and serve warm.

28) **Mixed Herb Cheese Bread**

Ingredients:

- 12 slice bread (1½ pounds)
- 1 cup lukewarm water
- 1½ tablespoons olive oil
- ¾ teaspoon table salt
- ¾ tablespoon sugar
- 2 cloves garlic, crushed
- 2 tablespoons mixed fresh herbs (basil, chives, oregano, rosemary, etc.)
- 3 tablespoons Parmesan cheese, grated
- 3 cups white bread flour
- 1⅔ teaspoons bread machine yeast
  Direction: PREP: 10 MINUTES PLUS FERMENTING TIME/MAKES 1 LOAF

✓ Preparing the Ingredients. Choose the size of loaf of your preference and then measure the ingredients.

✓ Add all of the ingredients mentioned previously in the list.

✓ Close the lid after placing the pan in the bread machine.

✓ Select the Bake cycle Turn on the bread machine.

✓ Select the White/Basic setting, select the loaf size, and the crust color.

✓ Press start. When the breadmaker cycle is complete, carefully remove the pan from the machine and allow it to cool before serving.

✓ Remove the bread from the pan, put in a wire rack to Cool about 5 minutes.

✓ Slice

29) **Blue Cheese Onion Bread**

Ingredients:

- 12 slice bread (1½ pounds)
- 1¼ cup water, at 80°F to 90°F 1 egg, at room temperature
- 1 tablespoon melted butter, cooled
- ¼ cup powdered skim milk

- 1 tablespoon sugar
- ¾ teaspoon salt
- ½ cup (2 ounces) crumbled blue cheese
- 1 tablespoon dried onion flakes
- 3 cups white bread flour
- ¼ cup instant mashed potato flakes
- 1 teaspoon bread machine or active dry yeast

Direction: PREP: 10 MINUTES PLUS FERMENTING TIME/MAKES 1 LOAF

✓ Preparing the Ingredients. Choose the size of loaf of your preference and then measure the ingredients.

✓ Add all of the ingredients mentioned previously in the list.

✓ Close the lid after placing the pan in the bread machine.

✓ Select the Bake Cycle Turn on the bread machine.

✓ Select the Quick/Rapid setting, select the loaf size, and the crust color.

✓ Press start.

✓ When the breadmaker cycle is complete, carefully remove the pan from the machine and allow it to cool before serving. Remove the bread from the pan, put in a wire rack to Cool about 10 minutes.

✓ Slice

30) *Cheddar and Bacon Bread*

Ingredients:

- 1⅓ cups water
- 2 Tbsp vegetable oil
- 1¼ tsp salt
- 2 Tbsp plus 1½ tsp sugar
- 4 cups bread flour
- 3 Tbsp nonfat dry milk
- 2 tsp dry active yeast
- 2 cups cheddar
- 8 slices crumbled bacon

Direction: PREP: 10 MINUTES PLUS FERMENTING TIME /MAKES 14 SLICES

✓ Preparing the Ingredients Add each ingredient to the bread machine except the cheese and bacon in the order and at the temperature recommended by your bread machine manufacturer.

✓ Select the Bake Cycle Close the lid, select the basic bread, medium crust setting on your bread machine, and press start.

✓ Add the cheddar cheese and bacon 30 to 40 minutes into the cycle.

✓ Take out the baked bread from the bread machine and allow it to cool on a cooling rack.

31) *Basil Cheese Bread*

Ingredients:

- 12 slice bread (1½ pounds)
- 1 cup lukewarm milk
- 1 tablespoon unsalted butter, melted
- 1 tablespoon sugar
- 1 teaspoon dried basil

- ¾ teaspoon table salt
- ¾ cup sharp Cheddar cheese, shredded
- 3 cups white bread flour
- 1½ teaspoons bread machine yeast.

Direction: PREP: 10 MINUTES PLUS FERMENTING TIME /MAKES 1 LOAF

✓ Preparing the Ingredients. Choose the size of loaf of your preference and then measure the ingredients.

✓ Add all of the ingredients mentioned previously in the list.

✓ Close the lid after placing the pan in the bread machine.

✓ Select the Bake Cycle Turn on the bread machine.

✓ Select the Quick/Rapid setting, select the loaf size, and the crust color.

✓ Press start. When the breadmaker cycle is complete, carefully remove the pan from the machine and allow it to cool before serving.

✓ Remove the bread from the pan, put in a wire rack to Cool about 5 minutes.

✓ Slice

32) *Double Cheese Bread*

Ingredients:

- 8 slices bread (1 pound)
- ¾ cup plus 1 tablespoon milk, at 80°F to 90°F
- 2 teaspoons butter, melted and cooled
- 4 teaspoons sugar
- ⅔ teaspoon salt
- ⅓ teaspoon freshly ground black pepper
- Pinch cayenne pepper
- 1 cup (4 ounces) shredded aged sharp Cheddar cheese
- ⅓ cup shredded or grated Parmesan cheese
- 2 cups white bread flour
- ¾ teaspoon bread machine or instant yeast

Direction: PREP: 10 MINUTES PLUS FERMENTING TIME /MAKES 1 LOAF

✓ Preparing the Ingredients. Choose the size of loaf of your preference and then measure the ingredients.

✓ Add all of the ingredients mentioned previously in the list.

✓ Close the lid after placing the pan in the bread machine.

✓ Select the Bake Cycle Turn on the bread machine. Select the Quick/Rapid setting, select the loaf size, and the crust color.

✓ Press start.

✓

✓ When the breadmaker cycle is complete, carefully remove the pan from the machine and allow it to cool before serving.

✓ Remove the bread from the pan, put in a wire rack to Cool about 5 minutes.

✓ Slice

✓

33) *American Cheese Beer Bread*

- 16 slice bread (2 pounds)
- 1⅔ cups warm beer
- 1½ tablespoons sugar
- 2 teaspoons table salt
- 1½ tablespoons unsalted butter, melted
- ¾ cup American cheese, shredded
- ¾ cup Monterrey Jack cheese, shredded
- 4 cups white bread flour
- 2 teaspoons bread machine yeast

Direction: PREP: 10 MINUTES PLUS FERMENTING TIME /MAKES 1 LOAF

✓ Preparing the Ingredients. Choose the size of loaf of your preference and then measure the ingredients.
✓ Add all of the ingredients mentioned previously in the list.
✓ Close the lid after placing the pan in the bread machine.
✓ Select the Bake Cycle Turn on the bread machine. Select the Quick/Rapid setting, select the loaf size, and the crust color.
✓ Press start.
✓ When the breadmaker cycle is complete, carefully remove the pan from the machine and allow it to cool before serving.
✓ Remove the bread from the pan, put in a wire rack to Cool about 5 minutes.
✓ Slice
✓

34) **Mozzarella and Salami Bread**

Ingredients:

- 12 slice bread (1½ pounds)
- 1 cup water plus 2 tablespoons, at 80°F to 90°F
- ½ cup (2 ounces) shredded mozzarella cheese
- 2 tablespoons sugar
- 1 teaspoon salt
- 1 teaspoon dried basil
- ¼ teaspoon garlic powder
- 3¼ cups white bread flour
- 1½ teaspoons bread machine or instant yeast
- ¾ cup finely diced hot German salami

Direction: PREP: 10 MINUTES PLUS FERMENTING TIME /MAKES 1 LOAF

✓ Preparing the Ingredients. Add all ingredients except the salami in your bread machine according to the manufacturer's instructions.
✓ Set the machine to Basic/White bread, then pick light or medium crust and push Start.
✓ Remove the bucket from the machine after the loaf is complete.
✓ Choose a baking cycle When your machine indicates or 5 minutes before the second kneading cycle is complete, add the salami.
✓ Allow the bread to cool for 5 minutes before slicing.
✓ Shake the bucket gently to dislodge the loaf, then turn it out onto a cooling rack.

35) **Simple Cottage Cheese Bread**

Ingredients:

- 12 slice bread (1½ pounds)
- ½ cup water, at 80°F to 90°F
- ¾ cup cottage cheese, at room temperature
- 1 egg, at room temperature
- 2 tablespoons butter, melted and cooled
- 1 tablespoon sugar
- 1 teaspoon salt
- ¼ teaspoon baking soda
- 3 cups white bread flour 2
- teaspoons bread machine or instant yeast

Direction: PREP: 10 MINUTES PLUS FERMENTING TIME /MAKES 1 LOAF

✓ Preparing the Ingredients. Choose the size of loaf of your preference and then measure the ingredients.
✓ Add all of the ingredients mentioned previously in the list.
✓ Close the lid after placing the pan in the bread machine.
✓ Select the Bake Cycle Turn on the bread machine.
✓ Select the White/Basic setting, select the loaf size, and the crust color.
✓ Press start. When the breadmaker cycle is complete, carefully remove the pan from the machine and allow it to cool before serving.
✓ Remove the bread from the pan, put in a wire rack to Cool about 5 minutes.
✓ Slice

36) **Parmesan Cheddar Bread**

Ingredients:

- 12 slice bread (1½ pounds)
- 1¼ cups lukewarm milk
- 1 tablespoon unsalted butter, melted
- 2 tablespoons sugar
- 1 teaspoon table salt
- ½ teaspoon freshly ground black pepper
- Pinch cayenne pepper
- 1½ cups shredded aged sharp Cheddar cheese
- ½ cup shredded or grated Parmesan cheese
- 3 cups white bread flour
- 1¼ teaspoons bread machine yeast

Direction: PREP: 10 MINUTES PLUS FERMENTING TIME /MAKES 1 LOAF

✓ Preparing the Ingredients. Choose the size of loaf of your preference and then measure the ingredients.
✓ Add all of the ingredients mentioned previously in the list.
✓ Close the lid after placing the pan in the bread machine.
✓ Select the Bake Cycle Turn on the bread machine.
✓ Select the Quick/Rapid setting, select the loaf size,

and the crust color.

✓ Press start.

✓ When the breadmaker cycle is complete, carefully remove the pan from the machine and allow it to cool before serving.

✓ Remove the bread from the pan, put in a wire rack to Cool about 5 minutes.

✓ Slice

37) *Chile Cheese Bacon Bread*

Ingredients:

- 8 slices bread (1 pound)
- ⅓ cup milk, at 80°F to 90°F
- 1 teaspoon melted butter, cooled
- 1 tablespoon honey
- 1 teaspoon salt
- ⅓ cup chopped and drained green chiles
- ⅓ cup grated Cheddar cheese
- ⅓ cup chopped cooked bacon
- 2 cups white bread flour
- 1⅓ teaspoons bread machine or instant yeast

Direction: PREP: 10 MINUTES PLUS FERMENTING TIME /MAKES 1 LOAF

✓ Preparing the Ingredients. Choose the size of loaf of your preference and then measure the ingredients.

✓ Add all of the ingredients mentioned previously in the list.

✓ Close the lid after placing the pan in the bread machine.

✓ Select the Bake Cycle Turn on the bread machine.

✓ Select the Quick/Rapid setting, select the loaf size, and the crust color.

✓ Press start.

✓ When the breadmaker cycle is complete, carefully remove the pan from the machine and allow it to cool before serving.

✓ Remove the bread from the pan, put in a wire rack to Cool about 5 minutes.

✓ Slice

38) *Honey Goat Cheese Bread*

Ingredients:

- 12 slice bread (1½ pounds)
- 1 cup lukewarm milk
- 1½ tablespoons honey
- 1 teaspoon table salt
- 1 teaspoon freshly cracked black pepper
- ¼ cup goat cheese, shredded or crumbled
- 3 cups white bread flour
- 1½ teaspoons bread machine yeast

Direction: PREP: 10 MINUTES PLUS FERMENTING TIME /MAKES 1 LOAF

✓ Preparing the Ingredients. Choose the size of loaf of your preference and then measure the ingredients.

✓ Add all of the ingredients mentioned previously in the list. Close the lid after placing the pan in the bread

machine.

✓ Select the Bake Cycle Turn on the bread machine.

✓ Select the Quick/Rapid setting, select the loaf size, and the crust color.

✓ Press start.

✓ When the breadmaker cycle is complete, carefully remove the pan from the machine and allow it to cool before serving. Remove the bread from the pan, put in a wire rack to Cool about 5 minutes.

✓ Slice

39) *Italian Parmesan Bread*

Ingredients:

- 8 slices bread (1 pound)
- ¾ cup water, at 80°F to 90°F
- 2 tablespoons melted butter, cooled
- 2 teaspoons sugar
- ⅔ teaspoon salt
- 1⅓ teaspoons chopped fresh basil
- 2⅔ tablespoons grated Parmesan cheese
- 2⅓ cups white bread flour
- 1 teaspoon bread machine or instant yeast

Direction: PREP: 10 MINUTES PLUS FERMENTING TIME /MAKES 1 LOAF

✓ Preparing the Ingredients. Choose the size of loaf of your preference and then measure the ingredients.

✓ Add all of the ingredients mentioned previously in the list.

✓ Close the lid after placing the pan in the bread machine.

✓ Select the Bake Cycle Turn on the bread machine.

✓ Select the Quick/Rapid setting, select the loaf size, and the crust color.
Press start.

✓ When the breadmaker cycle is complete, carefully remove the pan from the machine and allow it to cool before serving.

✓ Remove the bread from the pan, put in a wire rack to Cool about 5 minutes.

✓ Slice

40) *Rich Cheddar Bread*

Ingredients:

- 12 slice bread (1½ pounds)
- 1 cup milk, at 80°F to 90°F
- 2 tablespoons butter, melted and cooled
- 3 tablespoons sugar
- 1 teaspoon salt
- ½ cup (2 ounces) grated aged Cheddar cheese
- 3 cups white bread flour
- 2 teaspoons bread machine or instant yeast

Direction: PREP: 10 MINUTES PLUS FERMENTING TIME /MAKES 1 LOAF

✓ Preparing the Ingredients. Choose the size of loaf of your preference and then measure the ingredients.

- ✓ Add all of the ingredients mentioned previously in the list.
- ✓ Close the lid after placing the pan in the bread machine.
- ✓ Select the Bake Cycle Turn on the bread machine.
- ✓ Select the Quick/Rapid setting, select the loaf size, and the crust color.
- ✓ Press start.
- ✓ When the breadmaker cycle is complete, carefully remove the pan from the machine and allow it to cool before serving.
- ✓ Remove the bread from the pan, put in a wire rack to Cool about 5 minutes.
- ✓ Slice

41)   Feta Oregano Bread

Ingredients:

- 8 slice bread (1 pounds)
- ⅔ cup milk, at 80°F to 90°F
- 2 teaspoons melted butter, cooled
- 2 teaspoons sugar
- ⅔ teaspoon salt
- 2 teaspoons dried oregano
- 2 cups white bread flour
- 1½ teaspoons bread machine or instant yeast
- ⅔ cup (2½ ounces) crumbled feta cheese

Direction: PREP: 10 MINUTES PLUS FERMENTING TIME /MAKES 1 LOAF

- ✓ Preparing the Ingredients. Choose the size of loaf of your preference and then measure the ingredients.
- ✓ Add all of the ingredients mentioned previously in the list.
- ✓ Close the lid after placing the pan in the bread machine.
- ✓ Select the Bake Cycle Turn on the bread machine. Select the Quick/Rapid setting, select the loaf size, and the crust color.
- ✓ Press start. When the breadmaker cycle is complete, carefully remove the pan from the machine and allow it to cool before serving.
- ✓ Remove the bread from the pan, put in a wire rack to Cool about 5 minutes.
- ✓ Slice

42)   Goat Cheese Bread

Ingredients:

- 8 slices bread (1 pound)
- ⅔ cup milk, at 80°F to 90°F
- 2⅔ tablespoons goat cheese, at room temperature
- 1 tablespoon honey
- ⅔ teaspoon salt
- ⅔ teaspoon freshly cracked black pepper
- 2 cups white bread flour
- 1 teaspoon bread machine or instant yeast

Direction: PREP: 10 MINUTES PLUS FERMENTING

TIME /MAKES 1 LOAF

- ✓ Preparing the Ingredients. Choose the size of loaf of your preference and then measure the ingredients.
- ✓ Add all of the ingredients mentioned previously in the list.
- ✓ Close the lid after placing the pan in the bread machine. Select the Bake Cycle Turn on the bread machine.
- ✓ Select the Quick/Rapid setting, select the loaf size, and the crust color.
- ✓ Press start. When the breadmaker cycle is complete, carefully remove the pan from the machine and allow it to cool before serving.
- ✓ Remove the bread from the pan, put in a wire rack to Cool about 5 minutes.
- ✓ Slice

43)   Mozzarella-Herb Bread

Ingredients:

- 12 slice bread (1½ pounds)
- 1¼ cups milk, at 80°F to 90°F
- 1 tablespoon butter, melted and cooled
- 2 tablespoons sugar
- 1 teaspoon salt
- 2 teaspoons dried basil
- 1 teaspoon dried oregano
- 1½ cups (6 ounces) shredded mozzarella cheese
- 3 cups white bread flour
- 2¼ teaspoons bread machine or instant yeast

Direction: PREP: 10 MINUTES PLUS FERMENTING TIME /MAKES 1 LOAF

- ✓ Preparing the Ingredients. Choose the size of loaf of your preference and then measure the ingredients.
- ✓ Add all of the ingredients mentioned previously in the list.
- ✓ Close the lid after placing the pan in the bread machine.
- ✓ Select the Bake cycle Turn on the bread machine.
- ✓ Select the Quick/Rapid setting, select the loaf size, and the crust color.
- ✓ Press start.
- ✓ When the breadmaker cycle is complete, carefully remove the pan from the machine and allow it to cool before serving.
- ✓ Remove the bread from the pan, put in a wire rack to Cool about 5 minutes. Slice

44)   Olive Loaf

Ingredients:

- 1 cup plus 2 tablespoons water
- 1 tablespoon olive oil 3
- cups bread flour
- 2 tablespoons instant nonfat dry milk
- 1 tablespoon sugar
- 1 1/4 teaspoons salt

- 1/4 teaspoon garlic powder
- 2 teaspoons active dry yeast
- 2/3 cup grated parmesan cheese
- 1 cup pitted Greek olives, sliced and drained
  Direction: PREP: 10 MINUTES PLUS FERMENTING TIME /MAKES 1 LOAF

✓ Preparing the Ingredients Add ingredients, except yeast, olives and cheese, to bread maker in order listed above.

✓ Make a well in the flour; pour the yeast into the hole.

✓ Select the Bake Cycle Select Basic cycle, light crust color, and press Start; do not use delay cycle.

✓ Just before the final kneading, add the olives and cheese.

✓ Remove and allow to cool on a wire rack for 15 minutes before serving.

45) *Wine and Cheese Bread*

Ingredients:

- 3/4 cup white wine
- 1/2 cup white cheddar or gruyere cheese, shredded
- 1 1/2 tablespoons butter
- 1/2 teaspoon salt
- 3/4 teaspoon sugar
- 2 1/4 cups bread flour
- 1 1/2 teaspoons active dry yeast
  Direction: PREP: 10 MINUTES PLUS FERMENTING TIME /MAKES 1 LOAF

✓ Preparing the Ingredients Add liquid ingredients to the bread maker pan.

✓ In a large bread pan, combine all dry ingredients except yeast.

✓ Use your fingers to form a well-like hole in the flour where you will pour the yeast; yeast must never come into contact with a liquid when you are adding the ingredients.

✓ Carefully pour the yeast into the well.

✓ Select the Bake Cycle Select Basic bread setting, light crust color, and press Start.

✓ Before serving, cool completely on a wire rack.

46) *Garlic and Herb Bread*

Ingredients: 1 POUND LOAF

- Unsalted butter, diced 1 tbsp
- Lukewarm 1% milk 1 cup
- White all-purpose flour 1 ½ tsp
- Italian seasoning 2 ¼ cups
- Garlic powder 3 tsp
- Sugar 1 tbsp
- Salt 1 ½ tsp
- Instant dry yeast 2 tsp
  Direction: Time: 2 hours and 10 minutes / Prep Time: 10 minutes / Cook Time: 2 hours

✓ Add the ingredients to the bread machine in the sequence stated above or as directed in the instruction manual for your bread maker.

✓ Select the basic setting and the function for medium crust. When the bread is finished, transfer it to a drying rack to cool somewhat before serving.

✓ Tip(s): If you are not a big lover of garlic, you may add two teaspoons of garlic powder to the recipe instead.

47) *Pepperoni and Cheese Bread*

Ingredients: 1 POUND LOAF

- Lukewarm water ½ cup and 1 tbsp
- Mozzarella cheese 4 tbsp
- Sugar 1 tbsp
- Garlic salt ¾ tsp
- Dried oregano ¾ tsp
- All-purpose flour 1 ⅔ cup
- Active dry yeast ¾ tsp
- Diced pepperoni ⅓ cup
  Direction: 3 hours and 10 minutes / Prep Time: 10 minutes / Cook Time: 3 hours

✓ Add all ingredients, except the pepperoni, to the bread machine, either in the order listed or according to your bread machine's instruction manual.

✓ Select the basic bread setting and the medium crust function.

✓ Add the pepperoni just before your bread machine reaches its last kneading cycle (most machines will indicate this with a sound).

✓ When the bread is finished, turn it out onto a drying rack to cool before serving.

✓ TIP(S): This recipe does not work well with the delay timer feature.

✓ Adding an extra ½ or 1 tbsp of vegetable oil can lift the flavor, if necessary.

✓ Cheese amounts can be tripled to increase the flavor.

✓ Any Italian seasoning can be substituted for the oregano.

48) *Quick Bake Italian Bread*

Ingredients: 1 POUND LOAF

- Lukewarm water ¾ cup
- Unsalted butter, softened 1 tbsp
- Plain bread flour 2 cups
- Powdered milk 1 ½ tbsp
- Dried marjoram ¾ tsp
- Dried basil ¾ tsp
- Dried thyme ½ tsp
- Salt 1 pinch
- Sugar ½ tbsp
- Instant dry yeast 2 tsp
  Direction: 1 hour and 45 minutes / Prep Time: 14 minutes / Cook Time: 1 hour and 20 minutes

✓ Add the ingredients to the bread machine in the sequence stated above or as directed in the instruction manual for your bread maker.

✓ Select the quick or rapid setting and medium crust function.

✓ When ready, turn the bread out onto a drying rack

and allow it to cool, then serve.

✓ Tip(s): Ensure that your olives have been patted dry before using them in this recipe as olive brine affects the yeast.

49) *Ciabatta*

Ingredients: 1 POUND LOAF

- Lukewarm water ¾ cup
- Extra-virgin olive oil ½ tbsp
- All-purpose flour 1 ½ cups
- Salt ¾ tsp
- Sugar ½ tsp
- Bread machine yeast ¾ tsp

Direction: 2 hours and 40 minutes / Prep Time: 2 hours and 10 minutes / Cook Time: 30 minutes

✓ Add the ingredients to the bread machine in the sequence stated above or as directed in the instruction manual for your bread maker.

✓ Select the dough cycle. When the dough is ready, place it onto a floured surface.

✓ Cover the dough with a ceramic or glass dish and allow it to rest for ten minutes.

✓ Shape the dough an oval shape.

✓ Split into two oval shapes when doubling up on the recipe.

✓ Place onto a greased baking tray, cover with a cloth and allow to rest for a further 30 minutes or until it has doubled in size.

✓ Allow the dough to rest in a dry, warm area of your kitchen.

✓ Preheat your oven to 425 F.

✓ Using the bottom end of a wooden spoon make small indents on the top of each Loaf.

✓ Drive the spoon down into the dough until it touches the baking tray. Then bake for 30 minutes at 350 °F.

✓ Sprinkle water lightly over the top of the loaves every 10 minutes while baking.

✓ When ready, turn the bread out onto a drying rack and allow it to cool, then serve.

✓ TIP(S): This is a sticky dough, so do not add extra flour though you may feel the need to do so.

50) **Bacon and Cheese Bread**

Ingredients: 1 POUND LOAF

- Egg, lightly beaten ½
- Lukewarm water   ½ cup
- Unsalted butter, diced   ½ tbsp
- Shredded cheddar cheese   ½ cup
- Bacon bits 2 tbsp
- Salt ½ tsp
- Sugar 1 tbsp
- Active dry yeast 1 tsp

Direction: 3 hours and 10 minutes / Prep Time: 10 minutes / Cook Time: 3 hours

✓ Add the ingredients to the bread machine in the sequence stated above or according to the instructions in your bread machine's instruction manual.

✓ Select the basic cycle and light crust function.

✓ When the bread is finished, flip it out onto a drying rack and allow it to cool slightly before serving.

✓ Tip(s): Feel free to use other varieties of cheese or make a mixture for added flavor. You may also swap the bacon bits with real, pan crisped bacon bits instead.

51) **Spiced Jalapeno Cheese Bread**

Ingredients: 1 POUND LOAF

- Lukewarm water ½ cup
- Milk powder 2 tbsp
- Unsalted butter   1 ½ cup
- Plain bread flour 2 tbsp
- Cheddar cheese ½ cup
- Jalapeno pepper, finely diced ½ cup
- Granulated brown sugar 1 tbsp
- Salt 1 tsp
- Bread machine yeast ¾ tsp

Direction: 3 hours and 10 minutes / Prep Time: 10 minutes / Cook Time: 3 hours

✓ Combine the water and instant milk powder first, then add it to your bread machine.

✓ Add the remaining ingredients to the bread machine in the sequence stated above or according to the instructions in your bread machine's instruction manual.

✓ Choose the default setting and the soft crust option.

✓ When the bread is finished, flip it out onto a drying rack and allow it to cool slightly before serving.

✓ TIP(S): I removed the seeds from the jalapeno pepper before using it in this recipe. If you like spicy foods, you may add more peppers or leave the seeds in, depending on

✓ your taste

Nuts & Seeds Breads

52) Rye Bread with Caraway
Ingredients: 1 POUND LOAF

- Lukewarm water ¾ cup
- Unsalted butter, diced 1 tbsp
- Molasses 1 tbsp
- Rye flour ½ cup
- Plain bread flour 1 cup
- Whole wheat flour ½ cup
- Milk powder 1 tbsp
- Salt ¾ tsp
- Brown sugar 1 tbsp
- Caraway seeds ¼
- Instant dry yeast 1 ¼ tsp

Direction: 4 hours and 5 minutes / Prep Time: 5 minutes / Cook Time: 4 hours

- ✓ Add the ingredients to the bread machine in the sequence stated above or as directed in the instruction manual for your bread maker.
- ✓ Select whole wheat as the grain type and the medium crust as the crust type.
- ✓ When the bread is finished, flip it out onto a drying rack and allow it to cool slightly before serving.
- ✓ Tip(s): The sweetener can be substituted for the sugar, and the butter can be replaced with extra-virgin olive oil.

53) Sunflower and Flax Seed Bread
Ingredients: 1 POUND LOAF

- Lukewarm water ⅔ cup
- Butter, softened 1 tbsp
- Honey 1 ½ tbsp
- Bread flour ¾ cup
- Whole wheat flour ⅔ cup
- Salt ½ tsp
- Active dry yeast ½ tsp
- Flax seeds ¼ cup
- Sunflower seeds   ¼ cup

Direction: TIME: 3 hours and 10 minutes / Prep Time: 10 minutes / Cook Time: 3 hours

- ✓ All ingredients (excluding the sunflower seeds) should be added to the bread machine in the sequence specified or according to the instructions in your bread machine's instruction manual.
- ✓ Choose between the basic bread setting and the soft or medium crust option.
- ✓ Add the sunflower seeds just before your bread machine reaches its last kneading cycle (most machines will notify you with a sound at this point).
- ✓ When the bread is finished, turn it out onto a drying rack to cool before serving.
- ✓ TIP(S): Flax needs to be finely ground before it is good for you; that's why we add it in at the beginning, and hold only the sunflowers back for the final kneading cycle.
- ✓ Salt can be doubled for a stronger flavor.

54) Sweet Mixed Nut Bread
Ingredients: 1 POUND LOAF

- Lukewarm water ⅔ cup
- Olive oil   1 ⅓ tbsp
- Honey 1 ⅓ tbsp
- Molasses 1 ⅓ tbsp
- Salt   1 tsp
- Whole wheat flour ⅔ cup
- Plain bread flour 1 ⅓ cups
- Active dry yeast 1 ½ tsp
- Pecan nuts ¼ cup
- Walnuts ¼ cup

Direction: 3 hours and 10 minutes / Prep Time: 10 minutes / Cook Time: 3 hours

- ✓ All ingredients (excluding the pecans and walnuts) should be added to the bread machine in the sequence specified or according to the instructions included with your bread maker.
- ✓ Choose the basic cycle and the soft crust function.
- ✓ Add your pecans and walnuts just before the last kneading cycle.
- ✓ When the bread is finished, turn it out onto a drying rack to cool before serving.
- ✓ Tip(s): Although it's always wise to check your dough within the first 10-15 minutes of a bread cycle, for this recipe it is recommended that you check your dough 5 minutes after mixing commences.
- ✓ As usual, add 1 tbsp of water if too chunky, or 1 tbsp of flour if too sticky.

55) Multigrain Sandwich Loaf
Ingredients: 1 POUND LOAF

- Milk, warmed ½ cup
- Unsalted butter 2 tbsp
- Plain bread flour 1 ½ cups
- Multigrain cereal ½ cup
- Granulated brown sugar ¼ cup
- Salt ¾ tsp
- Bread machine yeast ¾ tsp

Direction: 3 hours and 10 minutes / Prep Time: 10 minutes / Cook Time: 3 hours

- ✓ Add the ingredients to the bread machine in the sequence stated above or as directed in the instruction manual for your bread maker. Choose the fundamental setting and the medium crust function. When the bread is finished, flip it out onto a drying rack and allow it to cool slightly before serving.
- ✓ Tip(s): When the Loaf is fresh out from the machine and still hot, brush the top generously with butter and press this into some extra crushed multigrain cereal.

56) Simple and Savory Mixed Seed Loaf
Ingredients: 1 POUND LOAF

- Lukewarm water   ⅔ cup

- Salt   ⅔ tsp
- Olive oil   1 tbsp and 1 tsp
- Whole wheat flour   ⅔ cup
- White bread flour 1 and ⅓ cups
- Active dry yeast 1 tsp
- Linseed 2 tsp
- Pumpkin seeds 2 tsp
- Sesame seeds 2 tsp
- Poppy seeds 2 tsp
- Sunflower seeds   2 tsp

Direction: 3 hours and 5 minutes / Prep Time: 5 minutes / Cook Time: 3 hours

✓ In the exact order specified, add all ingredients to your bread maker.

✓ The seeds may be put in any sequence as long as they follow the yeast.

✓ Select the fundamental bread option, as well as any crust function that interests you.

✓ When the bread is finished, transfer it to a drying rack to cool before serving.

✓ Tip(s): When adding seeds for a 1 ½ pound loaf, the 5 seeds mixed together should fill a ⅓ cup. You can substitute these seeds for any other ⅓ cup of seed mix, but the ones in the recipe are my favorite for this bread. Seed content for a 1 ½ pound loaf can be increased up to a ½ cup, but you must check your dough 10 minutes after kneading to ensure it has enough water.

57)   **Nut Bread**

Ingredients: 1 POUND LOAF

- Lukewarm water ⅔ cup
- Vegetable oil   ½ tbsp
- Lemon juice ½ tsp
- Salt   1 tsp
- Molasses   ⅙ cup
- Quick oatmeal   ⅓ cup
- Whole wheat flour   ½ cup
- Plain bread flour   1 ⅓ cup
- Walnuts   1 ½ cups
- Instant dry yeast   1 ½ tsp

Direction: 3 hours and 15 minutes / Prep Time: 15 minutes / Cook Time: 3 hours

✓ Add the ingredients to the bread machine in the sequence stated above or according to the instructions in your bread machine's instruction manual.

✓ Select the fundamental setting and the soft crust option.

✓ When ready, flip the bread out onto a drying rack to cool slightly before serving.

✓ Tip(s): For a difference in flavor, swap out the walnuts for sliced almonds or mixed nuts. The molasses may be substituted with honey.

58)   **Pecan Cranberry Bread**

Ingredients:

- 12 slice bread (1½ pounds)
- 1⅛ cups lukewarm water
- 3 tablespoons canola oil
- ¾ tablespoon orange zest
- ¾ teaspoon apple cider vinegar
- 2 eggs, slightly beaten
- 2¼ tablespoons sugar
- ¾ teaspoon table salt
- 1½ cups white rice flour
- ½ cup nonfat dry milk powder
- ⅓ cup tapioca flour
- ⅓ cup potato starch
- ¼ cup corn starch
- ¾ tablespoon xanthan gum
- 1½ teaspoons bread machine yeast
- ½ cup dried cranberries
- ½ cup pecan pieces

Direction: PREP: 10 MINUTES /MAKES 1 LOAF

✓ Preparing the Ingredients. Choose the size of loaf of your preference and then measure the ingredients.

✓ Add all of the ingredients mentioned previously in the list, close the lid after placing the pan in the bread machine.

✓ Select the Bake Cycle Turn on the bread maker.

✓ Select the Gluten Free or Fruit/Nut (if your machine has this setting) setting, then the loaf size, and finally the crust color.

✓ Start the cycle. (If you don't have either of the above settings, use Basic/White.).

✓ When the machine signals to add ingredients, add the pecans and cranberries.

✓ (Some machines have a fruit/nut hopper where you can add the pecans and cranberries when you start the machine. During the baking process, the machine will automatically add them into the dough).

✓ When the bread maker cycle is complete, carefully remove the pan from the machine and allow it to cool before serving.

✓ Remove the bread from the pan, put in a wire rack to cool for at least 10 minutes, and slice.

59)   **Almond and Dates Sweet Bread**

Ingredients: 1 POUND LOAF

- Lukewarm water ⅔ cup
- Vegetable oil 1 tbsp
- Honey 1 ⅓ tbsp
- Salt ¼ tsp
- Rolled oats   ½ cup
- Whole wheat flour ½ cup
- Bread flour ½ cup
- Active dry yeast   1 tsp
- Dates, chopped and pitted ⅓ cup

- *Almonds, chopped   ⅓ cup*

Direction: 3 hours and 10 minutes / Prep Time: 10 minutes / Cook Time: 3 hours

- ✓ *All ingredients (excluding the dates and almonds) should be added to the bread machine in the sequence specified or according to the instructions included with your bread maker.*

- ✓ *Select the nut and raisin flavor profile, as well as the soft crust option.*

- ✓ *Add the dates and almonds just before the last kneading cycle of your bread machine begins (most machines will indicate this with a sound).*

- ✓ *When the bread is finished, transfer it to a drying rack to cool before serving.*

- ✓ *TIP(S): The dates can be swapped out with any dried fruit you desire. For a chunkier date or fruit texture in your bread, throw the dates in 2 minutes before the bread is finished, rather than just before the final kneading cycle.*

Special Breads And Cakes

60) Candied Fruits Bread

Ingredients:

- Orange juice - 1 cup
- Lukewarm water - ½ cup
- Butter - 2½ tbsp.,
- softened Powdered milk - 2 tbsp.
- Brown sugar - 2½ tbsp.
- Kosher salt - 1 tsp.
- Whole-grain flour - 4 cups
- Bread machine yeast - 1½ tsp.
- Candied fruits - ¾ cup (pineapple, coconut, papaya)
- Walnuts - ¼ cup, chopped
- All-purpose flour - 1 tbsp. for packing candied fruits
- Almond flakes - ¼ cup

Direction: PREP: 10 MINUTES /MAKES 1 LOAF

- ✓ Preparing the Ingredients Put the candied fruit water, then dry on a paper towel and roll in flour.
- ✓ Choose the size of loaf of your preference and then measure the ingredients.
- ✓ Add all of the ingredients mentioned previously in the list, (except almonds and fruit). Close the lid after placing the pan in the bread machine.
- ✓ Select the Bake Cycle Turn on the bread machine. Select the Wheat/Whole-Grain bread setting, select the loaf size, and the crust color.
- ✓ Press start.
- ✓ When the breadmaker cycle is complete, carefully remove the pan from the machine and allow it to cool before serving.
- ✓ Remove the bread from the pan, put in a wire rack to cool for at least 5 minutes, and slice.

61) Blueberry Honey Bread

Ingredients:

- 16 slice bread (2 pounds)
- 1 cup plain yogurt
- ⅔ cup lukewarm water
- ¼ cup honey
- 4 teaspoons unsalted butter, melted
- 1½ teaspoons lime zest
- ⅔ teaspoon lemon extract
- 4 cups white bread flour
- 2¼ teaspoons bread machine yeast
- 2 teaspoons table salt
- 1⅓ cups dried blueberries

Direction: PREP: 10 MINUTES /MAKES 1 LOAF

- ✓ Preparing the Ingredients. Choose the size of loaf of your preference and then measure the ingredients.
- ✓ Add all of the ingredients mentioned previously in the list, except for the blueberries.
- ✓ Close the lid after placing the pan in the bread machine.
- ✓ Set your oven to the Bake setting. Turn on the breadmaker. Simply choose White/Basic or Fruit/Nut (if your machine has this setting) and then the loaf size and crust color that you desire.

- ✓ Press start.
- ✓ When the machine signals to add ingredients, add the blueberries.
- ✓ When the breadmaker cycle is complete, carefully remove the pan from the machine and allow it to cool before serving.
- ✓ Remove the bread from the pan, put in a wire rack to cool for at least 10 minutes, and slice.

62) Saffron Tomato Bread

Ingredients:

- 1 teaspoon bread machine yeast
- 2½ cups wheat bread machine flour
- 1 Tablespoon panifarin
- 1½ teaspoon kosher salt
- 1½ Tablespoon white sugar
- 1 Tablespoon extra-virgin olive oil
- 1 Tablespoon tomatoes, dried and chopped
- 1 Tablespoon tomato paste
- ½ cup firm cheese (cubes)
- ½ cup feta cheese
- 1 pinch saffron
- 1½ cups serum

Direction: Preparation Time: 3 hours 30 minutes
Cooking Time: 15minutes Servings: 10

- ✓ Add 1 tbsp. olive oil and 1 tbsp. dried tomatoes five minutes before cooking is finished. Mix the tomato paste into the mixture.
- ✓ Place the dry and liquid ingredients, excluding any additives, into the bread machine pan and follow the bread machine's directions.
- ✓ Pay special attention to the amount of each ingredient. A cup, spoon, and kitchen scale are all you need to get the job done.
  4 Set the baking program to BASIC and the crust type to MEDIUM.
- ✓ 5 Add the additives after the beep or place them in the dispenser of the bread machine.
- ✓ Remove the bread from the pan by shaking it. Use a spatula if required. Take a kitchen towel and cover the bread.
- ✓ Let it rest for an hour.
- ✓ On the other hand, you can put it on a wire rack and let it cool down.

63) Cardamon Bread

Ingredients:

- ½ cup milk, at 80°F to 90°F
- 1 egg, at room temperature
- 1 teaspoon melted butter, cooled
- 1 teaspoons honey
- ⅔Teaspoon salt
- ⅔ Teaspoon ground cardamom
- 2 cups white bread flour
- ¾ teaspoon bread machine or instant yeast

- ✓ Put the ingredients in your bread maker according to the manufacturer's instructions.
- ✓ Press Start after setting the machine to Basic/White bread and choose between a light or medium crust.
- ✓ Make sure that the bread is done before taking the bucket out of the machine.
- ✓ Allow the loaf to cool for five minutes before serving.
- ✓ To remove the loaf, gently shake the bucket, and then turn it out onto a cooling rack.

64) **Herb Bread**

Ingredients:

- 3/4 to 7/8 cup milk
- 1 tablespoon Sugar
- 1 teaspoon Salt
- 1 tablespoon Butter or margarine
- 1/3 cup chopped onion
- 2 cups bread flour
- 1/2 teaspoon Dried dill
- 1/2 teaspoon Dried basil
- 1/2 teaspoon Dried rosemary
- 11/2 teaspoon Active dry yeast

Direction: Preparation Time: 1 hour 20 minutes Cooking Time: 50 minutes (20+30 minutes) Servings: 1 loaf

- ✓ Add all the ingredients to the bread pan. The rapid bake cycle should be used after medium crus. Pressing the start button activates the process.
- ✓ As soon as you hear straining sounds in your machine or see the dough becoming stiff and dry after 5-10 minutes, add 1 tablespoon of liquid at a time until the dough is smooth, soft, and slightly tacky to touch.
- ✓ Then you can proceed with the rest of the recipe.
- ✓ Remove the bread from the pan once it has risen and cooled for a few minutes. Let cool for an hour before cutting into slices.

65) **Original Italian Herb Bread**

Ingredients:

- 1 cup water at 80 degrees F
- ½ cup olive brine
- 1½ tablespoons butter
- 2 tablespoons sugar
- 1 teaspoons salt
- 5 ⅓ cups flour
- 1 teaspoons bread machine yeast
- 20 olives, black/green
- 1½ teaspoons Italian herbs

Direction: Preparation Time: 2hours 40 minutes Cooking Time: 50 minutes Servings: 2 loaves

- ✓ Slice the olives thinly.
- ✓ Add all of the ingredients (excluding olives) to your bread machine, following the manufacturer's instructions.
- ✓ For medium crust, select the French bread setting on your bread maker and set the crust type to medium.
- ✓ Start by pressing the START button.
- ✓ Add olives when the maker beeps.
- ✓ Be patient and let the process play out.
- ✓ Wait for the loaf to cool down for 5 minutes before removing the bucket.
- ✓ Remove the bread by gently shaking the bucket.
- ✓ Slicing and serving are the final steps.

66) **Oregano Mozza-Cheese Bread**

Ingredients:

- 1 cup (milk + egg) mixture
- ½ cup mozzarella cheese
- 2¼ cups flour
- ¾cup whole grain flour
- 2 Tablespoons sugar
- 1 teaspoon salt
- 1 teaspoons oregano
- 1½ teaspoons dry yeast

Direction: Preparation Time: 2hours 50 minutes Cooking Time: 50 minutes Servings: 2 loaves

- ✓ Set your bread machine on dough cycle and add all of the ingredients.
- ✓ Set your bread machine's program to Basic/White Bread and choose a dark crust type.
- ✓ Start by pressing the START button.
- ✓ Wait for the cycle to complete before moving on to the next one.
- ✓ Wait for the loaf to cool down for 5 minutes before removing the bucket.
- ✓ Remove the bread by gently shaking the bucket.
- ✓ Slicing and serving are the final steps.

67) **Cumin Bread**

Ingredients:

- 1/3 cups bread machine flour, sifted
- 1½ teaspoon kosher salt
- 1½ Tablespoon sugar
- 1 Tablespoon bread machine yeast
- 1¾ cups lukewarm water
- 1 Tablespoon black cumin
- 1 Tablespoon sunflower oil

Direction: Preparation Time: 3hours 30minutes Cooking Time: 15 minutes Servings: 8

- ✓ Place the dry and liquid ingredients in a baking pan and bake according to the manufacturer's instructions.
- ✓ Use the BASIC baking software and a MEDIUM crust type.
- ✓ Adjust the flour and liquid in the recipe if the dough is excessively dense or wet.
- ✓ The pan should be taken out of the bread machine and allowed to cool for 5 minutes once the program

has finished.

- ✓ Remove the bread from the pan by shaking it. A spatula can be used if necessary.
- ✓ A kitchen towel can be used to wrap the bread, then put it in the fridge for an hour. Cool it on a wire rack, if necessary.

68) Blueberry Oatmeal Bread

Ingredients:

- ¾ cup milk, at 80°F to 90°F
- 1 egg, at room temperature
- 2¼ tablespoons melted butter, cooled
- 1½ tablespoons honey
- ½ cup rolled oats
- 2 ⅓ cups white bread flour
- 1⅛ teaspoons salt
- 1½ teaspoons bread machine or instant yeast
- ½ cup dried blueberries

Direction: PREP: MINUTES MAKES LOAF 12 SLICE READ (1½ pounds)

- ✓ Preparing the Ingredients. As instructed by your bread machine's owner's manual, put in all of your ingredients, except for the blueberries.
- ✓ Choose light or medium crust and push Start when the machine is set to Basic/White bread.
- ✓ When the machine tells you to, or five minutes before the second kneading cycle is complete, add the blueberries.
- ✓ The Bake Cycle must be chosen. Remove the bucket from the machine after the loaf is finished baking.
- ✓ Take a 5-minute break from the loaf's cooling process.
- ✓ After removing the loaf, gently shake the bucket to remove the loaf, and then transfer it to the cooling rack.

69) Rosemary Cranberry Pecan Bread

Ingredients:

- 1 ⅓ cups water, plus 2 Tbsp water
- 2 Tbsp butter
- 2 tsp salt
- 4 cups bread flour
- ¾ cup dried sweetened cranberries
- ¾ cup toasted chopped pecans
- 2 Tbsp. non-fat powdered milk
- ¼ cup sugar
- 2 tsp yeast

Direction: PREP: 10 MINUTES /MAKES 14 SLICES

- ✓ Preparing the Ingredients In the order and at the temperature specified by the maker of your bread machine, add each ingredient to the bread machine..
- ✓ Select the Bake Cycle Close the lid, select the basic bread, medium crust setting on your bread machine and press start.

- ✓ Take out the baked bread from the bread machine and allow it to cool on a cooling rack.
- ✓

70) Cranberry Walnut Wheat Bread

Ingredients:

- 1 cup warm water
- 1 tablespoon molasses
- 2 tablespoons butter
- 1 teaspoon salt
- 2 cups 100% whole wheat flour
- 1 cup unbleached flour
- 2 tablespoons dry milk
- 1 cup cranberries
- 1 cup walnuts, chopped
- 2 teaspoons active dry yeast

Direction: PREP: 10 MINUTES /MAKES 14 SLICES

- ✓ Preparing the Ingredients To begin, add the liquid ingredients to the breadmaker pan. Add the dry ingredients, save for the yeast, walnuts and cranberries.
- ✓ Toss the yeast into the center of the bread flour and stir to combine. Once you've put the pan in the bread machine, close the top and press start.
- ✓ The Bake Cycle should be chosen. Make a selection for your favorite crust color, then press the Start button to bake your wheat bread. After the first kneading cycle is complete, add cranberries and walnuts.
- ✓ The bread is done baking when it comes out of the oven and has cooled down fully on a cooling rack.

71) Fragrant Orange Bread

Ingredients:

- 1 cup milk, at 80°F to 90°F
- 3 tablespoons freshly squeezed orange juice, at room temperature
- 3 tablespoons sugar
- 1 tablespoon melted butter, cooled
- 1 teaspoon salt
- 3 cups white bread flour
- Zest of 1 orange
- 1¼ teaspoons bread machine or instant yeast

Direction: PREP: 10 MINUTES MAKES 1 LOAF12 SLICE BREAD (1½pounds)

- ✓ Preparing the Ingredients.
- ✓ Put the ingredients in your bread maker according to the manufacturer's instructions.
- ✓ Choose the Bake Cycle Set the machine to Basic/White bread, choose between light or medium crust, then push Start.
- ✓ When the loaf is done, remove the bucket from the machine.
- ✓ Let the loaf cool for 5 minutes. Gently shake the bucket to remove the loaf, and turn it out onto a rack to cool.

72) Moist Oatmeal Apple Bread

Ingredients:

- ⅔ cup milk, at 80°F to 90°F
- ¼ cup unsweetened applesauce, at room temperature
- 1 tablespoon melted butter, cooled
- 1 tablespoon sugar
- 1 teaspoon salt
- ½ teaspoon ground cinnamon
- Pinch ground nutmeg
- ¼ cup quick oats
- 2¼ cups white bread flour
- 2¼ teaspoons bread machine or active dry yeast

Direction: PREP: 10 MINUTES MAKES 1 LOAF12 SLICE BREAD (1½pounds)

- ✓ Preparing the Ingredients. Your bread machine's instructions will tell you how to put the ingredients in. Set the machine to make Basic/White bread with a light or medium crust, then hit the Start button to get it going.
- ✓ Make sure that the bread is done before taking the bucket out of the machine.
- ✓ The Bake Cycle should be picked as an option. Time to let the bread cool for five minutes. Remove the loaf by gently shaking the pail and transferring it to a cooling rack.

73) Whole Wheat Banana Bread with Caramel Glaze

Ingredients:

- 2 cups white whole wheat flour
- 1 teaspoon baking soda
- ½ teaspoon baking powder
- ½ teaspoon salt
- ½ cup butter, softened
- ½ cup granulated sugar
- ½ cup packed brown sugar
- 2 eggs
- 1 ⅓ cups mashed very ripe bananas (3 medium)
- ½ cup chopped pecans, toasted glaze
- ½ cup packed brown sugar
- 3 tablespoons whipping cream
- 2 tablespoons butter, cut up
- 1 tablespoon light corn syrup
- ½ cup chopped pecans, toasted

Direction: PREP: 10 MINUTES /MAKES 1 LOAF

- ✓ Preparing the Ingredients. Put the ingredients in your bread maker according to the manufacturer's instructions.
- ✓ Program the machine for Basic/White bread, select light or medium crust, and press Start.
- ✓ When the loaf is done, remove the bucket from the machine. Let the loaf cool for 5 minutes.
- ✓ Gently shake the bucket to remove the loaf, and turn it out onto a rack to cool.

- ✓ Select the Bake Cycle Cool completely, about 2 hours.
- ✓ Meanwhile, in 1-quart saucepan, combine all glaze ingredients except pecans.
- ✓ Bring to a boil over medium heat, stirring frequently, until sugar has melted.
- ✓ Boil, without stirring, 45 to 60 seconds or until thickened.
- ✓ Pour into small bowl; refrigerate 30 to 40 minutes or until cool enough to spread, stirring occasionally.
- ✓ Spread caramel over top of cooled bread; sprinkle ½ cup chopped pecans over caramel.
- ✓ Let stand until set. To toast pecans, bake in ungreased shallow pan at 325°F for 7 to 11 minutes, stirring occasionally, until light brown.
- ✓ When stirring the caramel, make sure all of the sugar is dissolved before it boils and thickens, or crystallization can occur.
- ✓ If there is sugar that has not dissolved on the side of the pan, use a pastry brush dipped in water to wash the sugar crystals down into the caramel before boiling.

74) Orange Cranberry Bread

Ingredients:

- ¾ cup milk, at 80°F to 90°F
- ¾ cup sugar
- ⅔ cup melted butter, cooled
- 2 eggs, at room temperature
- ¼ cup freshly squeezed orange juice, at room temperature
- 1 tablespoon orange zest
- 1 teaspoon pure vanilla extract
- 2¼ cups all-purpose flour
- 1 cup sweetened dried cranberries
- 1½ teaspoons baking powder
- ½ teaspoon baking soda
- ½ teaspoon salt
- ¼ teaspoon ground nutmeg

Direction: PREP: 10 MINUTES MAKES 1 LOAF12 SLICE BREAD (1½pounds)

- ✓ Preparing the Ingredients. Place all of the ingredients for your bread machine into the machine. Select the baking mode.
- ✓ Press the Start button to begin making bread.
- ✓ Toss together the dry ingredients while the wet ones are mixing in a medium bowl with the flour and cranberries.
- ✓ Add the dry ingredients when the initial quick mixing is complete and the machine signals.
- ✓ Remove the bucket from the machine after the loaf is done baking. Time to let the bread cool for five minutes.
- ✓ To remove the loaf, gently shake the bucket, and then turn it out onto a cooling rack.

75) Cardamom Cranberry Bread

Ingredients:

- 1¾ cups water
- 2 tbsp. brown sugar
- 1½ tsp salt
- 2 tbsp. coconut oil
- 4 cups flour
- 2 tsp cinnamon
- 2 tsp cardamom
- 1 cup dried cranberries
- 2 tsp yeast

Direction: PREP: 10 MINUTES /MAKES 1 LOAF

✓ Preparing the Ingredients Add each ingredient except the dried cranberries to the bread machine in the order and at the temperature recommended by your bread machine manufacturer.

✓ Select the Bake Cycle Close the lid, select the basic bread, medium crust setting on your bread machine and press start. Add the dried cranberries 5 to 10 minutes before the last kneading cycle ends.

✓ Take out the baked bread from the bread machine and allow it to cool on a cooling rack.

76) Harvest Fruit Bread

Ingredients:

- 1 cup plus 2 tbsp. water (70°F to 80°F)
- 1 egg
- 3 tbsp. butter, softened
- ¼ cup packed brown sugar
- 1½ tsp salt
- ¼ tsp ground nutmeg
- Dash allspice
- 3¾ cups plus 1 tbsp. bread flour
- 2 tsp active dry yeast
- 1 cup dried fruit (dried cherries, cranberries and/or raisins)
- ⅓ cup chopped pecans

Direction: PREP: 10 MINUTES /MAKES 14 SLICES

✓ Preparing the Ingredients Add each ingredient except the fruit and pecans to the bread machine in the order and at the temperature recommended by your bread machine manufacturer.

✓ Select the Bake Cycle Close the lid, select the basic bread, medium crust setting on your bread machine, and press start.

✓ Just before the final kneading, add the fruit and pecans.

✓ Take out the baked bread from the bread machine and allow it to cool on a cooling rack.

77) Fragrant Herb Bread

Ingredients:

- 1⅛ cups water, at 80°F to 90°F
- 1½ tablespoons melted butter, cooled

- 1½ tablespoons sugar
- 1 teaspoon salt
- 3 tablespoons skim milk powder
- 1 teaspoon dried thyme
- 1 teaspoon dried chives
- 1 teaspoon dried oregano
- 3 cups white bread flour
- 1¼ teaspoons bread machine or instant yeast

Direction: PREP: 10 MINUTES MAKES 1 LOAF12 SLICE BREAD (1½pounds)

✓ Preparing the Ingredients. Put the ingredients in your bread maker according to the manufacturer's instructions.

✓ Program the machine for Basic/White bread, select light or medium crust, and press Start.

✓ Select the Bake Cycle Remove the bucket from the machine after the loaf is complete. Allow the bread to cool for 5 minutes before slicing. Shake the bucket gently to dislodge the loaf, then turn it out onto a cooling rack.

78) Super Spice Bread

Ingredients:

- 1 ⅓ cups lukewarm milk
- 2 eggs, at room temperature
- 2 tablespoons unsalted butter, melted
- 2 ⅔ tablespoons honey
- 1 ⅓ teaspoons table salt
- 4 cups white bread flour
- 1 ⅓ teaspoons ground cinnamon
- ⅔ teaspoon ground cardamom
- ⅔ teaspoon ground nutmeg
- 2¼ teaspoons bread machine yeast

Direction: PREP: 10 MINUTES MAKES 1 LOAF16 SLICE BREAD (2 pounds)

✓ Preparing the Ingredients. Measure out the ingredients for the loaf size you want to bake.

✓ In the sequence stated above, add the ingredients to the bread pan.

✓ Close the bread machine's lid and place the pan inside.

✓ Start the bread machine. " Select the White/Basic setting, then the loaf size, and finally the crust color, to get the desired result. Reset the loop.

✓ Choose the Bake Cycle you want. Carefully remove the pan from the machine once the cycle has done and the bread has been baked.

✓ Keep your hands away from the handle, as it will be extremely hot. Let it cool down for a while.

✓ Once it's out of the pan, allow it to cool for at least 10 minutes before cutting into it.

79) Swiss Olive Bread

Ingredients:

- 1 cup lukewarm milk
- 1½ tablespoons unsalted butter, melted

- *1 teaspoon minced garlic*
- *1½ tablespoons sugar*
- *1 teaspoon table salt*
- *¾ cup Swiss cheese, shredded*
- *3 cups white bread flour*
- *1 teaspoon bread machine yeast*
- *⅓ cup chopped black olives*

Direction: PREP: 10 MINUTES PLUS FERMENTING TIMEMAKES 1 LOAF12SLICE BREAD (1½ pounds)

- ✓ *Preparing the Ingredients. Measure out the ingredients for the loaf you want to bake.*
- ✓ *In the bread pan, combine the other ingredients, except for the olives, in the sequence stated above. Close the bread machine's lid and put the pan inside.*
- ✓ *Start the bread machine.*
- ✓ *Select the Bake Cycle To begin, select the White/Basic or Fruit/Nut (if your machine has this choice) setting, followed by the loaf size, and finally the crust color setting. Set up a new loop.*
- ✓ *To add ingredients, simply follow the machine's instructions.*
- ✓ *At the beginning of the baking process, some machines offer an area where you may add olives and they will be incorporated into your finished product as it bakes.*
- ✓ *When the cycle is finished and the bread is baked, carefully remove the pan from the machine.*
- ✓ *Use a potholder as the handle will be very hot. Let rest for a few minutes.*
- ✓ *Remove the bread from the pan and allow to cool on a wire rack for at least 10 minutes before slicing.*

80) **Christmas Bread**

Ingredients:

- *1¼ cups warm whole milk (70°F to 80°F)*
- *½ tsp lemon juice*
- *2 tbsp. butter, softened*
- *2 tbsp. sugar*
- *1½ tsp salt*
- *3 cups bread flour*
- *2 tsp active dry yeast*
- *¾ cup golden raisins*
- *¾ cup raisins*
- *½ cup dried currants*
- *1½ tsp grated lemon zest*
- *Glaze: ½ cup powdered sugar*
- *1½ tsp 2% milk*
- *1 tsp melted butter*
- *¼ tsp vanilla extract*

Direction: PREP: 10 MINUTES /MAKES 8 SLICES

- ✓ *Preparing the Ingredients Add each ingredient except the raisins, currants, and lemon zest to the bread machine in the order and at the temperature recommended by your bread machine manufacturer.*
- ✓ *Select the Bake Cycle Close the lid, select the sweet loaf, low crust setting on your bread machine, and press start.*
- ✓ *Just before the final kneading, add the raisins, currants and lemon zest.*
- ✓ *Take out the baked bread from the bread machine and allow it to cool on a cooling rack.*
- ✓ *Combine the glaze ingredients in a bowl. Drizzle over the cooled bread*

81) **Golden Brown**

Ingredients:

- *¾ cup +1 tablespoon water, lukewarm between 80 and 90°F*
- *2 tablespoons unsalted butter, melted*
- *1 egg, beaten*
- *2 tablespoons sugar*
- *1 ½ teaspoons salt*
- *3 ¼ cups white bread flour*
- *1 ½ teaspoons bread machine yeast or rapid rise yeast*

For oven baking

- *1 egg yolk*
- *2 tablespoons cold water*
- *1 tablespoon poppy seed (optional)*

Direction: PREP: 10 MINUTES MAKES 1 LOAF12 SLICE BREAD (1½pounds)

- ✓ *Preparing the Ingredients. Measure out the ingredients for the loaf size you want to bake.*
- ✓ *The order in which you add the ingredients to the bread pan is as follows: Take out the bread machine's pan and put the lid on.*
- ✓ *Select the Bake Cycle Turn on the bread maker. Select the Dough setting, then the loaf size, and finally the crust color. Start the cycle.*
- ✓ *Lightly flour a working surface and prepare a large baking sheet by greasing it with cooking spray or vegetable oil or line with parchment paper or a silicone mat.*
- ✓ *Preheat the oven to 375°F and place the oven rack in the middle position.*
- ✓ *After the dough cycle is done, carefully remove the dough from the pan and place it on the working surface. Divide dough in three even parts.*
- ✓ *Roll each part into 13-inch-long cables for the 1 ½ pound Challah bread or 17-inch for the 2-pound loaf. Arrange the dough cables side by side and start braiding from its middle part.*
- ✓ *In order to make a seal, pinch ends and tuck the ends under the braid.*
- ✓ *Arrange the loaf onto the baking sheet; cover the sheet with a clean kitchen towel. Let rise for 45-60 minutes or more until it doubles in size.*
- ✓ *In a mixing bowl, mix the egg yolk and cold water to make an egg wash.*
- ✓ *Gently brush the egg wash over the loaf. Sprinkle top with the poppy seed, if desired.*
- ✓ *Bake for about 25-30 minutes or until loaf turns golden brown and is fully cooked.*

82)   Irish Yogurt Bread

Ingredients:

- 1¾ cups all-purpose flour
- ½ cup dried currants or raisins
- 1½ teaspoons baking powder
- ¼ teaspoon baking soda
- ¼ teaspoon salt
- 1 container (6 oz) lemon burst,
- orange crème
- French vanilla yogurt
- 2 tablespoons vegetable oil

Direction: PREP: 10 MINUTES /MAKES 8 WEDGES

- ✓ Preparing the Ingredients. Make your bread machine according to the manufacturer's guidelines.
- ✓ You can choose between a light or medium crust and hit the Start button after setting the machine to make basic/white bread.
- ✓ Select the Bake Cycle Remove the bucket from the machine when the bread is done. Time to let the loaf cool for five minutes.
- ✓ Remove the loaf from the bucket with a little shake, and then place it on a rack to cool.

83)   White Chocolate Cranberry Bread

Ingredients:

- ¾ cup plus 2 tablespoons milk, at 80°F to 90°F
- 1 egg, at room temperature
- 1½ tablespoons melted butter, cooled
- 1 teaspoon pure vanilla extract
- 2 tablespoons sugar
- ¾ teaspoon salt
- 3 cups white bread flour
- 1 teaspoon bread machine or instant yeast
- ½ cup white chocolate chips
- ⅓ cup sweetened dried cranberries

Direction: PREP: 10 MINUTES PLUS FERMENTING TIME MAKES 1 LOAF12 SLICE BREAD (1½ pounds)

- ✓ Preparing the Ingredients. Add all of the ingredients, except the chocolate chips and cranberries, to your bread machine in accordance with the manufacturer's instructions.
- ✓ Select a Bake Cycle You can select a light or medium crust by pressing the Start button.
- ✓ Remove the bucket from the machine once the loaf is done baking. Add the white chocolate chips and cranberries when the machine tells you to or 5 minutes before the last knead cycle is complete.
- ✓ Time to let the bread cool for 5 minutes. Turn out onto a cooling rack after removing the loaf from the bucket.

84)   Italian Easter Cake

Ingredients:

- 1¾ cups wheat flour
- 2½ tbsp. quick-acting dry yeast
- 8 tbsp. sugar
- ½ tsp salt
- 3 chicken eggs
- ¾ cup milk
- 3 tbsp. butter
- 1 cup raisins

Direction: PREP: 10 MINUTES PLUS FERMENTING TIME /MAKES 4 SLICES

- ✓ Preparing the Ingredients Add each ingredient except the raisins to the bread machine in the order and at the temperature recommended by your bread machine manufacturer.
- ✓ Select the Bake cycle.
- ✓ Close the lid, select the sweet loaf, low crust setting on your bread machine, and press start.
- ✓ When the dough is kneading, add the raisins.
- ✓ Take out the baked bread from the bread machine and allow it to cool on a cooling rack.

85)   Eggnog Bread

Ingredients:

- ¾ cup eggnog, at 80°F to 90°F
- ¾ tablespoon melted butter, cooled
- 1 tablespoon sugar
- ⅔ teaspoon salt
- ¼ teaspoon ground cinnamon
- ¼ teaspoon ground nutmeg
- 2 cups white bread flour
- ¾ teaspoon bread machine or instant yeast

Direction: PREP: 10 MINUTES PLUS FERMENTING TIME MAKES 1 LOAF8 SLICE BREAD (1 pound)

- ✓ Preparing the Ingredients. Put the ingredients in your bread maker according to the manufacturer's instructions.
- ✓ Choose the Bake Cycle Set the machine to Basic/White bread, choose between light or medium crust, then push Start.
- ✓ Make sure that the bread is done before taking the bucket out of the machine. Time to let the bread cool for five minutes.
- ✓ To remove the loaf, gently shake the bucket, and then turn it out onto a cooling rack.
- ✓ Basil Pizza Dough Ingredients 1 cup lukewarm water 3 tablespoons olive oil 1 teaspoon table salt 1½ teaspoons sugar 1½ teaspoons basil, dried 3 cups white bread flour or all-purpose flour 1½ teaspoons bread machine yeast Directions
- ✓ Preparing the Ingredients. Measure your ingredients to determine how much dough you want to make. The order in which you add the ingredients to the bread pan is as follows:
- ✓ Closing the bread machine's lid after placing the pan inside is sufficient. The Bake Cycle should be picked as an option. Start the bread machine.
- ✓ Select the Dough setting, then the dough size. "' The machine should be turned on now. Carefully remove the dough from the pan when it's done baking.
- ✓ A pizza crust should be rolled out on a lightly floured surface, then cut into desired shapes.

- ✓ Allow 10–15 minutes for this to happen.
- ✓ Add your favorite pizza sauce, toppings, cheese, etc. on the pizza crust before baking.
- ✓ 15–20 minutes at 400°F or 204°C, or until the edges begin to brown.

86) **Milk Honey Sourdough Bread**

Ingredients:

- ½ cup lukewarm milk
- 2 cups sourdough starter
- ¼ cup olive oil
- 2 tablespoons honey
- 1 ⅓ teaspoons salt
- 4 cups white bread flour
- 1 ⅓ teaspoons bread machine yeast

Direction: PREP: 10 MINUTES PLUS FERMENTING TIME MAKES 1 LOAF16 SLICE BREAD (2 pounds)

- ✓ Preparing the Ingredients. Measure out the ingredients for the loaf size you want to bake. The order in which you add the ingredients to the bread pan is as follows:
- ✓ Closing the bread machine's lid after placing the pan inside is sufficient.
- ✓ Click on the Bake button. Start the bread machine.
- ✓ Finally, choose a crust color by selecting White/Basic as your preset.
- ✓ Begin the process. Carefully remove the pan from the machine once the cycle has done and the bread has been baked.
- ✓ Use a potholder to protect your hands from the handle's heat. Let it cool down for a while.
- ✓ At least 10 minutes before slicing, remove the bread from the pan and place it on a cooling rack.

87) **Cherry Christmas Bread**

Ingredients:

- 1 cup + 1 tablespoon lukewarm milk
- 1 egg, at room temperature
- 2 tablespoons unsalted butter, melted
- 3 tablespoons light brown sugar
- ⅛ teaspoon ground cinnamon
- 4 cups white bread flour, divided
- 1½ teaspoons bread machine yeast
- ⅔ cup candied cherries
- ½ cup chopped almonds
- ½ cup raisins, chopped

Direction: PREP: 10 MINUTES PLUS FERMENTING TIME MAKES 1 LOAF16 SLICE BREAD (2 pounds)

- ✓ Preparing the Ingredients. Measure out the ingredients for the loaf size you want to bake.
- ✓ In a bread pan, combine all of the ingredients except the cherries, raisins, and almonds.
- ✓ Closing the bread machine's lid after placing the pan inside is sufficient.
- ✓ Start the bread machine. " Depending on the type of bread machine you have, you can select either the White/Basic or Fruit/Nut (if applicable) setting, as well as the loaf size and crust color.
- ✓ Reset the loop.
- ✓ Choose Bake Cycle and add cherries, raisins and almonds when machine tells you to.
- ✓ The cherries, raisins, and almonds can be added to the machine's fruit/nut hopper when you start it up.). If you choose, you can also manually add them at this point.)
- ✓ Carefully remove the pan from the machine once the cycle has done and the bread has been baked.
- ✓ Use a potholder to protect your hands from the handle's heat. Let it cool down for a while.
- ✓ At least 10 minutes before slicing, remove the bread from the pan and place it on a cooling rack.

88) **Maple-Walnut Twists**

Ingredients:

- Dough
- 1 cup water
- ¼ butter, softened
- 1 egg
- 3½ cups bread flour
- ⅓ cup granulated sugar
- 1 teaspoon salt
- 1½ teaspoons bread machine or fast-acting dry yeast Filling
- ¼ cup finely chopped walnuts
- 2 tablespoons maple-flavored syrup
- 2 tablespoons butter, softened
- ½ teaspoon ground cinnamon Icing
- 1 cup powdered sugar
- ½ teaspoon maple extract
- About 1 tablespoon milk

Direction: PREP: 10 MINUTES PLUS FERMENTING TIME /MAKES 1 LOAF

- ✓ Preparing the Ingredients. Make sure you follow the manufacturer's instructions when it comes to putting the ingredients in the bread machine pan.
- ✓ To bake, select the Dough/Manual cycle from the Bake menu. Avoid using the delay cycle.
- ✓ Remove the dough from the pan by rubbing it with a little flour.
- ✓ Underneath a lightly floured surface, cover and let rest for 10 minutes.
- ✓ In small bowl, mix all filling ingredients.
- ✓ Grease 13×9-inch pan. Roll or pat dough into 16×10-inch rectangle on lightly floured surface.
- ✓ Put a half of the filling in the middle third of the rectangle and spread it out evenly.
- ✓ To assemble, spread remaining filling over the dough and fold in the outer third.
- ✓ Fold the remaining third of the dough over the filling; pinch the border to seal.
- ✓ Slice sixteen 1-inch strips crosswise.
- ✓ Twist the strips in opposing directions while holding

them at the ends.

- ✓ Place strips about 1 inch apart in pan, forming 2 rows of 8 strips each.
- ✓ Cover and let rise in warm place 50 to 60 minutes or until doubled in size.
- ✓ An indentation may be seen when the dough is pressed.
- ✓ Heat oven to 350°F. Bake 35 to 40 minutes or until golden brown. In small bowl, mix all icing ingredients until smooth and thin enough to drizzle.
- ✓ Drizzle icing over warm twists.
- ✓ Serve warm.

89) Bread Machine Brioche
Ingredients:

- ½ cup plus 1 tablespoon milk, at 80°F to 90°F
- 3 eggs, at room temperature
- 2 tablespoons sugar
- ¾ teaspoon salt
- 3 cups white bread flour
- 1½ teaspoons bread machine or instant yeast
- ½ cup (1 stick) butter, softened

Direction: PREP: 10 MINUTES PLUS FERMENTING TIME MAKES 1 LOAF12 SLICE BREAD (1½ pounds)

- ✓ Preparing the Ingredients. Put the ingredients in your bread maker according to the manufacturer's instructions. Program the machine for Basic/White bread, select light crust, and press Start.
- ✓ Cut the butter into tablespoon-sized pieces.
- ✓ Select the Bake Cycle About 10 minutes before the end of your first kneading cycle, begin adding the butter, 1 tablespoon each minute.
- ✓ Make sure that the bread is done before taking the bucket out of the machine. Time to let the bread cool for five minutes.
- ✓ Remove the loaf from the bucket with a little shake, and let it cool on a rack.

90) Traditional Paska
Ingredients:

- ¾ cup milk, at 80°F to 90°F
- 2 eggs, at room temperature
- 2 tablespoons butter, melted and cooled
- ¼ cup sugar
- 1 teaspoon salt
- 2 teaspoons lemon zest
- 3 cups white bread flour
- 2 teaspoons bread machine or instant yeast

Direction: PREP: 10 MINUTES PLUS FERMENTING TIME MAKES 1 LOAF12 SLICE BREAD (1½ pounds)

- ✓ Preparing the Ingredients. Put the ingredients in your bread maker as instructed by the manufacturer.
- ✓ Select a Baking Cycle You can select a light or medium crust by pressing the Start button after setting the machine to Basic/White bread mode.
- ✓ Make sure that the bread is done before taking the

bucket out of the machine.

- ✓ Allow the loaf to cool for five minutes before serving.
- ✓ To remove the loaf, gently shake the bucket, and then turn it out onto a cooling rack.

91) Raisin and Nut Paska
Ingredients:

- ¾ cup milk, at 80°F to 90°F
- 2 eggs, at room temperature
- 2 tablespoons butter, melted and cooled
- ¼ cup sugar
- 1 teaspoon salt
- 2 teaspoons lemon zest
- 3 cups white bread flour
- 2 teaspoons bread machine or instant yeast
- ⅓ cup slivered almonds
- ⅓ cup golden raisins

Direction: PREP: 10 MINUTES PLUS FERMENTING TIME MAKES 1 LOAF12 SLICE BREAD (1½ pounds)

- ✓ Preparing the Ingredients. Place the ingredients, except the almonds and raisins, in your bread machine as recommended by the manufacturer.
- ✓ Choose the Bake Cycle Set the machine to Basic/White bread, choose between light or medium crust, then push Start.
- ✓ When the loaf is done, remove the bucket from the machine.
- ✓ Add the almonds and raisins when the machine signals or 5 minutes before the second kneading cycle is finished.
- ✓ Let the loaf cool for 5 minutes. Gently shake the bucket to remove the loaf, and turn it out onto a rack to cool.

92) Honey Cake
Ingredients:

- ⅓ cup brewed coffee, cooled to room temperature
- ½ cup (1 stick) butter, melted and cooled
- ½ cup honey
- ¾ cup sugar
- ¼ cup dark brown sugar
- 2 eggs, at room temperature
- 2 tablespoons whiskey
- ¼ cup freshly squeezed orange juice, at room temperature
- 1 teaspoon pure vanilla extract
- 2 cups all-purpose flour
- ½ tablespoon baking powder
- ½ tablespoon ground cinnamon
- ½ teaspoon baking soda
- ¼ teaspoon ground allspice
- ¼ teaspoon salt
- ¼ teaspoon ground cloves

Direction: PREP: 10 MINUTES PLUS FERMENTING

- ✓ *Preparing the Ingredients. Place the coffee, butter, honey, sugar, brown sugar, eggs, whiskey, orange juice, and vanilla in your bread machine.*
- ✓ *Press the Start button after selecting the Bake Cycle Program for Quick/Rapid Bread on the machine.*
- ✓ *Baking soda, cinnamon and spices can all be added at this point while the wet ingredients are still being mixed.*
- ✓ *Add the dry ingredients when the initial quick mixing is complete and the machine indicates.*
- ✓ *Make sure that the bread is done before taking the bucket out of the machine. Time to let the bread cool for five minutes.*
- ✓ *Remove the loaf from the bucket with a little shake, and let it cool on a rack.*

93) *Christmas Fruit Bread*

Ingredients:

- ¾ cup plus 1 tablespoon milk, at 80°F to 90°F
- 2 ⅔ tablespoons melted butter, cooled
- ⅓ teaspoon pure vanilla extract
- ⅛ teaspoon pure almond extract
- 2 tablespoons light brown sugar
- ⅔ teaspoon salt
- 1 teaspoon ground cinnamon
- 2 cups white bread flour
- ⅔ teaspoon bread machine or instant yeast
- ⅓ cup dried mixed fruit
- ⅓ cup golden raisins

Direction: PREP: 10 MINUTES PLUS FERMENTING TIME MAKES 1 LOAF8 SLICE BREAD (1 pound)

- ✓ *Preparing the Ingredients. Place the ingredients, except the dried fruit and raisins, in your bread machine as recommended by the manufacturer.*
- ✓ *Choose the Bake Cycle Set the machine to Basic/White bread, choose between light or medium crust, then push Start.*
- ✓ *A few minutes before the end of the second kneading cycle, add dried fruit and raisins to the dough.*
- ✓ *Remove the bucket from the machine once the loaf is done baking.*
- ✓ *Take a 5-minute break from the loaf's cooling process. After removing the loaf, gently shake the bucket and then transfer it to a cooling rack.*

94) *Stollen*

Ingredients:

- ¾ cup milk, at 80°F to 90°F
- 1 egg, at room temperature
- 1½ tablespoons butter, melted and cooled
- 2¼ tablespoons light brown sugar
- ⅛ teaspoon ground cinnamon
- 3 cups white bread flour, divided
- 1⅛ teaspoons bread machine or instant yeast

- ½ cup red and green candied cherries
- ⅓ cup chopped almonds
- ⅓ cup raisins

Direction: PREP: 10 MINUTES PLUS FERMENTING TIME MAKES 1 LOAF12 SLICE BREAD (1½ pounds)

- ✓ *Preparing the Ingredients. Place the ingredients, except the candied fruit, nuts, raisins, and ¼ cup of the flour, in your bread machine as recommended by the manufacturer.*
- ✓ *Choose the Bake Cycle Set the machine to Basic/White bread, choose between light or medium crust, then push Start.*
- ✓ *In a small bowl, stir together the candied cherries, almonds, raisins, and ¼ cup of flour.*
- ✓ *When the machine signals or 5 minutes before the second kneading cycle is complete, add the raisins, candied citrus fruit, and flour.*
- ✓ *Make sure that the bread is done before taking the bucket out of the machine.*
- ✓ *Allow the bread to cool for five minutes before slicing.*
- ✓ *To remove the loaf, gently shake the bucket, and then turn it out onto a cooling rack.*

95) *Julekake*

Ingredients:

- ⅔ cup milk, at 80°F to 90°F
- 1 egg, at room temperature
- ⅓ cup butter, melted and cooled
- 2 ⅔ tablespoons honey
- ⅓ teaspoon salt
- ⅓ teaspoon ground cardamom
- ¼ teaspoon ground cinnamon
- 2¼ cups white bread flour,
- 1 tablespoon 1½ teaspoons bread machine or instant yeast
- ⅓ cup golden raisins
- ⅓ cup candied citrus fruit
- 2 ⅔ tablespoons candied cherries

Direction: PREP: 10 MINUTES PLUS FERMENTING TIME MAKES 1 LOAF8 SLICE BREAD (1 pound)

- ✓ *Preparing the Ingredients. Place the ingredients, except the raisins, candied citrus fruit, and 1 tablespoon of flour, in your bread machine as recommended by the manufacturer.*
- ✓ *Choose the Bake Cycle Set the machine to Basic/White bread, choose between light or medium crust, then push Start.*
- ✓ *Toss the raisins, candied citrus fruit, and 1 tablespoon of flour together in a small bowl.*
- ✓ *When the machine signals or 5 minutes before the second kneading cycle is complete, add the raisins, candied citrus fruit, and flour.*
- ✓ *Make sure that the bread is done before taking the bucket out of the machine.*
- ✓ *Allow the bread to cool for five minutes before slicing.*
- ✓ *To remove the loaf, gently shake the bucket, and then*

turn it out onto a cooling rack.

96) __Spiked Eggnog Bread__

Ingredients:

- 1 cup eggnog, at room temperature
- 1 cup sugar 2 eggs, at room temperature
- ½ cup (1 stick) butter, at room temperature
- 1 tablespoon dark rum
- 1½ teaspoons pure vanilla extract
- ½ teaspoon rum extract
- 2¼ cups all-purpose flour
- 2 teaspoons baking powder
- ¼ teaspoon ground cinnamon
- ½ teaspoon ground nutmeg
- ½ teaspoon salt

Direction: PREP: 10 MINUTES PLUS FERMENTING TIME MAKES 1 LOAF12 SLICE BREAD (1½ pounds)

- ✓ *Preparing the Ingredients. Place the eggnog, sugar, eggs, butter, rum, vanilla, and rum extract in your bread machine.*
- ✓ *Select the Bake Cycle Once you've selected Quick/Rapid bread, hit Start.*
- ✓ *In a small bowl, combine the flour, baking powder, cinnamon, nutmeg, and salt while mixing the liquid ingredients.*
- ✓ *Add the dry ingredients when the initial quick mixing is complete and the machine indicates.*
- ✓ *Make sure that the bread is done before you take its container from the machine.*
- ✓ *For 5 minutes, let the loaf cool. Remove the loaf by gently shaking the bucket, then transfer it to a cooling rack.*

97) __Zucchini Pecan Bread__

Ingredients:

- 2eggs, at room temperature
- ½ cup melted butter, cooled
- ¾ cup shredded zucchini
- ½ cup packed light brown sugar
- 2 tablespoons sugar
- 1½ cups all-purpose flour
- 1 teaspoon ground cinnamon
- ½ teaspoon salt
- ½ teaspoon baking powder
- ½ teaspoon baking soda
- ¼ teaspoon ground allspice
- ½ cup chopped pecans

Direction: PREP: 10 MINUTES PLUS FERMENTING TIME MAKES 1 LOAF12 SLICE BREAD (1½ pounds)

- ✓ *Preparing the Ingredients. Put the ingredients in your bread maker according to the manufacturer's instructions.*
- ✓ *Program the machine for Quick/Rapid bread and press Start.*
- ✓ *When the mixing is done, use a rubber spatula to scrape down the sides of the bucket, then stir.*

- ✓ *Select the Bake cycle.*
- ✓ *Make sure that the bread is done before taking the bucket out of the machine. Time to let the bread cool for five minutes.*
- ✓ *To remove the loaf, gently shake the bucket, and then turn it out onto a cooling rack.*
- ✓ *Wrap the loaf in plastic wrap after it is completely cooled and store it in the refrigerator.*

98) __Lemon Poppy Seed Bread__

Ingredients:

- ¾ cup water, at 80°F to 90°F
- 1 egg, at room temperature
- ¼ cup freshly squeezed lemon juice, at room temperature
- 3 tablespoons melted butter, cooled
- 3 tablespoons sugar
- 2 teaspoons lemon zest
- 1 teaspoon salt
- 3 cups white bread flour
- 2 tablespoons poppy seeds
- 1¼ teaspoons bread machine or instant yeast

Direction: PREP: 10 MINUTES PLUS FERMENTING TIME MAKES 1 LOAF12 SLICE BREAD (1½ pounds)

- ✓ *Preparing the Ingredients. Place the ingredients in your bread maker as instructed by the manufacturer.*
- ✓ *You can choose between a light or medium crust and hit the Start button after setting the machine to make basic/white bread.*
- ✓ *When the loaf is done, remove the bucket from the bread maker.*
- ✓ *Let the loaf cool for 5 minutes.*
- ✓ *Gently shake the bucket to remove the loaf, and turn it out onto a rack to cool.*

99) __Ham and Cheese Bread__

Ingredients:

- 1 cup plus 2 tablespoons water, at 80°F to 90°F
- 2 tablespoons sugar
- 1½ teaspoons salt
- 2 teaspoons dried oregano
- ½ cup (2 ounces) shredded Swiss cheese
- 3¼ cups white bread flour
- 1½ teaspoons bread machine or active dry yeast
- ⅔ cup diced smoked ham

Direction: PREP: 10 MINUTES PLUS FERMENTING TIME MAKES 1 LOAF12 SLICE BREAD (1½ pounds)

- ✓ *Preparing the Ingredients. Place the ingredients, except for the ham, in your bread machine according to the manufacturer's instructions.*
- ✓ *You can choose between a light or medium crust and hit the Start button after setting the machine to make basic/white bread.*
- ✓ *Choose the Bake cycle. "*
- ✓ *The ham should be added to the dough about five minutes before the second kneading cycle concludes.*

- ✓ Remove the bucket from the machine after the loaf is done baking.
- ✓ For 5 minutes, let the loaf cool. Remove the loaf by gently shaking the bucket, then transfer it to a cooling rack.

100) *Wild Rice Hazelnut Bread*

Ingredients:

- ½ cup milk, at 80°F to 90°F
- 2 teaspoons melted butter, cooled
- 2 teaspoons honey
- ⅔ teaspoon salt
- ⅓ cup cooked wild rice, cooled
- ⅓ cup whole-wheat flour
- ⅔ teaspoon caraway seeds
- 1 cup plus 1 tablespoon white bread flour
- 1 teaspoon bread machine or instant yeast
- ⅓ cup chopped hazelnuts

Direction: PREP: 10 MINUTES PLUS FERMENTING TIME MAKES 1 LOAF8 SLICE BREAD (1 pound)

- ✓ Preparing the Ingredients. Put the ingredients in your bread maker as instructed by the manufacturer.
- ✓ To bake white bread in a bread machine, set the bake cycle to "Light Crust" and press "Start."
- ✓ Make sure that the bread is done before taking the bucket out of the machine. Time to let the bread cool for five minutes.
- ✓ To remove the loaf, gently shake the bucket, and then turn it out onto a cooling rack.

101) *Rum Raisin Bread*

Ingredients:

- 2 tablespoons dark rum
- ½ cup raisins
- ½ cup plus 2 tablespoons milk, at 80°F to 90°F
- 1 egg, at room temperature
- 1 tablespoon melted butter, cooled
- 2 teaspoons light brown sugar
- 1 teaspoon salt
- ½ teaspoon rum flavored extract
- 2 cups white bread flour
- 1½ teaspoons bread machine or instant yeast

Direction: PREP: 10 MINUTES PLUS FERMENTING TIME MAKES 1 LOAF8 SLICE BREAD (1 pound)

- ✓ Preparing the Ingredients. In a small bowl, stir together the rum and raisins, and let the fruit soak for 30 minutes; drain the raisins.
- ✓ Place the ingredients, except the soaked raisins, in your bread machine as recommended by the manufacturer.
- ✓ Choose the Bake Cycle Set the machine to Basic/White bread, choose between light or medium crust, then push Start.
- ✓ After 5 minutes of kneading, add the raisins to the dough, according to the machine's instructions.
- ✓ Remove the bucket from the machine after the loaf is done baking.

- ✓ Take a 5-minute break from the loaf's cooling process. After removing the loaf, gently shake the bucket and then transfer it to a cooling rack.

102) *Oatmeal Coffee Bread*

Ingredients:

- 1 cup water, at 80°F to 90°F
- 1½ tablespoons Kahlúa or other coffee liqueur
- ¼ cup honey
- ¾ teaspoon salt
- ¾ cup quick oats
- 2¼ cups white bread flour
- 1 ⅔ teaspoons bread machine or instant yeast

Direction: PREP: 10 MINUTES PLUS FERMENTING TIME MAKES 1 LOAF12 SLICE BREAD (1½ pounds)

- ✓ Preparing the Ingredients. Place the ingredients in your bread machine as recommended by the bread machine manufacturer.
- ✓ Choose the Bake Cycle Set the machine to Basic/White bread, choose between light or medium crust, then push Start.
- ✓ When the loaf is done, remove the bucket from the machine. Let the loaf cool for 5 minutes.
- ✓ Gently shake the bucket to remove the loaf, and turn it out onto a rack to cool.

103) *Banana Coconut Bread*

Ingredients:

- 2 ripe bananas, mashed
- ⅔ cup milk, at 80°F to 90°F
- ⅓ cup melted butter, cooled
- 2 eggs, at room temperature
- ⅔ cup sugar
- ⅔ teaspoon pure vanilla extract
- ⅔ teaspoon pure almond extract
- 1 ⅔ cups all-purpose flour
- ⅔ cup shredded sweet coconut
- 1 teaspoon baking soda
- 1 teaspoon baking powder
- ⅓ teaspoon salt

Direction: PREP: 10 MINUTES PLUS FERMENTING TIME MAKES 1 LOAF12 SLICE BREAD (1½ pounds)

- ✓ Preparing the Ingredients. Place the bananas, milk, butter, eggs, sugar, vanilla, and almond extract in your bread machine.
- ✓ Press the Start button after selecting the Bake Cycle Program for Quick/Rapid Bread on the machine.
- ✓ Mix together the flour, coconut, baking soda and baking powder and salt in a small bowl while the wet ingredients are being mixed.
- ✓ Add the dry ingredients when the initial quick mixing is complete and the machine signals.
- ✓ Make sure that the bread is done before taking the bucket out of the machine.
- ✓ Allow the loaf to cool for five minutes before serving.

✓ To remove the loaf, gently shake the bucket, and then turn it out onto a cooling rack.

104) **Coffee Molasses Bread**

Ingredients:

- ½ cup brewed coffee, at 80°F to 90°F
- ½ cup evaporated milk, at 80°F to 90°F
- 1 tablespoon melted butter, cooled
- 1½ tablespoons honey
- ½ tablespoon dark molasses
- ½ tablespoon sugar
- 2 teaspoons unsweetened cocoa powder
- ½ teaspoon salt
- 1⅛ cups whole-wheat bread flour
- 1⅛ cups white bread flour
- 1⅛ teaspoons bread machine or instant yeast

Direction: PREP: 10 MINUTES PLUS FERMENTING TIME MAKES 1 LOAF8 SLICE BREAD (1 pound)

✓ Preparing the Ingredients. Put the ingredients in your bread maker as instructed by the manufacturer.

✓ Press the Start button and select the Bake cycle.

✓ Program the machine for Sweet bread.

✓ Remove the bucket from the machine after the loaf is done baking.

✓ Time to let the bread cool for five minutes. After removing the loaf, gently shake the bucket and place the bread on a cooling rack.

✓

105) **Panettone**

Ingredients:

- ¾ cup warm water
- 6 Tbsp vegetable oil
- 1½ tsp salt
- 4 Tbsp sugar
- 2 eggs
- 3 cups bread flour
- 1 (¼ ounce) package Fleishman's yeast
- ½ cup candied fruit
- ⅓ cup chopped almonds
- ½ tsp almond extract

Direction: PREP: 10 MINUTES /MAKES 1 LOAF

✓ Preparing the Ingredients.

✓ In the order and at the temperature specified by the maker of your bread machine, add each ingredient to the bread machine.

✓ Select the Bake cycle Close the lid, select the sweet loaf, low crust setting on your bread machine, and press start.

✓ When the bread machine has finished baking, remove the bread and put it on a cooling rack

106) **Challah Bread**

Ingredients:

- 1 cup +¾ teaspoon water, lukewarm between 80 and 90°F

- 2 ½ tablespoons unsalted butter, melted
- 2 small eggs, beaten
- 2 ½ tablespoons sugar
- 1 ¾ teaspoons salt
- 4 ½ cups white bread flour
- 2 teaspoons bread machine yeast or rapid rise yeast

Direction: PREP: 10 MINUTES MAKES 1 LOAF16 SLICE BREAD (2 pounds)

✓ Preparing the Ingredients. Measure your ingredients and choose the size of loaf you want to make.

✓ In the sequence stated above, add the ingredients to the bread pan.

✓ Close the lid on the bread maker and place the pan inside.

✓ Activate the Bake cycle.

✓ Start the bread machine.

✓ Select the Whole Wheat/Wholegrain option first, followed by the loaf size and crust color. Begin the cycle.

✓ When the cycle is complete and the bread is done baking, remove the pan from the machine with caution.

✓ Because the handle will be quite hot, use a potholder.

✓ Allow to cool for a few minutes.

✓ Remove the bread from the pan and cool for at least 10 minutes on a wire rack before slicing.

107) **Dry Fruit Cinnamon Bread**

Ingredients:

- 1¼ cups lukewarm milk
- ¼ cup unsalted butter, melted
- ½ teaspoon pure vanilla extract
- ¼ teaspoon pure almond extract
- 3 tablespoons light brown sugar
- 1 teaspoon table salt
- 2 teaspoons ground cinnamon
- 3 cups white bread flour
- 1 teaspoon bread machine yeast
- ½ cup dried mixed fruit
- ½ cup golden raisins, chopped

Direction: PREP: 10 MINUTES MAKES 1 LOAF12 SLICE BREAD (1½pounds)

✓ Preparing the Ingredients.

✓ Measure your ingredients and choose the size of loaf you want to make.

✓ In the order given above, add all of the ingredients to the bread pan except the mixed fruit and raisins.

✓ Close the lid on the bread maker and place the pan inside.

✓ Activate the Bake cycle. Start the bread machine.

✓ Select the White/Basic or Fruit/Nut setting, then the loaf size, and finally the crust color (if your machine has this function).

✓ Begin the cycle.

✓ When the machine says to add ingredients, add the raisins and mixed fruit.

- ✓ (When you start the machine, some machines feature a fruit/nut hopper where you can put the mixed fruit and raisins.)
- ✓ During the baking process, the machine will mechanically add them to the dough.)
- ✓ When the cycle is complete and the bread is done baking, remove the pan from the machine with caution.
- ✓ Because the handle will be quite hot, use a potholder.
- ✓ Allow to cool for a few minutes. Remove the bread from the pan and cool for at least 10 minutes on a wire rack before slicing.

108)   **Festive Raspberry Rolls**

Ingredients:

- ⅓ cup milk
- ⅓ cup water
- 3 tablespoons butter, softened
- 1 egg
- 2 cups bread flour
- ⅓ cup sugar
- ½ teaspoon salt
- 1¾ teaspoons bread machine or fast-acting dry yeast
- 3 tablespoons raspberry preserves

Direction: PREP: 10 MINUTES PLUS FERMENTING TIME /MAKES 12 ROLLS

- ✓ Preparing the Ingredients. Measure carefully, placing all ingredients except preserves in bread machine pan in the order recommended by the manufacturer.
- ✓ Select the Bake Cycle Select Dough/Manual cycle.
- ✓ Do not use delay cycle. Remove dough from pan, using lightly floured hands.
- ✓ Cover and let rest 10 minutes on lightly floured surface. Grease 12 regular-size muffin cups.
- ✓ Roll or pat dough into 15×10-inch rectangle. Spread preserves over dough to within ¼ inch of edges.
- ✓ Starting with 15-inch side, roll up dough; pinch edge of dough into roll to seal.
- ✓ Stretch and shape roll to make even.
- ✓ Cut roll into 12 equal slices.
- ✓ Place slices, cut side up, in muffin cups.
- ✓ Using kitchen scissors, snip through each slice twice, cutting into fourths.
- ✓ Gently spread dough pieces open.
- ✓ Cover and let rise in warm place about 25 minutes or until doubled in size.
- ✓ Dough is ready if indentation remains when touched.
- ✓ Heat oven to 375°F. Bake 15 to 20 minutes or until golden brown. Immediately remove from pan to cooling rack.
- ✓ Serve warm or cool.

109)   **Beer Pizza Dough**

Ingredients:

- 1 cup beer, at room temperature
- 3 tablespoons olive oil
- 1 tablespoon sugar
- 1 teaspoon table salt
- 3 cups white bread flour or all-purpose flour
- 1½ teaspoons bread machine yeast

Direction: PREP: 10 MINUTES PLUS FERMENTING TIME MAKES 1 LOAF12 SLICE BREAD (1½ pounds)

- ✓ Preparing the Ingredients. Measure your ingredients and choose the size of dough you want to make.
- ✓ In the sequence stated above, add the ingredients to the bread pan.
- ✓ Close the lid on the bread maker and place the pan inside.
- ✓ Activate the Bake cycle. Start the bread machine.
- ✓ Select the Dough option, followed by the dough size.
- ✓ Activate the machine. When the cycle is complete, remove the dough from the pan with care.
- ✓ Place the dough on a lightly floured surface and roll out to the desired thickness of pizza crust.
- ✓ Allow 10–15 minutes to pass.
- ✓ Add your favorite pizza sauce, toppings, cheese, and other ingredients to the top.
- ✓ Bake for 15–20 minutes at 400°F or 204°C, or until the edges are lightly brown.

110)   **Whole-Wheat Challah**

Ingredients:

- ¾ cup water, at 80°F to 90°F
- ⅓ cup melted butter, cooled
- 2 eggs, at room temperature
- 1½ teaspoons salt
- 3 tablespoons sugar
- 1 cup whole-wheat flour
- 2 cups white bread flour
- 1 ⅔ teaspoons bread machine or instant yeast

Direction: PREP: 10 MINUTES PLUS FERMENTING TIME MAKES 1 LOAF12 SLICE BREAD (1½ pounds)

- ✓ Preparing the Ingredients. Put the ingredients in your bread maker according to the manufacturer's instructions.
- ✓ Choose the Bake Cycle Set the machine to Basic/White bread, choose between light or medium crust, then push Start.
- ✓ When the loaf is done, remove the bucket from the machine. Let the loaf cool for 5 minutes.
- ✓ Gently shake the bucket to remove the loaf, and turn it out onto a rack to cool.

111)   **Panettone Bread**

Ingredients:

- ¾ cup milk, at 80°F to 90°F
- ¼ cup melted butter, cooled
- 2 eggs, at room temperature
- 2 teaspoons pure vanilla extract
- 2 tablespoons sugar
- 1½ teaspoons salt
- 3¼ cups white bread flour

- 2 teaspoons bread machine or instant yeast
- ¼ cup candied lemon peel
- ¼ cup candied orange peel

  Direction: PREP: 10 MINUTES MAKES 1 LOAF 12 SLICE BREAD (1½ pounds)

✓ Preparing the Ingredients.

✓ Place the ingredients, except the candied fruit peel, in your bread machine as recommended by the manufacturer.

✓ Select the Bake Cycle Program the machine for Sweet bread, select light or medium crust, and press Start.

✓ When the machine signals, add the peel, or place in the nut/raisin hopper and let the machine add the peel automatically.

✓ When the loaf is done, remove the bucket from the machine. Let the loaf cool for 5 minutes.

✓ Gently shake the bucket to remove the loaf, and turn it out onto a rack to cool.

112) **Portuguese Sweet Bread**

Ingredients:

- ⅔ cup milk, at 80°F to 90°F
- 1 egg, at room temperature
- 4 teaspoons butter, softened
- ⅓ cup sugar
- ⅔ teaspoon salt
- 2 cups white bread flour
- 1½ teaspoons bread machine or instant yeast

  Direction: PREP: 10 MINUTES PLUS FERMENTING TIME MAKES 1 LOAF8 SLICE BREAD (1 pound)

✓ Preparing the Ingredients. Follow the manufacturer's directions for putting the ingredients in your bread machine.

✓ Select the Bake cycle and push the Start button.

✓ Remove the bucket from the machine once the loaf is completed.

✓ Allow for a 5-minute cooling period.

✓ To remove the loaf, gently shake the bucket and place it on a cooling rack.

113) **Pecan Maple Bread**

Ingredients:

- 1½ cups (3 sticks) butter, at room temperature
- 4 eggs, at room temperature
- ⅔ cup maple syrup
- ⅔ cup sugar
- 3 cups all-purpose flour
- 1 cup chopped pecans
- 2 teaspoons baking powder
- ½ teaspoon salt

  Direction: PREP: 10 MINUTES PLUS FERMENTING TIME MAKES 1 LOAF16 SLICE BREAD (2 pounds)

✓ Preparing the Ingredients. Place the butter, eggs, maple syrup, and sugar in your bread machine.

✓ Activate the Bake mode.

✓ Press the Start button after programming the machine for Quick/Rapid bread.

✓ In a small mixing basin, combine the flour, pecans, baking powder, and salt while the wet ingredients are mixing.

✓ After the machine has signaled that the initial quick mixing is complete, add the dry ingredients.

✓ Remove the bucket from the machine when the bread is done.

✓ Allow the loaf to cool for 5 minutes before serving.

✓ To remove the loaf from the bucket, gently shake it out and place it on a cooling rack.

114) **Nana's Gingerbread**

Ingredients:

- ⅔ cup buttermilk, at 80°F to 90°F
- 1 egg, at room temperature
- 2 ⅔ tablespoons dark molasses
- 2 teaspoons melted butter, cooled
- 2 tablespoons sugar
- 1 teaspoon salt
- 1 teaspoon ground ginger
- ⅔ teaspoon ground cinnamon
- ⅓ teaspoon ground nutmeg
- ⅛ teaspoon ground cloves
- 2 ⅓ cups white bread flour
- 1 ⅓ teaspoons bread machine or active dry yeast

  Direction: PREP: 10 MINUTES PLUS FERMENTING TIME MAKES 1 LOAF8 SLICE BREAD (1 pounds)

✓ Preparing the Ingredients. Follow the manufacturer's directions for putting the ingredients in your bread machine.

✓ Select the Bake cycle and push the Start button.

✓ Remove the bucket from the machine once the loaf is completed. Allow for a 5-minute cooling period.

✓ To remove the loaf, gently shake the bucket and place it on a cooling rack.

115) **Coffee Caraway Seed Bread**

Ingredients:

- ¾ cup lukewarm water
- ⅓ cup brewed coffee, lukewarm
- 1½ tablespoons balsamic vinegar
- 1½ tablespoons olive oil
- 1½ tablespoons dark molasses
- ¾ tablespoon light brown sugar
- ¾ teaspoon table salt
- 1½ teaspoons caraway seeds
- 3 tablespoons unsweetened cocoa powder
- ¾ cup dark rye flour
- 1¾ cups white bread flour
- 1½ teaspoons bread machine yeast

  Direction: PREP: 10 MINUTES PLUS FERMENTING TIME MAKES 1 LOAF12 SLICE BREAD (1½ pounds)

✓ Preparing the Ingredients. Measure your ingredients

and choose the size of loaf you want to make.

- ✓ In the sequence stated above, add the ingredients to the bread pan.
- ✓ Close the lid on the bread maker and place the pan inside.
- ✓ Activate the Bake cycle. Start the bread machine.
- ✓ Select the Whole Wheat/Wholegrain option first, followed by the loaf size and crust color. Begin the cycle.
- ✓ Carefully remove the pan from the machine once the cycle has completed and the bread has baked.
- ✓ Because the handle will be quite hot, use a potholder. Allow to cool for a few minutes.
- ✓ Remove the bread from the pan and allow to cool down on a wire rack for at least 10 minutes or more before slicing.

116)   Sun-Dried Tomato Rolls

Ingredients:

- ¾ cup warm milk (105°F to 115°F)
- 2 cups bread flour
- ¼ cup chopped sun-dried tomatoes in oil, drained,
- 1 tablespoon oil reserved
- 1 tablespoon sugar
- 1 teaspoon salt
- 1½ teaspoons bread machine yeast

Direction: PREP: 10 MINUTES PLUS FERMENTING TIME /MAKES 12 ROLLS

- ✓ Preparing the Ingredients. Measure carefully, placing all ingredients in bread machine pan in the order recommended by the manufacturer.
- ✓ Select Dough/Manual cycle. Do not use delay cycle.
- ✓ Remove dough from pan; place on lightly floured surface.
- ✓ Cover and let rest 10 minutes.
- ✓ Select the Bake Cycle Lightly grease cookie sheet with shortening or spray with cooking spray.
- ✓ Gently push fist into dough to deflate.
- ✓ Divide dough into 12 equal pieces. Shape each piece into a ball. Place balls about 2 inches apart on cookie sheet.
- ✓ Cover and let rise in warm place 30 to 45 minutes or until almost doubled in size. Heat oven to 350°F.
- ✓ Bake 12 to 16 minutes or until golden brown. Remove from cookie sheet to cooling rack.
- ✓ Serve warm or cool.

117)   Cinnamon Beer Bread

Ingredients:

- 2 cups beer, at room temperature
- 1 cup unsalted butter, melted
- ⅓ cup honey
- 4 cups all-purpose flour
- 1 ⅓ teaspoons table salt
- ⅓ teaspoon ground cinnamon

- 1 ⅓ tablespoons baking powder

Direction: PREP: 10 MINUTES PLUS FERMENTING TIME MAKES 1 LOAF16 SLICE BREAD (2 pounds)

- ✓ Preparing the Ingredients. Measure your ingredients and choose the size of loaf you want to make.
- ✓ In the sequence stated above, add the ingredients to the bread pan.
- ✓ Close the lid on the bread maker and place the pan inside.
- ✓ Activate the Bake cycle. Start the bread machine.
- ✓ Choose Quick/Rapid, then the loaf size, and finally the crust color. Begin the cycle.
- ✓ When the cycle is complete and the bread is done baking, remove the pan from the machine with caution.
- ✓ Because the handle will be quite hot, use a potholder.
- ✓ Allow to cool for a few minutes.
- ✓ Remove the bread from the pan and cool for at least 10 minutes on a wire rack before slicing.

118)   French Butter Bread

Ingredients:

- ½ cup + 1 tablespoon lukewarm milk
- 3 eggs, at room temperature
- 2 tablespoons sugar
- ¾ teaspoon table salt
- ½ cup unsalted butter, melted
- 3 cups white bread flour
- 1½ teaspoons bread machine yeast

Direction: PREP: 10 MINUTES PLUS FERMENTING TIME MAKES 1 LOAF12 SLICE BREAD (1½ pounds)

- ✓ Preparing the Ingredients. Measure your ingredients and choose the size of loaf you want to make.
- ✓ In the sequence stated above, add the ingredients to the bread pan.
- ✓ Close the lid on the bread maker and place the pan inside.
- ✓ Activate the Bake cycle. Start the bread machine.
- ✓ Choose the White/Basic setting first, then the loaf size, and lastly the crust color.
- ✓ Begin the cycle. Carefully remove the pan from the machine once the cycle has completed and the bread has baked.
- ✓ Because the handle will be quite hot, use a potholder. Allow to cool for a few minutes.
- ✓ Remove the bread from the pan and cool for at least 10 minutes on a wire rack before slicing.

119)   Holiday Chocolate Bread

Ingredients:

- ⅞ cup lukewarm milk
- 1 egg, at room temperature
- 1½ tablespoons unsalted butter, melted
- 1 teaspoon pure vanilla extract
- 2 tablespoons sugar
- ¾ teaspoon table salt

- 3 cups white bread flour
- 1 teaspoon bread machine yeast
- ½ cup white chocolate chips
- ⅓ cup dried cranberries

Direction: PREP: 10 MINUTES PLUS FERMENTING TIME MAKES 1 LOAF12 SLICE BREAD (1½ pounds)

- ✓ Preparing the Ingredients. Measure your ingredients and choose the size of loaf you want to make.
- ✓ In the order mentioned above, add all of the ingredients to the bread pan except the chocolate chips and cranberries.
- ✓ Close the lid on the bread maker and place the pan inside.
- ✓ Activate the Bake Cycle. Start the bread machine.
- ✓ Select the White/Basic or Fruit/Nut setting, then the loaf size, and finally the crust color (if your machine has this function).
- ✓ Begin the cycle.
- ✓ Add the chocolate chips and cranberries when the machine says it's time to add ingredients.
- ✓ (Some machines feature a fruit/nut hopper where you can put the chocolate chips and cranberries when you start the machine; the machine will add them to the dough automatically during the baking process.)
- ✓ When the cycle is complete and the bread is done baking, remove the pan from the machine with caution.
- ✓ Because the handle will be quite hot, use a potholder.
- ✓ Allow to cool for a few minutes.
- ✓ Remove the bread from the pan and cool for at least 10 minutes on a wire rack before slicing.

120) New Year Spiced Bread

Ingredients:

- ⅓ cup brewed coffee, cooled to room temperature
- ½ cup unsalted butter, melted
- ½ cup honey
- ¾ cup sugar
- ¼ cup dark brown sugar
- 2 eggs, at room temperature
- 2 tablespoons whiskey
- ¼ cup orange juice, at room temperature
- 1 teaspoon pure vanilla extract
- 2 cups all-purpose flour
- ½ tablespoon ground cinnamon
- ½ teaspoon baking soda
- ¼ teaspoon ground allspice
- ¼ teaspoon table salt
- ¼ teaspoon ground cloves
- ½ tablespoon baking powder

Direction: PREP: 10 MINUTES PLUS FERMENTING TIME MAKES 1 LOAF12 SLICE BREAD (1½ pounds)

- ✓ Preparing the Ingredients. Measure your ingredients and choose the size of loaf you want to make.
- ✓ In the sequence stated above, add the ingredients to

the bread pan.

- ✓ Close the lid on the bread maker and place the pan inside.
- ✓ Activate the Bake Cycle. Start the bread machine.
- ✓ Choose Quick/Rapid, then the loaf size, and finally the crust color. Begin the cycle.
- ✓ When the cycle is complete and the bread is done baking, remove the pan from the machine with caution.
- ✓ Because the handle will be quite hot, use a potholder.
- ✓ Allow to cool for a few minutes.
- ✓ Remove the bread from the pan and cool for at least 10 minutes on a wire rack before slicing.

121) Cocoa Holiday Bread

Ingredients:

- ¾ cup brewed coffee, lukewarm
- ⅓ cup evaporated milk, lukewarm
- 1½ tablespoons unsalted butter, melted
- 2¼ tablespoons honey
- ¾ tablespoon dark molasses
- ¾ tablespoon sugar
- 1 tablespoon unsweetened cocoa powder
- ¾ teaspoon table salt
- 1 ⅔ cups whole-wheat bread flour
- 1 ⅔ cups white bread flour
- 1 ⅔ teaspoons bread machine yeast

Direction: PREP: 10 MINUTES PLUS FERMENTING TIME MAKES 1 LOAF12 SLICE BREAD (1½ pounds)

- ✓ Preparing the Ingredients. Measure your ingredients and choose the size of loaf you want to make.
- ✓ In the sequence stated above, add the ingredients to the bread pan.
- ✓ Close the lid on the bread maker and place the pan inside.
- ✓ Activate the Bake Cycle. Start the bread machine.
- ✓ Choose the Sweet option first, then the loaf size, and then the crust color.
- ✓ Begin the cycle. Carefully remove the pan from the machine once the cycle has completed and the bread has baked.
- ✓ Because the handle will be quite hot, use a potholder. Allow to cool for a few minutes.
- ✓ Remove the bread from the pan and cool for at least 10 minutes on a wire rack before slicing.

122) Holiday Eggnog Bread

Ingredients:

- 1⅛ cups eggnog, at room temperature
- 1⅛ tablespoons unsalted butter, melted
- 1½ tablespoons sugar
- 1 teaspoon   table salt
- ⅓ teaspoon ground cinnamon
- ⅓ teaspoon ground nutmeg
- 3 cups white bread flour

- 1 ⅓ teaspoons bread machine yeast
  Direction: PREP: 10 MINUTES PLUS FERMENTING TIME MAKES 1 LOAF12 SLICE BREAD (1½ pounds)

✓ Preparing the Ingredients. Measure your ingredients and choose the size of loaf you want to make.

✓ In the sequence stated above, add the ingredients to the bread pan.

✓ Close the lid on the bread maker and place the pan inside.

✓ Activate the Bake Cycle. Start the bread machine.

✓ Choose Quick/Rapid, then the loaf size, and finally the crust color. Begin the cycle.

✓ When the cycle is complete and the bread is done baking, remove the pan from the machine with caution.

✓ Because the handle will be quite hot, use a potholder.

✓ Allow to cool for a few minutes.

✓ Remove the bread from the pan and cool for at least 10 minutes on a wire rack before slicing.

123) **Easter Bread**

Ingredients:

- 1 cup lukewarm milk
- 2 eggs, at room temperature
- 2 ⅔ tablespoons unsalted butter, melted
- ⅓ cup sugar
- 1 teaspoon table salt
- 2 ⅓ teaspoons lemon zest
- 4 cups white bread flour
- 2¼ teaspoons bread machine yeast
  Direction: PREP: 10 MINUTES PLUS FERMENTING TIME MAKES 1 LOAF16 SLICE BREAD (2 pounds)

✓ Preparing the Ingredients. Measure your ingredients and choose the size of loaf you want to make.

✓ In the sequence stated above, add the ingredients to the bread pan.

✓ Close the lid on the bread maker and place the pan inside.

✓ Activate the Bake cycle. Start the bread machine.

✓ Choose the White/Basic setting first, then the loaf size, and lastly the crust color.

✓ Begin the cycle. Carefully remove the pan from the machine once the cycle has completed and the bread has baked.

✓ Because the handle will be quite hot, use a potholder.

✓ Allow to cool for a few minutes.

✓ Remove the bread from the pan and cool for at least 10 minutes on a wire rack before slicing.

124) **Hot Buttered Rum Bread**

Ingredients:

- ¾ cup water, at 80°F to 90°F 1 egg, at room temperature
- 3 tablespoons butter, melted and cooled
- 3 tablespoons sugar
- 1 tablespoon rum extract

- 1¼ teaspoons salt
- 1 teaspoon ground cinnamon
- ¼ teaspoon ground nutmeg
- 3 cups white bread flour
- 1 teaspoon bread machine or instant yeast
  Direction: PREP: 10 MINUTES PLUS FERMENTING TIME MAKES 1 LOAF12 SLICE BREAD (1½ pounds)

✓ Preparing the Ingredients. Put the ingredients in your bread maker according to the manufacturer's instructions.

✓ Program the machine for Sweet bread and press Start.

✓ Select the Bake cycle When the loaf is done, remove the bucket from the machine.

✓ Let the loaf cool for 5 minutes.

✓ Gently shake the bucket to remove the loaf, and turn it out onto a rack to cool.

125) **Raisin Bran Bread**

Ingredients:

- 1⅛ cup milk, at 80°F to 90°F
- 2¼ tablespoons melted butter, cooled
- 3 tablespoons sugar
- 1½ teaspoons salt
- ⅓ cup wheat bran
- 2 ⅔ cups white bread flour
- 1½ teaspoons bread machine or instant yeast
- ¾ cup raisins
  Direction: PREP: 10 MINUTES PLUS FERMENTING TIME MAKES 1 LOAF12 SLICE BREAD (1½ pounds)

✓ Preparing the Ingredients. Place the ingredients, except the raisins, in your bread machine as recommended by the manufacturer.

✓ Choose the Bake Cycle Set the machine to Basic/White bread, choose between light or medium crust, then push Start.

✓ When the machine signals, add the raisins, or put them in the nut/raisin hopper and let your machine add them automatically.

✓ When the loaf is done, remove the bucket from the machine.

✓ Let the loaf cool for 5 minutes.

✓ Gently shake the bucket to remove the loaf, and turn it out onto a rack to cool.

126) **Mustard Rye Bread**

Ingredients:

- 1¼ cups water, at 80°F to 90°F
- ¼ cup Dijon mustard
- 1½ tablespoons melted butter, cooled
- 1 tablespoon sugar
- ¾ teaspoon salt
- 1½ cups rye flour
- 2 cups white bread flour
- 1 teaspoon bread machine or instant yeast
  Direction: PREP: 10 MINUTES PLUS FERMENTING

- ✓ *Preparing the Ingredients. Put the ingredients in your bread maker according to the manufacturer's instructions.*
- ✓ *Choose the Bake Cycle Set the machine to Basic/White bread, choose between light or medium crust, then push Start.*
- ✓ *When the loaf is done, remove the bucket from the machine.*
- ✓ *Let the loaf cool for 5 minutes.*
- ✓ *Gently shake the bucket to remove the loaf, and turn it out onto a rack to cool.*

127) Sausage Herb Bread

Ingredients:

- 1 cup water, at 80°F to 90°F
- 1½ tablespoons olive oil
- 1½ tablespoons sugar
- 1⅛ teaspoons salt
- ⅓ teaspoon dried basil
- ⅓ teaspoon dried oregano
- ½ cup cooked chopped Italian sausage
- 3 cups white bread flour
- 1½ teaspoons bread machine or instant yeast

Direction: PREP: 10 MINUTES PLUS FERMENTING TIME MAKES 1 LOAF12 SLICE BREAD (1½ pounds

- ✓ *Preparing the Ingredients. Follow the manufacturer's directions for putting the ingredients in your bread machine.*
- ✓ *Set the machine to Basic/White bread, choose light or medium crust, then click the Start button.*
- ✓ *Activate the Bake mode on the oven.*
- ✓ *Remove the bucket from the machine once the loaf is completed.*
- ✓ *Allow for a 5-minute cooling period.*
- ✓ *To remove the loaf, gently shake the bucket and place it on a cooling rack.*

128) Spinach Feta Bread

Ingredients:

- ⅓ cup cooked chopped spinach, well-drained, cooled
- ¼ cup water, at 80°F to 90°F
- 1 small egg, at room temperature
- 1½ tablespoons melted butter, cooled
- ¾ tablespoon sugar
- ¾ teaspoon salt
- ⅛ teaspoon freshly ground black pepper
- 2 tablespoons oat bran
- 1½ cups white bread flour
- 1⅛ teaspoons bread machine or instant yeast
- ¼ cup crumbled feta cheese

Direction: PREP: 10 MINUTES PLUS FERMENTING TIME MAKES 1 LOAF8 SLICE BREAD (1 pound)

- ✓ *Preparing the Ingredients. Place the ingredients, except the feta cheese, in your bread machine as recommended by the manufacturer.*

- ✓ *Choose the Bake Cycle Set the machine to Basic/White bread, choose between light or medium crust, then push Start.*
- ✓ *When the machine beeps or 5 minutes before the second kneading cycle ends, add the cheese.*
- ✓ *Remove the bucket from the machine after the loaf is done.*
- ✓ *Allow 5 minutes for the bread to cool.*
- ✓ *Remove the loaf from the bucket with a little shake and place it on a cooling rack.*

129) Bacon Corn Bread

Ingredients:

- 1 cup milk, at room temperature
- 2 eggs, at room temperature
- ¼ cup butter, at room temperature
- 1 cup sugar
- 2 cups all-purpose flour
- 1 cup cornmeal
- 1 tablespoon baking powder
- 1 teaspoon salt
- 1 cup cooked crumbled bacon

Direction: PREP: 10 MINUTES PLUS FERMENTING TIME MAKES 1 LOAF12 SLICE BREAD (1½ pounds)

- ✓ *Ingredients Preparation. In your bread machine, mix the milk, eggs, butter, and sugar.*
- ✓ *Select the Bake Cycle and press Start to program the machine for Quick/Rapid bread. While the wet ingredients are combining, in a small bowl, combine the flour, cornmeal, baking powder, salt, and bacon.*
- ✓ *After the initial rapid mixing has been completed and the machine indicates, add the dry ingredients.*
- ✓ *Remove the bucket from the machine once the loaf is finished.*
- ✓ *Allow 5 minutes for the bread to cool.*
- ✓ *Shake the bucket gently to extract the loaf, then put it out onto a rack to cool.*

130) Cherry Pistachio Bread

Ingredients:

- ½ cup water, at 80°F to 90°F
- 1 egg, at room temperature
- 2 tablespoons butter, softened
- 2 tablespoons packed dark brown sugar
- ¾ teaspoon salt
- ¼ teaspoon ground nutmeg
- Dash allspice
- 1¾ cups plus 1 tablespoon white bread flour
- 1 teaspoon bread machine or active dry yeast
- ½ cup dried cherries
- ¼ cup chopped unsalted pistachios

Direction: PREP: 10 MINUTES PLUS FERMENTING TIME MAKES 1 LOAF8 SLICE BREAD (1 pound)

- ✓ *Preparing the Ingredients. Place the ingredients, except the cherries and pistachios, in your bread* machine as recommended by the manufacturer.

- ✓ Choose the Bake Cycle Set the machine to Basic/White bread, choose between light or medium crust, then push Start.
- ✓ Just before the final kneading is over or when the machine signals, add the cherries and pistachios.
- ✓ When the loaf is done, remove the bucket from the machine.
- ✓ Let the loaf cool for 5 minutes.
- ✓ Gently shake the bucket to remove the loaf, and turn it out onto a rack to cool.

131) Easy Honey Beer Bread

Ingredients:

- 12 ounces beer, at room temperature
- ⅓ cup melted butter, cooled
- ¼ cup honey
- 3 cups all-purpose flour
- 1 tablespoon baking powder
- 1 teaspoon salt
- ¼ teaspoon ground cinnamon

Direction: PREP: 10 MINUTES PLUS FERMENTING TIME MAKES 1 LOAF12 SLICE BREAD (1½ pounds)

- ✓ Ingredients Preparation. In your bread machine, combine the beer, butter, and honey.
- ✓ Bake is the cycle to choose.
- ✓ Start the machine and program it for Quick/Rapid bread.
- ✓ While the wet ingredients are combining, in a small bowl, whisk together the flour, baking powder, salt, and cinnamon.
- ✓ After the initial rapid mixing has been completed and the machine indicates, add the dry ingredients.
- ✓ Remove the bucket from the machine once the loaf is finished.
- ✓ Allow 5 minutes for the bread to cool. Shake the bucket gently to extract the loaf, then put it out onto a rack to cool.

132) Pear Sweet Potato Bread

Ingredients:

- ⅓ cup plus 1 tablespoon milk, at 80°F to 90°F
- ⅓ cup shredded peeled pear
- ⅓ cup mashed cooked sweet potato, cooled
- 1½ tablespoons melted butter, cooled
- 1½ tablespoons sugar
- ¾ teaspoon salt
- ¼ teaspoon ground cinnamon
- ¼ teaspoon ground nutmeg
- ⅛ teaspoon ``ground ginger
- 2 cups white bread flour
- ⅔ teaspoons bread machine or instant yeast

Direction: PREP: 10 MINUTES PLUS FERMENTING TIME MAKES 1 LOAF8 SLICE BREAD (1 pound)

- ✓ Ingredients Preparation. Combine the ingredients in your bread machine according to the manufacturer's instructions.

- ✓ Select the Bake Cycle Program for Sweet bread on the machine and push Start.
- ✓ Remove the bucket from the machine once the loaf is finished.
- ✓ Allow 5 minutes for the bread to cool.
- ✓ Shake the bucket gently to extract the loaf, then put it out onto a rack to cool.

133) Honey Pound Cake

Ingredients:

- 1 cup butter, unsalted
- 1/4 cup honey
- Two tablespoons whole milk
- Four eggs, beaten
- 1 cup of sugar
- 2 cups flour

Direction: Preparation Time: 5 minutes Cooking Time: 2 hours 50 minutes Servings: 12 - 16

- ✓ Bring the butter to room temperature and cut into 1/2-inch cubes. Add all ingredients to the bread machine in the order listed (butter, honey, milk, eggs, sugar, and flour).
- ✓ Press Sweetbread setting follow by light crust colour, then press Start.
- ✓ Take out the cake on the bread pan using a rubber spatula as soon as it's finished.
- ✓ Cool on a rack and serve with your favorite fruit.

134) Carrot Cake Bread

Ingredients:

- Nonstick cooking spray
- 1/4 cup vegetable oil
- Two large eggs, room temperature
- 1/2 teaspoon pure vanilla extract
- 1/2 cup sugar
- 1/4 cup light brown sugar
- 1/4 cup of crushed pineapple with juice (from a can or fresh)
- 1 1/4 cups unbleached, all-purpose flour
- One teaspoon baking powder
- 1/4 teaspoon baking soda
- 1/4 teaspoon salt
- One teaspoon ground cloves
- 3/4 teaspoon ground cinnamon
- 1 cup freshly grated carrots
- 1/3 cup chopped pecans
- 1/3 cup golden raisins

Direction: Preparation Time: 5 minutes Cooking Time: 1 hour 20 minutes Servings: 12 - 16

- ✓ Coat the inside of the bread pan with nonstick cooking spray. Add all of the ingredients, in the order listed, to the bread pan.
- ✓ Select Express Bake, medium crust color, and press Start.
- ✓ While the batter is mixing, scrape the bread pan's

sides with a rubber spatula to incorporate ingredients fully.

✓ When baked, remove from bread pan and place on a wire rack to cool completely before slicing and serving.

135)   Lemon Cake

Ingredients:

- Three large eggs, beaten
- 1/3 cup 2% milk
- 1/2 cup butter, melted
- 2 cups all-purpose flour
- Three teaspoons baking powder
- 1 1/3 cup sugar
- One teaspoon vanilla extract
- Two lemons, zested

For the glaze:

- 1 cup powdered sugar
- Two tablespoons lemon juice, freshly squeezed

Direction: Preparation Time: 5 minutes Cooking Time: 2 hours 50 minutes Servings: 12

✓ Prepare the glaze by whisking the powder sugar and lemon juice together in a small mixing bowl and set aside.

✓ Add all remaining ingredients to the baking pan in the order listed. Select the Sweetbread, medium color crust, and press Start.

✓ When baked, transfer the baking pan to a cooling rack.

✓ When the cake has cooled, gently shake the cake out into a serving plate. Glaze the cold cake and serve.

136)   Insane Coffee Cake

Ingredients:

- 7/8 cup of milk
- 1/4 cup of sugar
- One teaspoon salt
- One egg yolk
- One tablespoon butter
- 2 1/4 cups bread flour
- Two teaspoons of active dry yeast

For the topping:

- Two tablespoons butter, melted
- Two tablespoons brown sugar
- One teaspoon cinnamon

Direction: Preparation Time: 15 minutes Cooking Time: 2 hours Servings: 10 - 12

✓ Set the topping ingredients aside, then add the other ingredients to the bread pan in the order above.

✓ Set the bread machine to the Dough process.

✓ Butter a 9-by-9-inch glass baking dish and pour the dough into the container.

✓ Cover with a towel and rise for about 10 minutes.

✓ Preheat an oven to 375°F. Brush the dough with melted butter.

✓ Put brown sugar and cinnamon in a bowl, mix it well, and then sprinkle on top of the coffee cake.

✓ Let the topped dough rise, uncovered, for another 30 minutes.

✓ Place in oven and bake for 35 minutes or until a wooden toothpick inserted into the center comes out clean and dry.

✓ When baked, let the coffee cake rest for 10 minutes.

✓ Carefully remove the coffee cake from the dish with a rubber spatula, slice, and serve

137)   Chocolate Marble Cake

Ingredients:

- 1 1/2 cups water
- 1 1/2 teaspoons vanilla extract
- 1 1/2 teaspoons salt
- 3 ½ cups bread flour
- 1 ½ teaspoon instant yeast
- 1 cup semisweet chocolate chips

Direction: Preparation Time: 15 minutes Cooking Time: 3 hours 45 minutes Servings: 12 - 16

✓ Set the chocolate chips aside and add the other ingredients to your bread maker's pan. Program the machine for Sweetbread and then press Start.

✓ Check the dough after 15 minutes of kneading; you should have a smooth ball, soft but not sticky.

✓ Add the chocolate chips about 3 minutes before the end of the second kneading cycle.

✓ Once baked, remove with a rubber spatula and cool on a rack before serving.

138)   Pumpkin Spice Cake

Ingredients:

- 1 cup of sugar
- 1 cup canned pumpkin
- 1/3 cup vegetable oil
- One teaspoon vanilla extract
- Two eggs
- 1 1/2 cups all-purpose flour
- Two teaspoons baking powder
- 1/4 teaspoon salt
- One teaspoon ground cinnamon
- 1/4 teaspoon ground nutmeg
- 1/8 teaspoon ground cloves
- Shortening, for greasing pan

Direction: Preparation Time: 5 minutes Cooking Time: 2 hours 50 minutes Servings: 12

✓ Grease bread maker pan and kneading blade generously with shortening.

✓ Add all ingredients to the pan in the order listed above.

✓ Select the Rapid cycle and press Start. Open the lid three minutes into the cycle.

✓ Carefully scrape the pan's downsides with a rubber spatula; close the lid to continue the process.

- Cool the baked cake for 10 minutes on a wire rack before slicing.

139) *Lemon Blueberry Quick Bread*

Ingredients:

- 2 cups all-purpose flour
- 1 1/2 teaspoons baking powder
- 1/2 teaspoon salt
- One tablespoon lemon zest
- 1 cup of sugar
- 1/2 cup unsalted butter, softened T
- wo large eggs
- Two teaspoons pure vanilla extract
- 1/2 cup whole milk
- 1 1/2 cups blueberries

For the crumb topping:

- 1/3 cup sugar
- Three tablespoons all-purpose flour
- Two tablespoons butter, melted
- Nonstick cooking spray

Direction: Preparation Time: 20 minutes Cooking Time: 2 hours Servings: 10 – 12

- Spray bread maker pan with nonstick cooking spray and lightly flour.
- Combine crumb topping ingredients and set aside.
- In a small bowl, put the whisk together with flour, baking powder and salt and set aside.
- In a large bowl, put the sugar and lemon zest, then mix them.
- Add butter and beat until light and fluffy.
- Add eggs, vanilla and milk.
- Add flour mixture and mix until combined.
- Stir in blueberries and spread batter evenly into bread maker pan.
- Top with crumb topping; select Sweetbread, light colour crust, and press Start.
- When the cake is made, cool it on a wire rack for 15 minutes and serves warm

140) *French Ham Bread*

Ingredients:

- 3 1/3 cups wheat flour
- 1 cup ham
- ½ cup of milk powder
- 1 ½ tablespoons sugar
- One teaspoon yeast, fresh
- One teaspoon salt
- One teaspoon dried basil
- 1 1/3 cups water
- Two tablespoons olive oil

Direction: Preparation Time: 30-45 minutes Cooking Time: 2 hours Servings: 8

- Cut ham into cubes of 0.5-1 cm (approximately ¼ inch). Put all ingredients in the bread maker from the following order: water, olive oil, salt, sugar, flour, milk powder, ham, and yeast.
- Put all the ingredients according to the instructions in your bread maker.
- Basil put in a dispenser or fill it later, at the signal in the container.
- Turn on the bread maker.
- After the end of the baking cycle, leave the bread container in the bread maker to keep warm for 1 hour.
- Then your delicious bread is ready!

141) *Meat Bread*

Ingredients:

- 2 cups boiled chicken
- 1 cup milk
- 3 cups flour
- One tablespoon dry yeast
- one egg
- One teaspoon sugar
- ½ tablespoon salt
- Two tablespoons oil

Direction: Preparation Time: 1 hour 30 minutes Cooking Time: 1 hour 30minutes Servings: 8

- Pre-cook the meat. You can use a leg or fillet.
- Separate meat from the bone and cut it into small pieces.
- Pour all ingredients into the bread maker according to the instructions.
- Add chicken pieces now.
- The program is Basic.
- This bread is perfectly combined with dill and butter

142) *Onion Bacon Bread*

Ingredients:

- 1 ½ cups water
- Two tablespoons sugar
- Three teaspoons dry yeast
- 4 ½ cups flour
- One egg
- Two teaspoons salt
- One tablespoon oil
- Three small onions, chopped
- 1 cup bacon

Direction: Preparation Time: 1 hour 30 minutes Cooking Time: 1 hour 30 minutes Servings: 8

- Cut the bacon. Put all ingredients into the machine.
- Set it to the Basic program.
- Enjoy this tasty bread!

143) *Fish Bell Pepper Bran Bread*

Ingredients:

- 2 ½ cups flour

- ½ cup bran
- 1 1/3 cups water
- 1 ½ teaspoons salt
- 1 ½ teaspoons sugar
- 1 ½ tablespoon mustard oil
- One ¼ teaspoons dry yeast
- Two teaspoons powdered milk
- 1 cup chopped bell pepper
- ¾ cup chopped smoked fish
- One onion

Direction: Preparation Time: 1 hour 30 minutes Cooking Time: 1 hour 30 minutes Servings: 8

✓ Grind onion and fry until golden brown.
✓ Cut the fish into small pieces and the pepper into cubes.!
✓ Load all the ingredients in the bucket.
✓ Turn on the baking program.
✓ Bon Appetite

144) **Sausage Bread**

Ingredients:

- 1 ½ teaspoons dry yeast
- 3 cups flour
- One teaspoon sugar
- 1 ½ teaspoons salt
- 1 1/3 cups whey
- One tablespoon oil
- 1 cup chopped smoked sausage

Direction: Preparation Time: 2 hours Cooking Time: 2 hours Servings: 8

✓ Fold all the ingredients in the order that is recommended specifically for your model.
✓ Set the required parameters for baking bread.
✓ When ready, remove the delicious hot bread.
✓ Wait until it cools down and enjoy sausage.

145) **Milk Sweet Bread**

Ingredients:

- 1 cup lukewarm milk
- 1 egg, at room temperature
- 2 tablespoons butter, softened
- ½ cup sugar
- 1 teaspoon table salt
- 3 cups white bread flour
- 2¼ teaspoons bread machine yeast

Direction: PREP: 10 MINUTES PLUS FERMENTING TIME MAKES 1 LOAF 12 SLICE BREAD (1½ pounds)

✓ Preparing the Ingredients. Measure your ingredients and choose the size of loaf you want to make.
✓ In the sequence stated above, add the ingredients to the bread pan.
✓ Close the lid of the bread maker and place the pan inside.
✓ Choose the Bake option.

✓ Start the bread machine.
✓ Choose the Sweet option first, then the loaf size, and finally the color of the crust.
✓ Begin the cycle.
✓ Carefully remove the pan from the machine once the cycle has completed and the bread has baked.
✓ Because the handle will be quite hot, use a potholder.
✓ Allow to cool for a few minutes.
✓ Remove the bread from the pan and cool for at least 10 minutes on a wire rack before slicing.

146) **Miniature Brioche**

Ingredients:

- ¼ cup water
- 3 tablespoons butter, softened
- 2 eggs
- 2½ cups bread flour
- ¼ cup sugar
- ¾ teaspoon salt
- 1 teaspoon grated orange or lemon peel
- 2½ teaspoons bread machine yeast
- 1 tablespoon milk
- 1 egg yolk Coarse
- sugar crystals

Direction: PREP: 10 MINUTES PLUS FERMENTING TIME /MAKES 12 MINI BRIOCHE

✓ Preparing the Ingredients. Place all ingredients in bread machine pan in the order recommended by the manufacturer, except milk, egg yolk, and sugar crystals.
✓ Refrigerate for at least 4 hours but no more than 24 hours after covering with plastic wrap. 12 regular-size muffin cups should be greased.
✓ Knead the dough. Cut the dough into 16 pieces.
✓ Make a ball out of each piece.
✓ Cut each of the four balls into three pieces and roll into small balls.
✓ 12 large balls should be placed in each muffin cup.
✓ With your thumb, flatten each and make an indentation in the center. In each indentation, place one small ball.
✓ Choose the Bake option. Select the Dough/Manual cycle from the drop-down menu.
✓ Use the delay cycle sparingly.
✓ Grease a medium mixing bowl. Place the dough in the bowl and turn it to grease all sides.
✓ Cover and let rise for 50 to 60 minutes in a warm place, or until doubled in size.
✓ Preheat the oven to 350°F.
✓ Brush the tops of the rolls with a mixture of milk and egg yolk.
✓ Sugar crystals are sprinkled on top.
✓ Preheat oven to 350°F and bake for 15 to 20 minutes, or until golden brown.
✓ Remove the pan from the oven and place it on a cooling rack.
✓ Serve immediately.

147) Apple Butter Bread

Ingredients:

- ⅔ cup milk, at 80°F to 90°F
- ⅓ cup apple butter, at room temperature
- 4 teaspoons melted butter, cooled
- 2 teaspoons honey
- ⅔ teaspoon salt
- ⅔ cup whole-wheat flour
- 1½ cups white bread flour
- 1 teaspoon bread machine or instant yeast

Direction: PREP: 10 MINUTES PLUS FERMENTING TIME MAKES 1 LOAF 8 SLICE BREAD (1 pound)

✓ Getting the Ingredients Ready. Put the ingredients in your bread maker according to the manufacturer's instructions.

✓ Select the Bake option.

✓ Set the machine to Basic/White bread, choose light or medium crust, and start the machine.

✓ Remove the bucket from the machine once the loaf is finished.

✓ Allow the loaf to cool for 5 minutes before serving.

✓ To remove the loaf from the bucket, gently shake it out and place it on a cooling rack.

148) Buttermilk Pecan Bread

Ingredients:

- ¾ cup buttermilk, at room temperature
- ¾ cup butter, at room temperature
- 1 tablespoon instant coffee granules
- 3 eggs, at room temperature
- ¾ cup sugar
- 2 cups all-purpose flour
- ½ tablespoon baking powder
- ½ teaspoon table salt
- 1 cup chopped pecans

Direction: PREP: 10 MINUTES PLUS FERMENTING TIME MAKES 1 LOAF 12 SLICE BREAD (1½ pounds)

✓ Preparing the Ingredients. Measure your ingredients and choose the size of loaf you want to make.

✓ In the sequence stated above, add the ingredients to the bread pan.

✓ Close the lid of the bread maker and place the pan inside.

✓ Choose the Bake option. Start the bread machine.

✓ Choose the Quick/Rapid setting first, then the loaf size, and lastly the crust color.

✓ Begin the cycle. Carefully remove the pan from the machine once the cycle has completed and the bread has baked.

✓ Because the handle will be quite hot, use a potholder. Allow to cool for a few minutes.

✓ Remove the bread from the pan and cool for at least 10 minutes on a wire rack before slicing.

149) Brown Sugar Date Nut Swirl Bread

Ingredients:

- 1 cup milk
- 1 large egg
- 4 tablespoons butter
- 4 tablespoons sugar
- 1 teaspoon salt
- 4 cups flour
- 1 ⅔ teaspoons yeast

For the filling:

- ½ cup packed brown sugar
- 1 cup walnuts, chopped
- 1 cup Medjool dates, pitted and chopped
- 2 teaspoons cinnamon
- 2 teaspoons clove spice
- 1 ⅓ tablespoons butter
- Powdered sugar, sifted

Direction: PREP: 10 MINUTES PLUS FERMENTING TIME /MAKES 1 LOAF

✓ Preparing the Ingredients Add wet ingredients to the bread maker pan.

✓ Combine flour, sugar, and salt in a mixing bowl and pour into the pan.

✓ In the center of the dry ingredients, make a well and add the yeast.

✓ Choose the Bake option.

✓ Press Start after selecting the Dough cycle.

✓ Allow the dough to rest in a warm location after punching it down.

✓ Set aside the brown sugar, walnuts, dates, and spices.

✓ On a lightly floured surface, roll the dough into a rectangle. Brush with a spoonful of butter and then stuff with the filling.

✓ Begin rolling the dough from the short end to produce a jelly roll shape. Cover the roll and place it in a greased loaf pan.

✓ Allow it to rise in a warm location for about 30 minutes, or until nearly doubled in size.

✓ Preheat oven to 350°F and bake for 30 minutes.

✓ During the last 10 minutes of cooking, cover with foil.

✓ Allow to cool for 15 minutes before sprinkling with powdered sugar and serving.

150) Sugared Doughnuts

Ingredients:

- ⅔ cup milk
- ¼ cup water
- ¼ cup butter, softened
- 1 egg 3 cups bread flour
- ¼ cup sugar
- 1 teaspoon salt
- 2½ teaspoons bread machine or fast-acting dry yeast

- Vegetable oil
- Additional sugar, if desired

Direction: PREP: 30 MINUTES PLUS FERMENTING TIME /MAKES 20 DOUGHNUTS

- ✓ Preparing the Ingredients. Measure carefully, placing all ingredients except vegetable oil and additional sugar in bread machine pan in the order recommended by the manufacturer.
- ✓ Select the Bake cycle Select Dough/Manual cycle.
- ✓ Do not use delay cycle. Remove dough from pan, using lightly floured hands.
- ✓ Cover and let rest 10 minutes on lightly floured board.
- ✓ Roll dough to ¾a-inch thickness on lightly floured board.
- ✓ Cut with floured doughnut cutter.
- ✓ Cover and let rise on board 35 to 45 minutes or until slightly raised.
- ✓ In deep fryer or heavy Dutch oven, heat 2 to 3 inches' oil to 375°F.
- ✓ Fry doughnuts in oil, 2 or 3 at a time, turning as they rise to the surface.
- ✓ Fry 2 to 3 minutes or until golden brown on both sides.
- ✓ Transfer to a cooling rack after removing from oil using a slotted spoon.
- ✓ Roll warm doughnuts in sugar

151) <u>Cherry–White Chocolate Almond Twist</u>

Ingredients:

- Bread dough
- ½ cup maraschino cherries
- ¾ cup plus 2 tablespoons water
- 1 teaspoon almond extract
- 2 tablespoons butter
- 3¼ cups bread flour
- 2 tablespoons sugar
- 1 teaspoon salt
- 2 teaspoons bread machine yeast or fast-acting dry yeast filling
- ½ cup chopped white baking chips
- ⅓ cup chopped slivered almonds
- 2 tablespoons sugar
- 2 tablespoons butter, softened
- ¼ cup maraschino cherries, well drained Glaze
- ½ cup powdered sugar
- 2 to 4 teaspoons reserved maraschino cherry juice

Direction: PREP: 25 MINUTES PLUS FERMENTING TIME /MAKES 16 SERVINGS

- ✓ Preparing the Ingredients. Drain ½ cup cherries thoroughly; reserve 2 to 4 teaspoons cherry juice for glaze.
- ✓ Measure carefully, placing ½ cup cherries and remaining bread dough ingredients in bread machine pan in the order recommended by the manufacturer.
- ✓ Select the Bake cycle Select Dough/Manual cycle. Do not use delay cycle.
- ✓ Remove dough from pan, using lightly floured hands. Cover and let rest 10 minutes on lightly floured surface.
- ✓ In small bowl, mix baking chips, almonds and 2 tablespoons sugar.
- ✓ Grease large cookie sheet with shortening.
- ✓ On floured surface, roll dough into 15×10-inch rectangle. Spread 2 tablespoons butter over dough.
- ✓ Sprinkle with almond mixture and ¼ cup cherries; press into dough.
- ✓ Starting with 15-inch side, roll up dough; press to seal seam. Place, seam side down, on cookie sheet.
- ✓ Cut roll lengthwise in half.
- ✓ Place halves, filling side up and side by side, on cookie sheet; twist together gently and loosely.
- ✓ Pinch ends to seal. Cover and let rise in warm place about 45 minutes or until doubled in size.
- ✓ Heat oven to 350°F. Bake 30 to 35 minutes or until golden brown.
- ✓ Remove from cookie sheet to cooling rack.
- ✓ Cool 20 minutes.
- ✓ In small bowl, stir powdered sugar and enough cherry juice for drizzling consistency.
- ✓ Drizzle over coffee cake.

152) <u>Barmbrack Bread</u>

Ingredients:

- ⅔ cup water, at 80°F to 90°F
- 1 tablespoon melted butter, cooled
- 2 tablespoons sugar
- 2 tablespoons skim milk powder
- 1 teaspoon salt
- 1 teaspoon dried lemon zest
- ¼ teaspoon ground allspice
- ⅛ teaspoon ground nutmeg
- 2 cups white bread flour
- 1½ teaspoons bread machine or active dry yeast
- ½ cup dried currants

Direction: PREP: 10 MINUTES PLUS FERMENTING TIME MAKES 1 LOAF8 SLICE BREAD (1 pound)

- ✓ Getting the Ingredients Ready. Place all of the ingredients, except the currants, in your bread machine according to the manufacturer's instructions.
- ✓ Select the Bake option.
- ✓ Set the machine to Basic/White bread, choose light or medium crust, and start the machine.
- ✓ When your machine signals or the second kneading cycle begins, add the currants.
- ✓ Remove the bucket from the machine once the loaf is finished.
- ✓ Allow the loaf to cool for 5 minutes before serving.
- ✓ To remove the loaf from the bucket, gently shake it out and place it on a cooling rack.

153) Allspice Currant Bread

Ingredients:

- 1½ cups lukewarm water
- 2 tablespoons unsalted butter, melted
- ¼ cup sugar
- ¼ cup skim milk powder
- 2 teaspoons table salt
- 4 cups white bread flour
- 1½ teaspoons dried lemon zest
- ¾ teaspoon ground allspice
- ¼ teaspoon ground nutmeg
- 2½ teaspoons bread machine yeast
- 1 cup dried currants

Direction: PREP: 10 MINUTES PLUS FERMENTING TIME MAKES 1 LOAF16 SLICE BREAD (2 pounds)

- ✓ Getting the Ingredients Ready Measure your ingredients and choose the size of loaf you want to make.
- ✓ In the order given above, add all of the ingredients to the bread pan except the dried currants.
- ✓ Close the lid of the bread maker and place the pan inside.
- ✓ Choose the Bake option. Start the bread machine.
- ✓ Select the White/Basic or Fruit/Nut setting, then the loaf size, and finally the crust color (if your machine has this function). Begin the cycle.
- ✓ Add the dried currants when the machine says it's time to add ingredients.
- ✓ (Some machines have a fruit/nut hopper where the dried currants can be placed when the machine is turned on.)
- ✓ During the baking process, the machine will mechanically incorporate them into the dough.
- ✓ Carefully remove the pan from the machine once the cycle has completed and the bread has baked.
- ✓ Because the handle will be quite hot, use a potholder. Allow to cool for a few minutes.
- ✓ Remove the bread from the pan and cool for at least 10 minutes on a wire rack before slicing.

154) Beer and Pretzel Bread

Ingredients:

- ¾ cup regular or nonalcoholic beer
- ⅓ cup water
- 2 tablespoons butter, softened
- 3 cups bread flour
- 1 tablespoon packed brown sugar
- 1 teaspoon ground mustard
- 1 teaspoon salt
- 1½ teaspoons bread machine yeast
- ½ cup bite-size pretzel pieces, about 1×¾ inch, or pretzel rods, cut into 1-inch pieces

Direction: PREP: 10 MINUTES PLUS FERMENTING TIME /MAKES 12 SLICES

- ✓ Preparing the Ingredients. Measure carefully, placing all ingredients except pretzels in bread machine pan in order recommended by the manufacturer.
- ✓ Select the Bake cycle Select Basic/White cycle.
- ✓ Use Medium or Light crust color.
- ✓ Do not use delay cycle.
- ✓ Add pretzels 5 minutes before the last kneading cycle ends.
- ✓ Remove baked bread from pan; cool on cooling rack.

155) Crusty Honey Bread

Ingredients:

- 1 cup minus 1 tablespoon water, at 80°F to 90°F
- 1½ tablespoons honey
- 1⅛ tablespoons melted butter, cooled
- ¾ teaspoon salt
- 2 ⅔ cups white bread flour
- 1½ teaspoons bread machine or instant yeast

Direction: PREP: 10 MINUTES PLUS FERMENTING TIME MAKES 1 LOAF12 SLICE BREAD (1½ pounds)

- ✓ Getting the Ingredients Ready Place the ingredients in your bread maker according to the manufacturer's instructions.
- ✓ Choose the Bake option. Press Start after programming the machine for Basic/White bread and selecting light or medium crust.
- ✓ Remove the bucket from the machine after the loaf is done.
- ✓ Allow 5 minutes for the bread to cool.
- ✓ Remove the loaf from the bucket with a little shake and place it on a cooling rack.

156) Sage-Raisin Wheat Bread

Ingredients:

- 1¼ cups water
- 2 tablespoons butter, softened
- 1½ cups bread flour
- 1½ cups whole wheat flour
- 2 tablespoons sugar
- 1½ teaspoons salt
- ¾ teaspoon crumbled dried sage leaves
- 1¾ teaspoons bread machine or fast-acting dry yeast
- ¾ cup golden raisins
- 1 egg, beaten

Direction: PREP: 15 MINUTES PLUS FERMENTING TIME /MAKES 16 SLICES

- ✓ Getting the Ingredients Ready Carefully measure all ingredients, except the raisins and egg, and place them in the bread machine pan in the manufacturer's recommended order.
- ✓ At the Raisin/Nut signal, add raisins. Select the Dough/Manual cycle from the drop-down menu.
- ✓ Use the delay cycle sparingly.
- ✓ Using lightly greased hands, remove the dough from the pan.
- ✓ Cover and set aside on a lightly floured surface for 10 minutes. Choose the Bake option.

- ✓ Using a big cookie sheet, grease it.
- ✓ One-third of the dough should be cut off and shaped into a tiny ball (about 3 inches).
- ✓ Form the rest of the dough into a big ball (about 5 inches).
- ✓ Place the large ball on the cookie sheet and the mini ball on top of it.
- ✓ Push into the middle of the little ball with your thumb and first two fingers, pushing through the dough until it almost touches the cookie sheet.
- ✓ Cover and let rise for 30 to 45 minutes in a warm area, or until doubled in size.
- ✓ If the indentation stays when the dough is touched, it is ready.
- ✓ Preheat the oven to 400 degrees Fahrenheit.
- ✓ Brush the egg all over the loaf.
- ✓ Cut 14-inch-deep vertical slits on the sides of each ball about 2 inches apart using a serrated knife.
- ✓ Bake for 18 to 20 minutes, or until a hollow sound can be heard when the loaf is tapped.

157) Asiago Dinner Rolls

Ingredients:

- 2 tablespoons sugar
- 2 packages (1/4 ounce each) active dry yeast
- 2 teaspoons garlic salt
- 1 teaspoon Italian seasoning
- 3-3/4 to 4-1/4 cups all-purpose flour
- 1 cup 2% milk
- 1/2 cup water
- 4 tablespoons butter, divided
- 1 large egg
- 3/4 cup shredded Asiago cheese, divided

Direction: Serving: 1-1/2 dozen. | Prep: 45mins | Cook: 20mins |

- ✓ Combine 2 cups of flour, Italian seasoning, garlic salt, yeast, and sugar in a large bowl.
- ✓ Heat 2 tablespoons butter, water and milk to 120° to 130° in a small saucepan.
- ✓ Add to the dry ingredients and then beat for 2 minutes on medium speed.
- ✓ Put in egg and then beat for two more minutes.
- ✓ Mix in enough leftover flour and 1/2 cup of cheese to make a soft dough (the dough will be sticky).
- ✓ Transfer the dough to a floured surface and knead for about 6 to 8 minutes until elastic and smooth.
- ✓ Put into a greased bowl and flip once to grease the top.
- ✓ Use in plastic wrap to cover and allow to rise for about 30 minutes in a warm place until doubled.
- ✓ Punch the dough down and turn it on a lightly floured surface.
- ✓ Then divide and form into 18 balls. Roll every ball into a 12-inch rope and then tie to form a loose knot.
- ✓ Tuck the ends under.
- ✓ Put into a greased baking sheets, placing three inches apart.

- ✓ Melt the leftover butter and brush over the rolls.
- ✓ Top with the remaining cheese.
- ✓ Allow to rise for about 15 minutes in a warm place until almost doubled.
- ✓ Preheat an oven to 375°.
- ✓ Bake until turned golden brown for about 20 to 25 minutes and rotate the pans halfway through baking.
- ✓ Transfer from the pans onto wire racks and then serve warm

158) Best Dinner Rolls

Ingredients:

- 1/4 cup sugar
- 1 package (1/4 ounce) active dry yeast
- 1-1/4 teaspoons salt
- 4-1/2 to 5 cups all-purpose flour
- 1 cup whole milk
- 1/2 cup water
- 2 tablespoons butter
- 2 large eggs
- 1 large egg, lightly beaten

FOR EVERYTHING DINNER ROLLS:

- 1 teaspoon kosher salt
- 1 teaspoon dried minced garlic
- 1 teaspoon dried minced onion 1 teaspoon poppy seeds
- 1 teaspoon sesame seeds

FOR PARM- GARLIC DINNER ROLLS:

- 2 tablespoons grated Parmesan cheese
- 1/2 teaspoon dried minced garlic

FOR ALMOND HERB DINNER ROLLS:

- 2 tablespoons chopped sliced almonds
- 1/2 teaspoon kosher salt
- 1/2 teaspoon dried basil
- 1/2 teaspoon dried oregano

Direction: Serving: 2 dozen. | Prep: 35mins | Cook: 10mins |

- ✓ Combine 2 cups of flour, salt, yeast and sugar in a big bowl. Heat butter, water and milk in a small saucepan to 120-130 degrees.
- ✓ Put to the dry ingredients; mix for 3 minutes on moderate speed. Put in 2 eggs; beat for 2 minutes on high.
- ✓ Mix in sufficient leftover flour to make a soft dough; dough will become sticky.
- ✓ Transfer dough to a floured area; knead for 6 to 8 minutes, till pliable and smooth.
- ✓ Put in a greased bowl, flipping one time to coat the surface.
- ✓ Put on plastic wrap to cover and allow to rise in a warm area for an hour till doubled in size.
- ✓ Dough must be beaten down.
- ✓ Transfer to a slightly floured area; split and from dough into 2 dozen rounds.
- ✓ Put in 2 greased baking pans, 13x9 inches in size.

- ✓ Put on kitchen towels to cover; allow to rise in a warm area for half an hour till doubled in size.
- ✓ Preheat the oven to 375°. Brush lightly beaten egg on rolls.
- ✓ On the top, scatter rolls toppings of your preference.
- ✓ Bake till golden brown, or about 10 to 15 minutes.
- ✓ Transfer from the pans onto the wire racks; serve while warm.

159) *Butternut Squash Dinner Rolls*

Ingredients:

- 2 tablespoons plus 1 teaspoon active dry yeast
- 3/4 teaspoon plus 1 cup sugar, divided
- 1/2 cup warm water (110° to 115°)
- 2 cups warm milk (110° to 115°)
- 1/4 cup butter, softened
- 2 cups mashed cooked butternut squash
- 2 teaspoons salt
- 1/4 cup toasted wheat germ
- 10 to 11-1/2 cups all-purpose flour
- Additional butter

Direction: Serving: 5 dozen. | Prep: 30mins | Cook: 15mins |

- ✓ In a large bowl, dissolve 3/4 teaspoon sugar and yeast in warm water;
- ✓ allow 5 minutes to rest.
- ✓ Add the butter, milk, squash, the remaining sugar and salt; mix until smooth.
- ✓ Add 4 cups flour and wheat germ; beat until smooth. In order to form a soft dough, stir in enough of the remaining flour.
- ✓ On a floured surface, place dough; knead for around 6 to 8 minutes until elastic and smooth.
- ✓ In a greased bowl, place dough and turning once to grease top.
- ✓ Allow to rise while covering in a warm place for around 1 hour until doubled.
- ✓ Punch dough down and divide into thirds;
- ✓ cut each portion into 20 pieces.
- ✓ Form into balls.
- ✓ Transfer onto greased baking sheets.
- ✓ Allow to rise, covered, for approximately 30 minutes until doubled.
- ✓ Bake at 350° for nearly 15 to 17 minutes or until it has the color of golden brown.
- ✓ Use butter for brushing.
- ✓ Take away to wire racks.

160) *Caraway Rye Dinner Rolls*

Ingredients:

- 1-1/4 cups rye flour
- 1/2 cup wheat germ
- 2 tablespoons caraway seeds
- 1 package (1/4 ounce) active dry yeast
- 1 teaspoon salt

- 3 cups all-purpose flour
- 1 cup 2% milk
- 1/2 cup water
- 3 tablespoons butter
- 2 tablespoons honey
- 1/3 cup finely chopped onion

EGG WASH:

- 1 egg
- 2 teaspoons water

Direction: Serving: 1-1/2 dozen. | Prep: 35mins | Cook: 15mins |

- ✓ In a large mixing basin, combine 1 cup all-purpose flour and the first 5 ingredients. In a small saucepan, heat the honey, butter, water, and milk to 120-130 degrees.
- ✓ Add to the dry ingredients and beat on medium speed for 3 minutes.
- ✓ In a large mixing bowl, combine enough remaining all-purpose flour and onion to make a soft dough (the dough will get sticky).
- ✓ Turn the dough out onto a floured surface and knead for 6 to 8 minutes, or until malleable and smooth.
- ✓ Place in an oiled mixing bowl and flip once to grease the top.
- ✓ Allow to rise in a warm environment for about an hour, or until doubled.
- ✓ Punch down the dough.
- ✓ Spread a thin layer of flour on a work surface, then split and roll into 18 balls.
- ✓ Place on buttered baking pans, ensuring a 2-inch spacing between them.
- ✓ Cover with a kitchen towel and leave to rise in a warm room for about 45 minutes, or until nearly doubled.
- ✓ Preheat the oven to 400°F.
- ✓ In a small dish, whisk together the water and egg, then brush on top of the rolls.
- ✓ Preheat oven to 350°F and bake for 11–14 minutes, or until gently browned.
- ✓ Allow to cool on wire racks.

161) *Crescent Dinner Rolls*

Ingredients:

- 1 package (1/4 ounce) active dry yeast
- 1/4 cup warm water (110° to 115°)
- 1 tablespoon plus 1/2 cup sugar, divided
- 3/4 cup warm milk (110° to 115°)
- 3 large eggs, lightly beaten
- 1/2 cup butter, softened
- 1 teaspoon salt
- 5 to 5-1/2 cups all-purpose flour
- Melted butter

Direction: Serving: 2 dozen. | Prep: 40mins | Cook: 10mins |

- ✓ Melt yeast in warm water in a big bowl.
- ✓ Add 1 tbsp. sugar; stand for 5 minutes.

- ✓ Add leftover sugar, salt, butter, eggs and milk;
- ✓ mix in enough flour to make a stiff dough.
- ✓ Turn it on a floured surface; knead for 6-8 minutes till elastic and smooth.
- ✓ Put into a greased bowl;
- ✓ turn once to grease the top.
- ✓ Cover; rise for 1 1/2 hours till doubled in a warm place.
- ✓ Punch down the dough; divide into thirds.
- ✓ Roll each into a 12-in.
- ✓ circle and cut each circle into 8 wedges.
- ✓ Brush with melted butter; from wide end, roll up the wedges.
- ✓ Put on greased baking sheets, 2-in. apart, pointed end down.
- ✓ Cover; rise for 30 minutes till doubled in a warm place.
- ✓ Bake for 10-12 minutes till golden brown at 375°.
- ✓ Transfer from pans onto wire racks.

162) **Dinner Rolls**

Ingredients:

- 1 cup Milk, scalded and cooled
- 4-6 tablespoons Butter
- 1 packet Yeast
- 4 tablespoon Sugar
- 1 cup Water, lukewarm
- 1 tablespoon Salt
- 1 Egg, beaten
- 4-6 cups Flour

Direction: Serving: | Prep: 1hours | Cook: 6hours |

- ✓ To prepare: Add 1 tbsp. sugar and yeast to water and allow to dissolve.
- ✓ Add melted butter into the milk.
- ✓ Add leftover sugar, egg and salt to the covered mixing bowl together with yeast and milk mixtures.
- ✓ Add flour and stir until the dough achieves a workable consistency.
- ✓ Flour or water as necessary so that the dough will not become too stiff or sticky.
- ✓ Allow to rise for 3 hours in a covered bowl. Beat down as needed.
- ✓ Roll the dough flat and use cup's rim to cut into rounds.
- ✓ Brush the rounds lightly, then fold.
- ✓ Allow to rise for 2 hours in greased pans.
- ✓ Bake for about 15 minutes at 425 degrees until the rolls are browned a little.
- ✓ To prepare the cinnamon rolls, roll the dough flat and sprinkle a generous amount of butter pieces, brown sugar and cinnamon on top.
- ✓ Roll and slice into about 1-inch thick pieces and bake in the tins as mentioned above.

163) **Golden Dinner Rolls**

Ingredients:

- 1/2 small (about 4 ounces/112 grams) orange-fleshed sweet potato (also called yam)
- 1 1/2 cups plus 1 tablespoon (8 ounces/224 grams) unbleached all-purpose flour
- 1/3 cup plus 4 teaspoons (3.5 ounces/98 grams) water, room temperature (70°F to 90°F)
- 1 1/2 teaspoons honey
- 3/4 teaspoon instant yeast (also known as rapid- rise or bread machine yeast)
- 1 1/2 tablespoons non-fat dry milk powder
- 1 tablespoon unsalted butter, softened,
- plus 6 tablespoons unsalted butter, melted and cooled
- 3/4 teaspoon fine sea salt stand mixer fitted with whisk attachment and dough hook,
- 3-quart or larger bowl or dough-rising container, masking tape, dough scraper or spatula, heavy baking sheet, baking stone or second heavy baking sheet, aluminum-foil-lined cast-iron pan or heavy rimmed baking pan

Direction: Serving: Makes one dozen dinner rolls | Prep: | Cook: |

- ✓ Baking and mashing potato: Preheat an oven to 375°F.
- ✓ Pierce the potato in several places with fork.
- ✓ Wrap with aluminum foil and then bake for about 50 minutes until easily pierce with fork.
- ✓ Peel and mash once cooled enough to handle. Save half cup (4.5 ounces) of mashed potato and get rid of the remainder or keep for another use.
- ✓ Making the dough starter (sponge): whisk together 1/4 teaspoon yeast, honey, 1/3 cup plus 4 teaspoons (3.5 ounces/98 grams) water and 1/2 cup plus 1 tablespoon (3 ounces/84 grams) flour in the bowl of stand mixer that is fitted with a whisk attachment for about 2 minutes until very smooth.
- ✓ The sponge will have consistency of thick batter).
- ✓ Scrape down the sides of the bowl.
- ✓ Whisk together milk powder, remaining 1/2 teaspoon yeast and remaining 1 cup (5 ounces/140 grams) flour in a medium bowl.
- ✓ Sprinkle the mixture over the flour mixture (sponge) in the bowl of mixer to make a blanket on top the sponge.
- ✓ Tightly cover the bowl with plastic wrap and allow to sit for at least 1 hour, best if left to sit up to 4 hours. (You can make the starter ahead and chill while tightly covered with plastic wrap overnight.
- ✓ No need to heat the starter to room temperature before use).
- ✓ Mixing the dough: Attach the dough hook to the stand mixer.
- ✓ Add 1 tablespoon of softened butter and mashed sweet potato to the starter and combine on low for about 1 minute until you have a rough dough.
- ✓ Scrape down the sides of the bowl and then tightly cover in plastic wrap.
- ✓ Allow the dough to sit for 20 minutes to rest.

- ✓ Sprinkle salt on top the dough and then knead on low for 7 to 10 minutes until it is smooth, shiny, and a bit sticky to touch.
- ✓ Scrape down the sides of the bowl. (In case the dough is too sticky, place onto a work surface that is lightly floured and then knead in a little flour. If it is too stiff, pour in a little cold water and then knead briefly.)
- ✓ First rise: Oil a 3-quart or larger bowl (or dough-rising container) lightly with nonstick vegetable-oil spray or vegetable oil.
- ✓ Place the dough into the bowl and then lightly oil or spray the top of the dough.
- ✓ Mark the outside of the bowl with tape to about double the current height of the dough.
- ✓ Tightly cover the bowl in plastic wrap and allow the dough to rise for about an hour in a warm place (75°F to 80°F) until it is doubled in size.
- ✓ Second rising: using an oiled spatula or dough scraper, transfer the dough to a lightly oiled work surface.
- ✓ Stretch the bottom of the dough gently and then fold up to the middle.
- ✓ Repeat this with the right side, left side, and top.
- ✓ Round the dough package and place into bowl with the smooth side up.
- ✓ The dough should be lightly sprayed or oiled.
- ✓ Mark the outside of the bowl with tape to about double the current height of the dough.
- ✓ Then divide into four equal pieces with a lightly oiled bench scraper, ensure each weighs approximately four ounces (112 grams).
- ✓ Then divide every piece into three pieces and each should weigh around 1.3 ounces (36 grams).
- ✓ Keep the rest of the dough covered while you work with each batch. Roll one piece of dough in between your palms with lightly floured hands to create a smooth, 1 3/4-inch-wide ball.
- ✓ Pinch an indentation at the bottom of ball tightly to seal.
- ✓ Repeat this to make the remaining balls.
- ✓ Place melted butter into a small bowl. Dunk each dough ball in the melted butter and coat all the sides.
- ✓ Place into the prepared baking sheet, placing about two inches apart, sealed-side-down.
- ✓ Use nonstick vegetable- oil spray or vegetable oil to lightly coat the sheet of plastic wrap and then cover the pan gently with the oiled wrap.
- ✓ Allow the rolls to rise in a warm location for approximately 45 minutes, or until a depression fills in very slowly and doubles in size when pressed with a finger.
- ✓ Baking the rolls: once the dough is rising, set the rack close to the bottom of the oven and then place a heavy baking sheet or baking stone on top.
- ✓ Onto the floor of an oven, place aluminum foil-lined cast-iron pan or heavy rimmed baking pan and preheat an oven for 1 hour to 400°F.
- ✓ Quickly place the baking sheet of the rolls into the hot baking stone and add half cup of ice cubes onto the pan beneath.

Bake the rolls and rotate the pan 180 degrees halfway through for about 12 minutes until turned golden brown and a skewer comes out clean when inserted in the centers (the temperature at the center should register about 190°F).
- ✓ Remove the rolls from the baking sheet onto a rack and cool completely at room temperature.
- ✓ You can serve while still warm or lukewarm

164)   Hawaiian Dinner Rolls

Ingredients:

- 1 can (8 ounces) crushed pineapple, undrained
- 1/4 cup warm pineapple juice (70° to 80°)
- 1/4 cup water (70° to 80°)
- 1 large egg
- 1/4 cup butter, cubed
- 1/4 cup nonfat dry milk powder
- 1 tablespoon sugar
- 1-1/2 teaspoons salt
- 3-1/4 cups bread flour
- 2-1/4 teaspoons active dry yeast
- 3/4 cup sweetened shredded coconut

Direction: Serving: 15 rolls. | Prep: 35mins | Cook: 15mins |

- ✓ Place the first 10 ingredients in the bread machine pan in the sequence indicated by the manufacturer.
- ✓ Select a dough setting.
- ✓ Check dough after 5 minutes of stirring; if necessary, add 1-2 tablespoons flour/water.
- ✓ Add the coconut just before the final kneading; the machine may provide an audible signal.
- ✓ The dough should be turned out onto a lightly floured surface and covered when the cycle is complete.
- ✓ Allow for 10 minutes of resting time before dividing into 15 portions.
- ✓ Roll each into a ball and place in a greased 13x9-inch baking pan.
- ✓ Cover and let rise for 45 minutes in a warm area until doubled. At 375°F, bake for 15-20 minutes, or until golden brown.

165)   Herb Buttermilk Dinner Rolls

Ingredients:

- 1 package (1/4 ounce) active dry yeast
- 1/4 cup warm water (110° to 115°)
- 3/4 cup warm buttermilk (110° to 115°)
- 4 tablespoons butter, melted, divided
- 2 tablespoons sugar
- 1-1/2 teaspoons salt
- 1/2 teaspoon dried basil
- 1/2 teaspoon dried marjoram
- 1/2 teaspoon dried thyme
- 1/4 teaspoon baking soda
- 1 large egg

- 2-3/4 to 3-1/4 cups all-purpose flour
  Direction: Serving: 2 dozen. | Prep: 20mins | Cook: 25mins |

✓ Melt the yeast in a bowl of warm water. 2 tbsp. butter, buttermilk, and the remaining 7 ingredients are added.

✓ 2 cups flour 2 cups flour 2 cups flour 2 cups flour 2 cups flour 2 cups flour 2 cups flour 2 cups flour 2 cups flour 2 cups Mix in enough remaining flour to produce a sticky, soft dough.

✓ Knead for 6-8 minutes on a heavily floured surface, until elastic and smooth.

✓ Place it in an oiled bowl and turn once to grease the surface.

✓ Cover and let rise in a warm place for 75 minutes, or until doubled.

✓ Knead the dough.

✓ Turn it out onto a lightly floured board and cut it into four pieces.

✓ Divide each part into six pieces and roll each one into a ball.

✓ Place it in a greased 13x9-inch baking pan.

✓ Cover and let rise for 50 minutes, or until doubled in size. Preheat the oven to 375 °F and bake the rolls for 25-30 minutes, or until golden brown.

✓ Allow to cool for 5 minutes. Remove from pan to wire rack and brush with remaining butter.

166) **Herbed Accordian Dinner Rolls**

Ingredients:

- 2 packages (1/4 ounce each) active dry yeast
- 1/2 cup warm water (110° to 115°)
- 1 teaspoon plus 1/3 cup sugar, divided
- 1-1/4 cups warm 2% milk (110° to 115°)
- 1/2 cup butter, melted
- 2 large eggs
- 1- 1/2 teaspoons salt
- 6 to 6-1/2 cups all-purpose flour
- 3 tablespoons butter, softened
- 1 teaspoon Italian seasoning
- 1 large egg white, beaten

Direction: Serving: 2 dozen. | Prep: 30mins | Cook: 20mins |

✓ In a large mixing basin, dissolve the yeast in warm water with a teaspoon of sugar.

✓ Combine the remaining sugar, 3 cups flour, salt, eggs, melted butter, and milk in a mixing bowl and whisk until smooth.

✓ To form a soft dough, add enough remaining flour.

✓ Transfer to a floured surface and knead for 6 to 8 minutes, or until smooth and malleable.

✓ Place in a greased mixing bowl and flip once to coat the surface.

✓ Cover and leave to rise for an hour in a warm place until it has doubled in size.

✓ Deflate the dough and place it on a floured surface.

✓ Divided into four sections.

✓ Roll each component into a 14x6-inch rectangle.

✓ Combine Italian spice and softened butter in a bowl and sprinkle over dough.

✓ Every rectangle should be scored crosswise at 2-inch intervals.

✓ On score lines with marks as a guide, fold the dough accordion-style backward and forward.

✓ Make 6 one-inch sections from the folded dough.

✓ Place the pieces, cut side down, in oiled muffin cups.

✓ Wrap loosely in plastic wrap.

✓ Refrigerate for at least 8 hours or overnight.

✓ Preheat the oven to 375 °F.

✓ Before baking, remove the cover and let aside for 10 minutes at room temperature.

✓ Using the egg white, give it a brushing. For 18 to 22 minutes, bake until golden brown.

✓ Place the wire racks on top of the pans.

167) **Homemade Golden Dinner Rolls**

Ingredients:

- 5-1/2 to 6 cups all-purpose flour
- 1/2 cup sugar
- 2 packages (1/4 ounce each) active dry yeast
- 1-1/2 teaspoons salt
- 1 cup milk
- 2/3 cup water
- 1/4 cup butter, softened
- 2 eggs
- Melted butter

Direction: Serving: 2 dozen. | Prep: 45mins | Cook: 15mins |

✓ Melt the yeast in a bowl of warm water. 2 tbsp. butter, buttermilk, and the remaining 7 ingredients are added. 2 cups flour 2 cups flour 2 cups flour 2 cups flour 2 cups flour 2 cups flour 2 cups flour 2 cups flour 2 cups flour 2 cups.

✓ Mix in enough remaining flour to produce a sticky, soft dough.

✓ Knead for 6-8 minutes on a heavily floured surface, until elastic and smooth.

✓ Place it in an oiled bowl and turn once to grease the surface.

✓ Cover and let rise in a warm place for 75 minutes, or until doubled.

✓ Knead the dough.

✓ Turn it out onto a lightly floured board and cut it into four pieces.

✓ Divide each part into six pieces and roll each one into a ball.

✓ Place it in a greased 13x9-inch baking pan.

✓ Cover and let rise for 50 minutes, or until doubled in size.

✓ Preheat the oven to 375 °F and bake the rolls for 25-30 minutes, or until golden brown. Allow to cool for 5 minutes.

✓ Remove from pan to wire rack and brush with remaining butter.

168)   *Italian Dinner Rolls*

Ingredients:

- 3-1/2 to 4 cups all-purpose flour
- 2 tablespoons sugar
- 1 package (1/4 ounce) active dry yeast
- 1-1/2 teaspoons garlic salt
- 1 teaspoon onion powder
- 1 teaspoon Italian seasoning
- 1 teaspoon dried parsley flakes
- 1 cup 2% milk
- 1/2 cup water
- 4 tablespoons butter, divided
- 1 egg
- 3/4 cup grated Parmesan cheese, divided

Direction: Serving: 15 rolls. | Prep: 20mins | Cook: 20mins |

- ✓ In a large mixing bowl, combine the seasonings, yeast, sugar, and 1/2 cup flour.
- ✓ In a small saucepan, heat 2 tablespoons butter, 2 tablespoons water, and 2 tablespoons milk to 120-130°.
- ✓ Combine the wet and dry ingredients in a mixing bowl and beat until well combined.
- ✓ On medium speed, beat in the egg for 3 minutes. Combine leftover flour and 1/2 cup of cheese to make a soft dough.
- ✓ Knead for 6-8 minutes, or until elastic and smooth, on a floured surface.
- ✓ Place it in an oiled mixing bowl and turn it once to grease the surface.
- ✓ Cover and set aside for 15 minutes to allow the flavors to mingle.
- ✓ Dough must be beaten down.
- ✓ Divide the dough into 15 pieces on a lightly floured surface.
- ✓ Make a ball out of each of the pieces.
- ✓ Melt the remaining butter and dip the tops of the balls in it.
- ✓ Cover and bake in a greased 13x9-inch baking pan. Allow 10 minutes for rest.
- ✓ Cook for 20-25 minutes at 375 degrees until golden brown.
- ✓ Cool on wire racks after removing the pans.

169)   *Maple Oat Dinner Rolls*

Ingredients:

- 1 package (1/4 ounce) active dry yeast
- 1/2 cup warm water (110° to 115°), divided
- 1/2 cup warm strong brewed coffee (110° to 115°)
- 1/2 cup old-fashioned oats
- 1/4 cup sugar
- 1/4 cup maple syrup
- 1 egg
- 3 tablespoons shortening
- 1 teaspoon salt
- 3 to 3-1/2 cups bread flour
- 1 tablespoon butter, melted

Direction: Serving: 2 dozen. | Prep: 25mins | Cook: 25mins |

- ✓ In a large mixing basin, dissolve the yeast in 1/4 cup warm water.
- ✓ 2 cups flour, remaining water, salt, shortening, egg, syrup, sugar, oats, and coffee, whisked together until smooth.
- ✓ Add enough remaining flour to make a soft dough.
- ✓ Turn out onto a floured surface and knead for 6 to 8 minutes, or until malleable and smooth.
- ✓ Place in an oiled mixing bowl and flip once to grease the top.
- ✓ Allow to rise for about one hour in a warm environment until it has doubled in size.
- ✓ Punch down the dough.
- ✓ Turn out onto a floured surface and cut into four pieces.
- ✓ Divide each portion into six parts and roll each one into a ball.
- ✓ Place in a 13x9-inch baking pan that has been sprayed with nonstick cooking spray.
- ✓ Allow to rise for about 30 minutes, or until doubled in size.
- ✓ Preheat oven to 350°F and bake for 25–30 minutes, or until golden brown.
- ✓ Brush the rolls with butter.
- ✓ Remove it from the pan and place it on a wire rack to cool.
- ✓ Serve while the dish is still warm.

170)   *Mom's Dinner Rolls*

Ingredients:

- 1/4 cup finely chopped onion
- 4 garlic cloves, minced
- 1/4 cup butter, cubed
- 1 teaspoon dried basil
- 1 teaspoon dried oregano
- 1/2 teaspoon each dried marjoram, parsley flakes and tarragon
- 1 package (1/4 ounce) active dry yeast
- 3/4 cup warm water (110° to 115°)
- 1 teaspoon sugar
- 1 teaspoon salt
- 2 cups all-purpose flour
- 1 egg, lightly beaten

Direction: Serving: 2 dozen. | Prep: 25mins | Cook: 20mins |

- ✓ In a small frying pan, melt the butter and sauté the garlic and onion until soft.
- ✓ Allow to cool before adding herbs.
- ✓ In a food processor, dissolve the yeast in warm water, then add the onion mixture, salt, and sugar, and process until smooth.
- ✓ Process until the dough forms a smooth ball, then add the flour and cover.

- ✓ Knead it for 6-8 minutes on a floured surface, until dough is flexible and smooth.
- ✓ Place it in an oiled mixing bowl and flip it once to grease the surface.
- ✓ Allow it to rise in a warm environment for about an hour, or until it has doubled in size.
- ✓ Split the dough into 24 pieces after punching it down and transferring it to a flat surface.
- ✓ Each one should be formed into a ball and placed 2 inches apart on greased baking trays.
- ✓ Allow it to rise in a warm place for about 30 minutes, until it has doubled in size. Using an egg, brush it.
- ✓ Allow it to bake at 350 degrees for 20 to 25 minutes, or until golden brown.
- ✓ Transfer the mixture to wire racks after removing it from the pans.
- ✓ It's best served hot

171)   **No Fuss Dinner Rolls**

Ingredients:

- 1 package (1/4 ounce) active dry yeast
- 1-1/2 cups warm milk (110° to 115°)
- 1 egg
- 2 tablespoons butter, melted
- 2 tablespoons sugar
- 1 teaspoon salt
- 4 cups all-purpose flour
- Melted butter

Direction: Serving: about 15 rolls. | Prep: 15mins | Cook: 15mins |

- ✓ Dissolve the yeast in warm milk in a big bowl.
- ✓ Add 2 cups of flour, salt, sugar, butter and egg and beat it for 3 minutes on medium speed.
- ✓ Mix in leftover flour (the batter will get stiff).
- ✓ Avoid kneading.
- ✓ Put cover and allow it to rest for 15 minutes.
- ✓ Stir down the dough.
- ✓ Fill the greased muffin cups 3/4 full.
- ✓ Put cover and allow it to rise for about 30 minutes in a warm area, until it doubles.
- ✓ Let it bake for 12 to 15 minutes at 400 degrees or until it turns golden brown, then brush it with melted butter.
- ✓ Allow it to cool for 1 minute prior to taking it out from the pans and transferring to wire racks.

172)   **Oatmeal Dinner Rolls**

Ingredients:

- 2 cups water
- 1 cup quick-cooking oats
- 3 tablespoons butter
- 1 package (1/4 ounce) active dry yeast
- 1/3 cup warm water (110° to 115°)
- 1/3 cup packed brown sugar

- 1 tablespoon sugar
- 1-1/2 teaspoons salt
- 4-3/4 to 5-1/4 cups all-purpose flour

Direction: Serving: 1-1/2 dozen. | Prep: 40mins | Cook: 20mins |

- ✓ Boil water in a big saucepan; put in butter and oats.
- ✓ Cook and mix for a minute.
- ✓ Take away from heat; cool till lukewarm. In a large dish, dissolve the yeast in warm water.
- ✓ Add 4 cups flour, salt, sugars, and oat mixture in a large mixing bowl until smooth.
- ✓ Add enough remaining flour to form a soft dough.
- ✓ Transfer to a floured surface and knead for 6 to 8 minutes, or until smooth and malleable.
- ✓ Place in an oiled basin, flipping once to coat the surface with oil.
- ✓ Cover and allow to double in size for an hour in a warm environment.
- ✓ Allow dough to deflate for 10 minutes. 18 rounds should be formed.
- ✓ Divide evenly between two oiled 9-inch round baking pans.
- ✓ Cover and allow to double in size for 45 minutes.
- ✓ Bake at 350° for 20 to 25 minutes, or until golden brown.
- ✓ Transfer the baked goods from the pan to the wire racks.

173)   **Parmesan Herb Dinner Rolls**

Ingredients:

- 12 frozen bread dough dinner rolls
- 1/2 cup grated Parmesan cheese
- 2 garlic cloves, minced
- 1-1/2 teaspoons Italian seasoning
- 1/4 teaspoon dill weed
- 1/4 cup butter, melted

Direction: Serving: 1 dozen. | Prep: 10mins | Cook: 15mins |

- ✓ Put rolls onto greased baking sheet; thaw in the fridge, covered, overnight or for 2 hours at room temperature.
- ✓ Mix dill, Italian seasoning, garlic and cheese in a small bowl.
- ✓ Brush butter on rolls; sprinkle cheese mixture.
- ✓ Use plastic wrap to loosely cover; rise for 1-hour till doubled in a warm place. Preheat an oven to 350°F.
- ✓ Bake till golden brown for 15-20 minutes.
- ✓ Transfer it from pan onto wire rack and serve warm.

174)   **Pillow Soft Dinner Rolls**

Ingredients:

- 4-1/2 teaspoons active dry yeast
- 1/2 cup warm water (110° to 115°)
- 2 cups warm milk (110° to 115°)
- 6 tablespoons shortening

- 2 large eggs
- 1/4 cup sugar
- 1-1/2 teaspoons salt
- 7 to 7-1/2 cups all-purpose flour

Direction: Serving: 2 dozen. | Prep: 30mins | Cook: 20mins |

- ✓ In a large mixing basin, dissolve the yeast in warm water.
- ✓ Combine 3 cups flour, salt, sugar, eggs, shortening, and milk in a mixing bowl and whisk until smooth.
- ✓ Add enough remaining flour to form a soft dough.
- ✓ Transfer the dough to a floured surface and knead for approximately 6 to 8 minutes (it will become sticky), or until it becomes elastic and smooth.
- ✓ Place it in a greased bowl and turn it once to coat the top with grease.
- ✓ Cover and allow it to double in size for about an hour in a warm environment. Punch the dough down.
- ✓ It should be transferred to a lightly floured board and then divided into 24 pieces.
- ✓ Each should be rolled. Arrange it on buttered baking pans 2 inches apart.
- ✓ Cover and leave it rise for approximately 30 minutes, or until it doubles in size.
- ✓ Bake for 20–25 minutes at 350 degrees, or until golden brown.
- ✓ Transfer to racks made of wire.

175) Rosemary Garlic Dinner Rolls

Ingredients:

- 1 cup water (70° to 80°)
- 2 tablespoons butter, softened
- 1 egg, lightly beaten
- 3 tablespoons sugar
- 1 tablespoon dried rosemary, crushed
- 2 teaspoons dried minced garlic
- 1 teaspoon salt
- 3-1/4 cups bread flour
- 1 package (1/4 ounce) active dry yeast

Direction: Serving: 16 rolls. | Prep: 15mins | Cook: 15mins |

- ✓ Put all the ingredients in the bread machine pan in the order given by the manufacturer.
- ✓ Choose the dough setting (after five minutes of mixing, check the dough and pour in 1 to 2 tablespoons of flour or water if necessary).
- ✓ Once the cycle is done, flip the dough on a surface that is lightly floured.
- ✓ Separate into 16 parts and then form into balls.
- ✓ Distribute among 2 greased 9-inch round baking pans.
- ✓ Cover the pans and leave the balls to rise for about 30 minutes until doubled. Bake them for 12 to 15 minutes at 375° or until they turned golden brown.
- ✓ Transfer from the pans onto wire racks.
- ✓

176) Sweet Milk Dinner Rolls

Ingredients:

- 1 package (1/4 ounce) active dry yeast
- 2 cups warm milk (110° to 115°)
- 1/2 cup sugar
- 2 tablespoons butter, melted
- 1 teaspoon salt
- 4 to 5 cups all-purpose flour

Direction: Serving: 16 rolls. | Prep: 20mins | Cook: 35mins |

- ✓ Melt yeast in warm milk in a big bowl.
- ✓ Add 3 cups flour, salt, butter and sugar; beat till smooth.
- ✓ To make a soft dough, add enough leftover flour.
- ✓ Turn it out onto the floured surface and knead for 6-8 minutes, or until smooth and elastic.
- ✓ Place it in an oiled bowl; turn once to grease the surface.
- ✓ Cover and set aside for 1 hour in a warm place to double in size.
- ✓ Punctuate dough.
- ✓ Turn it onto the floured surface; divide it to 16 pieces.
- ✓ Form each to a ball; put onto greased baking sheets, 2-in. apart.
- ✓ Cover; rise for 30 minutes' till doubled.
- ✓ Bake at 350°F for 35-40 minutes, or until golden brown. Transfer from pans onto wire racks and serve warm.

177) Whole Wheat Dinner Rolls

Ingredients:

- 3/4 cup whole milk
- 3/4 cup water
- 1/4 cup (1/2 stick) unsalted butter, room temperature
- 3 cups (or more) white whole wheat flour* or regular whole wheat flour
- 3/4 cup instant mashed potato flakes
- 1/4 cup nonfat dry milk powder
- 3 tablespoons sugar
- 2 1/4 teaspoons quick-rising active dry yeast (from two 1/4-ounce envelopes)
- 1 1/4 teaspoons salt
- 1 large egg yolk
- 1 large egg white, whisked with 1 tablespoon water (for glaze)
- 3 to 4 tablespoons quick-cooking oats

Direction: Serving: Makes 16 | Prep: | Cook: |

- ✓ Simmer 3/4 cup water and 3/4 cup whole milk in a small saucepan; take off heat.
- ✓ Add butter; mix till melted. To inside of pan, attach instant-read thermometer; cool milk till thermometer reads 120- 130°F.
- ✓ Meanwhile, whisk salt, yeast, sugar, dry milk powder, potato flakes and 3 cups flour to blend in a

big bowl.

- ✓ Add warm milk mixture; mix to blend. Stir in egg yolk.
- ✓ Knead it till dough comes together and is sticky in bowl.
- ✓ Turn onto floured work surface; knead, adding extra flour as needed by tablespoonful's, for 8 minutes till elastic, smooth and not sticky.
- ✓ In buttered bowl, put dough; turn to coat.
- ✓ Use plastic wrap to cover bowl then kitchen towel; rise for 1-1 1/2 hours till doubled in volume in a draft-free, warm place. Butter a small baking sheet/13x9x2-in. metal baking pan.
- ✓ Turn dough onto floured work surface; halve. Lightly knead each piece till smooth. Cut every dough half to 8 even pieces.
- ✓ Roll every piece till nearly smooth ball.
- ✓ In 4 crosswise and 4 lengthwise rows, put dough rounds in prepped pan, 3/4-1-in. apart.
- ✓ They won't fill the pan. Use a kitchen towel to cover shaped rolls; rise in draft-free warm area for 1 hour 15 minutes till rolls expand to touch each other and nearly double in volume.
- ✓ Put rack in middle of oven; preheat to 350°F.
- ✓ Brush egg- white glaze on rolls gently; generously sprinkle oats.
- ✓ Bake dinner rolls for 28 minutes till light golden brown; cool rolls for 5 minutes in pan.
- ✓ Pull rolls apart; cool for 15 minutes on rack.
- ✓ You can make it 8 hours ahead. Fully cool rolls; wrap in foil.
- ✓ Stand in room temperature.
- ✓ Rewarm the foil-wrapped rolls for 10 minutes in 350°F oven, if you want, or serve them at room temperature.
- ✓ You can make them ahead and keep frozen for 2 weeks. In foil, wrap; put into re-sealable plastic bag

178) **Zucchini Dinner Rolls**

Ingredients:

- 1 cup shredded peeled zucchini
- 1 teaspoon salt, divided
- 3-1/2 cups all-purpose flour, divided
- 1 package (1/4 ounce) quick-rise yeast
- 5 tablespoons grated Parmesan cheese, divided
- 1 teaspoon sugar
- 1 cup warm water (120° to 130°)
- 1/4 cup butter, softened

Direction: Serving: 2 dozen. | Prep: 25mins | Cook: 20mins |

- ✓ In a small bowl, add zucchini, then sprinkle 1/2 teaspoon salt on top. Allow to stand for 5 minutes, then drain.
- ✓ In the meantime, mix together leftover salt, sugar, 2 tbsp. cheese, yeast and 3 cups flour in a separate bowl.
- ✓ Add zucchini, then toss to blend.
- ✓ Mix together butter and water, then add to the dry

ingredients.

- ✓ Incorporate the remaining flour until a soft dough forms.
- ✓ Turn out onto a floured surface and knead for approximately 6 to 8 minutes, or until malleable and smooth.
- ✓ Place in a cooking spray-coated bowl, flipping once to oil the top.
- ✓ Cover and allow to double in size for approximately an hour in a warm area.
- ✓ Divide the dough in half and shape each half into 12 balls.
- ✓ Place in a greased 13x9-inch baking sheet and sprinkle with remaining cheese.
- ✓ Restart the procedure. Cover and allow to double in around 45 minutes in a warm environment.
- ✓ Bake at 375 degrees for 20 to 25 minutes, or until golden brown.
- ✓ Take out of the pan, then transfer to a wire rack.

179) **Almond Chocolate Crescents**

Ingredients:

- 1/4 cup almond paste
- 3/4 cup semisweet chocolate chips
- 1 tablespoon shortening
- 1 tube (8 ounces) refrigerated crescent rolls

Direction: Serving: 8 rolls. | Prep: 15mins | Cook: 15mins |

- ✓ Split the almond paste into 8 pieces; form each piece into a small log. Reserve. Melt shortening and chocolate chips in a microwave; mix until becomes smooth. Unfold crescent dough; divide into triangles. Scatter each with 1 tablespoon chocolate mixture; reserve the left mixture for sprinkling.,
- ✓ Put one-piece almond paste at a broad end of each triangle.
- ✓ Then roll up and put point side down 2 inches apart on a baking sheet which is ungreased; to form a crescent curve ends.
- ✓ Place inside the preheated oven for 11-13 minutes or until golden brown in color.
- ✓ Then put on a wire rack to fully cool.
- ✓ Sprinkle with left chocolate mixture.

180) **Apricot Cheese Crescents**

Ingredients:

- 2 cups all-purpose flour
- 1/2 teaspoon salt
- 1 cup cold butter
- 1 cup (8 ounces) 4% cottage cheese

FILLING:

- 1 package (6 ounces) dried apricots
- 1/2 cup water
- 1/2 cup sugar

TOPPING:

- 3/4 cup finely chopped almonds

- 1/2 cup sugar
- 1 egg white, lightly beaten
  Direction: Serving: 4-1/2 dozen. | Prep: 60mins | Cook: 15mins |

✓ Mix salt and flour in a big bowl; mash in butter till crumbly.

✓ Put in cottage cheese; combine thoroughly.

✓ Form into an-inch rounds.

✓ Place cover and chill for a few hours to overnight.

✓ For filling, in saucepan, mix water and apricots.

✓ Put on cover and let simmer for twenty minutes.

✓ Allow to cool for ten minutes. Put into blender; place cover and on high speed, blend till smooth.

✓ Turn onto bowl; mix in sugar.

✓ Place cover and refrigerate.

✓ For the topping, mix sugar and almonds; reserve.

✓ Roll rounds on floured area into 2-1/2-inch circles.

✓ Scoop approximately a teaspoon of filling to each.

✓ Fold the dough on top of filling and press edges to enclose.

✓ Put on oiled baking sheets. Brush egg white on tops; scatter with mixture of almond. Bake for 12 to 15 minutes at 375° or till browned lightly.

181)   Basil Garlic Crescents

Ingredients:

- 1/2 cup 4% cottage cheese
- 1/2 cup butter, softened
- 3 ounces' cream cheese, softened
- 1-1/2 cups all-purpose flour
- 2 tablespoons olive oil
  1 cup grated Parmesan cheese
- 2 tablespoons minced fresh basil or 2 teaspoons dried basil
- 1 teaspoon garlic powder
  Direction: Serving: 2 dozen. | Prep: 30mins | Cook: 20mins |

✓ Add cream cheese, butter and cottage cheese to a food processor, tighten the lid and blend until smooth.

✓ Add flour, cover and blend until the mixture can be shaped into a ball.

✓ Cut the dough into 2 parts.

✓ Take them to a floured surface, roll each out into a 10-inch round.

✓ Brush oil over.

✓ Dredge garlic powder, basil and Parmesan cheese on top.

✓ Divide each round into 12 wedges.

✓ Roll wedges from wide end and lay them, pointed side down, 2 inches away from one another on lubricated baking sheets.

✓ Bend the ends of each to shape a crescent.

✓ Set oven at 350° and bake until they turn golden brown, or for 20 to 25 minutes.

✓ Take them to wire racks.

✓ Serve while still warm.

182)   Buttery Crescents

Ingredients:

- 2 packages (1/4 ounce each) active dry yeast
- 2 cups warm whole milk (110° to 115°)
- 2 large eggs, lightly beaten
- 1/4 cup butter, melted and cooled
- 3 tablespoons sugar
- 1 teaspoon salt
- 6-1/2 to 7 cups all-purpose flour
- Additional melted butter, optional
  Direction: Serving: 3 dozen. | Prep: 25mins | Cook: 15mins |

✓ Melt yeast in milk in a big bowl.

✓ Add 4 cups flour, sugar, salt, butter and eggs; beat till smooth.

✓ To make a soft dough, add enough leftover flour.

✓ Turn it out onto a floured surface and knead for 6-8 minutes, or until the dough is elastic and smooth.

✓ Place it in an oiled bowl and turn once to grease the top.

✓ Cover; allow to double in size for 1 hour in a warm environment.

✓ Punch down dough; divide to thirds.

✓ Roll every portion to a 12-in. circle then cut every circle to 12 wedges.

✓ Roll wedges from the broad end; place on buttered baking pans, pointed end down.

✓ Cover; rise for 30 minutes' till doubled.

✓ Bake it at 400° till golden brown for 12-14 minutes.

✓ If desired, brush with butter.

183)   Cheese Crescents

Ingredients:

- 4-1/4 cups all-purpose flour
- 1 cu (4 ounces) finely shredded cheddar cheese
- 2 tablespoons plus 1-1/2 teaspoons sugar
- 1 package (1/4 ounce) active dry yeast
- 1-1/2 teaspoons salt
- 1-1/2 teaspoons Italian seasoning
- 1-1/2 cups 2% milk
- 2 tablespoons butter
- 1 egg yolk
- 1 tablespoon water
  Direction: Serving: 3 dozen. | Prep: 30mins | Cook: 20mins |

✓ Mix Italian seasoning, salt, yeast, sugar, cheese and 3 cups flour in a big bowl.

✓ Heat butter and milk for 120-130° in a small saucepan.

✓ Add to the dry ingredients; beat till smooth.

✓ Add enough remaining flour to form a stiff dough.

✓ Turn it out onto the floured surface and knead for 6-8 minutes, or until smooth and elastic.

✓ Place it in an oiled bowl; turn once to grease the surface.

- ✓ Cover and allow to double in size for 1 hour in a warm environment.
- ✓ Punch down dough.
- ✓ Turn it onto the lightly floured surface; divide to thirds.
- ✓ Roll every portion to 12-in. circle then cut every circle to 12 wedges.
- ✓ From the wide end, roll up wedges; put, point side down, on greased baking sheets, 2-in. apart.
- ✓ To make a crescent shape, curve ends; cover. Rise for about 45 minutes.
- ✓ Beat water and egg yolk; brush on crescents.
- ✓ Bake it at 375° till golden brown for 16-18 minutes.
- ✓ Transfer from pans onto wire racks.

184) Cherry Crescents
Ingredients:

- 2 cups all-purpose flour
- 1/2 teaspoon salt
- 1 cup cold butter, cubed
- 1 egg yolk, lightly beaten
- 1 cup (8 ounces) sour cream
- 1 can (21 ounces) cherry pie filling
- 1/2 teaspoon almond extract
- Confectioners' sugar

Direction: Serving: 4 dozen. | Prep: 20mins | Cook: 20mins |

- ✓ Mix flour and salt in a large bowl.
- ✓ Whisk in butter until mixture achieves a coarse crumbs texture.
- ✓ Add egg yolk and sour cream, and mix well.
- ✓ Place in the refrigerator for hours or overnight.
- ✓ Roughly slice cherries in the pie filling and transfer to a small dish.
- ✓ Add extract then leave aside for later use.
- ✓ Cut doughs into 4 parts.
- ✓ Roll each dough part into a 12-inch circle on a slightly floured work surface.
- ✓ Make 12 wedges from the circle. Scoop in a teaspoon filling at the wide end.
- ✓ Roll up starting from the wide end and arrange an inch apart, point side down, on ungreased baking sheets.
- ✓ Form a crescent shape by curving the ends.
- ✓ Bake at 375°F for about 20-24 minutes or until color is golden brown.
- ✓ Remove pastries from pan right away and transfer to a cooling rack to cool.
- ✓ Sprinkle with confectioner's sugar.

185) Chocolate Cinnamon Crescents
Ingredients:

Cinnamon Sugar:
- 2 cups white sugar
- 8 teaspoons ground cinnamon

Dough:

- 1 cup white sugar
- 1-pound margarine
- 2 eggs
- 1 cup milk
- 5 cups all-purpose flour
- 2 teaspoons baking powder

Glaze:
- 2 cups white sugar
- 1 teaspoon vanilla extract
- 2 cups water
- 3 tablespoons cornstarch
- 1 (16 ounce) package semisweet chocolate chips, melted

Direction: Serving: 80 | Prep: 45mins | Cook: 20mins |

- ✓ Preheat an oven to 190°C/375°F and grease 2 baking sheets.
- ✓ Whisk cinnamon and 2 cups sugar; put aside. To make a dough, beat baking powder, flour, milk, eggs, margarine and 1 cup sugar in a big bowl; divide dough to 10 balls.
- ✓ Onto work surface, spread sugar mixture and prepped cinnamon.
- ✓ Roll each dough ball using rolling pin on cinnamon sugar, making each to 14-in. circle.
- ✓ Cut every circle to 8 wedges. Starting at wide side, rolling towards tip, roll every wedge to crescent.
- ✓ Put rolls onto prepped baking sheets. In preheated oven, bake crescents for 20 minutes till lightly browned and set.
- ✓ As crescents bake, boil cornstarch, 2 cups water, vanilla and 2 cups sugar in a saucepan; cook till thick.
- ✓ On baked crescent rolls, brush glaze; set glaze for 5 minutes.
- ✓ On glazed crescents, drizzle melted chocolate.
- ✓ Serve warm, if desired.

186) Cinnamon Walnut Crescents
Ingredients:

- 3 large egg yolks
- 1 cup sour cream
- 1 package (1/4 ounce) active dry yeast
- 3 cups all-purpose flour
- 1/2 teaspoon salt
- 1 cup cold butter
- 1 cup finely chopped walnuts
- 1 cup sugar
- 2 teaspoons ground cinnamon
- Confectioners' sugar icing, optional

Direction: Serving: about 5 dozen. | Prep: 35mins | Cook: 20mins |

- ✓ Beat yolks in a small bowl; mix in yeast and sour cream.
- ✓ Stand for about 10 minutes.
- ✓ Mix salt and flour in a big bowl; cut in butter till it looks like coarse crumbs.

- ✓ Add the sour cream mixture; mix well.
- ✓ Form to a ball; use plastic wrap to cover.
- ✓ Refrigerate it for 8 hours up to overnight.
- ✓ Mix cinnamon, sugar and walnuts; sprinkle 1/4 of the mixture onto a flat surface.
- ✓ Divide the dough to 4 portions; put aside 3.
- ✓ Roll 1 portion to 8-in. circle on walnut-sprinkled surface; flip the dough.
- ✓ Press the walnut mixture in both sides. Cut to 16 wedges.
- ✓ Starting with a wide end, roll up every wedge to a crescent shape.
- ✓ Put it, point down, onto greased baking sheets, 1-in. apart.
- ✓ Repeat thrice more with leftover dough and walnut mixture.
- ✓ Bake it at 350° till golden brown for 20-25 minutes; cool on wire racks. If desired, drizzle with icing.

187) Golden Crescents

Ingredients:

- 2 packages (1/4 ounce each) active dry yeast
- 3/4 cup warm water (110° to 115°)
- 1/2 cup sugar
- 2 large eggs
- 1/4 cup butter, softened
- 2 tablespoons shortening
- 1 teaspoon salt
- 4 to 4-1/2 cups all-purpose flour
- 2 tablespoons melted butter plus additional as needed, divided

Direction: Serving: 2 dozen. | Prep: 25mins | Cook: 10mins |

- ✓ In a large basin, dissolve yeast in warm water.
- ✓ Combine 2 cups flour, salt, shortening, softened butter, sugar, and egg in a large mixing bowl and whisk until smooth.
- ✓ Add enough remaining flour to form a soft dough.
- ✓ Turn it out onto the floured surface and knead for 6-8 minutes, or until smooth and elastic.
- ✓ Place it in an oiled bowl; turn once to grease the surface.
- ✓ Cover with plastic wrap and let rise in a warm area for 1 1/2 hours until doubled.
- ✓ Dough should be punched down and halved.
- ✓ Each part should be rolled into a 12-inch circle and brushed with 1 tablespoon melted butter; cut into 12 wedges.
- ✓ Roll up wedges starting at the broad end; place, point side down, on oiled baking pans 2 inches apart.
- ✓ Curve ends to form crescents; cover.
- ✓ Continue rising for 45 minutes, or until doubled.
- ✓ For 8-10 minutes, bake at 375° until brown.
- ✓ Brush with additional melted butter if desired.

188) Lemon Nut Crescents

Ingredients:

- 1 tube (8 ounces) refrigerated crescent rolls
- 3 tablespoons butter, softened, divided
- 1/3 cup chopped nuts
- 1 tablespoon grated lemon zest
- 1/4 cup sugar
- 1/4 cup sour cream
- 1 tablespoon thawed lemonade concentrate

Direction: Serving: 8 rolls. | Prep: 10mins | Cook: 10mins |

- ✓ Unroll the crescent roll dough; separate to 8 triangles. Spread it with 1 tbsp. butter.
- ✓ Mix lemon zest and nuts; sprinkle on dough.
- ✓ Roll to crescents; put onto ungreased baking sheet.
- ✓ Bake it at 375° till golden brown for 10-12 minutes.
- ✓ Meanwhile, mix leftover butter, lemonade concentrate, sour cream and sugar in a saucepan; boil, occasionally mixing.
- ✓ Brush on warm rolls.

189) Onion Crescents

Ingredients:

- 1 package (1/4 ounce) active dry yeast
- 1 cup warm milk (110° to 115°)
- 1/2 cup butter, softened
- 1/2 cup sugar
- 2 large eggs
- 1/2 cup dried minced onion
- 1/2 teaspoon salt
- 3-1/2 to 4-1/2 cups all-purpose flour
- 2 tablespoons butter, melted

Direction: Serving: 2 dozen. | Prep: 30mins | Cook: 10mins |

- ✓ In a small basin, dissolve yeast in hot milk.
- ✓ In a large mixing basin, combine the sugar and butter.
- ✓ Add eggs and whisk until mixed.
- ✓ Add 2 cups flour, yeast mixture, salt, and onion.
- ✓ Add enough leftover flour to form a soft dough by whisking.
- ✓ Turn dough out onto a floured surface and knead for approximately 6-8 minutes, or until smooth and elastic.
- ✓ Transfer to an oiled bowl, flipping once to coat the top with grease.
- ✓ Cover with plastic wrap and leave to rise for approximately an hour until doubled in a warm environment.
- ✓ The dough should be pounded.
- ✓ Divide into two parts and turn out onto a lightly floured surface.
- ✓ Each circular should be rolled out to a 12-inch diameter and cut into 12 wedges.
- ✓ Begin by rolling each wedge from the wide end.

- ✓ Arrange the dough, point side down, 2 inches apart on greased baking pans.
- ✓ Conceal crescents with a curve.
- ✓ Cover the dough with a kitchen towel and leave to rise for approximately 30 minutes until doubled in a warm location.
- ✓ To begin, preheat the oven to 400°.
- ✓ Cook for 8-12 minutes, or until golden brown.
- ✓ Brush pans with melted butter and then move to wire racks to cool.

190) **Orange Crescents**

Ingredients:

- 1 package (1/4 ounce) active dry yeast
- 1/4 cup warm water (110° to 115°)
- 3/4 cup sugar, divided
- 1 teaspoon salt
- 2 large eggs
- 1/2 cup sour cream
- 1/2 cup butter, melted, divided
- 3-1/4 to 3-3/4 cups all- purpose flour
- 2 tablespoons grated orange zest

GLAZE:

- 3/4 cup sugar
- 1/4 cup butter
- 2 tablespoons orange juice
- 1/2 cup sour cream

Direction: Serving: 2 dozen. | Prep: 30mins | Cook: 20mins |

- ✓ In a large basin, dissolve yeast in water.
- ✓ Combine 2 cups flour, 6 tablespoons butter, sour cream, eggs, salt, and 1/4 cup sugar in a mixing bowl and whisk until smooth.
- ✓ Add sufficient remaining flour to form a soft dough.
- ✓ Turn onto a floured area and knead for approximately 6-8 minutes, or until smooth and elastic.
- ✓ Place in a greased bowl, swirling once to coat the top with melted butter.
- ✓ Cover and let to double in a warm spot for approximately 1-1/2 hours. Punch the dough down.
- ✓ Turn out onto a lightly floured surface and cut in half.
- ✓ Each part should be rolled into a 12-inch circle and brushed with the remaining butter.
- ✓ Combine the remaining sugar and orange zest; sprinkle over butter.
- ✓ Each circular should be cut into 12 wedges.
- ✓ Roll the wedges from the broad end; place on prepared baking pans 2 inches apart, pointed side down.
- ✓ Curve the ends downward to create a crescent shape; cover.
- ✓ In a warm environment, rise for 45 minutes until doubled.
- ✓ Bake at 350° for 20-30 minutes, or until golden brown.

- ✓ Transfer the baked goods from the pans to the wire racks.
- ✓ In a small saucepan, bring the glaze ingredients to a boil; stir and cook for 3 minutes.
- ✓ Place warm rolls on a cooling rack. Refrigerate

191) **Quick Easy Pumpkin Crescents**

Ingredients:

- 1-3/4 cups all-purpose flour
- 2 teaspoons baking powder
- 1/4 teaspoon baking soda
- 1/4 teaspoon ground nutmeg
- 1/8 teaspoon salt
- 1/8 teaspoon ground ginger
- 1-1/2 teaspoons ground cinnamon, divided
- 3/4 cup canned pumpkin
- 3 tablespoons canola oil
- 2 tablespoons brown sugar
- 2 tablespoons sugar
- 4 tablespoons butter, melted, divided

Direction: Serving: 16 rolls. | Prep: 15mins | Cook: 10mins |

- ✓ Preheat an oven to 400°.
- ✓ Whisk first 6 ingredients in big bowl; mix 1/2 tsp. cinnamon in.
- ✓ Whisk brown sugar, oil and pumpkin in another bowl; mix into flour mixture till just moist.
- ✓ Mix leftover cinnamon and sugar in small bowl; keep 2 tsp. cinnamon-sugar for topping.
- ✓ Turn out dough on lightly floured surface; gently knead 10 times.
- ✓ Halve; roll every portion to 10-in. circle.
- ✓ Brush 1 tbsp. melted butter on each circle; sprinkle 2 tsp. cinnamon-sugar over.
- ✓ Cut each to 8 wedges. From wide ends, roll up wedges; put, point side down, on greased baking sheet, 1-in. apart.
  Curve to make crescents; brush leftover butter on tops then sprinkle leftover cinnamon-sugar over.
- ✓ Bake till golden brown, about 9-11 minutes; transfer from pan onto wire rack then serve warm.

192) **Sausage Crescent Rolls**

Ingredients:

- 1 pound fresh, ground spicy pork sausage
- 1 (8 ounce) package cream cheese
- 2 (8 ounce) packages refrigerated crescent rolls
- 1 egg white, lightly beaten
- 1 tablespoon poppy seeds

Direction: Serving: 20 | Prep: 25mins | Cook: 20mins |

- ✓ Preheat the oven to 350°F (175°C).
- ✓ Put the sausage in a medium- sized skillet and let it cook until it turns light brown in color; drain off any excess oil.
- ✓ Mix in the cream cheese while the temperature of the

cooked sausage is still hot; mix until the cheese has fully melted and the consistency of the mixture is creamy.

✓ Allow it to fully cool down.

✓ Separate the crescent rolls from each other and form it into 2 rectangles.

✓ Stuff the prepared sausage mixture in the shape of a lengthwise log in the middle of each of the rectangles.

✓ Fold the long sides of the rectangular crescent rolls over the sausage mixture filling.

✓ Put it onto an ungreased cookie sheet with the seam side facing down.

✓ Use a brush to coat it with egg white then top it off with poppy seeds.

✓ Put it in the preheated oven and let it bake for 20 minutes until the crust turns golden in color.

✓ Cut it into 1 1/2-inch slices once it has fully cooled down.

193) **_Sour Cream Crescents_**

Ingredients:

- 2 teaspoons active dry yeast
- 1/3 cup warm water (110° to 115°)
- 1/2 cup sugar
- 1/2 teaspoon salt
- 1 cup butter, softened
- 1 cup (8 ounces)
- sour cream
- 2 egg
- s 4 cups all-purpose flour

Direction: Serving: 4 dozen. | Prep: 15mins | Cook: 15mins |

✓ Place yeast inside warm water in a large bowl until dissolved.

✓ Put in eggs, sour cream, butter, salt and sugar.

✓ Beat until smoothened. Add in 3 cups of flour and combine thoroughly.

✓ Whisk in the rest of the flour.

✓ Refrigerate, covered, for 6 hours to overnight. Punch down the dough.

✓ Transfer to a surface dusted with flour.

✓ Form each into a 10" circle; split circle into 12 wedges.

✓ Roll up the wedges, starting from wide end, and bring onto greased baking sheets, point side down, in a 3"-distance away from each other.

✓ Curve the ends to make a crescent.

✓ Allow to rise, covered, for about 90 minutes in a warm area until doubled in size.

✓ Bake for 15 minutes at 375 ° until golden brown.

✓ Take out of the pans, then move to wire racks.

194) **_Spinach Cheddar Crescent Bites_**

Ingredients:

- 1 cup chopped fresh spinach
- 1/2 cup shredded sharp cheddar cheese
- 1/3 cup spreadable spinach and artichoke cream cheese
- 1/4 cup dried cranberries
- 1/4 cup chopped pecans
- 1/4 teaspoon pepper
- 1/8 teaspoon salt
- 1 tube (8 ounces) refrigerated seamless crescent dough sheet
- 1 egg, lightly beaten
- Coarse sea salt

Direction: Serving: 16 appetizers. | Prep: 15mins | Cook: 10mins |

✓ Preheat an oven to 375°.

✓ Mix the initial 7 ingredients in a small bowl.

✓ Unroll the crescent dough to 1 long rectangle and cut to 16 rectangles.

✓ In middle of each rectangle, put 2 tsp. spinach mixture.

✓ Bring the dough edges over filling, pinching the seams to seal; form to a ball.

✓ Put, seam side down, onto greased baking sheets.

✓ Brush using egg; sprinkle coarse salt.

✓ Bake till golden brown for 10-12 minutes; serve warm.

✓ Keep leftovers refrigerated.

195) **_Swiss Onion Crescents_**

Ingredients:

- 1 tube (8 ounces) refrigerated crescent rolls
- 3 tablespoons shredded Swiss cheese, divided
- 2 tablespoons chopped green onion
- 1-1/2 teaspoons Dijon mustard

Direction: Serving: 8 rolls. | Prep: 15mins | Cook: 15mins |

✓ Unroll the crescent dough; separate to 8 triangles.

✓ Mix mustard, green onion and 2 tbsp. cheese; sprinkle 1 tsp. on each triangle.

✓ From the short side, roll put; put onto ungreased baking sheet, point side down.

✓ Curve it to a crescent shape then sprinkle leftover cheese.

✓ Bake it at 375° till golden brown for 11-13 minutes.

196) **_40 Minute Hamburger Buns_**

Ingredients:

- 2 tablespoons active dry yeast
- 1 cup plus 2 tablespoons warm water (110° to 115°)
- 1/3 cup vegetable oil
- 1/4 cup sugar
- 1 large egg
- 1 teaspoon salt
- 3 to 3-1/2 cups all-purpose flour

Direction: Serving: 1 dozen. | Prep: 20mins | Cook: 10mins |

✓ Melt yeast in warm water in a big bowl.

- ✓ Add sugar and oil; stand for about 5 minutes.
- ✓ Add enough flour to make a soft dough, salt and egg.
- ✓ Turn it onto the floured surface; knead for 3-5 minutes till elastic and smooth.
- ✓ Don't rise.
- ✓ Divide to 12 pieces; form each to a ball.
- ✓ Put it onto greased baking sheets, 3-in. apart.
- ✓ Cover; rest for about 10 minutes.
- ✓ Bake it at 425° till golden brown for 8-12 minutes.
- ✓ Transfer from pans onto wire racks; cool.

197) **Almond Filled Breakfast Rolls**

Ingredients:

- /2 cups all-purpose flour
- 1/4 cup plus 1 tablespoon sugar, divided
- 3/4 teaspoon salt
- 1/2 cup cold butter
- 1 package (1/4 ounce) active dry yeast
- 1/4 cup warm milk (110° to 115°)
- 1 cup warm heavy whipping cream (110° to 115°)
- 3 egg yolks, beaten

ALMOND FILLING:

- 3/4 cup almond cake and pastry filling
- 1/4 cup butter, softened

EGG WASH:

- 1 egg, beaten
- 1/2 cup slivered almonds

Direction: Serving: 28 rolls. | Prep: 35mins | Cook: 15mins |

- ✓ In a large bowl, blend salt, 1/4 cup of sugar, and flour.
- ✓ Cut in butter until crumbly.
- ✓ Dissolve yeast in warm milk in a small bowl.
- ✓ Put in the remaining sugar; allow to stand 5 minutes.
- ✓ Put in egg yolks and cream; combine well.
- ✓ Blend into dry ingredients; combine well.
- ✓ Do not knead.
- ✓ Cover and put in the refrigerator overnight.
- ✓ To make the filling, in a small bowl, whisk butter and almond paste until smooth.
- ✓ Punch the dough down; flour a surface and put the dough on.
- ✓ Separate into 2 portions.
- ✓ Shape each portion into a 12-inch square.
- ✓ Spread the filling to within 1/2-inch of edges.
- ✓ Roll up jellyroll style; pinch seams to secure.
- ✓ Slice each into 14 rolls.
- ✓ Arrange rolls, cut-side up, on oiled baking sheets.
- ✓ In a warm area, let rise, covered, for 45 minutes (dough won't double).
- ✓ Brush with egg; dust with almonds.
- ✓ Bake at 375° until golden, about 15 to 20 minutes.
- ✓ Take out of pans and place on wire racks to cool.

198) **Aniseed Yeast Rolls**

Ingredients:

- 5-1/4 to 5-3/4 cups all-purpose flour
- 3/4 cup packed brown sugar
- 1- 1/2 teaspoons salt
- 2 packages (1/4 ounce each) active dry yeast
- 4 teaspoons aniseed, divided
- 3/4 cup water
- 1/2 cup butter, cubed
- 6 eggs

Direction: Serving: 22 rolls. | Prep: 30mins | Cook: 20mins |

- ✓ Mix 3 tsp. aniseed, yeast, salt, brown sugar and 2 cups flour in a big bowl.
- ✓ Heat butter and water to 120-130° in a saucepan.
- ✓ Add to the dry ingredients; beat till just moist. Add 5 eggs; beat till smooth.
- ✓ Add enough remaining flour to form a soft dough.
- ✓ Turn it out onto the floured surface and knead for 6-8 minutes, or until smooth and elastic.
- ✓ Place it in the prepared bowl; turn once to grease the top.
- ✓ Cover; rise for 1 hour till nearly doubled in a warm place.
- ✓ Punch dough down.
- ✓ Turn onto the lightly floured surface then divide to 22 pieces.
- ✓ Form each to a ball; put on greased baking sheets, 2-in. apart.
- ✓ Cover and allow to rise for 30 minutes, or until nearly doubled.
- ✓ Brush remaining egg on dough.
- ✓ Sprinkle with remaining aniseed.
- ✓ Bake at 350°F for 20-22 minutes, or until golden brown.
- ✓ Transfer pans to wire racks to cool completely.

199) **Apple Cinnamon Rolls**

Ingredients:

- 4-1/2 to 5 cups all-purpose flour
- 1/3 cup sugar
- 1 package (1/4 ounce) active dry yeast
- 1/2 teaspoon salt
- 1 cup milk
- 1/3 cup butter, cubed
- 3 eggs

FILLING:

- 3/4 cup packed brown sugar
- 1/4 cup all- purpose flour
- 1 tablespoon ground cinnamon
- 1/2 cup cold butter
- 1 cup grated peeled apple
- 1/2 cup chopped pecans

GLAZE:

- 1 cup confectioners' sugar
- 2 tablespoons milk

Direction: Serving: 9 rolls. | Prep: 30mins | Cook: 30mins |

✓ Mix salt, yeast, sugar and 2 1/2 cups flour in a big bowl.

✓ Heat butter and milk to 120-130°F in saucepan.

✓ Mix with dry ingredients and whisk until barely moistened. Beat in eggs until smooth.

✓ Combine enough remaining flour to form a soft dough.

✓ Turn out onto a floured surface and knead for 6-8 minutes, or until the dough is elastic and smooth.

✓ Place in an oiled bowl, turn once to coat the top with grease, and cover.

✓ In a warm location, rise for 1 hour until doubled in size.

✓ In a bowl, combine cinnamon, flour, and brown sugar.

✓ Cut butter in till crumbly; put aside.

✓ Punch down dough. Turn on floured surface; rest for 10 minutes.
Roll to 12-in. square.

✓ Within 1/2-in. of edges, sprinkle crumble mixture.

✓ Top with pecans and apple. Roll up like a jellyroll.

✓ To seal, pinch seams.

✓ Slice to 9 slices. Put in 13x9-in. greased baking dish, cut side up. Cover.

✓ Refrigerate for 2-24 hours. Uncover.

✓ Let stand for 30 minutes at room temperature before baking.

✓ Bake for 30-35 minutes till golden brown at 350°F.

✓ Mix glaze ingredients; drizzle on rolls. Serve warm.

200) **Apple Sticky Buns**

Ingredients:

- 4 cups all-purpose flour
- 2 packages (1/4 ounce each) active dry yeast
- 1/4 cup sugar
- 1 teaspoon salt
- 3/4 cup milk
- 1/4 cup water
- 1/4 cup butter, cubed
- 1 egg
- 1-1/2 cups finely chopped peeled apples

TOPPING:

- 1 cup packed brown sugar
- 3/4 cup butter, cubed
- 3/4 cup chopped walnuts or pecans
- 1 tablespoon water
- 1 tablespoon corn syrup
- 1 teaspoon ground cinnamon

Direction: Serving: 12-16 | Prep: 35mins | Cook: 30mins |

✓ In a large mixing basin, combine the salt, sugar,

yeast, and 1 1/2 cups flour. In a saucepan, heat the butter, water, and milk to 120-130 °.

✓ Combine with the dry ingredients and beat until barely moistened.

✓ Beat in the egg until smooth.

✓ Combine apples and any remaining flour. Eliminate kneading.

✓ Cover and allow to rise in a warm environment for 30 minutes.

✓ Meanwhile, in a saucepan, combine the topping ingredients and bring to a boil, stirring constantly until incorporated.

✓ Fill a 13x9-inch dry baking dish halfway with batter.

✓ Reduce the volume of the dough by stirring.

✓ Scoop pieces of dough the size of walnuts on top of the nut mixture.

✓ Cover and let aside for 30 minutes to rise.

✓ Bake at 375 ° for 30 to 35 minutes, or until golden brown.

✓ Allow it stand for 1 minute before inverting onto a large serving plate.

201) **Apple Raisin Egg Rolls**

Ingredients:

- 4 medium tart apples, peeled and sliced
- 1/4 cup raisins
- 1/2 teaspoon ground cinnamon
- 2 tablespoons butter
- 1 tablespoon cornstarch
- 1 cup unsweetened apple juice
- 3 tablespoons honey
- 16 egg roll wrappers
- Oil for deep-fat frying Vanilla ice cream

Direction: Serving: 16 servings. | Prep: 15mins | Cook: 5mins |

✓ Sauté cinnamon, raisins and apples in butter till tender in a big skillet.

✓ Mix honey, juice and cornstarch till smooth; mix into apple mixture.

✓ Boil on medium heat; mix and cook till thick for 1-2 minutes.

✓ Take off heat; cool. In the middle of 1 egg roll wrapper, put 1/4 cup apple mixture.

✓ Fold bottom corner over the filling.

✓ Fold the sides toward the center over filling.

✓ Use water to moisten leftover corner; to seal, tightly roll up.

✓ Repeat with leftover wrappers and apple mixture. Stand for about 15 minutes.

✓ Heat 1-in. oil to 375° in an electric skillet.

✓ Several at a time, fry turnovers till golden brown for 1-2 minutes per side.

✓ Drain on paper towels then serve with ice cream.

202) Asparagus Ham Cheese Rolls

Ingredients:

- 3 to 4 cups all-purpose flour
- 2 tablespoons sugar
- 1 package (1/4 ounce) active dry yeast
- 1 teaspoon salt
- 1/2 cup milk
- 1/2 cup water
- 2 tablespoons vegetable oil
- 2 egg whites, divided
- 1 egg
- 1-pound fresh asparagus, trimmed and cut into 1/2-inch pieces
- 1 block (4 ounces) cheddar cheese, cubed
- 2 cups diced fully cooked lean ham

Direction: Serving: 2 dozen. | Prep: 20mins | Cook: 20mins |

- ✓ Mix salt, yeast, sugar and 2 1/2 cups flour in a big bowl.
- ✓ Heat oil, water and milk to 120°-130° in a saucepan.
- ✓ Add to the dry ingredients and beat till just moist.
- ✓ Add egg and 1 egg white; beat till smooth.
- ✓ Add enough remaining flour to form a soft dough.
- ✓ Turn out onto a floured board and knead for 6-8 minutes, or until smooth and elastic.
- ✓ Place in an oiled bowl and turn once to coat the top with grease.
- ✓ Cover and allow to double in size for 1 hour in a warm environment.
- ✓ Punch the dough down and turn it out onto a lightly floured board.
- ✓ Cover; stand for 15 minutes. Meanwhile, boil asparagus and 1/2-in. water in a saucepan.
- ✓ Lower the heat; cover. Simmer for 3-5 minutes and drain.
- ✓ Divide the dough into 24 pieces and roll each piece to a 5-in. circle.
- ✓ Put 1 tbsp. ham, cheese cube and few asparagus pieces in the middle of every circle.
- ✓ Around the filling, wrap the dough; to seal, pinch the seams.
- ✓ Put rolls on baking sheets coated in cooking spray, 2-in. apart, and seam side down.
- ✓ Cover; rise for 30 minutes' till doubled in a warm place.
- ✓ Beat leftover egg white; brush on rolls.
- ✓ Bake till golden brown for 18-20 minutes at 350°.
- ✓ Transfer to wire racks and refrigerate leftovers.

203) Bacon Buns

Ingredients:

- 10 bacon strips, diced
- 1/3 cup chopped onion
- 1 package (16 ounces) hot roll mix
- 1 egg, lightly beaten

- ✓ Cook onion and bacon in a skillet on medium heat till onion is tender and bacon is crisp; drain on the paper towels.
- ✓ Follow the package directions to prep roll mix.
- ✓ Turn dough onto floured surface; knead for 5 minutes till elastic and smooth.
- ✓ Place it in an oiled bowl and turn once to grease the top.
- ✓ Cover and let rise in a warm place for 40 minutes, or until doubled.
- ✓ Divide dough to 18 pieces. Roll each piece out to 5-in. circle on a floured surface.
- ✓ Put 1 tbsp. bacon filling over each.
- ✓ Fold the dough around the filling, shaping every piece to a small loaf; to seal, pinch edges.
- ✓ Place seam side down on prepared baking pans.
- ✓ Use plastic wrap coated in cooking spray to loosely cover; rise for 20-30 minutes in a warm place.
- ✓ Brush egg on buns; bake it at 350°till golden brown for 20-25 minutes.
- ✓ Transfer from pans onto wire racks then serve warm; keep leftovers refrigerated.

204) Bacon Cheese Pinwheel Rolls

Ingredients:

- 2 packages (1/4 ounce each) active dry yeast
- 2 teaspoons plus 1/2 cup sugar, divided
- 2 cups warm water (110° to 115°), divided
- 1 cup warm milk (110° to 115°)
- 2/3 cup butter, melted
- 2 large eggs, lightly beaten
- 2 teaspoons salt
- 8-3/4 to 9-1/4 cups all-purpose flour
- 1 pound sliced bacon, diced
- 1/2 cup finely chopped onion
- 4 cups shredded cheddar cheese

Direction: Serving: 4 dozen. | Prep: 30mins | Cook: 25mins |

- ✓ Melt 2 tsp. sugar and yeast in 1 cup of warm water in a big bowl.
- ✓ Allow to sit for 5 minutes.
- ✓ Mix the remaining sugar and water, 7 cups flour, salt, eggs, butter, and milk in a mixing bowl and whisk until smooth.
- ✓ To make a soft dough, add extra remaining flour.
- ✓ Knead for 6-8 minutes on a floured surface, or until elastic and smooth.
- ✓ Turn once to butter the top of the greased basin.
- ✓ In a warm environment, cover and rise for one hour until doubled.
- ✓ Meanwhile, cook bacon till crisp in a skillet on medium heat.
- ✓ Put on paper towels; drain. Keep 1 tbsp. drippings for later.
- ✓ Put aside bacon.

- ✓ Cook onion in drippings till tender then put aside.
- ✓ Punch down dough.
- ✓ Turn on lightly floured surface and divide to fourths; roll every portion to 15x10-in. rectangle.
- ✓ Sprinkle 1/4 cheese, 2 tbsp. onion and 1/3 cup bacon on each.
- ✓ Starting at long side, roll up like a jellyroll.
- ✓ Seal by pinching the seam. Cut each to 12 slices; put on ungreased baking sheets, 2-in. apart, cut side down.
- ✓ Rise with cover for 30 minutes' till doubled.
- ✓ Preheat oven to 350°F and bake for 25-30 minutes, or until golden brown.
- ✓ Refrigerate after transferring from pans to wire racks.

205) **Bacon Onion Oatmeal Buns**

Ingredients:

- 1/2-pound bacon strips, diced
- 2 large onions, finely chopped
- 1 cup water
- 1 cup milk
- 1 cup quick-cooking oats
- 1/4 cup molasses
- 3 tablespoons canola oil
- 2 teaspoons salt
  2 tablespoons active dry yeast
- 1/2 cup packed brown sugar, divided
- 1/3 cup warm water (110° to 115°)
- 1 egg
- 2 cups whole wheat flour
- 4 to 4-1/2 cups bread flour

Direction: Serving: 3 dozen. | Prep: 50mins | Cook: 15mins |

- ✓ Cook the bacon over medium heat, in a large skillet until it is crisp.
- ✓ Transfer to paper towels using a slotted spoon, drain.
- ✓ Sauté the onions in the drippings.
- ✓ Then drain and put aside. In the meantime, bring milk and water just to boil in a small saucepan.
- ✓ Pour the boiling liquid over oats in a large bowl.
- ✓ Add salt, oil and molasses.
- ✓ Allow to until the mixture cools to 110°-115°, stirring sometimes.
- ✓ Dissolve 1 tablespoon brown sugar and yeast in warm water in a large bowl.
- ✓ Add the leftover brown sugar, 3-1/2 cups bread flour, whole wheat flour, egg, oatmeal mixture, onions and bacon.
- ✓ Beat until the mixture is smooth.
- ✓ Add enough remaining flour to make a soft dough (the dough should be sticky).
- ✓ Transfer to a floured surface and then knead for about 6 to 8 minutes until elastic and smooth.
- ✓ Put into a greased bowl and flip once to grease the top.

- ✓ Cover the dough and allow to rise in a warm place for about 1 hour until doubled.
- ✓ Transfer the dough to a lightly floured surface after punching it down.
- ✓ Separate into 36 pieces.
- ✓ Form each piece into a ball and then put on greased baking sheets, 2 inches apart.
- ✓ Cover the balls and allow to rise for 30 minutes until doubled.
- ✓ Bake for 12-15 minutes at 375° or until turned golden brown. Cool for one minute, transfer from the pans to wire racks.

206) **Baker's Dozen Yeast Rolls**

Ingredients:

- 2 to 2-1/2 cups all-purpose flour
- 2 tablespoons sugar
- 1 package (1/4 ounce) quick-rise yeast
- 1/2 teaspoon salt
- 3/4 cup warm water (120° to 130°)
- 2 tablespoons plus 4 teaspoons butter, melted, divided
- 3/4 cup shredded sharp cheddar cheese
- 2 teaspoons honey
- 1/8 teaspoon garlic salt

Direction: Serving: 13 rolls. | Prep: 25mins | Cook: 15mins |

- ✓ Mix salt, yeast, sugar and 1-1/2 cups flour in a big bowl.
- ✓ Put in 2 tablespoons of butter and water; beat for 3 minutes on moderate speed or till smooth.
- ✓ Mix in the cheese and sufficient leftover flour to make a soft dough.
- ✓ Transfer to a slightly floured area; knead for 4 to 6 minutes, till pliable and smooth.
- ✓ Put on cover and allow to sit for 10 minutes.
- ✓ Split into 13 portions. From each into a round.
- ✓ Put into an oiled 9-inch round baking pan.
- ✓ Put on cover and allow to rise in a warm area for half an hour till doubled in size.
- ✓ Preheat the oven to 375°.
- ✓ Let rolls bake till slightly browned for 11 to 14 minutes.
- ✓ Mix the rest of butter, the garlic salt and honey; brush on top of rolls.
- ✓ Transfer from the pan onto the wire rack.

207) **Basil Cloverleaf Rolls**

Ingredients:

- 2 to 3 cups all-purpose flour, divided
- 1 cup whole wheat flour
- 1/2 cup sugar
- 1 package (1/4 ounce) active dry yeast
- 3 to 4 teaspoons dried basil
- 1 teaspoon celery salt
- 2 medium potatoes, peeled and cubed

- 1-1/2 cups water
- 1/4 cup butter, melted
- 2 eggs, beaten

GLAZE:

- 1 egg yolk
- 1 tablespoon water

Direction: Serving: 2 dozen. | Prep: 30mins | Cook: 20mins |

✓ Mix together celery salt, basil, yeast, sugar, whole wheat flour and 2 cups all-purpose flour in a bowl, then put aside.

✓ Bring water and potatoes into a saucepan and let it cook until tender.

✓ Drain and set aside 1 cup of the cooking liquid, then cool the liquid to 120-130 degrees.

✓ In the meantime, mash or rice the potatoes, then measure 1 cup (chill the leftover potato in the fridge for later use).

✓ Mix together the mashed potato, eggs, butter and potato liquid, then add to dry ingredients and beat smoothened.

✓ Add enough of the leftover flour until a soft dough forms.

✓ Turn out onto a floured surface and knead for 8-10 minutes, or until the dough is smooth and flexible.

✓ Put in a bowl coated with cooking spray, flipping once to grease the top.

✓ Put on a cover and let chill in the fridge overnight or for a maximum of 3 days, then punch down every day.

✓ To bake, punch down the dough.

✓ From the dough, pinch off small parts, then roll into 1-inch balls.

✓ Put 3 balls each in greased muffin cups.

✓ Allow it rise for 1 1/2 to 2 hours, or until it has doubled in size.

✓ Beat the water and egg yolk, then brush on top of the rolls.

✓ Bake for 20 minutes at 375 degrees or until golden brown.

✓ Take it out of the pans and cool on the wire racks

208) Beautiful Brown Rolls

Ingredients:

- 2 cups boiling water
- 1 cup quick-cooking oats
- 2 packages (1/4 ounce each) active dry yeast
- 1/4 cup warm water (110° to 115°)
- 2 eggs, beaten
- 1/2 cup molasses
- 1/2 cup vegetable oil
- 1/3 cup sugar
- 1/2 teaspoon salt
- 5-3/4 to 6-1/4 cups all-purpose flour
- Melted butter

Direction: Serving: 3 dozen. | Prep: 20mins | Cook: 20mins |

✓ Mix oats and boiling water in a big bowl; let cool to lukewarm, or 110° to 115°.

✓ In the meantime, in warm water, dissolve yeast; mix into mixture of oat.

✓ Put in salt, sugar, oil, molasses and eggs.

✓ To get a soft dough, add enough flour.

✓ Transfer to a floured surface and knead for 6 to 8 minutes, or until smooth and malleable.

✓ Place in a greased mixing bowl and flip once to coat the surface.

✓ Cover and leave to rise for an hour in a warm place until it has doubled in size.

✓ The dough should be deflated.

✓ Make 36 rolls by dividing the dough into 36 parts.

✓ Place on grease-coated baking sheets.

✓ Cover and allow to rise for 30 minutes or until doubled in size.

✓ Preheat oven to 375°F and bake for 20 to 25 minutes.

✓ Using butter, coat the entire surface.

✓ Allow to cool completely on wire racks.

209) Best Ever Cinnamon Rolls

Ingredients:

- 1 package (1/4 ounce) active dry yeast
- 1 cup warm fat-free milk (110° to 115°)
- 2 egg whites
- 1/3 cup sugar
- 3 tablespoons vegetable oil
- 1/2 teaspoon salt
- 2-1/2 to 2-3/4 cups all-purpose flour
- 1 cup whole wheat flour
- 1/4 cup butter, softened
- 1/3 cup packed brown sugar
- 1 teaspoon ground cinnamon

ICING:

- 1 cup confectioners' sugar
- 4 to 5 teaspoons orange juice

Direction: Serving: 1-1/2 dozen. | Prep: 35mins | Cook: 25mins |

✓ In a large mixing basin, dissolve yeast in warm milk.

✓ Combine the whole wheat flour, 1 cup all-purpose flour, salt, oil, sugar, and egg whites in a mixing bowl and whisk until smooth.

✓ To make a solid dough, add enough remaining all-purpose flour.

✓ Knead for 6-8 minutes on a lightly floured surface, or until elastic and smooth.

✓ Put in a bowl that has been sprayed with cooking spray and turn once to coat the top. Cover.

✓ In a warm environment, rise for 1 hour until doubled.

✓ Knead the dough. Turn out onto a lightly floured surface and cut in half.

✓ Each piece should be rolled into a 12x9-inch rectangle.

✓ Using butter, coat the pan.

- ✓ Combine the cinnamon and brown sugar in a bowl.
- ✓ Sprinkle dough within 1/2-inch of the edges. Roll up jellyroll manner, starting with the long side.
- ✓ Pinch the seams together to seal them.
- ✓ Each half should be cut into 9 slices.
- ✓ Place cut side down in two 9-inch round baking pans sprayed with cooking spray.
- ✓ Cover. Rise for 40 minutes, or until doubled in size.
- ✓ At 350°, bake for 25-30 minutes, or until golden brown.
- ✓ Cool on wire racks.
- ✓ To make the icing, combine confectioners' sugar with just enough juice to make a dripping consistency.
- ✓ Drizzle over the rolls.

210) *Big Batch Yeast Rolls*

Ingredients:

- 2 packages (1/4 ounce each) active dry yeast
- 1/2 cup warm water (110° to 115°)
- 2-1/2 cups warm 2% milk (110° to 115°)
- 1/2 cup butter, melted
- 1/2 cup mashed potato flakes
- 1 cup sugar
- 3 eggs
- 2-1/2 teaspoons salt
- 7 to 7-1/2 cups all-purpose flour
- 1 tablespoon cold water

  Direction: Serving: 3 dozen. | Prep: 50mins | Cook: 15mins |

- ✓ In a large mixing basin, dissolve yeast in warm water.
- ✓ In a separate bowl, combine the butter and milk, then add the potato flakes.
- ✓ 1 minute of standing in a mixing bowl, combine 3 cups flour, salt, 2 eggs, sugar, and milk mixture; beat until smooth.
- ✓ Make a soft dough with the remaining flour.
- ✓ Knead for 6-8 minutes on a floured surface, or until elastic and smooth.
- ✓ Place in an oiled bowl and turn once to grease the top.
- ✓ Cover and let rise in a warm place for 1 hour, or until doubled.
- ✓ Divide dough into 36 pieces after punching it down.
- ✓ Make each one into a ball. Place 2 inches apart on prepared baking pans. Cover and let rise for 30 minutes, or until doubled in size. Brush the rolls with a mixture of cold water and the remaining egg. Preheat oven to 350°F and bake for 12-15 minutes, or until golden brown.

211) *Bite Size Cinnamon Roll Cookies*

Ingredients:

- 1/2 cup packed brown sugar
- 4 teaspoons ground cinnamon
- 1-1/4 cups butter, softened

- 4 ounces' cream cheese, softened
- 1-1/2 cups sugar
- 2 large eggs
- 2 teaspoons vanilla extract
- 2 teaspoons grated orange zest
- 4-1/4 cups all-purpose flour
- 1 teaspoon baking powder
- 1 teaspoon active dry yeast
- 1/2 teaspoon salt

GLAZE:

- 1 cup confectioners' sugar
- 2 tablespoons 2% milk
- 1 teaspoon vanilla extract

  Direction: Serving: 6 dozen. | Prep: 60mins | Cook: 10mins |

- ✓ Mix cinnamon and brown sugar till blended in a small bowl.
- ✓ Cream sugar, cream cheese and butter till fluffy and light in a big bowl.
- ✓ Beat orange zest, vanilla and eggs in. Whisk salt, yeast, baking powder and flour in another bowl.
- ✓ Beat into creamed mixture slowly.
- ✓ Divide dough to 4 portions.
- ✓ Roll each to 8x6-in. rectangle on lightly floured surface.
- ✓ Sprinkle 2 tbsp. brown sugar mixture on.
- ✓ Tightly roll up, beginning with long side, like a jellyroll.
- ✓ Use plastic to wrap. Refrigerate till firm for 1 hour.
- ✓ Preheat an oven to 350°F. Crosswise, cut dough to 3/8-in. slices.
- ✓ Put on greased baking sheets, 1-in. apart.
- ✓ Bake till bottoms are light brown for 8-10 minutes.
- ✓ Transfer from pans onto wire racks; completely cool.
- ✓ Whisk glaze ingredients in a small bowl.
- ✓ Dip cookie tops in glaze. Let stand till set. Keep in airtight container.

212) *Blooming Sweet Rolls*

Ingredients:

- 10 frozen bread dough dinner rolls, thawed
- 3-1/2 teaspoons currant jelly, divided
- 1 teaspoon mint jelly, divided
- 1 cup confectioners' sugar
- 1 tablespoon milk
- 1-1/2 teaspoons butter, melted
- 1/8 teaspoon almond extract

  Direction: Serving: 10 servings. | Prep: 20mins | Cook: 15mins |

- ✓ Put on roll in middle of the greased baking sheet.
- ✓ Form 6 rolls to ovals; put around the middle roll, making a flower.
- ✓ Roll 1 of the leftover rolls to 5-in. rope for stem; place the rope to touch the flower.
- ✓ Form leftover rolls to leaves; put on each of the

stem's sides.

- ✓ Cover; rise for 30 minutes' till doubled in a warm place.
- ✓ Create an indentation in middle of every petal and the flower center using a wooden spoon end's handle; fill it with 1/4 tsp. currant jelly.
- ✓ In the middle of every leaf, make an indentation; fill it with 1/4 tsp. mint jelly.
- ✓ Bake it at 350° till golden brown for 15-20 minutes.
- ✓ Transfer from pan onto wire rack carefully.
- ✓ Use leftover jelly to fill indentations.
- ✓ Whisk extract, butter, milk and confectioners' sugar in a small bowl; drizzle on warm sweet rolls.

213)   **Bow Tie Wheat Rolls**

Ingredients:

- 3 tablespoons active dry yeast
- 5 cups warm water (110° to 115°)
- 2/3 cup honey
- 2/3 cup olive oil
- 1 tablespoon salt
- 9-1/2 to 10 cups whole wheat flour

Direction: Serving: 3 dozen. | Prep: 40mins | Cook: 15mins |

- ✓ In warm water, dissolve the yeast in big bowl.
- ✓ Put in 6 cups flour, salt, oil and honey.
- ✓ On a moderate speed, beat until smooth.
- ✓ Stir in enough residual flour to make a soft dough; the mixture will get sticky as a result.
- ✓ Knead for 6–8 minutes, until flexible and smooth, on a floured surface.
- ✓ Put in bowl greased with cooking spray, flipping one time to cover the surface.
- ✓ Cover and leave to rise for an hour in a warm place until it has doubled in size.
- ✓ Split dough into 4 parts.
- ✓ Roll 3 parts into rectangles, 12x5 inches in size.
- ✓ Slice each part, making a dozen rectangles, 2-1/2x2 inches in size.
- ✓ Roll the rest of the dough, making a rectangle, 18x5 inches in size.
- ✓ Slice into 36 half-inch-wide straps.
- ✓ To make bow ties, wrap around the middle of every rectangle with a strip.
- ✓ Put on baking sheets covered in cooking spray.
- ✓ Put on cover and allow to rise in a warm area for half an hour till doubled in size.
- ✓ Pinch middles to resemble bow ties.
- ✓ Bake till golden brown, or about 12 to 14 minutes at 350°.
- ✓ Transfer onto the wire racks

214)   **Bran Buns**

Ingredients:

- 1 cup All-Bran
- 2 cups water, divided

- 2 tablespoons active dry yeast
- 8 tablespoons sugar, divided
- 2 eggs
- 3/4 cup vegetable oil
- 2 teaspoons salt
- 5-1/2 to 6 cups all-purpose flour

Direction: Serving: 2 dozen. | Prep: 25mins | Cook: 15mins |

- ✓ In a bowl, put bran.
- ✓ Heat a cup of water to about 120°-130°; to soften, put on cereal.
- ✓ Put aside. In a bowl, put yeast.
- ✓ Heat leftover water to about 110°-115° then put on yeast to melt.
- ✓ Add 2 tbsp. sugar.
- ✓ Allow to stand for 5 minutes.
- ✓ Add leftover sugar, bran mixture, salt, oil and eggs; stir well.
- ✓ To get a soft dough, add enough flour.
- ✓ Turn on floured surface, kneading for 6-8 minutes till elastic and smooth.
- ✓ Put into greased bowl; turn once to grease the top.
- ✓ Rise with cover for 1 1/2 hours till doubled in a warm place.
- ✓ Punch down dough; turn on lightly floured surface then divide to 24 pieces.
- ✓ Form each to a ball.
- ✓ Put on greased baking sheets, 2-in. apart; cover.
- ✓ Rise for 30 minutes' till doubled. Bake till golden brown for 15-20 minutes at 350°.
- ✓ Transfer from pans onto wire racks; cool.

215)   **Bran Refrigerator Rolls**

Ingredients:

- 1-3/4 cups boiling water
- 1 cup all-bran cereal
- 2 packages (1/4 ounce each) active dry yeast
- 1/4 cup warm water
- 1/2 cup shortening
- 1/2 cup sugar
- 1-1/2 teaspoons salt
- 2 eggs
- 5-1/2 to 6 cups all-purpose flour

Direction: Serving: 3-1/2 dozen. | Prep: 25mins | Cook: 15mins |

- ✓ In a small bowl, mix the bran and boiling water, then set aside to cool.
- ✓ In a separate bowl, dissolve the yeast in warm water and set aside.
- ✓ In a mixing dish, cream together the salt, sugar, and shortening, then add the eggs.
- ✓ Stir in the yeast mixture thoroughly.
- ✓ After each addition of 2 cups flour and bran mixture, stir well.
- ✓ Slowly incorporate the remaining flour until a soft

dough forms.

- ✓ *Knead it for about 6 to 8 minutes on a lightly floured board, until it becomes flexible and smooth.*
- ✓ *Place it in an oiled mixing bowl and turn it once to grease the top.*
- ✓ *Cover and chill in the refrigerator overnight.*
- ✓ *Roll out the dough after punching it down.*
- ✓ *Place it in muffin tins or baking trays that have been buttered.*
- ✓ *Allow it to rise for 1 to 1 1/2 hours, or until it has doubled in size.*
- ✓ *Allow it to bake for 15 minutes at 375°F, or until light brown.*
- ✓ *Remove it from the pan and cool on wire racks.*

216) **Bread Machine Crescent Rolls**

Ingredients:

- *1/2 cup warm 2% milk (70° to 80°)*
- *1/4 cup water (70° to 80°)*
- *1 egg, lightly beaten*
- *1 teaspoon salt*
- *1/4 cup butter, softened*
- *3/4 cup warm mashed potatoes (prepared with milk and butter)*
- *1/4 cup sugar*
- *4-1/4 cups bread flour*
- *1-1/2 teaspoons active dry yeast*
- *Additional butter, melted*

Direction: Serving: 2 dozen. | Prep: 25mins | Cook: 10mins |

- ✓ *Put the initial 9 ingredients in a bread machine in the order recommended by manufacturer.*
- ✓ *Choose the dough setting (after 5 minutes of mixing, check the dough, then add 1-2 tbsp. of water or flour if necessary).*
- ✓ *Once the cycle has been completed, flip the dough onto a surface covered with a thin layer of flour.*
- ✓ *Split in half and roll each part into a 12-inch round.*
- ✓ *Slice each round into 12 wedges, then roll up the wedges from the wide end.*
- ✓ *Put on the greased baking sheets, pointed side down, keeping a 2"-distance away from each other.*
- ✓ *Form a crescent shape by curving the ends down.*
- ✓ *Allow to rise for 20 to 25 minutes, or until doubled in size.*
- ✓ *Bake at 400 degrees for 10 to 15 minutes, or until golden brown.*
- ✓ *Transfer to wire racks. Brush melted butter on the warm rolls*

217) **Brown Rice Yeast Rolls**

Ingredients:

- *6 to 7 cups all-purpose flour*
- *1/2 cup cornmeal*
- *2 packages (1/4 ounce each) active dry yeast*
- *1 teaspoon salt*
- *1/4 teaspoon baking soda*
- *2 cups water*
- *1/2 cup honey*
- *1/4 cup butter, cubed*
- *2 cups cooked brown rice*

Direction: Serving: 2-1/2 dozen. | Prep: 30mins | Cook: 15mins |

- ✓ *Mix together the baking soda, salt, yeast, cornmeal and 4 cups of flour in a big bowl.*
- ✓ *Heat the butter, honey and water in a small saucepan to 120-130 degrees.*
- ✓ *Mix it with the dry ingredients and beat until smooth.*
- ✓ *Add enough remaining flour and rice to make a soft dough.*
- ✓ *Knead it for about 6 to 8 minutes on a floured surface, until it becomes elastic and smooth.*
- ✓ *Place it in an oiled mixing bowl and turn it once to grease the top.*
- ✓ *Cover and let it rise for approximately an hour in a warm place until it has doubled in size.*
- ✓ *Punch the dough down. Split it into 30 pieces after turning it out onto a lightly floured surface.*
- ✓ *Make each one into a roll.*
- ✓ *Place the cookies 2 inches apart on buttered baking pans.*
- ✓ *Allow it to rise for about 30 minutes, or until it has doubled in size. Bake at 375 degrees for 12 to 15 minutes, or until golden brown.*
- ✓ *Remove it from the pans and place it on wire racks to cool.*

218) **Butterfluff Rolls**

Ingredients:

- *1 package (1/4 ounce) active dry yeast*
- *1/4 cup warm water (110° to 115°)*
- *1 cup warm buttermilk (110° to 115°)*
- *1/4 cup sugar*
- *1/4 cup shortening*
- *2 eggs*
- *1-1/2 teaspoons salt*
- *1/2 teaspoon baking soda*
- *4 to 4-1/2 cups all-purpose flour*

GLAZE:

- *1 egg 1*
- *tablespoon water*

Direction: Serving: 1-1/2 dozen. | Prep: 20mins | Cook: 15mins |

- ✓ *In a large mixing basin, dissolve the yeast in warm water.*
- ✓ *Combine 2 cups flour, baking soda, salt, eggs, shortening, sugar, and buttermilk in a mixing bowl and whisk until smooth.*
- ✓ *Add enough remaining flour to make a soft dough.*
- ✓ *Knead it for about 6 to 8 minutes on a floured surface, until it becomes elastic and smooth.*

- ✓ It should be cut into 18 pieces. Roll each into a 9-inch rope, then coil the ends in opposite directions toward the middle to form a "S" shape.
- ✓ Place the cookies 3 inches apart on buttered baking pans.
- ✓ Allow it to rise in a warm place for about 40 minutes, or until it has doubled in size.
- ✓ In a small bowl, whisk together the water and egg, then brush it over the rolls.
- ✓ Preheat oven to 350°F and bake for 15 to 20 minutes, or until golden brown.
- ✓ Remove it from the pans and set it to cool on wire racks.

219) **Buttermilk Biscuit Rolls**

Ingredients:

- • 2 cups all-purpose flour
- • 2-1/2 teaspoons baking powder
- • 1/8 teaspoon salt
- • 1/3 cup butter-flavored shortening
- • 3/4 cup buttermilk

Direction: Serving: 10 biscuits. | Prep: 15mins | Cook: 10mins |

- ✓ Mix salt, baking powder and flour in a bowl; cut in shortening till crumbly.
- ✓ Mix in buttermilk till just moist. Knead for 1 minute on a floured surface.
- ✓ Roll it to 1/2-in. thick; use a 2 1/2-in. biscuit cutter to cut.
- ✓ Put it onto the greased baking sheet and bake it at 450° till golden brown for 10-12 minutes

220) **Buttermilk Rolls**

Ingredients:

- • 1 package (1/4 ounce) active dry yeast
- • 1/4 cup warm water (110° to 115°)
- • 1-1/2 cups warm buttermilk (110° to 115°)
- • 1/2 cup canola oil
  3 tablespoons sugar
- • 1 teaspoon salt
- • 1/2 teaspoon baking soda
- • 4-1/2 cups all-purpose flour

Direction: Serving: 1-1/2 dozen. | Prep: 20mins | Cook: 15mins |

- ✓ Dissolve yeast in water in a big bowl.
- ✓ Beat in the 2 cups of flour, baking soda, salt, sugar, oil and buttermilk until smoothened.
- ✓ Mix in enough flour until a soft dough forms.
- ✓ Flip out onto a floured surface and knead for about 6 to 8 minutes until pliable and smooth.
- ✓ Put in a bowl coated with cooking spray, flipping once to grease the top.
- ✓ Put on a cover and allow to rise for around 1 1/2 hours in a warm area until doubled. Punch down the dough.
- ✓ Split into 18 pieces, then roll into balls.

- ✓ Put on greased baking sheets.
- ✓ Put on a cover and allow to rest for around 30 minutes until doubled.
- ✓ Bake for 15 to 20 minutes at 400 °F or until golden brown.
- ✓ Let cool on wire racks.

221) **Butterscotch Pecan Cinnamon Rolls**

Ingredients:

- • 1 cup warm 2% milk (70° to 80°)
- • 1/4 cup warm water (70° to 80°)
- • 1 large egg
- • 1/4 cup butter, softened
- • 1/4 cup instant butterscotch pudding mix
- • 1 tablespoon sugar
- • 1 teaspoon salt
- • 4-1/4 cups bread flour
- • 1 tablespoon active dry yeast
- • 1/4 cup finely chopped pecans
- • 1/4 cup milk chocolate chips

FILLING:

- • 1/4 cup butter, softened
- • 1 cup packed brown sugar
- • 1/4 cup finely chopped pecans
- • 1/4 cup milk chocolate chips
- • 2 teaspoons ground cinnamon

ICING:

- • 3/4 cup confectioners' sugar
- • 2 tablespoons butter, softened
- • 1-1/2 teaspoons 2% milk
- • 1/4 teaspoon vanilla extract

Direction: Serving: 1 dozen. | Prep: 45mins | Cook: 25mins |

- ✓ Put the first nine ingredients in the bread machine pan according to the order recommended by the machine's manufacturer.
- ✓ Use the dough setting (after five minutes of mixing, check the dough and add one to two tablespoons of flour or water if necessary).
- ✓ Before the last kneading (the machine may signal this audibly), pour in pecans and chips.
- ✓ Once the cycle has ended, turn the dough on a surface that is well-floured.
- ✓ Roll to form an 18x12-inch rectangle and then spread with butter.
- ✓ Mix the cinnamon, chips, pecans, and brown sugar.
- ✓ Top onto the dough to within half inch of edges.
- ✓ Roll up jellyroll style, beginning with a long side and then pinch the seam to seal.
- ✓ Slice into 12 pieces.
- ✓ Transfer onto a 13x9-inch baking pan that is greased placing the cut side down.
- ✓ Cover the pan and allow rising for about half an hour until doubled.

- ✓ Bake for 25-30 minutes at 350 °F or until golden brown.
- ✓ Let it cool in the pan for five minutes before inverting on a serving plate.
- ✓ Mix the icing ingredients in a small bowl.
- ✓ Drip over warm rolls.

222) **Buttery Rolls**

Ingredients:

- 1 cup warm milk (70° to 80°)
- 1/2 cup butter, softened
- 1/4 cup sugar
- 2 eggs
- 1-1/2 teaspoons salt
- 4 cups bread flour
- 2-1/4 teaspoons active dry yeast

Direction: Serving: 2 dozen. | Prep: 30mins | Cook: 13mins |

- ✓ Place all of the ingredients in the bread machine pan according to the manufacturer's instructions.
- ✓ On the machine, select Dough (after 5 minutes of the cycle, check on the dough and put 1-2 tablespoons of flour or water if necessary).
- ✓ Place the dough on a clean surface that has been lightly dusted with flour when the machine has completed the entire cycle.
- ✓ Slice the dough into 24 pieces and shape each piece into a ball.
- ✓ Put the dough balls in a 9x13-inch baking pan that is greased.
- ✓ Cover the dough balls and allow it to rise in volume in a warm area for 15 minutes.
- ✓ Put in the preheated 375°F oven and bake for 13-16 minutes until it turns golden brown in color.

223) **Candied Fruit Hot Cross Buns**

Ingredients:

- 2 packages (1/4 ounce each) active dry yeast
- 2 cups warm milk (110° to 115°)
- 6 tablespoons butter, softened
- 2 eggs, lightly beaten
- 3/4 cup sugar
- 1 teaspoon salt
- 6 to 6-1/2 cups all-purpose flour
- 1 cup chopped mixed candied fruit
- 2 teaspoons ground cinnamon
- 1 egg yolk
- 2 tablespoons water

ICING:

- 1-1/4 cups confectioners' sugar
- 2 tablespoons milk
- 1 tablespoon butter, melted
- 1/4 teaspoon vanilla extract

Direction: Serving: 3 dozen. | Prep: 30mins | Cook:

15mins |

- ✓ Dissolve yeast in warm water in a large mixing bowl.
- ✓ In a large mixing basin, combine 4 cups flour, salt, butter, sugar, buttermilk, and heated milk.
- ✓ Beat on medium speed until smooth.
- ✓ Using the leftover flour, make a sticky, soft dough.
- ✓ Knead on a floured surface for 6-8 minutes, or until elastic and smooth.
- ✓ Turn once to coat the surface of the mixture in a greased mixing bowl.
- ✓ Cover. Rise for 1 hour in a warm place until it has doubled in size.
- ✓ Make the dough by kneading it.
- ✓ Activate the floured surface by pressing down on it.
- ✓ Brush the dough with butter and roll it out to an 18x12-inch rectangle. In a mixing bowl, combine the cinnamon, coffee granules, and brown sugar.
- ✓ Within 1/2-inch of the edges, sprinkle dough.
- ✓ Starting with the long side, roll up jellyroll style.
- ✓ To seal the seam, pinch it together. Cut the cake into 12 wedges.
- ✓ In a greased 13x9-inch baking sheet, place the cut side down.
- ✓ Cover and allow the dough to double in size for 30 minutes.
- ✓ Preheat the oven to 350 °F (180 °C). Cook until golden brown, about 22-28 minutes.
- ✓ Allow the pan to cool on a wire rack.
- ✓ Whisk together the icing ingredients in a small mixing bowl until smooth.
- ✓ Serve on buns that have been heated.

224) **Cappuccino Cinnamon Rolls**

Ingredients:

- 1 package (1/4 ounce) active dry yeast
- 1 cup warm water (110° to 115°)
- 3/4 cup warm milk (110° to 115°) 1/2 cup warm buttermilk (110° to 115°)
- 3 tablespoons sugar
- 2 tablespoons butter, softened
- 1-1/4 teaspoons salt
- 5-1/2 to 6 cups all-purpose flour

FILLING:

- 1/4 cup butter, melted
- 1 cup packed brown sugar
- 4 teaspoons instant coffee granules
- 2 teaspoons ground cinnamon

ICING:

- 1-1/2 cups confectioners' sugar
- 2 tablespoons butter, softened
- 1 to 2 tablespoons milk
- 2 teaspoons instant cappuccino mix, optional
- 1/2 teaspoon vanilla extract

Direction: Serving: 1 dozen. | Prep: 45mins | Cook: 25mins |

- ✓ In a large mixing basin, dissolve yeast in warm water.
- ✓ Combine 4 cups flour, salt, butter, sugar, buttermilk, and warm milk in a large mixing bowl.
- ✓ On medium speed, beat until smooth.
- ✓ Make a sticky soft dough using the leftover flour.
- ✓ Knead for 6-8 minutes on a floured surface, or until elastic and smooth.
- ✓ Place in a greased mixing bowl and turn once to coat the top.
- ✓ Cover in a warm location, rise for 1 hour until doubled in size.
- ✓ Knead the dough. Activate the floured surface.
- ✓ Roll out to an 18x12-inch rectangle and brush with butter.
- ✓ Combine the cinnamon, coffee granules, and brown sugar in a bowl.
- ✓ Sprinkle dough within 1/2-inch of the edges.
- ✓ Roll up jellyroll manner, starting with the long side.
- ✓ Pinch the seam to seal it. Cut into 12 slices.
- ✓ Place cut side down in a greased 13x9-inch baking sheet.
- ✓ Cover and allow 30 minutes for the dough to double in bulk.
- ✓ Preheat the oven to 350 °F.
- ✓ Cook for 22-28 minutes, or until golden brown.
- ✓ Place the pan on a wire rack to cool.
- ✓ In a small mixing basin, whisk together the icing ingredients until smooth.
- ✓ Spread on heated buns and serve.

225) Caramel Pecan Rolls

Ingredients:

- 2 cups milk
- 1/2 cup water
- 1/2 cup sugar
- 1/2 cup butter
- 1/3 cup cornmeal
- 2 teaspoons salt
- 7 to 7-1/2 cups all-purpose flour
- 2 packages (1/4 ounce each) active dry yeast
- 2 large eggs

TOPPING:

- 2 cups packed brown sugar
- 1/2 cup butter
- 1/2 cup milk
- 1/2 to 1 cup chopped pecans

FILLING:

- 1/4 cup butter, softened
- 1/2 cup sugar
- 2 teaspoons ground cinnamon

Direction: Serving: 2 dozen. | Prep: 40mins | Cook: 20mins |

- ✓ Mix the initial 6 ingredients in saucepan; boil, mixing often.

- ✓ Put aside to let cool to 120° to 130°.
- ✓ Mix yeast and 2 cups of flour in bowl.
- ✓ Put in the cooled mixture of cornmeal; mix till smooth on low.
- ✓ Put in a cup flour and eggs; combine for a minute.
- ✓ To make a soft dough, add extra remaining flour.
- ✓ Transfer dough to a floured surface and knead for 6 to 8 minutes, or until smooth and malleable.
- ✓ Place in an oiled basin, flipping once to coat the surface with oil.
- ✓ Cover and leave to rise for an hour in a warm place until it has doubled in size.
- ✓ In saucepan, mix the initial 3 ingredients for topping; boil, mixing from time to time.
- ✓ Put into 2 oiled baking pans, 13x9 inches in size.
- ✓ Scatter with pecans; put aside Deflate dough; halve.
- ✓ Roll every portion into a rectangle, 12x15 inches in size; spread butter over.
- ✓ Cinnamon and sugar should be mixed together and sprinkled over the butter.
- ✓ Roll dough up starting at a long side; press seams and tuck ends beneath.
- ✓ Slice every roll into a dozen pieces.
- ✓ Put a dozen pieces in every baking pan, cut side facing down.
- ✓ Cover and allow to rise for half an hour in a warm environment, until almost doubled.
- ✓ At 375°, bake until golden brown, about 20 to 25 minutes.
- ✓ Cool for a minute; flip onto serving platter.

226) Caramel Rolls

Ingredients:

- Dough:
- 3/4 cup water
- 2 tablespoons butter
- 2 cups white bread flour
- 2 tablespoons white sugar
- 1 1/2 tablespoons nonfat dry milk powder
- 1 teaspoon fast-rising dry yeast
- 1/2 teaspoon salt

Sauce:

- 1/2 cup brown sugar
- 1/4 cup light corn syrup
- 1/4 cup butter
- 1/4 cup chopped pecans (optional)

Filling:

- 1/4 cup butter, softened
- 1/2 teaspoon ground cinnamon

Direction: Serving: 12 | Prep: 45mins | Cook: 23mins |

- ✓ Respectively, mix water, 2 tablespoon butter, bread flour, the white sugar, milk powder, and the yeast in bread machine's bucket.
- ✓ Choose dough cycle. Remove dough from machine after 1 hour 45 minutes after cycle is done.
- ✓ Stir and cook 1/4 cup butter, light corn syrup and

brown sugar in saucepan on medium heat for 3 minutes till sugar melts.

- ✓ Put sauce in 8-in. square baking pan. Sprinkle pecans on.
- ✓ Turn out dough on floured surface; punch down.
- ✓ Roll to 8x12-in. rectangle.
- ✓ Use 1/4 cup butter to dot. Sprinkle cinnamon.
- ✓ Roll up.
- ✓ Pinch seams together. Cut roll to 1 1/2-in. thick slices.
- ✓ Put slices in pan over sauce.
- ✓ Put aside for 1-hour till doubled in size.
- ✓ Preheat an oven to 190°C/375°F.
- ✓ In preheated oven, bake rolls for 20-25 minutes till golden brown.
- ✓ In pan, cool for no longer than 3 minutes.
- ✓ Put waxed paper sheet over pan.
- ✓ Invert so pecans and sauce are on top.

227) *Caramel Pecan Cinnamon Rolls*

Ingredients:

- 2 packages (1/4 ounce each) active dry yeast
- 1 cup warm 2% milk (110° to 115°)
- 2 large eggs
- 5 tablespoons butter, melted 1/2 cup sugar
- 1 teaspoon salt
- 5 cups all-purpose flour
  CARAMEL SAUCE:
- 1 cup butter, cubed
- 2 cups packed brown sugar
- 1/4 cup corn syrup
- 1/2 to 3/4 cup chopped pecans

FILLING:
- 2 tablespoons butter, melted
- 1/2 cup sugar
- 1 teaspoon ground cinnamon
  Direction: Serving: 15 servings. | Prep: 20mins | Cook: 30mins |

- ✓ In a large mixing basin, dissolve yeast in warm milk.
- ✓ Combine 3 cups flour, salt, sugar, butter, and eggs in a mixing bowl.
- ✓ Blend until completely smooth.
- ✓ Make a soft dough with the remaining flour.
- ✓ Knead for 6-8 minutes on a lightly floured surface, or until elastic and smooth.
- ✓ Turn once to butter the top of the greased basin.
- ✓ Cover and let rise for 1 hour in a warm area till doubled in size.
- ✓ Meanwhile, sauce: Melt butter in a big saucepan.
- ✓ Mix corn syrup and brown sugar in; boil for 2 minutes, constantly mixing, on medium heat.
- ✓ Put in 13x9-in. greased baking dish. Sprinkle pecans on; put aside.
- ✓ Punch down dough. Turn on floured surface.
- ✓ Roll to 17x15-in. rectangle. Within 1/2-in. of edges, spread butter.

- ✓ Mix cinnamon and sugar; sprinkle on dough.
- ✓ Roll up, beginning with long side, jellyroll style.
- ✓ To seal, pinch seam.
- ✓ Slice to 15 slices. Put on caramel sauce, cut side down; cover.
- ✓ Let rise for 30 minutes' till doubled in size.
- ✓ Bake for 30-35 minutes till golden brown at 350°F.
- ✓ Let stand for 5 minutes. Invert on serving platter.

228) *Caraway Cloverleaf Rolls*

Ingredients:

- 2 packages (1/4 ounce each) active dry yeast
- 1-1/2 cups warm water (110° to 115°)
- 1 cup whole wheat flour
- 1/2 cup sugar
- 1/2 cup vegetable oil
- 2 teaspoons caraway seeds
- 1-1/2 teaspoons salt
- 3-1/2 to 4 cups all-purpose flour
  Direction: Serving: 2 dozen. | Prep: 30mins | Cook: 15mins |

- ✓ In a large mixing basin, dissolve yeast in water.
- ✓ Add 2 cups all-purpose flour, salt, caraway, oil, sugar and whole wheat flour, then beat until smoothened.
- ✓ Add enough of the leftover all-purpose flour until a soft dough forms.
- ✓ Flip over onto a surface dusted with flour and knead for about 6 to 8 minutes until pliable and smooth.
- ✓ Put in a bowl coated with cooking spray, flipping once to grease the top.
- ✓ Allow to rise for about an hour in a warm environment until it has doubled in size.
- ✓ Punch the dough down.
- ✓ Turn out onto a flour-dusted work surface.
- ✓ Split in half, then into 36 pieces for each half.
- ✓ Form into balls and place three per muffin cup in oiled muffin tins.
- ✓ Allow to rise for about 30 minutes, or until doubled in size.
- ✓ Bake at 375 degrees for 15 to 18 minutes, or until golden brown.
- ✓ Remove it from the pans and place it on wire racks to cool.

229) *Caraway Rye Rolls*

Ingredients:

- 2 packages (1/4 ounce each) active dry yeast
- 1/2 cup warm water (110° to 115°)
- 2 cups warm
- 4% cottage cheese (110° to 115°)
- 1/2 cup sugar
- 2 eggs, lightly beaten
- 2 tablespoons caraway seeds

- 2 teaspoons salt
- 1/2 teaspoon baking soda
- 1 cup rye flour
- 3 to 4 cups all-purpose flour

Direction: Serving: 2 dozen. | Prep: 15mins | Cook: 20mins |

- ✓ Dissolve the yeast in warm water in a large bowl.
- ✓ Add the 1 cup all- purpose flour, rye flour, baking soda, salt, caraway seeds, eggs, sugar, and cottage cheese.
- ✓ Beat until the mix is smooth.
- ✓ Slowly mix in enough of the leftover all-purpose flour to make a sticky batter (don't knead).
- ✓ Cover and let rise for about 1 hour in a warm place until doubled.
- ✓ Stir the dough down and transfer to a lightly floured surface.
- ✓ Separate into 24 pieces and then put in muffin cups that are well-greased.
- ✓ Allow to rise for about 35 minutes, or until doubled in size.
- ✓ Preheat the oven to 350°F and bake for 18 to 20 minutes, or until golden brown.
- ✓ Allow to cool for one minute before removing from the pans and placing on wire racks.

230) **Cheddar Bacon Swirled Rolls**

Ingredients:

- 2/3 cup warm whole milk (70° to 80°)
- 4-1/2 teaspoons water
- 4 teaspoons butter, softened
- 1/2 teaspoon lemon juice
- 1 tablespoon sugar
- 1/2 teaspoon salt
- 1-3/4 cups all-purpose flour
- 3 tablespoons mashed potato flakes
- 1 package (1/4 ounce) active dry yeast
- 1/2 cup shredded cheddar cheese

FILLING:

- 1 cup finely chopped onion
- 1/4 teaspoon salt
- 1/8 teaspoon pepper
- 3 tablespoons butter
- 8 bacon strips, cooked and crumbled (equals 1/2 cup)

Direction: Serving: 9 servings. | Prep: 30mins | Cook: 30mins |

- ✓ Put the first nine ingredients in bread machine pan in the order endorsed by manufacturer.
- ✓ Use the dough setting (after five minutes of mixing, check the dough and you can add one to two tablespoons of flour or water if necessary).
- ✓ Add in cheese just before the last kneading (the machine may signal this audibly).
- ✓ As the dough is processing, you can prepare the filling.
- ✓ Over medium heat, cook onion, pepper and salt in

butter in a large skillet until the onion becomes translucent (do not brown) and tender.

- ✓ Mix in the bacon bits.
- ✓ Then remove from heat and let to cool.
- ✓ After the cycle is finished, flip the dough on a surface that is lightly floured.
- ✓ Then fold to form a 12x8-inch rectangle.
- ✓ Pour the onion mixture to within half inch of the edges.
- ✓ Fold up using jellyroll style, beginning with a long side and then pinch the seam to seal.
- ✓ Chop into nine rolls.
- ✓ Transfer into a 9-in. square baking pan that is greased and put the cut side up.
- ✓ Cover the rolls and allow to rise in a warm place for about half an hour until doubled.
- ✓ Bake for about 30-35 minutes at 375 degrees F or until golden brown. Transfer from the pan onto a wire rack. Serve while still warm.

231) **Cheese Filled Garlic Rolls**

Ingredients:

- 1 loaf (1 pound) frozen bread dough, thawed
- 24 cubes part-skim mozzarella cheese (3/4 inch each, about 10 ounces)
- 3 tablespoons butter, melted
- 2 teaspoons minced fresh parsley
- 1 garlic clove, minced
- 1/2 teaspoon Italian seasoning
- 1/2 teaspoon crushed red pepper flakes
- 2 tablespoons grated Parmigiano-Reggiano cheese

Direction: Serving: 2 dozen. | Prep: 20mins | Cook: 15mins |

- ✓ Divide dough to 24 portions.
- ✓ Form each portion around the cheese cube to fully cover; to seal, pinch.
- ✓ Put each roll, seam side down, into a greased muffin cup.
- ✓ Use kitchen towels to cover; rise for 30 minutes' till doubled in a warm place. Preheat your oven to 350°F.
- ✓ Mix pepper flakes, Italian seasoning, garlic, parsley and butter in a small bowl. Brush on rolls; sprinkle cheese.
- ✓ Bake for 15-18 minutes till golden brown.
- ✓ Before removing from the pans, cool for 5 minutes; serve warm

232) **Cherry Nut Breakfast Rolls**

Ingredients:

- 2 packages (1/4 ounce each) active dry yeast
- 1 cup warm water (110°-115°)
- 1/2 cup butter, melted
- 1/2 cup sugar
- 3 large eggs, beaten

- *1/2 teaspoon salt*
- *4-1/2 to 5 cups all-purpose flour, divided*

FILLING:

- *3 cups fresh or frozen pitted tart red cherries, chopped*
- *2/3 cup sugar*
- *3 tablespoons cornstarch*
- *1/4 teaspoon almond extract*
- *1/3 cups finely chopped almonds*
- *Few drops red food coloring, optional*

ICING:

- *1/2 cup confectioners' sugar*
- *1/2 to 2 teaspoons whole milk*
- *1/2 teaspoon butter, softened*
- *1/2 teaspoon almond extract*

Direction: Serving: 12 rolls. | Prep: 30mins | Cook: 25mins |

- ✓ *In a large mixing basin, dissolve the yeast in the water.*
- ✓ *Allow for a 5-minute rest period.*
- ✓ *Combine 3 cups flour, salt, eggs, sugar, and butter in a mixing bowl.*
- ✓ *Add enough remaining flour to make a soft dough.*
- ✓ *Turn it out onto a floured area and knead it for 6 to 8 minutes, or until it is smooth and malleable.*
- ✓ *Place it in an oiled mixing bowl and turn it once to grease the top.*
- ✓ *Cover and chill for 2 hours in the refrigerator.*
- ✓ *Meanwhile, combine all of the filling ingredients in a pot and bring to a boil.*
- ✓ *Reduce the heat to low and simmer, stirring regularly, until it thickens.*
- ✓ *Allow time for it to cool.*
- ✓ *Turn the dough out onto a lightly floured work surface.*
- ✓ *Roll it out to a 14x16-inch rectangle and spread the filling on top. Starting with the long end, roll it up jelly roll style.*
- ✓ *It should be cut into 12 pieces.*
- ✓ *Place it cut side down in a greased 13x9-inch baking sheet.*
- ✓ *Allow it to rise for about 25 minutes, or until it almost doubles in size.*
- ✓ *Allow it to bake for 25 minutes at 375 degrees, or until golden brown.*
- ✓ *Remove it from the pan and set it aside to cool.*
- ✓ *Combine all of the frosting ingredients in a mixing bowl, then drizzle it over the warm rolls.*
- ✓ *Serve immediately.*

233) **Cherry Pineapple Sweet Rolls**

Ingredients:

- *1 cup pineapple tidbits*
- *1/2 cup pineapple juice, divided*
- *1 tube (13.9 ounces) refrigerated orange sweet rolls with icing*

- *1 teaspoon cornstarch*
- *1/4 cup chopped walnuts*
- *1/4 cup chopped maraschino cherries*

Direction: Serving: 8 servings. | Prep: 10mins | Cook: 20mins |

- ✓ *Mix and cook 2 tbsp. icing from the sweet rolls, 1/4 cup of pineapple juice and pineapple in a small saucepan on medium heat till icing melts.*
- ✓ *Mix leftover pineapple juice and cornstarch till smooth; mix into saucepan slowly.*
- ✓ *Boil; mix and cook till thick for 1 minute. Take off heat.*
- ✓ *Sprinkle cherries and walnuts into the 9-in. greased round baking pans; put pineapple mixture over.*
- ✓ *Put the sweet rolls on the top.*
- ✓ *Bake it at 375° till golden brown for 20-25 minutes.*
- ✓ *Invert onto serving platter immediately.*
- ✓ *If desired, drizzle leftover icing; serve warm.*

234) **Chicken Rolls**

Ingredients:

- *1 (8 ounce) package refrigerated crescent rolls*
- *1 (3 ounce) package cream cheese with chives, softened*
- *2 tablespoons butter*
- *1 cup shredded cooked chicken*
- *3/4 cup sliced fresh mushrooms*
- *1/2 teaspoon lemon pepper*
- *2 tablespoons butter, melted*
- *3 cups seasoned croutons, crushed*
- *1/3 cup drippings from a roast chicken*
- *1 tablespoon minced onion*
- *1/2 cup dry white wine*
- *1 cup chicken stock*
- *2 tablespoons cornstarch*
- *3 tablespoons chicken stock salt and ground black pepper to taste*

Direction: Serving: 4 | Prep: 25mins | Cook: 45mins |

- ✓ *Set an oven to preheat to 175°C (350°F).*
- ✓ *Roll it out and split up the crescent roll dough on a big baking tray.*
- ✓ *In a bowl, combine the butter and cream cheese until well blended.*
- ✓ *Mix in the lemon pepper, mushrooms and shredded chicken.*
- ✓ *Fill a tablespoonful of the chicken mixture to the crescent rolls.*
- ✓ *Roll up each piece starting with the wide end, then press and seal the top of the rolled dough.*
- ✓ *Brush butter on the rolls, then roll it in the crushed croutons.*
- ✓ *Put the coated rolls back into the baking tray.*
- ✓ *Let it bake for about 20 minutes in the preheated oven, until it turns golden brown in color.*
- ✓ *In a big frying pan, heat the drippings on medium-high heat.*

- ✓ Mix in the wine and onion and let it cook and stir for about 5 minutes, until much of the wine evaporates.
- ✓ Pour in 1 cup of the chicken stock and keep on cooking while stirring for about 15 minutes, until the sauce reduces by half.
- ✓ Lower the heat to low. In a small bowl, combine the leftover 3 tbsp. of chicken stock and cornstarch.
- ✓ Mix the cornstarch mixture into the frying pan for about 5 minutes, until it becomes thick.
- ✓ Sprinkle pepper and salt to season.
- ✓ Scoop the hot gravy on top of the chicken rolls prior to serving.

235)   Chive Pinwheel Rolls

Ingredients:

- 3-1/2 cups all-purpose flour
- 3 tablespoons sugar
- 1 package (1/4 ounce) active dry yeast
- 1-1/2 teaspoons salt
- 1 cup milk
- 1/3 cup canola oil
- 1/4 cup water
- 1/4 cup mashed potatoes (without added milk and butter)
- 1 large egg CHIVE

FILLING:

- 1 cup (8 ounces) sour cream
- 1 cup minced chives
- 1 large egg yolk
- Butter, melted

Direction: Serving: 15 rolls. | Prep: 25mins | Cook: 30mins |

- ✓ In a large mixing basin, combine the salt, yeast, sugar, and 2 1/2 cups flour.
- ✓ In a small saucepan, heat the mashed potatoes, water, oil, and milk to 120-130 degrees.
- ✓ Mix it together with the dry ingredients just until it's moistened.
- ✓ Beat in the egg until it is completely smooth.
- ✓ Add enough remaining flour to make a soft dough.
- ✓ Turn it out onto a floured area and knead it for 6 to 8 minutes, or until it is smooth and malleable.
- ✓ Place it in an oiled mixing bowl and turn it once to grease the top.
- ✓ Cover and let it rise in a warm place for approximately an hour, or until it doubles in size.
- ✓ On a floured board, roll out the dough into a 15x10-inch rectangle.
- ✓ In a mixing dish, combine the egg yolk, chives, and sour cream; distribute on top of the dough to within 1/2-inch of the edges.
- ✓ Start with a long side and wrap it up jellyroll style; squeeze the seam to close it.
- ✓ It should be cut into 1-inch pieces.
- ✓ Place it cut side down in a 13x9-inch baking sheet.
- ✓ Allow it to rise for about an hour, or until it has doubled in size.
- ✓ Allow it to bake for 30 to 35 minutes at 350°F, or until golden brown, before brushing it with butter.
- ✓ Place it on a wire rack to cool.
- ✓ Place any leftovers in the refrigerator.

236)   Chocolate Chip Filled Cinnamon Rolls

Ingredients:

- 2 packages (1/4 ounce each) active dry yeast
- 1-1/4 cups warm water (110° to 115°)
- 1-1/2 cups warm 2% milk (110° to 115°)
- 1/4 cup butter, softened
- 1 large egg
- 6 tablespoons honey
- 2 teaspoons salt
- 7 cups all-purpose flour

FILLING:

- 3 tablespoons butter, softened
- 1 cup packed brown sugar plus 2 tablespoons brown sugar
- 1-1/2 teaspoons ground cinnamon

GLAZE:

- 1-1/2 cups confectioners' sugar
- 3 tablespoons butter, softened
- 1/2 teaspoon vanilla extract
- 3 to 4 tablespoons 2% milk

Direction: Serving: 2 dozen. | Prep: 45mins | Cook: 25mins |

- ✓ In a large mixing basin, dissolve yeast in warm water and set aside for 5 minutes.
- ✓ Combine 3 cups flour, salt, eggs, butter, honey, and milk in a mixing bowl. On low, beat for 3 minutes.
- ✓ To make a soft dough, add extra remaining flour.
- ✓ Knead for 6-8 minutes on a floured surface, or until elastic and smooth.
- ✓ Place in a large oiled mixing bowl and turn once.
- ✓ Cover in a warm location, rise for 1 hour until doubled in size.
- ✓ Knead the dough.
- ✓ Turn out onto a floured surface and cut in half.
- ✓ Each one should be rolled into a 14x8-inch rectangle.
- ✓ Using butter, coat the pan.
- ✓ Combine the cinnamon, chips, and brown sugar in a mixing bowl.
- ✓ Sprinkle dough within 1/2-inch of the edges.
- ✓ Make a press into the dough.
- ✓ Roll up jellyroll manner, starting with the long side.
- ✓ Pinch the seam to seal it.
- ✓ Each one should be cut into 12 slices.
- ✓ Place cut side down in 2 greased 13x9-inch baking dishes.
- ✓ Cover. Allow 30 minutes for the dough to double in bulk.

- ✓ At 350°F, bake for 25-30 minutes, or until golden brown.
- ✓ Allow to cool for 5 minutes.
- ✓ Remove the pans from the oven and place them on wire racks to cool.
- ✓ In a large mixing bowl, combine vanilla, butter, confectioners' sugar, and enough milk to achieve desired consistency; drizzle over rolls.

237) <u>*Chocolate Cinnamon Rolls*</u>

Ingredients:
- 2 packages (1/4 ounce each) active dry yeast
- 1-1/2 cups warm water (110° to 115°), divided
- 1/2 cup butter, softened
- 1/2 cup sugar
- 1 teaspoon salt
- 4-1/2 to 4-3/4 cups all-purpose flour
- 2/3 cup baking cocoa

FILLING:
- 2 tablespoons butter, melted
- 1/3 cup sugar
- 1/2 teaspoon ground cinnamon
- 1 cup miniature semisweet chocolate chips
- 2/3 cup finely chopped nuts, optional

ICING:
- 2 cups confectioners' sugar
- 1/2 teaspoon vanilla extract
- 2 to 3 tablespoons milk
- Additional miniature semisweet chocolate chips, optional

Direction: Serving: 20 rolls. | Prep: 30mins | Cook: 25mins |

- ✓ Melt yeast in 1/2 cup warm water in a big bowl.
- ✓ Add leftover water, salt, sugar and butter.
- ✓ Mix cocoa and 2 1/2 cups flour in. Beat for 3 minutes till smooth on medium speed.
- ✓ Add enough residual flour to form a soft dough.
- ✓ Knead the dough for 6-8 minutes, or until smooth and elastic, on a lightly floured work surface.
- ✓ Place in an oiled bowl; turn once to coat the top with grease and cover.
- ✓ In a warm location, rise for 1 hour until doubled.
- ✓ Turn on lightly floured surface; halve.
- ✓ Roll every portion to 12x10-in. rectangle. Brush melted butter on.
- ✓ Mix nuts (optional), chocolate chips, cinnamon and sugar.
- ✓ Sprinkle dough within 1/2-inch of the edges.
- ✓ Roll up beginning with the long side in a jellyroll fashion.
- ✓ Pinch seams to seal.
- ✓ Each one should be sliced into ten slices.
- ✓ Place cut side down in a greased 15x10x1-inch baking sheet; cover.
- ✓ Continue rising for 45 minutes, or until doubled in size.
- ✓ Bake for 25-30 minutes till lightly browned at 375°F.
- ✓ Meanwhile, mix vanilla, confectioners' sugar and enough milk to get desired consistency in a small bowl.
- ✓ While slightly warm, spread on rolls.
- ✓ Sprinkle extra chocolate chips on if desired.

238) <u>*Chocolate Sticky Buns*</u>

Ingredients:
- 1 package (1/4 ounce) active dry yeast
- 1/3 cup warm water (110° to 115°)
- 3/4 cup warm milk (110° to 115°)
- 1/2 cup butter, softened
- 1/3 cup sugar
- 1 teaspoon salt
- 1 egg
- 4-1/2 to 5 cups all-purpose flour

SYRUP:
- 1 cup packed brown sugar
- 1/2 cup butter
- 1/4 cup corn syrup
- 3 tablespoons baking cocoa
- 1-1/2 cups chopped pecans

FILLING:
- 1/4 cup butter, melted
- 1 cup sugar
- 2 tablespoons baking cocoa
- 2 teaspoons ground cinnamon

Direction: Serving: 1-1/2 dozen. | Prep: 35mins | Cook: 20mins |

- ✓ Dissolve the yeast in warm water in a big bowl.
- ✓ Add the 1-1/2 cups flour, egg, salt, sugar, butter and milk.
- ✓ Beat it for 2 to 3 minutes on medium speed or until it becomes smooth.
- ✓ To make a soft dough, add enough remaining flour.
- ✓ Turn it out onto a floured area and knead for approximately 6 to 8 minutes, or until it becomes smooth and pliable.
- ✓ It should be placed in a greased bowl and turned once to coat the top in grease.
- ✓ Cover and set aside for approximately one hour in a warm atmosphere to double in size.
- ✓ Meanwhile, in a saucepan, combine the cocoa, corn syrup, butter, and brown sugar and bring to a boil.
- ✓ Let it cook and stir for a minute.
- ✓ Pour it into two greased 9-in square or round baking pans and sprinkle pecans on top.
- ✓ Put aside.
- ✓ Punch down the dough.
- ✓ Flip it onto a lightly floured surface, then split it in half.
- ✓ Roll each part into a 12x10-inch rectangle, then brush it using melted butter.

- ✓ Mix together the cinnamon, cocoa and sugar and sprinkle it on top of the rectangles to within 1/2-inch of the edges.
- ✓ Starting with a short side, roll it up jelly roll style, squeezing the seam to close it.
- ✓ Slice each roll into 9 pieces.
- ✓ Put it on top of the pecans and syrup, cut side down.
- ✓ Allow it to rise for about 40 minutes, or until it has doubled in size.
- ✓ Allow it to cool for 1 minute prior to turning it upside down onto serving platters.

239) *Christmas Tree Savory Rolls*

Ingredients:

- 4 to 4-1/2 cups all-purpose flour
- 2/3 cup sugar
- 1 tablespoon active dry yeast
- 2 teaspoons grated lemon peel
- 1 teaspoon salt
- 3/4 cup 2% milk
- 2/3 cup water
- 1/3 cup canola oil
- 1 tablespoon lemon juice

FILLING:

- 1 package (8 ounces) cream cheese, softened, divided
- 2 tablespoons mayonnaise
- 2 teaspoons lemon juice, divided
- 1 teaspoon lemon-pepper seasoning
- 1 teaspoon dried parsley flakes
- 1 can (6 ounces) crabmeat, drained, flaked and cartilage removed, optional
- 1 each small green and sweet red pepper
- 1 medium lemon

Direction: Serving: 1 tree (22 rolls). | Prep: 60mins | Cook: 25mins |

- ✓ Mix together salt, lemon peel, yeast, sugar, and 3 cups flour in a big bowl.
- ✓ Heat water and milk to 120-130 degrees in a small pot.
- ✓ Add lemon juice and oil, stirring together.
- ✓ Add to dry ingredients, whisk until smooth.
- ✓ Mix in enough remaining flour to make a soft dough.
- ✓ Transfer to a floured surface, knead for 6-8 minutes until elastic and smooth.
- ✓ Put into a greased bowl, turning once to make the top greased.
- ✓ Cover and put in a warm place. Allow to rise in 1 hour, until doubled in size.
- ✓ At the same time, whisk 4 ounces' cream cheese in a small bowl, until smooth.
- ✓ Add parsley, lemon-pepper, 1 teaspoon lemon juice, and mayonnaise.
- ✓ Combine thoroughly.
- ✓ Stir in crabmeat if you want, then put aside.
- ✓ Lightly flour a surface and put dough in.

- ✓ Roll out into a 22x14-inch rectangle.
- ✓ Arrange prepared filling to within 1/2 inch of edges.
- ✓ Pinch the seams to seal them after rolling up the long side. Slice into 22 slices.
- ✓ Use foil to cover a baking tray and grease thoroughly.
- ✓ Put a slice near the top center of the prepared baking tray.
- ✓ In the second row, put 2 slices with sides touching.
- ✓ Repeat, adding 1 slice for each row until there are 5 rows in the tree.
- ✓ Repeat the last row.
- ✓ For the trunk, center 2 remaining slices below last row.
- ✓ Cover and allow to rise for 30 minutes until doubled in size.
- ✓ Bake at 325 degrees until golden brown, about 25- 30 minutes.
- ✓ Carefully place rolls with foil on a wire jack to make them cool completely.
- ✓ At the same time, combine lemon juice and the remaining cream cheese in a small bowl until smooth.
- ✓ Make a small hole in the corner of plastic bag or pastry bag, pour in cream cheese mixture, then pipe onto the rolls for garland.
- ✓ Slice peppers in half lengthwise, take out seeds and stems.
- ✓ Cut out stars from peppers with a 1-1/2-inch star-shaped cookie cutter, put on the tree.
- ✓ Carefully take out a 2-inch piece of peel from lemon (lemon can be saved for another use).
- ✓ Cut out a star from lemon peel with a 2-inch star-shaped cookie cutter and put it on top of the tree.
- ✓ Take out foil and serve. Put leftovers in the fridge.

240) *Cinnamon Apple Rolls*

Ingredients:

- /2 cups sugar
- 3/4 cup water
- 3/4 cup unsweetened apple juice
- 1/4 cup butter, cubed
- 1/4 teaspoon ground cinnamon
- 1/4 teaspoon ground nutmeg
- 2 cups all-purpose flour
- 2 teaspoons baking powder
- 1/2 teaspoon salt
- 3/4 cup butter-flavored shortening
- 2/3 cup buttermilk

FILLING:

- 3 cups shredded peeled tart apples
- 1/4 cup sugar
- 1/2 teaspoon ground cinnamon

Direction: Serving: 1 dozen. | Prep: 25mins | Cook: 45mins |

- ✓ Put nutmeg, cinnamon, butter, apple juice, water and

sugar in big saucepan; boil. Stir and cook till liquid reduces to 2 cups or for 4-6 minutes.

- ✓ Put aside sauce.
- ✓ Mix salt, baking powder and flour in big bowl.
- ✓ Cut shortening in till mixture looks like coarse crumbs.
- ✓ Mix buttermilk in till just moistened.
- ✓ Turn on lightly floured surface then knead 8-10 times.
- ✓ Roll to 14x12-in. rectangle.
- ✓ Mix filling ingredients in small bowl.
- ✓ Within 1/2-in. of edges, spread over dough.
- ✓ Roll up, starting from long side, jellyroll style.
- ✓ To seal, pinch seam. Slice to 12 slices.
- ✓ Put in 13x9-in. greased baking dish, cut side down.
- ✓ Put sauce on rolls. Bake for 45-50 minutes or till toothpick exits cleanly at 350°.
- ✓ Serve warm.

241) **Cinnamon Bun Cookies**

Ingredients:

- 1 cup unsalted butter, softened
- 3/4 cup confectioners' sugar
- 1/3 cup granulated sugar
- 1-1/2 teaspoons grated orange zest
- 1/2 teaspoon salt
- 1 large egg
- 1 teaspoon vanilla extract
- 2-1/4 cups all-purpose flour

FILLING:

- 5 tablespoons unsalted butter, softened
- 1/4 cup packed brown sugar
- 1-1/2 teaspoons light corn syrup
- 1/2 teaspoon vanilla extract
- 2 tablespoons all-purpose flour
- 1 tablespoon ground cinnamon
- 1/2 teaspoon salt

GLAZE:

- 1 cup confectioners' sugar
- 1/4 cup light corn syrup
- 2 teaspoons vanilla extract
- 1 to 2 teaspoons water

Direction: Serving: about 4 dozen. | Prep: 30mins | Cook: 10mins |

- ✓ Cream initial 5 ingredients till fluffy and light.
- ✓ Beat vanilla and egg in.
- ✓ Beat flour in slowly.
- ✓ Roll dough between 2 waxed paper sheets on baking sheet to a 12-in. square.
- ✓ Keep it in the fridge for 30 minutes.
- ✓ Filling: beat vanilla, corn syrup, brown sugar and butter.
- ✓ Add salt, cinnamon and flour; stir well.
- ✓ Remove waxed paper top sheet. Within 1/4-in. of

edges, spread filling on dough.

- ✓ Tightly roll up jellyroll style using waxed paper, removing paper while rolling.
- ✓ Wrap in plastic.
- ✓ Freeze for 30 minutes till firm.
- ✓ Preheat an oven to 375°F.
- ✓ Unwrap.
- ✓ Crosswise, cut dough to 1/4-in. slices.
- ✓ Put on parchment paper-lined baking sheets, 2-in. apart.
- ✓ Bake for 10-12 minutes till edges are light brown.
- ✓ Cool for 5 minutes on pans.
- ✓ Transfer to wire racks; completely cool.
- ✓ GLAZE:
- ✓ Mix vanilla, corn syrup, confectioners' sugar and enough water to get preferred consistency.
- ✓ Drizzle/spread on cookies.
- ✓ Let stand till set at room temperature

242) **Cinnamon Cheese Roll Ups**

Ingredients:

- 1 loaf (16 ounces) thinly sliced white bread, crusts removed
- 1 package (8 ounces) cream cheese, softened
- 1 egg yolk
-
  3/4 cup confectioners' sugar
- 1 cup sugar
- 1-1/2 teaspoon ground cinnamon
- 3/4 cup butter, melted

Direction: Serving: 16 rollups. | Prep: 10mins | Cook: 20mins |

- ✓ Use a rolling pin to flatten bread.
- ✓ Mix confectioners' sugar, egg yolk and cream cheese in a bowl.
- ✓ Mix cinnamon and sugar in another bowl; put aside.
- ✓ On each bread's slice, spread 1 tablespoon cheese mixture.
- ✓ Roll up like a jellyroll. Dip into melted butter, then into cinnamon-sugar.
- ✓ Put on ungreased baking sheet.
- ✓ Bake for 20 minutes till golden brown at 350°.

243) **Cinnamon Chocolate Chip Rolls**

Ingredients:

- 4 packages (1/4 ounce each) active dry yeast
- 2-1/2 cups warm water (110° to 115°)
- 3 cups warm 2% milk (110° to 115°)
- 1/2 cup butter, softened
- 2 large eggs
- 3/4 cup honey
- 4 teaspoons salt
- 14 cups all-purpose flour
FILLING:

- 6 tablespoons butter, softened
- 2-1/4 cups packed brown sugar
- 1 package (12 ounces) miniature semisweet chocolate chips
- 3 teaspoons ground cinnamon

GLAZE:

- 3 cups confectioners' sugar
- 6 tablespoons butter, softened
- 1 teaspoon vanilla extract
- 6 to 8 tablespoons milk

Direction: Serving: 4 dozen. | Prep: 45mins | Cook: 25mins |

- ✓ In a large basin, mix the yeast and warm water and let it sit for 5 minutes.
- ✓ Slowly add 3 cups of flour and salt; mix on low speed for 3 minutes.
- ✓ To get a soft dough, add in enough of the remaining flour.
- ✓ Knead for 6-8 minutes, until elastic and smooth, on a floured surface.
- ✓ Turn once in a big, well-greased basin. Cover.
- ✓ In a warm environment, allow the dough to rise for an hour until it has doubled in size. Knead the dough.
- ✓ On a floured surface, knead the dough into a 14x8-inch rectangle and split into four equal pieces.
- ✓ On top of that, put some butter on there.
- ✓ Mix cinnamon, chips, and brown sugar into a paste.
- ✓ Sprinkle the dough over the edges, then press it into the dough.
- ✓ Pinch the seam to create a tight seal.
- ✓ Slice each one into 12 pieces.
- ✓ Put four 13x9-inch oiled baking plates, cut side down, in the oven for about an hour and 15 minutes.
- ✓ Cover. Double in size after 30 minutes of rising.
- ✓ Using a 350°F oven, bake for about 25-30 minutes, until the bread is golden brown.
- ✓ Cool for five minutes.
- ✓ Use a wire rack or a pan to transfer the food.
- ✓ Add enough milk to produce the appropriate consistency to a large bowl and mix well.
- ✓ Drizzle heated rolls with sauce.

244) *Cinnamon Crescent Rolls*

Ingredients:

- 6-1/2 to 7 cups all-purpose flour
- 2 packages (1/4 ounce each) active dry yeast
- 2 tablespoons sugar
- 1 teaspoon salt
- 1 cup butter, cubed
- 1 can (12 ounces) evaporated milk
- 1/2 cup shortening
- 1/4 cup water
- 3 egg yolks

FILLING:

- 1/2 cup sugar
- 1-1/2 teaspoons ground cinnamon
- 1/2 cup butter, softened, divided

GLAZE:

- 2 cups confectioners' sugar
- 3 to 4 tablespoons milk
- 1/2 teaspoon vanilla extract
- 2 tablespoons sugar
- 1/2 teaspoon ground cinnamon

Direction: Serving: 4 dozen. | Prep: 50mins | Cook: 15mins |

- ✓ Mix salt, sugar, yeast and 3 cups flour in a big bowl.
- ✓ Heat water, shortening, milk and butter to 120-130°F in a big saucepan. Just mix till it's a little wet.
- ✓ Add the egg yolks and continue to beat until the mixture is completely smooth.
- ✓ A soft, sticky dough can be formed by adding in enough of the remaining flour.
- ✓ Knead for 6-8 minutes, until elastic and smooth, on a floured surface.
- ✓ Gently turn the bowl gently to coat its surface with oil.
- ✓ Cover in a warm environment, allow the dough to rise for an hour until it has doubled in size.
- ✓ Set aside a small bowl of cinnamon and sugar. Punch down dough.
- ✓ Turn on lightly floured surface; knead 6 times.
- ✓ Divide the dough to 4 portions.
- ✓ Roll a portion to 12-in. circle. Spread 2 tbsp. butter.
- ✓ Sprinkle 2 tbsp. cinnamon-sugar.
- ✓ Slice to 12 wedges.
- ✓ From wide end, roll up each and put on ungreased baking sheets, 3-in. apart and point side down.
- ✓ Form crescents to curve ends. Repeat with leftover cinnamon- sugar, butter and dough.
- ✓ Cover and rise for 45 minutes' till doubled in size. Bake for 15-20 minutes till lightly browned at 350°F.
- ✓ Transfer to wire racks.
- ✓ Mix vanilla, milk and confectioners' sugar; drizzle on warm rolls.
- ✓ Mix cinnamon and sugar; sprinkle on rolls.

245) *Cinnamon Hot Cross Buns*

Ingredients:

- 2 packages (1/4 ounce each) active dry yeast
- 1/4 cup warm water (110° to 115°)
- 1 cup warm 2% milk (110° to 115°)
- 1/2 cup sugar
- 1/4 cup shortening
- 2 eggs
- 2 teaspoons salt
- 1 teaspoon ground cinnamon
- 1/4 teaspoon ground allspice
- 4-1/2 to 5 cups all-purpose flour

- 1 cup dried currants
- 1 egg white, lightly beaten

ICING:

- 1-3/4 cups confectioners' sugar
- 1/2 teaspoon vanilla extract
- 4 to 6 teaspoons 2% milk

Direction: Serving: 2 dozen. | Prep: 40mins | Cook: 15mins |

- ✓ Make sure to mix until it's a bit wet.
- ✓ Add the egg yolks and keep beating until the mixture is smooth.
- ✓ The remaining flour can be used to produce a soft, sticky dough.
- ✓ On a floured surface, knead for 6-8 minutes or until elastic and smooth.
- ✓ Pour some oil into the bowl and gently spin it around to coat the inside and outside surfaces.
- ✓ Cover to double in size, let the dough rise for an hour in a warm place.
- ✓ Set aside a tiny amount of cinnamon and sugar for later use.
- ✓ Transfer from pans on wire racks; cool.
- ✓ ICING:
- ✓ Mix vanilla, sugar and enough milk to get piping consistency.
- ✓ On each bun's top, pipe a cross

246) Cinnamon Potato Rolls

Ingredients:

- 3/4 cup sugar
- 3/4 cup hot mashed potatoes
- 1-1/2 cups warm water (110° to 115°)
- 2 packages (1/4 ounce each) active dry yeast
- 1/2 cup butter, softened
- 2 large eggs
- 2 teaspoons salt
- 6-1/2 cups all-purpose flour

FILLING:

- 1-1/3 cups packed brown sugar
- 1/2 teaspoon ground cinnamon
- 3 tablespoons heavy whipping cream
- 3 tablespoons butter, softened
- Vanilla icing, optional

Direction: Serving: 1-1/2 dozen. | Prep: 25mins | Cook: 35mins |

- ✓ Mix mashed potatoes and sugar in big bowl.
- ✓ Add yeast and water; stir well.
- ✓ Cover to rise for 1 hour in warm place.
- ✓ Meanwhile, mix filling ingredients; put aside.
- ✓ Mix dough down; beat salt, eggs and butter in.
- ✓ Mix flour in slowly.
- ✓ Turn out on lightly floured surface; knead for 6-8 minutes till elastic and smooth.
- ✓ Halve dough.
- ✓ Roll each piece to 12- in. square on floured surface.

- ✓ Within 1-in. of edges, spread filling on each square.
- ✓ Roll up like a jellyroll. Cut every roll to 9 slices.
- ✓ In each of two 9-in. greased square baking pans, put 9 rolls.
- ✓ Cover to rise for an hour in a warm environment to double in size. 35-40 minutes, or until golden brown at 350°, is the recommended baking time.
- ✓ If desired, drizzle with icing.

247) Cinnamon Roll Bunnies

Ingredients:

- 1 (16 ounce) package cinnamon roll dough with glaze (such as Immaculate®)
- 5 raisins

Direction: Serving: 5 | Prep: 15mins | Cook: 15mins |

- ✓ Preheat an oven to 175°C/350°F.
- ✓ Line parchment paper on baking sheet.
- ✓ Unroll 1 cinnamon roll dough; halve.
- ✓ Roll 1 half to make "body".
- ✓ Rotate roll so outer roll end is facing down.
- ✓ This makes the bunny's "front legs".
- ✓ Cut 1/3 of leftover dough off; roll up to make "tail".
- ✓ Roll last 2/3 of dough up to halfway point to make "head".
- ✓ Cut through leftover unrolled portion; fan pieces out to make "ears".
- ✓ Rub away cinnamon coating, wet dough then presses pieces together to attach the "head" and "tail" to the "body".
- ✓ Spread "ears" out, pinch them at tips to shape.
- ✓ Repeat using leftover rolls.
- ✓ Put "bunnies" on prepped baking sheet by lifting with scraper/spatula carefully.
- ✓ In preheated oven, bake for 15-18 minutes till golden brown.
- ✓ With "bunnies", slide parchment paper on rack; slightly cool.
- ✓ Spread glaze on warm "bunnies".
- ✓ Follow pattern of "ears" and swirls. Press raisins in middle of swirl on "head" to make "eyes".

248) Cinnamon Roll Coffee Cake

Ingredients:

- 1 pkg. (8 oz.) PHILADELPHIA Cream Cheese, softened
- 1 tsp. ground cinnamon
- 1 egg, separated
- 3/4 cup powdered sugar, divided
- 3/4 tsp. vanilla, divided
- 1 can (8 oz.) refrigerated crescent dinner rolls
- 2 tsp. milk
- 2 Tbsp. chopped PLANTERS Pecans, toasted

Direction: Serving: 8 servings | Prep: 15mins | Cook: |

- ✓ Mix 1/4 cup sugar, egg yolk, cinnamon, and cream cheese together until smooth.

- Unroll the crescent dough and place it in the middle of the baking pan.
- Seal the perforations and seams by pressing them together with your fingers. In 3- in. wide lengthwise strip down middle of dough, spread cream mixture within 1/4-in. of the short ends.
- Down both long dough's sides, make cuts, 1 1/2-in. apart, to within 1/2-in. cream cheese mixture.
- Starting at the short end of the opposite dough strip, bring the strips together over the filing.
- Gently twist in the center to hold. Brush the dough with whipped egg whites.
- Afterwards, allow to cool for 15 minutes before slicing.
- Drizzle over coffee cake after remaining vanilla, sugar, and milk have been combined.
- Mix in a few nuts.

249) Cinnamon Roll Cream Cheese Coffee Cake

Ingredients:

- 1/2 cup butter, softened
- 1 cup sugar
- 1 large egg
- 2 teaspoons vanilla extract
- 2-1/4 cups all-purpose flour
- 2 teaspoons baking powder
- 1 teaspoon ground cinnamon
- 1/2 teaspoon salt
- 3/4 cup 2% milk

CHEESECAKE FILLING:

- 2 packages (8 ounces each) cream cheese, softened
- 1/2 cup sugar 2 tablespoons all-purpose flour
- 3 teaspoons vanilla extract
- 2 large eggs, lightly beaten

CINNAMON FILLING:

- 1 cup packed brown sugar
- 1/3 cup butter, melted
- 2 tablespoons ground cinnamon

Direction: Serving: 16 servings. | Prep: 35mins | Cook: 01hours10mins |

- Set the oven temperature to 350 °F.
- To make a fluffy frosting, combine the sugar and the butter.
- Add vanilla and an egg and mix thoroughly.
- In another bowl, combine the salt, cinnamon, baking powder, and flour.
- When adding, alternate the milk with the flour and beat vigorously after each addition.
- In a 9-in. greased spring form pan, spread 3/4 of batter (it'll be thick). Put aside leftover batter.
- Beat flour, sugar and cream cheese till smooth in another bowl.
- Beat vanilla in.
- Add eggs.

- Beat till just combined on low speed.
- Put on batter.
- Stir cinnamon filling ingredients.
- By tablespoonful's, drop on cream cheese mixture.
- Use a knife to cut through cream cheese filing to swirl cinnamon filling.
- By tablespoonful's, drop reserved batter on filling.
- Put pan on the baking sheet. Bake for 70-80 minutes till center is nearly set.
- Loosely cover top with foil at final 30 minutes to avoid overbrowning if needed.
- Cool on a wire rack for ten minutes before serving.
- Run a knife around pan's edges carefully to loosen.
- Cool for 1 hour then remove pan sides.
- Serve warm and refrigerate leftovers.

250) Cinnamon Rolls In A Snap

Ingredients:

- 4-1/2 cups biscuit/baking mix
- 1-1/3 cups milk

FILLING:

- 2 tablespoons butter, softened
- 1/4 cup sugar
- 1 teaspoon ground cinnamon
- 1/3 cup raisins, optional

ICING:

- 2 cups confectioners' sugar
- 2 tablespoons milk
- 2 tablespoons butter, melted
- 1 teaspoon vanilla extract

Direction: Serving: 1 dozen. | Prep: 10mins | Cook: 10mins |

- Mix milk and biscuit mix in a big bowl; turn on floured surface then knead 8-10 minutes.
- Roll dough to 12x10-in. rectangle.
- Spread butter on.
- Mix raisins (optional), cinnamon and sugar; sprinkle on butter.
- From long side, roll up; pinch the seam to seal.
- Slice to 12 slices.
- Put on big baking sheet, cut side down.
- Bake for 10-12 minutes till golden brown at 450°.
- Meanwhile, mixing icing ingredients.
- Spread on warm rolls; serve while warm.

251) Cinnamon Sticky Bun Ice Cream

Ingredients:

- 1-3/4 cups whole milk
- 2/3 cup plus 2 cups sugar, divided
- 2 eggs, beaten
- 3 cups heavy whipping cream, divided
- 2 teaspoons ground cinnamon
- 1 teaspoon vanilla extract

- 1 cup butter, cubed
- 1/2 cup water
- 1 tablespoon corn syrup
- 2 baked cinnamon buns, cubed
- 9 tablespoons chopped pecans, toasted

Direction: Serving: 2-1/4 quarts. | Prep: 35mins | Cook: 25mins |

- ✓ Heat 2/3 cup sugar and milk till bubbles form around pan sides in big heavy saucepan.
- ✓ Whisk small amount of hot mixture in eggs; put all into pan, constantly whisking.
- ✓ Stir and cook on low heat till mixture coats back of spoon and reaches 160°F minimum.
- ✓ Take off heat. Transfer to bowl quickly.
- ✓ Put ice water in; mix for 2 minutes. Mix vanilla, cinnamon and 2 cups cream in.
- ✓ On custard surface, press waxed paper.
- ✓ Refrigerate for a few hours to overnight.
- ✓ Caramel: Mix corn syrup, water and butter in heavy saucepan.
- ✓ Stir and cook till butter melts on medium low heat.
- ✓ Add leftover sugar; stir and cook till sugar melts.
- ✓ Bring to a boil on medium heat without stirring then boil, don't stir, for 4 minutes.
- ✓ Continue to boil, constantly mixing, for 12-15 minutes till mixture is caramel-colored.
- ✓ Take off heat.
- ✓ Mix leftover cream in carefully till smooth; put aside. Cool.
- ✓ Fill ice cream freezer cylinder to 2/3 full.
- ✓ Follow manufacturer's directions to freeze.
- ✓ Refrigerate leftover mixture till freezing time.
- ✓ Layer 3 tbsp. pecans, 2/3 cup cinnamon buns, 1/2 cup caramel and layer 1/3 of ice cream in a big freezer container.
- ✓ Repeat twice.
- ✓ Swirl mixture; freeze till firm.
- ✓ Serve with leftover caramel

252) **Cinnamon Tea Rolls**

Ingredients:

- 1 tube (4 ounces) refrigerated crescent rolls
- 1 tablespoon sugar
- 1/8 teaspoon ground cinnamon
- 1/4 cup confectioners' sugar
- 1-1/4 teaspoons orange juice

Direction: Serving: 4 rolls. | Prep: 10mins | Cook: 10mins |

- ✓ Unroll crescent dough to a rectangle; seal perforations.
- ✓ Mix cinnamon and sugar; sprinkle on roll.
- ✓ Roll up, starting with short side, jellyroll style.
- ✓ To seal, pinch seam. Cut to 4 slices with a serrated knife.
- ✓ Put rolls in ungreased muffin cups, pinched side down.

- ✓ Bake for 10-12 minutes or till golden brown at 375°.
- ✓ Before transferring from pan to wire rack, cool for 5 minutes.
- ✓ Mix orange juice and confectioners' sugar in small bowl.
- ✓ Drizzle on rolls.

253) **Cinnamon Walnut Sticky Buns**

Ingredients:

- 2 packages (1/4 ounce each) active dry yeast
- 1-1/2 cups warm water (110° to 115°)
- 1 cup mashed potatoes (without added milk and butter)
- 1/2 cup sugar
- 1/2 cup butter, softened
- 2 large eggs
- 2 teaspoons salt
- 6 to 6-1/2 cups all-purpose flour

TOPPING:

- 1/4 cup butter
- 1 cup packed brown sugar
- 1 cup honey
- 1 teaspoon ground cinnamon
- 1 cup chopped walnuts

FILLING:

- 1/2 cup sugar
- 2 teaspoons ground cinnamon
- 2 tablespoons butter, melted

Direction: Serving: 2 dozen. | Prep: 60mins | Cook: 30mins |

- ✓ In a small dish, combine yeast and warm water and stir until dissolved.
- ✓ Gather all of the ingredients for the huge bowl and mix them together: 2 cups of flour; yeast mixture; salt, eggs, butter, sugar, and potatoes.
- ✓ Beat at a medium-low speed until the mixture is homogeneous.
- ✓ To produce a soft dough, add enough of the remaining flour.
- ✓ Using a floured surface, roll out the dough and knead it for 6 to 8 minutes, until it's elastic and supple.
- ✓ Gently turn the bowl gently to coat its surface with oil.
- ✓ Wrap the area in plastic wrap.
- ✓ Do not let it go to sleep for more than one hour.
- ✓ Topping: melt butter in small saucepan.
- ✓ Mix cinnamon, honey and brown sugar in. Divide mixture to 3 9-in. greased round baking pans, evenly spreading.
- ✓ Sprinkle walnuts on.
- ✓ Filling: mix cinnamon and sugar in a small bowl.
- ✓ Punch dough down. Turn on lightly floured surface; halve.
- ✓ Roll a portion to 18x12-in. rectangle. Within 1/2-in. of edges, brush 1 tbsp. melted butter Sprinkle 1/4 cup sugar mixture on.

- ✓ Starting from the long side, jellyroll-style, roll up the jellyroll-like shape.
- ✓ Pinch the seam to create a tight seal. Slice into twelve pieces.
- ✓ Repeat with leftover sugar mixture, butter and dough.
- ✓ In each pan, put 8 slices, cut side down. Use kitchen towels to cover.
- ✓ Rise for 30 minutes' till doubled.
- ✓ Preheat an oven to 350°F.
- ✓ Bake till golden brown for 30-35 minutes.
- ✓ Invert on serving plates immediately.
- ✓ Serve warm.

254) Cloverleaf Bran Rolls

Ingredients:

- 1 cup All-Bran
- 1 cup boiling water
- 2 packages (1/4 ounce each) active dry yeast
- 1 cup warm water (110° to 115°)
- 1 cup shortening
- 3/4 cup sugar
- 1 teaspoon salt
- 2 eggs, beaten
- 6 cups all-purpose flour

Direction: Serving: 2 dozen. | Prep: 40mins | Cook: 15mins |

- ✓ Combine boiling water and bran in a small bowl. Put aside.
- ✓ Dissolve the yeast in another bowl of warm water.
- ✓ Cream salt, sugar and shortening in large bowl.
- ✓ Put in yeast mixture and eggs; mix well.
- ✓ Put in 2 cups of flour and bran mixture; beat well.
- ✓ Make a soft dough by gradually adding enough remaining flour.
- ✓ Using a lightly floured surface, roll out the dough and knead it for 6 to 8 minutes, or until it is smooth and elastic.
- ✓ Coat the basin's surface with a thin layer of oil before turning.
- ✓ Allow to rise with a cover for 1 hour, until doubled.
- ✓ Punch the dough down.
- ✓ Turn onto the lightly floured surface.
- ✓ Separate into 6 portions; separate each into twelve pieces.
- ✓ Form each into ball; arrange 3 balls in each oiled muffin cups.
- ✓ Allow to rise with a cover until doubled, about 60 mins. Bake at 350°, until browned lightly, about 15 to 18 mins.
- ✓ Discard from the pans to the wire racks.

255) Cloverleaf Rolls

Ingredients:

- 3 tablespoons warm water (105–115°F)
- 1 (1/4-ounce) package active dry yeast (2 1/2 teaspoons)
- 3 tablespoons sugar
- 1 stick (1/2 cup) unsalted butter
- 1 cup whole milk
- 2 cups bread flour
- 1 1/2 teaspoons salt
- 1 1/2 to 2 cups all-purpose flour
- 1 large egg, lightly beaten with 2 teaspoons water
- About 1 tablespoon poppy seeds and/or toasted sesame seeds for sprinkling
- 2 muffin pans with a total of at least 18 (1/2-cup) muffin cups

Direction: Serving: Makes 18 rolls | Prep: | Cook: |

- ✓ Making the dough: in a small bowl, mix together one tablespoon sugar, yeast, and warm water until the yeast has dissolved.
- ✓ Allow to sit for about 5 minutes until foamy. (In case the mixture does not foam, get rid of it and start all over again with fresh yeast).
- ✓ In a small saucepan, melt 3/4 stick of butter, then pour in milk and heat to lukewarm.
- ✓ Use a wooden spoon to mix together salt, bread flour, butter mixture, remaining 2 tablespoons sugar and yeast mixture in a bowl until mixed well.
- ✓ Mix in about 1 1/2 cups all-purpose of flour or enough to form a slightly sticky dough.
- ✓ Butter a big bowl.
- ✓ Knead the dough onto a surface that is lightly floured for about 10 minutes and knead in more all-purpose flour if necessary to prevent the dough from sticking, until elastic and smooth (the dough should be slightly sticky).
- ✓ Shape the dough into a ball and place in the buttered bowl, flipping to coat.
- ✓ Allow the dough to rise with the bowl tightly covered with plastic wrap for about an hour in a draft-free place at warm room temperature until doubled in bulk.
- ✓ Making the rolls: Butter 18 muffin cups using leftover two tablespoons of butter.
- ✓ Turn out the dough onto a surface that is lightly floured and separate it into thirds.
- ✓ Working with one piece at a time (keep the leftover portions covered in plastic wrap), cut off tablespoon pieces of dough, and shape the pieces into balls.
- ✓ Place three balls into every buttered muffin cup.
- ✓ Allow the rolls to rise while covered loosely with kitchen towel (not terry cloth), for about 30 to 40 minutes at warm room temperature, in draft-free place until nearly doubled in bulk.
- ✓ As the rolls rise, place the oven rack in the center position and then preheat an oven to 400°F.
- ✓ Brush egg wash over the rolls lightly and top with seeds.
- ✓ Bake for 15 to 20 minutes until golden.
- ✓ Serve while still warm.
- ✓ Note: Rolls can be baked before 1 day and completely cooled, kept at room temperature while wrapped

well in foil.

- ✓ Preheat an oven to 350°F and then reheat it in foil in the oven for 15 to 20 minutes.

256) **Basil Dinner Rolls**

Ingredients:

- 1 package (1/4 ounce) active dry yeast
- 2-1/2 cups warm water (120° to 130°)
- 1 tablespoon sugar
- 2 teaspoons salt
- 7 to 7-1/2 cups all- purpose flour
- 1 cup chopped fresh basil
- 1/4 cup finely chopped walnuts
- 1/4 cup grated Parmesan cheese
- Melted butter

Direction: Serving: 32 rolls. | Prep: 30mins | Cook: 25mins |

- ✓ In a large basin, whisk together the yeast and warm water until it is completely dissolved.
- ✓ In a bowl, mix together 6 cups of flour, salt, and sugar.
- ✓ Mix in enough of the remaining flour to form a soft dough.
- ✓ It should be elastic and smooth when it is kneaded for around 6 to 8 minutes on a floured surface.
- ✓ To butter the top, place it in a greased basin and flip it over once to distribute the grease evenly throughout.
- ✓ Refrigerate overnight with the lid on.
- ✓ Make sure to knead the dough multiple times.
- ✓ Allow it to rest for 10 minutes before putting the cover on.
- ✓ In the meantime, combine the cheese, walnuts, and basil in a small bowl and set aside 2 tbsp. of the mixture for garnish.
- ✓ Make 32 balls out of the dough.
- ✓ Using a floured surface, flatten each ball into a 4-inch circle.
- ✓ Then, place 16 rolls on each of the two greased baking pans.
- ✓ Allow it to double in size for about 45 minutes under a cover.
- ✓ Sprinkle the remaining basil mixture on top of the toasted bread.
- ✓ Bake at 375 degrees Fahrenheit for 25 minutes, or until the crust is golden brown.
- ✓ Serve it at room temperature, if possible.

257) **Bread Machine Dinner Rolls**

Ingredients:

- 1 cup water (70° to 80°)
- 1/4 cup butter, cubed
- 1 egg
- 1-1/4 teaspoons salt
- 3-1/4 cups bread flour

- 1/4 cup sugar
- 3 tablespoons nonfat dry milk powder
- 1 package (1/4 ounce) quick-rise yeast

EGG WASH:

- 1 egg
- 4 teaspoons water

Direction: Serving: 2 dozen. | Prep: 25mins | Cook: 10mins |

- ✓ Put the initial 8 ingredients in a bread machine pan in the order recommended by manufacturer.
- ✓ Choose the dough setting.
- ✓ After 5 minutes of mixing, check the dough, then add 1-2 tbsp. of water or flour if necessary.
- ✓ Once the cycle has been completed, flip the dough onto a surface covered with a thin layer of flour.
- ✓ Split and form into 24 balls.
- ✓ Roll each into an 8-inch rope, then tie into a loose knot.
- ✓ Tuck the ends underneath.
- ✓ Put on greased baking sheets, keeping a 1/2-inch-distance away from each other.
- ✓ Cover using a kitchen towel and allow to rise for about 30 minutes in a warm area until doubled.
- ✓ Set an oven to 400 degrees and begin preheating. To make egg wash, whisk water and egg in a small bowl, then brush on top of the rolls.
- ✓ Bake for 8 to 9 minutes or until golden brown.
- ✓ Take out of the pans, then transfer to wire racks.
- ✓ Serve warm.

258) **Buttery Whole Wheat Dinner Rolls**

Ingredients:

- 1 tablespoon active dry yeast
- 3/4 cup warm water (110° to 115°)
- 1/3 cup sugar
- 1/3 cup nonfat dry milk powder
- 4 tablespoons butter, softened, divided
- 1 egg
- 1 teaspoon salt
- 2 cups whole wheat flour
- 1/2 to 1 cup bread flour

Direction: Serving: 16 rolls. | Prep: 30mins | Cook: 10mins |

- ✓ In a small dish, mix yeast and warm water and stir until dissolved.
- ✓ Toast 2 tablespoons of butter in a large skillet over medium heat; add milk powder and sugar; stir until blended.
- ✓ Use bread flour to create a soft, sticky dough.
- ✓ Knead for 6-8 minutes, until elastic and smooth, on a floured surface.
- ✓ Then, cover the bowl with a lid and turn it over once to coat the top.
- ✓ Rise in a warm location for an hour till doubled.
- ✓ Make use of the remaining butter by heating it in a

microwave-safe bowl.

- ✓ Using a lightly floured surface, roll out the dough and cut it into 16 equal pieces.
- ✓ Using a rolling pin, roll each into a ball.
- ✓ Disperse evenly over prepared baking sheets, with a 2-inch spacing between each. 30 minutes later, the dough will have doubled in size.
- ✓ Bake at 375° for 8-10 minutes, or until golden brown.
- ✓ Place wire racks below the prepared pans.

259) Cornmeal Dinner Rolls
Ingredients:

- 2 cups whole milk
- 1/2 cup sugar
- 1/2 cup butter, cubed
- 1/3 cup cornmeal
- 1-1/4 teaspoons salt
- 1 package (1/4 ounce) active dry yeast
- 1/4 cup warm water (110° to 115°)
- 2 large eggs
- 4-3/4 to 5-3/4 cups all-purpose flour

TOPPING:

- 2 tablespoons butter, melted
- 1 tablespoon cornmeal
  Direction: Serving: 2-1/2 dozen. | Prep: 35mins | Cook: 15mins |

- ✓ Mix salt, cornmeal, butter, sugar, and milk together in a large saucepan.
- ✓ Bring to a boiling over medium heat, stirring frequently.
- ✓ Lower the heat.
- ✓ Cook, stirring, for 5 to 8 minutes until thickened.
- ✓ Allow to cool to 110° to 115°.
- ✓ Dissolve yeast in a small bowl of warm water.
- ✓ Combine 2 cups of flour, yeast mixture, cornmeal mixture, and eggs in a large bowl; beat until no lumps remain.
- ✓ To produce a smooth, elastic dough, gradually add in the remaining flour.
- ✓ Dough is ready to be kneaded when it's elastic and smooth, so transfer it to a floured work area.
- ✓ Lay dough in a greased bowl, flipping once to grease the top.
- ✓ Use plastic wrap to cover dough; allow to rise for approximately 60 minutes in a warm spot until dough is twice the size.
- ✓ Punch dough down.
- ✓ Transfer to a work surface lightly coated with flour.
- ✓ Cut dough into 30 balls.
- ✓ Arrange them 2 inches apart on oiled baking sheets.
- ✓ Place a clean kitchen towel over dough to cover; allow to rise for about 45 minutes in a warm spot until dough is twice the size.
- ✓ Remove covers; brush dough with melted butter and scatter with cornmeal.

- ✓ Bake for 13 to 17 minutes at 375° until golden brown.
- ✓ Transfer from pans to wire racks;
- ✓ serve warm

260) Dilly Onion Dinner Rolls
Ingredients:

- 1 package (1/4 ounce) active dry yeast
- 1/4 cup warm water (110° to 115°)
- 1 cup (8 ounces) 4% cottage cheese
- 1 large egg
- 2 tablespoons sugar
- 2 tablespoons dried minced onion
- 3 tablespoons butter, softened, divided
- 3 teaspoons dill seed, divided
- 1 teaspoon salt
- 2-1/4 to 2-1/2 cups all-purpose flour
  Direction: Serving: 1 dozen. | Prep: 30mins | Cook: 15mins |

- ✓ Dissolve yeast in warm water in a big bowl. Heat cottage cheese in a small saucepan to 110-115 degrees.
- ✓ Add 1 cup flour, salt, 2 tsp dill seed, 1 tbsp butter, onion, sugar, egg and cottage cheese into the yeast mixture and beat until thoroughly smoothened.
- ✓ Add enough remaining flour to make a stiff dough.
- ✓ Turn onto a floured surface and knead for 6–8 minutes, or until smooth and flexible.
- ✓ Place in a greased mixing bowl, flipping once to grease the top.
- ✓ Allow to rise for about one hour in a warm environment until it has doubled in size.
- ✓ Punch down the dough.
- ✓ Flip over onto a surface covered with a thin layer of flour, then split the dough in half.
- ✓ Roll each part into a 14x6-inch rectangle, then spread 1 tbsp. butter over.
- ✓ Score the dough widthwise at 2-inch intervals using the dull edge of a table knife.
- ✓ Make score marks widthwise across the dough using those marks as a guide.
- ✓ Fold the dough back and forth, accordion-style, along the creased lines.
- ✓ Slice folded dough into 1- inch pieces.
- ✓ Put each piece in a greased muffin cup, cut side down.
- ✓ Melt the leftover butter, then brush on top of the dough.
- ✓ Sprinkle the leftover dill seed on top.
- ✓ Cover and leave to rise for approximately 30 minutes, or until doubled.
- ✓ Bake at 375 degrees for 15 to 17 minutes, or until golden brown.
- ✓ Take out of the pan, then transfer to a wire rack.

261) *Dove Dinner Rolls*

Ingredients:

- 2 cups whole wheat pastry flour
- 1/2 cup sugar
- 3 packages (1/4 ounce each) active dry yeast
- 2 teaspoons salt
- 1 cup water
- 1 cup 2% milk
- 1/2 cup butter, cubed
- 1 large egg
- 4 to 4-1/2 cups bread flour

ASSEMBLY:

- 48 dried currants
- 24 slivered almonds
- 1 large egg
- 2 tablespoons 2% milk

Direction: Serving: 2 dozen. | Prep: 50mins | Cook: 10mins |

- ✓ Combine salt, yeast, sugar and pastry flour in a big bowl.
- ✓ Heat butter, milk and water in small saucepan to 120° to 130°.
- ✓ Put to the dry ingredients; beat for a minute on moderate speed.
- ✓ Put in egg; beat for 2 minutes on high.
- ✓ Mix in sufficient bread flour to make a soft dough; dough will become sticky.
- ✓ Knead for 6–8 minutes, until flexible and smooth, on a floured surface.
- ✓ Place in an oiled bowl and flip once to coat the surface with oil.
- ✓ Cover and set aside for 45 minutes to double in size in a warm location.
- ✓ Deflate dough.
- ✓ Rest for 15 minutes with cover.
- ✓ Transfer to a slightly floured area; split and form into 2 dozen rounds.
- ✓ Roll every round into a rope, 10-inch in length; tie to make one loose knot.
- ✓ Put an end up and tuck into the middle of roll to make a head.
- ✓ Flatten opposing end; make 4 slash using sharp knife to create 5 tail feathers.
- ✓ For the eyes, force 2 currants into the head and an almond for the beak.
- ✓ Put on oiled baking sheets, 2-inch away.
- ✓ Put kitchen towels to cover; allow to rise in a warm area till doubled in size, for half an hour.
- ✓ Preheat the oven to 400°.
- ✓ Beat milk and egg in small bowl; brush on top of rolls.
- ✓ Bake till golden brown, for 10 to 12 minutes.
- ✓ Transfer from the pans onto the wire racks; serve while warm.

262) *Grandma's Rosemary Dinner Rolls*

Ingredients:

- 1 package (1/4 ounce) active dry yeast
- 1/4 cup warm water (110° to 115°)
- 3 cups bread flour
- 2 tablespoons sugar
- 1 tablespoon minced fresh rosemary, divided
- 3/4 teaspoon salt
- 2/3 cup warm 2% milk (110° to 115°)
- 1 large egg
- 1/4 to 1/3 cup canola oil

EGG WASH:

- 1 large egg yolk
- 2 tablespoons 2% milk

Direction: Serving: 1 dozen. | Prep: 35mins | Cook: 20mins |

- ✓ Dissolve the yeast in warm water in a small bowl. In a food processor, put the salt, 2 tsp rosemary, sugar and flour, then pulse it until combined.
- ✓ Add the yeast mixture, egg and warm milk, put cover and pulse for 10 times or until it almost combined.
- ✓ Slowly add oil while processing, just until the dough pulls away from the sides and starts to form a ball.
- ✓ Process it for 2 minutes more to knead the dough (the dough will get very soft).
- ✓ Move the dough to a greased bowl and flip it once to grease the top.
- ✓ Cover with plastic wrap and let it rise in a warm place for approximately an hour, or until it doubles in size.
- ✓ Punch the dough down.
- ✓ Split and form the dough into 12 balls on a lightly floured surface.
- ✓ Make a 15-inch rope out of each.
- ✓ To make a coil, start at one end and loosely wrap the dough around itself.
- ✓ Pinch to seal the end by tucking it under.
- ✓ Place the cookies 2 inches apart on buttered baking pans.
- ✓ Allow it to rise for about 30 minutes, or until it has doubled in size.
- ✓ In a small dish, whisk together the milk and egg yolk, then brush it on top of the rolls.
- ✓ Finish with a sprinkling of the remaining rosemary.
- ✓ Preheat oven to 350°F and bake for 18 to 22 minutes, or until golden brown.
- ✓ Remove it from the pans and place it on wire racks to cool. Warm it up before serving.

263) *Heavenly Dinner Rolls*

Ingredients:

- 2 packages (1/4 ounce each) active dry yeast
- 1/4 cup warm water (110° to 115°)
- 4 cups warm milk (110° to 115°)

- 1 cup sugar
- 1 cup shortening
- 7 to 7-1/2 cups all-purpose flour, divided
- 2 teaspoons baking powder
- 1 teaspoon baking soda
- 1 teaspoon salt Melted
- butter, optional

Direction: Serving: about 5 dozen. | Prep: 20mins | Cook: 10mins |

- ✓ Melt yeast in water in a bowl.
- ✓ Add 4 cups flour, shortening, sugar and milk; beat till smooth.
- ✓ Cover; rise for 2 hours in a warm place.
- ✓ Add salt, baking soda, baking powder and enough leftover flour to make a slightly sticky, soft dough; cover.
- ✓ Refrigerate till needed.
- ✓ Turn onto a heavily floured surface then pat it to 1/2-in. thick.
- ✓ Use a biscuit cutter to cut/drop onto a greased baking sheets by 1/4 cupful.
- ✓ Cover; rise for 30 minutes till nearly doubled.
- ✓ Bake for 10-15 minutes at 350° till lightly browned.
- ✓ If desired, brush butter on tops; you can refrigerate the dough for up to 3 days.
- ✓ Each day, punch down

264) Herb Dinner Rolls

Ingredients:

- 1 package (1/4 ounce) active dry yeast
- 1/4 cup warm water (110° to 115°)
- 3/4 cup warm milk (110° to 115°)
- 2 tablespoons sugar
- 2 tablespoons shortening
- 1 egg, beaten
- 2 teaspoons celery seed
- 1 teaspoon rubbed sage
- 1 teaspoon salt
- 1/2 teaspoon ground nutmeg
- 3 to 3-1/2 cups all-purpose flour
- Melted butter

Direction: Serving: 2-1/2 dozen. | Prep: 35mins | Cook: 10mins |

- ✓ In water, dissolve the yeast in a bowl.
- ✓ Put in 3 cups flour, nutmeg, salt, sage, celery seed, egg, shortening, sugar and milk; beat till smooth.
- ✓ Add enough residual flour to form a soft dough.
- ✓ Transfer to a floured surface and knead for 6 to 8 minutes, or until smooth and malleable.
- ✓ Place in an oiled basin, flipping once to coat the surface with oil.
- ✓ Cover and allow to double in size for 90 minutes in a warm environment.
- ✓ Allow dough to deflate for 10 minutes.
- ✓ Form into 30 rounds; put on oiled baking sheets.

- ✓ Put on cover and allow to rise for 45 minutes' till doubled in size.
- ✓ Brush butter on tops.
- ✓ Bake till slightly browned, or about 10 to 12 minutes at 375°.
- ✓ Let cool on the wire racks.

265) Herbed Dinner Rolls

Ingredients:

- 1 cup water (70° to 80°)
- 2 tablespoons butter, softened
- 1 large egg
- 1/4 cup sugar
- 1 teaspoon salt
- 1/2 teaspoon each dried basil, oregano, thyme and rosemary, crushed
- 3-1/4 cups bread flour
- 2-1/4 teaspoons active dry yeast
- Additional butter, melted
- Coarse salt, optional

Direction: Serving: 16 rolls. | Prep: 20mins | Cook: 15mins |

- ✓ Put the water, butter, egg, sugar, salt, seasonings, flour and yeast respectively in the bread machine as recommended by manufacturer.
- ✓ Use the dough setting (after five minutes of mixing, check the dough and add one to two tablespoons of flour or water if necessary).
- ✓ Once the cycle has ended, turn the dough onto a surface that is lightly floured.
- ✓ Separate the dough into 16 portions and then shape each portion to form a ball.
- ✓ Transfer onto greased baking sheets placing two inches apart.
- ✓ Cover the dough and leave them to rise in a warm place for about half an hour until doubled.
- ✓ Bake for about 12 to 15 minutes at 375 degrees F or until turned golden brown.
- ✓ Brush with butter and then sprinkle with coarse salt if you preferred.
- ✓ Transfer from the pans to wire racks to cool.

266) Honey Squash Dinner Rolls

Ingredients:

- 2 packages (1/4 ounce each) active dry yeast
- 2 teaspoons salt
- 1/4 teaspoon ground nutmeg
- 6 to 6-1/2 cups all-purpose flour
- 1-1/4 cups 2% milk
- 1/2 cup butter, cubed
- 1/2 cup honey
- 1 package (12 ounces) frozen mashed winter squash, thawed (about 1-1/3 cups)
- 1 large egg, lightly beaten
- Poppy seeds, salted pumpkin seeds or pepitas, or sesame seeds

- ✓ Combine 3 cups of flour, nutmeg, salt and yeast in a big bowl.
- ✓ Heat honey, butter and milk in small saucepan to 120° to 130°.
- ✓ Put to the dry ingredients; whip for 2 minutes on moderate speed.
- ✓ Put in the squash; mix for 2 minutes on high. Add enough residual flour to form a soft dough; dough will get sticky.
- ✓ Transfer dough to a floured surface and knead for 6–8 minutes, or until smooth and malleable.
- ✓ Place in a lightly oiled bowl, turning once to coat the surface.
- ✓ Put on plastic wrap to cover and allow to rise in a warm area for an hour till doubled in size.
- ✓ Deflate the dough. Transfer to a slightly floured area; split and form into 2 dozen rounds.
- ✓ Distribute between 2 oiled 9-inch round baking pans.
- ✓ Put on kitchen towels to cover; allow to rise in warm area for 45 minutes' till doubled.
- ✓ Preheat the oven to 375°.
- ✓ Brush beaten egg on tops; scatter seeds over.
- ✓ Bake for 20 to 25 minutes till deep golden brown.
- ✓ Loosely cover in foil on the final 5 to 7 minutes if necessary to avoid excessive browning.
- ✓ Transfer from the pans onto the wire racks; serve while warm.

267)   *Lemon Drop Dinner Rolls*

Ingredients:

- 1 loaf (1 pound) frozen white or sweet bread dough, thawed
- 1/4 cup sugar
- 4-1/2 teaspoons grated lemon zest
- 1/8 teaspoon ground nutmeg
- 2 tablespoons butter, melted

Direction: Serving: 1 to 1-1/2 dozen. | Prep: 15mins | Cook: 15mins |

- ✓ Cut the dough into 12 to 18 parts; form into balls.
- ✓ Combine nutmeg, lemon zest and sugar in a small bowl.
- ✓ Dip the rolls' tops into the butter, followed by sugar mixture.
- ✓ Arrange, the sugar side facing up, into oiled muffin cups.
- ✓ On tops of the rolls, make 1/2-inch-deep cross.
- ✓ Allow to rise in warm place with a cover for 90 minutes or until doubled.
- ✓ Bake at 375° until golden brown, about 14 to 16 minutes.
- ✓ Take away from pan immediately; let cool on the wire racks.

268)   *Maple Pumpkin Dinner Rolls*

Ingredients:

- 1/2 cup cornmeal
- 1/4 cup packed brown sugar
- 1 package (1/4 ounce) quick-rise yeast
- 1/2 teaspoon salt
- 1/4 teaspoon pumpkin pie spice
- 2-1/2 to 3 cups all-purpose flour
- 3/4 cup plus 2 tablespoons milk, divided
- 1/4 cup maple syrup
- 4 tablespoons butter, divided
- 3/4 cup canned pumpkin

Direction: Serving: 16 rolls. | Prep: 30mins | Cook: 15mins |

- ✓ Mix 2 cups flour, pie spice, salt, yeast, brown sugar and cornmeal in big bowl.
- ✓ Heat 2 tbsp. butter and 3/4 cup milk in small saucepan to 120-130°; mix into dry ingredients.
- ✓ Combine pumpkin and enough remaining flour to form a sticky, soft dough.
- ✓ Turn dough onto a floured surface and knead for 6-8 minutes, or until elastic and smooth.
- ✓ Cover with plastic wrap and set aside for 10 minutes.
- ✓ Divide and shape dough into 16 balls; divide evenly between two oiled 9-inch round baking pans.
- ✓ Cover with kitchen towels and let stand for 1 hour or till doubled.
- ✓ Preheat an oven to 375°.
- ✓ Brush leftover milk on dough; bake till golden brown, about 12-15 minutes.
- ✓ Melt leftover butter; brush on top of hot rolls.
- ✓ Transfer from pans onto wire racks then serve warm

269)   *Mother's Dinner Rolls*

Ingredients:

- 2 packages (1/4 ounce each) active dry yeast
- 1 cup warm water (110° to 115°)
- 1 cup boiling water
- 1 cup shortening
- 3/4 cup sugar
- 1 teaspoon salt
- 2 large eggs, lightly beaten
- 7-1/2 to 8 cups all-purpose flour

Direction: Serving: 2-1/2 dozen. | Prep: 45mins | Cook: 20mins |

- ✓ Melt yeast in warm water in a small bowl.
- ✓ Meanwhile, mix salt, sugar, shortening and boiling water in a big bowl; stand till sugar dissolves and shortening melts for 3-4 minutes.
- ✓ Add eggs and yeast mixture; stir well.
- ✓ Add the 2 cups flour; beat till smooth.
- ✓ To make a soft dough, add enough leftover flour; don't knead.
- ✓ Put it into greased bowl; to grease top, turn once. Cover; refrigerate overnight.
- ✓ Turn the dough onto floured surface.
- ✓ Shape to 2 1/2-in. ball and roll to 5-in. rope; form to

knot.
- ✓ Repeat with leftover dough.
- ✓ Put onto greased baking sheet; cover.
- ✓ Rise for 30 minutes' till doubled in a warm place.
- ✓ Bake it at 350° till golden brown for 20-25 minutes.

270) at Dinner Rolls

Ingredients:

- 3 cups water, divided
- 1 cup quick-cooking oats
- 2/3 cup packed brown sugar
- 3 tablespoons butter
- 1-1/2 teaspoons salt
- 2 packages (1/4 ounce each) active dry yeast
- 5 to 5-3/4 cups all-purpose flour

Direction: Serving: 2 dozen. | Prep: 30mins | Cook: 20mins |

- ✓ 3 cups flour, 3 eggs, and the yeast mixture until smooth are incorporated into the shortening mixture.
- ✓ Continue adding flour until a soft dough forms. Turn the dough out onto a floured surface and knead for about 6 to 8 minutes, or until smooth and malleable.
- ✓ It should be placed in a greased bowl and turned once to coat the top in grease.
- ✓ Cover and set aside for approximately 45 minutes in a warm setting to double in size.
- ✓ Turn the dough out onto a lightly floured surface. Roll the dough out to a 1/2-inch thickness and cut with a 2-1/2-inch biscuit cutter.
- ✓ Circles should be folded in half and the edges sealed.
- ✓ Arrange it 2 inches apart on baking sheets prepared with cooking spray.
- ✓ Cover and set aside for about 30 minutes, or until the dough has doubled in size.
- ✓ Allow it to bake for 10 to 12 minutes, or until golden brown, at 400 degrees.
- ✓ Transfer to wire racks.
- ✓ It should be served warm and brushed with butter.

271) Parker House Dinner Rolls

Ingredients:

- 1/2 cup shortening
- 1/4 cup sugar
- 2 teaspoons salt
- 1-1/2 cups boiling water
- 2 tablespoons active dry yeast
- 1/2 cup warm water (110° to 115°)
- 3 eggs
- 6-3/4 to 7-1/4 cups all-purpose flour
- 1/4 cup butter, melted

Direction: Serving: 3 dozen. | Prep: 60mins | Cook: 10mins |

- ✓ In a large mixing basin, mix the salt, sugar, and shortening, then add the boiling water.
- ✓ Allow it to cool to a temperature of 110-115 degrees.

In warm water, dissolve the yeast.

- ✓ 3 cups flour, 3 eggs, and the yeast mixture until smooth are incorporated into the shortening mixture.
- ✓ Continue adding flour until a soft dough forms.
- ✓ Turn the dough out onto a floured surface and knead for about 6 to 8 minutes, or until smooth and malleable.
- ✓ It should be placed in a greased bowl and turned once to coat the top in grease.
- ✓ Cover and set aside for approximately 45 minutes in a warm setting to double in size.
- ✓ Turn the dough out onto a lightly floured surface. Roll the dough out to a 1/2-inch thickness and cut with a 2-1/2-inch biscuit cutter.
- ✓ Circles should be folded in half and the edges sealed.
- ✓ Arrange it 2 inches apart on baking sheets prepared with cooking spray.
- ✓ Cover and set aside for about 30 minutes, or until the dough has doubled in size.
- ✓ Allow it to bake for 10 to 12 minutes, or until golden brown, at 400 degrees.
- ✓ Transfer to wire racks. It should be served warm and brushed with butter.

272) Perfect Dinner Rolls

Ingredients:

- 1 tablespoon active dry yeast
- 2-1/4 cups warm water (110° to 115°)
- 1/3 cup sugar
- 1/3 cup shortening
- 1/4 cup powdered nondairy creamer
- 2-1/4 teaspoons salt
- 6 to 7 cups bread flour

Direction: Serving: 2 dozen. | Prep: 30mins | Cook: 15mins |

- ✓ In a large mixing basin, dissolve the yeast in warm water.
- ✓ Combine 5 cups flour, salt, creamer, shortening, and sugar in a mixing bowl and whisk until smooth.
- ✓ Add enough remaining flour to form a soft dough (the dough will get sticky).
- ✓ Turn out onto a floured surface and knead for approximately 6 to 8 minutes, or until malleable and smooth.
- ✓ Place in a basin covered with frying spray, flipping once to coat the top.
- ✓ Cover and allow to double in size for approximately an hour in a warm area.
- ✓ Punch the dough down.
- ✓ Turn out onto a floured surface and cut into 24 pieces.
- ✓ Each should be rolled.
- ✓ Arrange on buttered baking trays, ensuring a 2-inch spacing between each.
- ✓ Cover and leave to rise for approximately 30 minutes, or until doubled.
- ✓ In the meantime, preheat the oven to 350 degrees Fahrenheit.

- ✓ Bake for 12 to 15 minutes, or until lightly browned.
- ✓ Remove from the pans and place to wire racks.

273) **Pumpkin Dinner Rolls**

Ingredients:

- 3/4 cup milk
- 1/3 cup packed brown sugar
- 5 tablespoons butter, divided
- 1 teaspoon salt
- 1/2 cup warm water (110 to 115 °F /43 to 46 ° C)
- 2 (.25 ounce) packages active dry yeast
- 1 1/2 cups pumpkin puree
- 1 1/2 cups all-purpose flour, or more as needed
- 1 1/2 cups whole wheat flour
- 1/2 teaspoon ground cinnamon
- 1/4 teaspoon ground ginger
- 1/4 teaspoon ground nutmeg

Direction: Serving: 10 | Prep: 20mins | Cook: 24mins |

- ✓ Mix salt, 1 tbsp. butter, brown sugar and milk in small saucepan on medium heat; heat for 2-4 minutes to 43°C/110°F then take off heat.
- ✓ Mix yeast and warm water till yeast melts in bowl. Mix milk mixture and yeast mixture in big bowl.
- ✓ Add nutmeg, ginger, cinnamon, whole wheat flour, all-purpose flour and pumpkin puree; beat, adding extra all-purpose flour if necessary to make soft dough, till dough is smooth.
- ✓ Grease big bowl.
- ✓ On floured surface, turn dough; knead till elastic and smooth.
- ✓ Put dough in greased bowl; turn once to grease dough top.
- ✓ Cover; rise for 1 hour in warm place till doubled in size. Grease 9x13-in. baking dish.
- ✓ Punch down dough; divide to 10 pieces. Form each dough piece into ball; put dough balls on prepped baking dish.
- ✓ Cover; allow to rise for 30 minutes' till doubled in size.
- ✓ Preheat an oven to 190°C/375°F.
- ✓ Melt leftover butter in saucepan for 2-3 minutes on medium-low heat; brush melted butter on dough.
- ✓ In preheated oven, bake for 20-25 minutes till golden brown.
- ✓ Put rolls on wire rack; slightly cool.
- ✓ Serve

274) **Simply A Must Dinner Roll**

Ingredients:

- 5-1/2 to 6 cups all-purpose flour
- 1/2 cup sugar
- 1 tablespoon quick- rise yeast
- 2 teaspoons salt
- 1 cup 2% milk

- 1/2 cup canola oil
- 3 large eggs
- 2 tablespoons butter, melted

Direction: Serving: 3 dozen. | Prep: 40mins | Cook: 10mins |

- ✓ Mix salt, yeast, sugar and 3 cups flour in a big bowl.
- ✓ Heat oil and milk in small saucepan to 120 – 130 degrees.
- ✓ Put to the dry ingredients; beat till barely moistened.
- ✓ Beat in the eggs until smooth.
- ✓ Continue adding flour until a soft dough forms; dough will become sticky.
- ✓ Knead for 6 to 8 minutes, or until smooth and flexible, on a floured surface.
- ✓ Ten minutes later, cover and set aside.
- ✓ Divide dough into three equal parts.
- ✓ Each piece should be rolled into a 12-inch circular and brushed with butter.
- ✓ Each circle should be cut into a dozen wedges.
- ✓ Roll wedges up from the broad end and place 2 inches apart on prepared baking pans, point side facing down.
- ✓ Bend the ends to create crescents. Cover and allow to rise for a half hour or until nearly doubled.
- ✓ Bake till golden brown, or about 10 to 12 minutes at 400°.
- ✓ Transfer from the pans onto the wire racks.

275) **Tender Herb Dinner Rolls**

Ingredients:

- 3-1/2 to 4 cups all-purpose flour
- 3 tablespoons sugar
- 1 package (1/4 ounce) active dry yeast
- 2 teaspoons dried basil
- 1 teaspoon salt
- 1 teaspoon celery seed
- 1 teaspoon rubbed sage
- 1 teaspoon dried thyme
- 1/8 teaspoon ground ginger
- 1-1/4 cups milk
- ¼ cup shortening
- 1 egg

Direction: Serving: 2 dozen. | Prep: 15mins | Cook: 15mins |

- ✓ Mix the spices, yeast, sugar, and 1 1/2 cup flour in a large mixing basin.
- ✓ Heat the shortening and milk to 120-130 degrees in a saucepan.
- ✓ Combine the wet and dry ingredients in a mixing bowl and beat until combined.
- ✓ Beat in egg until smooth.
- ✓ Remaining flour should be added to produce a soft dough.
- ✓ Attempt to avoid kneading.
- ✓ Refrigerate, covered, for 2 hours.
- ✓ Punch down the dough.

- ✓ Turn the dough out onto a floured board and cut into 24 equal pieces.
- ✓ Each one should be rolled into a ball and placed on buttered baking sheets, leaving a 2-inch gap between them.
- ✓ Cover and set aside for approximately one hour in a warm environment to double in size.
- ✓ Bake for 12–14 minutes, or until golden brown, at 400 degrees.
- ✓ Remove the baked goods from the pans and cool completely on wire racks.

276) *Yeast Dinner Rolls*

Ingredients:

- 1 package (1/4 ounce) active dry yeast
- 1-1/2 cups warm water (110° to 115°)
- 1 can (12 ounces) evaporated milk
- 2 eggs
- 1/3 cup sugar
- 1/4 cup butter, melted
- 2 teaspoons salt
- 8 to 8-1/2 cups all-purpose flour
- Additional melted butter, optional

Direction: Serving: 32 rolls. | Prep: 20mins | Cook: 15mins |

- ✓ In a large mixing basin, dissolve the yeast in warm water. Combine 4 cups flour, salt, butter, sugar, eggs, and milk in a blender until smooth.
- ✓ Add flour in small amounts until a soft dough forms.
- ✓ Knead the dough for approximately 6 to 8 minutes, or until smooth and flexible, on a floured surface.
- ✓ It should be placed in an oiled bowl and turned once to lubricate the surface.
- ✓ Cover and lay aside in a warm place for 1 1/2 hours to double in size.
- ✓ Punctuate the dough in half. Divide each into eight rolls and arrange on a greased 13x9-inch baking sheet.
- ✓ Half of the 12 rolls should be placed in a greased 8-inch square baking tray.
- ✓ Cover and lay aside in a warm location for around 20 to 30 minutes to double in size.
- ✓ Bake for 15 to 20 minutes, or until golden brown in color, at 375 degrees.
- ✓ Alternatively, spread it with butter and serve it warm.

277) *Almond Crescents*

Ingredients:

- 1 cup slivered almonds, toasted
- 3/4 cup all-purpose flour
- 1/4 teaspoon salt
- 3/4 cup powdered sugar
- 1/2 cup (1 stick) unsalted butter, room temperature
- 1 1/2 teaspoons vanilla extract
- 1/4 teaspoon almond extract

Direction: Serving: Makes about 18 | Prep: | Cook: |

- ✓ Add salt, flour and nuts to a processor and finely grind them.
- ✓ Beat the vanilla and almond extracts, butter, and half a cup of powdered sugar in a big bowl using an electric mixer until light.
- ✓ Add in nut mixture and whisk until blended.
- ✓ Cover and put into a refrigerator for about an hour until firm.
- ✓ Set the oven to 350°F to preheat.
- ✓ Lightly grease 2 heavy big baking sheets with butter.
- ✓ Roll.
- ✓ 1 rounded tablespoonful of dough into cylinder and pinch to tape the ends to make each cookie.
- ✓ Arrange in crescent shape on baking sheet.
- ✓ Bake for about 15 minutes until the bottom of cookies become just golden.
- ✓ Move the baking sheets to racks to cool the cookies.
- ✓ Sift a quarter cup of powdered sugar over the cookies.
- ✓ These cookies can be made 3 days in advance.
- ✓ You just need to keep in airtight bags at room temperature.

278) *Apple Walnut Crescents*

Ingredients:

- 2 packages (8 ounces each) refrigerated crescent rolls
- 1/4 cup sugar
- 1 tablespoon ground cinnamon
- 4 medium tart apples, peeled and quartered
- 1/4 cup chopped walnuts
- 1/4 cup raisins, optional
- 1/4 cup butter, melted

Direction: Serving: 16 servings. | Prep: 15mins | Cook: 20mins |

- ✓ Preheat the oven to 375 ° F.
- ✓ Divide a crescent roll dough into 16 triangles after unfolding.
- ✓ Cinnamon and sugar should be combined; sprinkle about 1/2 teaspoon over each triangle.
- ✓ Roll up an apple quarter near the short side.
- ✓ Then transfer to a greased 15x10x1-inch baking pan.
- ✓ If desired, press raisins and walnuts into top of dough.
- ✓ Butter the top.
- ✓ Drizzle with the remainder of the cinnamon-sugar mixture.
- ✓ Bake for 20-24 minutes, or until golden brown.
- ✓ Serve immediately.

279) *Basil Sun Dried Tomato Crescents*

Ingredients:

- 2 tubes (8 ounces each) refrigerated crescent rolls
- 2/3 cup butter, softened

- 1/2 cup minced fresh basil
- 1/4 cup oil-packed sun-dried tomatoes, patted dry and finely chopped
- 1 teaspoon garlic powder

Direction: Serving: 16 rolls. | Prep: 15mins | Cook: 15mins |

✓ Preheat an oven to 375°.
✓ Unroll every tube of crescent dough; separate dough into 8 triangles.
✓ Mix leftover ingredients in a small bowl; spread on triangles.
✓ Roll up; put on ungreased baking sheets, 2-in. apart, point side down.
✓ To make crescents, curve; bake till golden brown for 11-13 minutes.

280) Butterscotch Crescents

Ingredients:

- 1 can (12 ounces) evaporated milk, divided
- 1 package (3-1/2 ounces) cook-and-serve butterscotch pudding mix
- 1/2 cup butter, cubed
- 1 package (1/4 ounce) active dry yeast
- 1/4 cup warm water
- (110° to 115°)
- 2 large eggs
- 2 teaspoons salt
- 5 to 5-1/2 cups all- purpose flour

FILLING:

- 2/3 cup packed brown sugar
- 2/3 cup sweetened shredded coconut
- 1/3 cup chopped pecans
- 1/4 cup butter, melted
- 2 tablespoons all-purpose flour

FROSTING:

- 1/4 cup packed brown sugar
- 2 tablespoons butter
- 1 cup confectioners' sugar
- 2 to 3 tablespoons hot water, optional

Direction: Serving: 3 dozen. | Prep: 50mins | Cook: 15mins |

✓ Put aside 2 tbsp. of evaporated milk for frosting.
✓ Mix the remaining evaporated milk and pudding mix in a saucepan until smooth.
✓ Bring the mixture to a boil over medium heat and stir constantly.
✓ Take away from heat and whisk in butter until the butter melts.
✓ Let it sit to cool to 110°-115°.
✓ In a large basin, dissolve yeast in water.
✓ Using an electric mixer, beat in 2 cups flour, salt, eggs, and pudding mixture until smooth.
✓ Incorporate enough of the remaining flour to form a soft dough.
✓ On a floured surface, knead the dough for 6-8

minutes, or until elastic and smooth.
✓ Place in an oiled bowl, turning once to grease the top.
✓ Cover and allow to double in about an hour in a warm environment.
✓ Punch the dough down.
✓ Divide into 3 portions.
✓ Roll out each portion into a 15-inch circle.
✓ Mix the filling ingredients and spread half a cupful over each circle.
✓ Slice each into 12 wedges and roll out each into a crescent shape, begin with the wide end.
✓ Arrange on greased baking sheets with the point side down.
✓ Cover and allow rising for about 45 minutes until doubled.
✓ Bake for 12-15 minutes at 375° until golden brown. Let cool on wire racks.
✓ To make the frosting, Mix the reserved evaporated milk, butter, brown sugar in a saucepan.
✓ Cook while stirring on low heat until smooth.
✓ Take away from heat and whisk in confectioners' sugar until smooth.
✓ Pour in water if necessary to reach the desired consistency.
✓ Frost the crescents.

281) Cardamom Crescents

Ingredients:

- 2 1/2 cups all-purpose flour
- 3/4 teaspoon ground cardamom
- 1/2 teaspoon ground cinnamon
- 1/2 teaspoon kosher salt
- 1 1/2 cups powdered sugar, divided
- 1 cup pecans
- 1 cup (2 sticks) unsalted butter, room temperature
- 1 tablespoon vanilla extract

Direction: Serving: Makes about 50 | Prep: | Cook: |

✓ Place racks in bottom and top thirds of the oven; heat the oven to 350°F.
✓ Line parchment paper on 2 baking sheets. In a medium size bowl, whip the initial 4 ingredients.
✓ Use a food processor to mix pecans and half cup of sugar; pulse to form a coarse meal.
✓ In medium bowl, whip vanilla and butter for 2 to 3 minutes with electric mixer till creamy.
✓ Put in the nut mixture; whip to incorporate.
✓ Put in the dry ingredients; mix thoroughly, dough will moisten yet remain crumbly.
✓ Turn onto a work counter; knead approximately 4 turns, to create a ball.
✓ Scoop out a rounded tablespoon dough; shape to make ball, then roll to a log, 1 1/2-inch length.
✓ Slowly curve to make crescent shape, pressing ends to patch, cookies might crack a bit.
✓ Redo with the rest of the dough, with approximately an-inch intervals on prepped sheets.

- ✓ Bake for 12 to 15 minutes, rotate sheets midway through, till undersides turn golden.
- ✓ In one wide, shallow bowl, sift leftover one cup of powdered sugar.
- ✓ Roll the still warm cookies softly in powdered sugar till coated, doing it in batches of approximately eight cookies each.
- ✓ Turn onto wire rack to cool down.
- ✓ Dust or roll powdered sugar on cooled cookies.
- ✓ May be done 5 days in advance.
- ✓ Keep at room temperature, airtight.

282) **_Cherry Cream Crescents_**

Ingredients:

- 1 package (8 ounces) cream cheese, softened
- 1 cup confectioners' sugar
- 1 egg, separated
- 2 tubes (8 ounces each) refrigerated crescent rolls
- 1 can (21 ounces) cherry pie filling

Direction: Serving: 16 rolls. | Prep: 20mins | Cook: 15mins |

- ✓ Beat together egg yolk, sugar and cream cheese in a bowl.
- ✓ Split dough into sixteen triangles, then arrange on baking sheets that lightly greased.
- ✓ Spread close to the edge of the short side of each triangle with 1 tbsp. of cream cheese mixture.
- ✓ Put 1 tbsp. of pie filling on top, then fold long point of triangle over filling and tuck beneath the dough.
- ✓ Beat egg white lightly and brush over rolls.
- ✓ Bake at 350 degrees until turn golden brown, about 15 to 20 minutes.

283) **_Chili Cornmeal Crescents_**

Ingredients:

- 1 package (1/4 ounce) active dry yeast
- 1-3/4 cups warm water (110° to 115°)
- 1-1/2 cups cornmeal
- 1/3 cup sugar
- 1 egg
- 2 tablespoons olive oil
- 1 tablespoon chili powder
- 1 teaspoon salt
- 4 to 4-1/2 cups all- purpose flour

Direction: Serving: 2 dozen. | Prep: 20mins | Cook: 20mins |

- ✓ Melt yeast in water in a big bowl.
- ✓ Put two cups flour, salt, chili powder, oil, egg, sugar, and cornmeal in a large mixing bowl and whisk until smooth.
- ✓ Add enough remaining flour to form a soft dough.
- ✓ Turn it out onto the floured surface and knead for 6-8 minutes, or until smooth and elastic.
- ✓ Place it in an oiled bowl; turn once to grease the surface.

- ✓ Cover; rise for 1-hour till doubled in a warm place.
- ✓ Punch down dough; halve.
- ✓ Roll every portion to a 12-in.
- ✓ circle then cut to 12 edges.
- ✓ Starting with wide end, roll up every wedge.
- ✓ Put onto greased baking sheet; curvet to a crescent shape then cover.
- ✓ Rise for 30 minutes' till doubled.
- ✓ Bake it at 375° till browned for 20 minutes; cool on wire racks.

284) **_Chocolate Filled Crescents_**

Ingredients:

- 1 (8 ounce) can Pillsbury® refrigerated crescent dinner rolls
- 1/2 cup mini chocolate chips Powdered sugar, if desired

Direction: Serving: 8 | Prep: 5mins | Cook: |

- ✓ Heat an oven to 350°F and separate dough to 8 triangles.
- ✓ On the wide end of every triangle, put 1 tbsp. chocolate chips.
- ✓ Starting at the triangle's shortest side, roll up, rolling to the opposite point; put onto ungreased cookie sheet.
- ✓ Bake it at 350°F till golden brown for 15-20 minutes; sprinkle powdered sugar.

285) **_Creamy Chocolate Crescents_**

Ingredients:

- 2 packages (3 ounces each) cream cheese, softened
- 1/4 cup butter, softened
- 1/2 cup confectioners' sugar
- 2 tablespoons cornstarch
- 2 cups (12 ounces) semisweet chocolate chips, melted
- 1 tablespoon butter, melted
- 1/2 teaspoon vanilla extract
- 4 tubes (8 ounces each) refrigerated crescent rolls

GLAZE:

- 2 eggs
- 1/2 teaspoon almond extract
- Confectioners' sugar, optional

Direction: Serving: about 2-1/2 dozen. | Prep: 25mins | Cook: 10mins |

- ✓ Gather all of the ingredients into a large basin and mix thoroughly.
- ✓ Beat in vanilla extract, melted chocolate, and cornstarch until smooth.
- ✓ Unroll the crescent roll dough and separate to triangles.
- ✓ Whisk extract, butter and eggs in a small bowl; brush some on dough.
- ✓ At a wide end of every triangle, drop rounded chocolate mixture tea-spoonful; from the wide end, roll up.
- ✓ Put it onto greased baking sheets, point side down;

slightly curve ends.

- ✓ Brush with leftover glaze.
- ✓ Bake it at 350° till golden for 10-15 minutes.
- ✓ Transfer from pans onto wire racks; cool.
- ✓ If desired, dust with confectioners' sugar

286) Herbed Cheddar Crescents

Ingredients:

- 4-1/4 cups all-purpose flour
- 1 cup shredded cheddar cheese
- 2 tablespoons plus 1-1/2 teaspoons sugar
- 2 packages (1/4 ounce each) active dry yeast
- 1-1/2 teaspoons Italian seasoning
- 1 teaspoon salt
- 1-1/2 cups whole milk
- 7 tablespoons butter, divided
- 1 large egg yolk
- 1 tablespoon water

Direction: Serving: 2 dozen. | Prep: 30mins | Cook: 15mins |

- ✓ Stir 3 cups flour, 3 tablespoons Italian spice and 1 tablespoon sugar in a large bowl.
- ✓ In a saucepan, heat 4 tbsp. of butter and milk to 120-130°.
- ✓ Toss in the wet ingredients and beat until well-combined.
- ✓ Make a soft dough by adding enough extra flour, but don't overwork it.
- ✓ A warm spot and a cover are all that's needed for this one.
- ✓ Knead the dough.
- ✓ Make three equal portions on a lightly floured surface.
- ✓ Each part should be rolled into a circle no more than 10 inches in diameter.
- ✓ Baste the dough with the melted butter that was left behind.
- ✓ Cut each round into eight equal pieces.
- ✓ Using a rolling pin, roll up the wide end into a log; place on prepared baking pans 2 inches apart, pointed side up.
- ✓ Curve the ends down to form a crescent shape.
- ✓ Until it has doubled, let it sit for 50 minutes covered.
- ✓ Brush the crescents with a mixture of water and egg yolk.
- ✓ For 15 to 20 minutes, bake it at 375° until it turns golden brown.
- ✓ Store the finished product in the refrigerator after you've removed it from the pans.

287) Mushroom Onion Crescents

Ingredients:

- 3 tablespoons butter, divided
- 1 cup sliced baby portobello mushrooms
- 1 medium onion, halved and sliced
- 3 garlic cloves, minced
- 1/3 cup grated Parmesan cheese
- 1 tablespoon minced fresh parsley
- 1 tube (8 ounces) refrigerated reduced-fat crescent rolls
- 1/2 cup shredded part-skim mozzarella cheese

Direction: Serving: 8 rolls. | Prep: 25mins | Cook: 10mins |

- ✓ Preheat the oven to 375 degrees.
- ✓ Heat 2 tablespoons butter in a big skillet on medium high heat.
- ✓ Add onion and mushrooms.
- ✓ Stir and cook until softened for 2-3 minutes.
- ✓ Lower heat to medium low.
- ✓ Stir and cook until onion is golden for 10-12 minutes.
- ✓ Put garlic.
- ✓ Cook for 1 more minute.
- ✓ Take off heat.
- ✓ Mix parsley and parmesan cheese in.
- ✓ Unroll the crescent dough.
- ✓ Separate them to triangles.
- ✓ At the wide end of every triangle, put 1 tbsp. mushroom mixture
- ✓ . Put 1 tbsp. mozzarella cheese on top.
- ✓ Roll up.
- ✓ Put on an ungreased baking sheet, 2-in. apart with the point side down.
- ✓ Curve the ends to make a crescent. Melt leftover butter then brush on top.
- ✓ Bake until golden brown for 10-12 minutes.
- ✓ Keep leftovers in the fridge.

288) Orange Coconut Crescents

Ingredients:

- 1 tube (8 ounces) refrigerated crescent rolls
- 2 tablespoons butter, softened
- 1/3 cup sweetened shredded coconut
- 1/3 cup sugar
- 1 tablespoon grated orange zest

GLAZE:

- 1/4 cup sugar
- 1/4 cup sour cream
- 2 tablespoons orange juice
- 2 tablespoons butter

Direction: Serving: 8 rolls. | Prep: 10mins | Cook: 20mins |

- ✓ Separate the crescent rolls; use butter to spread. Mix orange zest, sugar and coconut in a bowl; put 2 tbsp. aside for topping.
- ✓ Sprinkle leftover coconut mixture on butter.
- ✓ Roll up; put onto greased baking sheet, point side down.
- ✓ Bake it at 375° till golden brown for 16-18 minutes.
- ✓ Meanwhile, in a saucepan, mix glaze ingredients. Boil; boil till glossy for 3 minutes.

- ✓ Slightly cool; put on warm rolls.
- ✓ Sprinkle reserved coconut mixture

289) **Poppy Seed Crescents**

Ingredients:

- 1 package (1/4 ounce) active dry yeast
- 1/2 cup warm water (110° to 115°)
- 1 can (5 ounces) evaporated milk
- 1/4 cup sugar
- 1/4 cup butter, softened
- 1 egg
- 1 teaspoon salt
- 3 to 3-1/2 cups all-purpose flour

FILLING:

- 2 tablespoons sugar
- 2 tablespoons poppy seeds
- 2 tablespoons water
- 1/2 teaspoon grated lemon peel
- 1/4 teaspoon ground cinnamon

EGG WASH:

- 1 egg yolk
- 1 tablespoon water

Direction: Serving: 2 dozen. | Prep: 40mins | Cook: 15mins |

- ✓ In a large basin, mix yeast and warm water and allow to dissolve.
- ✓ The following ingredients should be combined and beaten to a smooth consistency: 2 cups of flour, salt, eggs, butter, sugar and milk.
- ✓ Add enough remaining flour to form a soft dough.
- ✓ The dough should be turned out onto a floured board and worked for 6-8 minutes until it is elastic and smooth.
- ✓ Turn it once to coat the top before placing it in the prepared basin.
- ✓ A warm spot and a cover are all that's needed for this one.
- ✓ In a small saucepan, combine all of the filling ingredients and bring to a boil, stirring frequently.
- ✓ Remove from the heat and set aside.
- ✓ Using a lightly floured surface, knead the dough until it is smooth.
- ✓ Roll out each half of the dough to a 12-inch circle.
- ✓ Spread the filling out to within half an inch of the edges of the wedges.
- ✓ Make 12 wedges out of each circle.
- ✓ Roll up the wedges starting from the wide end and place them 2-inches apart, point side up, on prepared baking pans.
- ✓ Curve the ends of the triangle to form a crescent shape. 30 minutes later, the dough will have doubled in size.
- ✓ Brush the rolls with a mixture of beaten egg yolk and water.
- ✓ If you want it golden brown, bake it for 15 to 20 minutes at 350° until it's done.

- ✓ Place wire racks below the prepared pans.

290) **Sausage Cheese Crescents**

Ingredients:

- 3-1/4 teaspoons active dry yeast
- 2 cups warm 2% milk (110° to 115°)
- 4 large eggs
- 1 cup mashed potato flakes
- 1 cup butter, softened
- 1/2 cup sugar
- 1 teaspoon salt
- 7 to 8 cups all-purpose flour
- 12 ounces Johnsonville® Ground Mild Italian sausage
- 3/4 cup shredded cheddar cheese

FINISHING:

- 1 large egg, beaten

Direction: Serving: 3 dozen. | Prep: 55mins | Cook: 15mins |

- ✓ Melt yeast in milk in a big bowl.
- ✓ Add 4 cups flour, salt, sugar, butter, potato flakes and eggs; beat for 3 minutes on medium speed.
- ✓ To make a sticky, soft dough, mix in enough leftover flour.
- ✓ Turn it onto floured surface; knead for 6-8 minutes till elastic and smooth.
- ✓ Put it into greased bowl; to grease top, turn once.
- ✓ Cover; rise for 1-hour till doubled in a warm place.
- ✓ Cook sausage in a big skillet on medium heat till not pink; drain.
- ✓ Put aside; cool.
- ✓ Punch down dough.
- ✓ Turn it onto lightly floured surface; divide to thirds.
- ✓ Roll every portion to 12- in. circle; sprinkle 1/4 cup cheese and 1 cup sausage
- ✓ . Cut every circle to 12 wedges.
- ✓ From the wide ends, roll up wedges; put, pointed side down, on greased baking sheets, 2-in. apart.
- ✓ To make crescents, curve ends.
- ✓ Cover; rise for 30 minutes' till doubled.
- ✓ Brush using eggs.
- ✓ Bake it at 375° till golden brown for 14-18 minutes.
- ✓ Serve warm.

291) **Savory Wheat Crescents**

Ingredients:

- 1 package (1/4 ounce) active dry yeast
- 1/2 cup warm water (110° to 115°)
- 8-1/2 teaspoons honey, divided
- 2 cups whole wheat flour
- 3/4 cup warm milk (110° to 115°)
- 6 tablespoons butter, softened, divided
- 1 egg

- *1 teaspoon salt*
- *1-3/4 to 2-1/4 cups all-purpose flour*
- *1/4 cup grated Parmesan cheese*
- *1/4 teaspoon garlic salt*
  Direction: Serving: 16 rolls. | Prep: 30mins | Cook: 15mins |
- ✓ *In a large basin, combine yeast and warm water and allow to dissolve.*
- ✓ *After 5 minutes, stir in 2 tbsp. honey.*
- ✓ *On medium speed, combine 1 cup all-purpose flour with the rest of the ingredients (except for the butter and milk) and beat for 3 minutes.*
- ✓ *Add enough leftover all-purpose flour to form a soft dough.*
- ✓ *The dough should be turned out onto a floured board and worked for 6-8 minutes until it is elastic and smooth.*
- ✓ *Put it in a greased bowl and turn it over once to coat the top with oil.*
- ✓ *A warm spot and a cover are all that's needed for this one.*
- ✓ *For 30 seconds, knead the dough on a floured surface once it has been punched down.*
- ✓ *Make a 12-inch circle out of it.*
- ✓ *Baste the dough with the melted butter that was left behind.*
- ✓ *Sprinkle the dough with garlic salt and parmesan. Cut into 16 wedges.*
- ✓ *The wide end should be rolled into a wedge and placed on a baking pan with the pointed end facing down.*
- ✓ *Create a crescent shape by bending the ends and covering them with tape.*
- ✓ *In a warm environment, rise for 20 minutes until you have doubled in size.*
- ✓ *At 400 degrees Fahrenheit, bake it for 12 to 15 minutes, or until it's browned and crispy.*
- ✓ *Cool on wire racks before removing from pans.*

292) **Spinach Crescents**

Ingredients:

- *1/2 cup sliced almonds*
- *1 package (10 ounces) frozen chopped spinach, thawed and squeezed dry*
- *1/2 cup grated Parmesan cheese*
- *1/4 cup chopped onion*
- *2 teaspoons olive oil*
- *1/4 teaspoon salt*
- *1/8 teaspoon pepper*
- *1 package (8 ounces) refrigerated crescent rolls*
  Direction: Serving: 8 servings. | Prep: 10mins | Cook: 15mins |
- ✓ *Finely chop almonds in a food processor.*
- ✓ *Add pepper, salt, oil, onion, cheese and spinach; cover.*
- ✓ *Process till blended well.*
- ✓ *Unroll; separate crescent dough to 8 pieces.*

- ✓ *Evenly spread spinach mixture on the dough within 1/8-in. of the edges.*
- ✓ *Roll it up; put onto greased baking sheet then bake it at 375° till golden brown for 15-18 minutes.*
- ✓ *Serve warm*

293) **Sweet Potato Crescents**

Ingredients:

- *2 packages (1/4 ounce each) active dry yeast*
- *1 cup warm water (110° to 115°)*
- *1 can (15-3/4 ounces) cut sweet potatoes, drained and mashed*
- *1/2 cup sugar*
- *1/2 cup shortening*
- *1 large egg*
- *1-1/2 teaspoons salt*
- *5 to 5-1/2 cups all-purpose flour*
- *1/4 cup butter, melted*
  Direction: Serving: 3 dozen. | Prep: 30mins | Cook: 15mins |
- ✓ *In a large basin, mix the yeast and water and let it sit for about 5 minutes.*
- ✓ *Sugar and sweet potatoes are incorporated into a dough that has been kneaded for many minutes.*
- ✓ *For 6-8 minutes, knead the dough on a floured surface.*
- ✓ *Put it in a greased bowl and turn it over once to coat the top with oil.*
- ✓ *In a warm place, cover and let rise for an hour until doubled.*
- ✓ *Roll out the dough and divide it in half. Each part should be rolled into a 12-inch circle and cut into 12 equal wedges.*
- ✓ *Brush on some butter.*
- ✓ *Rolled from the wide end, place the pointed end down on two baking pans that have been sprayed with cooking spray.*
- ✓ *Bake for 40 minutes, until doubled in size.*
- ✓ *For 13-15 minutes, bake it at 375° until golden brown.*
- ✓ *Place wire racks below the prepared pans.*

294) **Walnut Cheese Crescents**

Ingredients:

- *1 tablespoon butter, melted*
- *1/4 teaspoon onion powder*
- *1/8 teaspoon dill weed*
- *1/8 teaspoon paprika*
- *1 tube (8 ounces) refrigerated crescent rolls*
- *1/2 cup finely chopped walnuts*
- *1/4 cup grated Parmesan cheese*
  Direction: Serving: 8 servings. | Prep: 15mins | Cook: 10mins |
- ✓ *Mix paprika, dill, onion powder and butter in a small bowl; put aside.*
- ✓ *Unroll crescent dough and separate to 8 triangles.*

- ✓ Brush using butter mixture; to within 1/8-in. of the edges, sprinkle cheese and walnuts.
- ✓ From the wide end, roll up; put, point side down, onto ungreased baking sheet, 2-in. apart.
- ✓ To make crescents, curve ends.
- ✓ Bake it at 375° till golden brown for 8-10 minutes; serve warm.

295) Accordion Rye Rolls

Ingredients:

- 2 packages (1/4 ounce each) active dry yeast
- 1/2 cup warm water (110° to 115°)
- 1-1/2 cups warm milk (110° to 115°)
- 1/4 cup molasses
- 4 tablespoons butter, softened, divided
- 1 tablespoon sugar
- 1 tablespoon plus 1/2 teaspoon salt, divided
- 3 to 3-1/2 cups all-purpose flour
- 2-1/2 cups rye flour
- Vegetable oil
- 1 large egg white
- 2 teaspoons caraway seeds

Direction: Serving: 2 dozen. | Prep: 30mins | Cook: 20mins |

- ✓ In a large basin, mix the yeast and water.
- ✓ Sugar, salt, 2 tbsp butter, milk, and molasses are all mixed in with 2 cups of all-purpose flour and beaten to a smooth consistency.
- ✓ Using the remaining all-purpose flour and rye flour, create a soft dough by adding enough of each ingredient.
- ✓ Knead it on a floured board for about six to eight minutes, until it is flexible and smooth.
- ✓ To butter the top, place it in a greased basin and flip it over once to distribute the grease evenly throughout.
- ✓ Allow it to stand for 20 minutes with the cover on.
- ✓ The dough should be kneaded. On a lightly floured surface, flip it over and cut it into four equal pieces.
- ✓ Using the butter that's still left over, brush the 14x6-inch rectangles you've formed.
- ✓ A table knife with a dull edge can be used to score the dough at 2-inch intervals.
- ✓ Using the marks as a guide, score the dough in a horizontal direction.
- ✓ Back and forth along the folded lines, fold the dough accordion-style.
- ✓ In a muffin tin, place the cut side down of the folded dough into each cup.
- ✓ Apply a little coat of oil to the entire surface area.
- ✓ Wrap it with plastic wrap and secure it with tape.
- ✓ Refrigerate it for at least four to 24 hours.
- ✓ Remove the lid and let it sit for 10 minutes at room temperature before baking.
- ✓ Brush the egg white on top of the dough after beating it in a small bowl until it forms stiff peaks.

- ✓ Toss the remaining salt and caraway seeds on top of the finished dish.
- ✓ A light brown color can be achieved by baking it for 20 to 25 minutes at 375 degrees, or until it's crispy.
- ✓ Transfer it to wire racks after it's out of the pans.

296) Angel Rolls

Ingredients:

- 3-1/2 cups bread flour
- 2 tablespoons sugar
- 1 package (1/4 ounce) quick-rise yeast
- 1-1/4 teaspoons salt
- 1 teaspoon baking powder
- ½ teaspoon baking soda
- 1 cup buttermilk
- 1/2 cup canola oil
- 1/3 cup water
- Melted butter

Direction: Serving: 14 rolls. | Prep: 20mins | Cook: 15mins |

- ✓ In a large basin, mix 1 1/2 cups flour, baking soda, baking powder, salt, yeast, and sugar.
- ✓ In a small saucepan, bring the water, oil, and buttermilk to 120-130 degrees Fahrenheit.
- ✓ Add the wet ingredients to the dry and stir until they are just moistened.
- ✓ Make a soft dough by adding enough of the remaining flour.
- ✓ Make a ball of dough and knead it for 4 to 6 minutes until it's flexible.
- ✓ Allow to settle for 10 minutes before removing the cover.
- ✓ Using a floured biscuit cutter, cut the dough into 2-1/2-inch squares.
- ✓ Spray a baking sheet with cooking spray.
- ✓ Bake at 400° for 15 to 18 minutes, or until golden brown.
- ✓ Apply a thin layer of butter to the tops.
- ✓ To cool, remove from the pan and place on a wire rack.

297) Apple Cider Cinnamon Rolls

Ingredients:

- 3-1/4 cups all-purpose flour
- 1/4 cup sugar
- 1 package (1/4 ounce) quick-rise yeast
- 1/2 teaspoon salt
- 3/4 cup 2% milk
- 1/4 cup apple cider or juice
- 1/4 cup plus 1/3 cup butter, softened, divided
- 1 large egg
- 2 cups finely chopped peeled tart apples
- 1-1/4 cups packed brown sugar
  3/4 cup finely chopped walnuts

- 3 teaspoons ground cinnamon

APPLE CIDER CREAM CHEESE FROSTING:

- 2 cups apple cider or juice
- 1 cinnamon stick (3 inches)
- 1 package (8 ounces) cream cheese, softened
- 1/4 cup butter, softened
- 1 cup confectioners' sugar

Direction: Serving: 1 dozen. | Prep: 60mins | Cook: 30mins |

✓ In a large bowl, mix salt, yeast, sugar, and 2 1/4 cups flour.

✓ In a small saucepan, warm 1/4 cup butter, cider, and milk to 120-130°F.

✓ Slightly mix until it's just soaked, then add to the batter. Beat in the egg until it's smooth.

✓ Make a soft and sticky dough with the rest of the flour.

✓ Knead for 6-8 minutes, until elastic and smooth, on a floured surface.

✓ Cover. Then roll to a 15x10-inch rectangle and rest for ten minutes before continuing.

✓ Spread the remaining butter around the edges of the pan.

✓ In a bowl, combine the apple slices with the cinnamon, walnuts, brown sugar, and butter until well-combined.

✓ Starting from the long side, jellyroll-style, roll up the jellyroll-like shape.

✓ Pinch the seam to create a tight seal. Slice into twelve pieces.

✓ Prepare a 13x9-inch baking dish with cooking spray and place the cut side down in the pan.

✓ Cover.

✓ Allow yourself 30 minutes to rise and shine in a comfortable environment.

✓ Bake at 325° for 30 to 35 minutes, or until the bread is golden brown.

✓ Add the cider and cinnamon stick to a small saucepan and bring to a boil. 20 minutes of cooking time will provide 1/4 cup of liquid.

✓ Cool cider after removing cinnamon stick.

✓ In a large bowl, combine butter and cream cheese and beat until frothy.

✓ Reduced cider, confectioners' sugar, and butter, and beat until well-combined.

✓ Warm rolls should be topped with the mixture.

298) Apple Nutmeg Rolls

Ingredients:

- 1 loaf (1 pound) frozen bread dough, thawed
- 2 tablespoons butter, softened
- 1/4 cup packed brown sugar
- 1/4 cup finely chopped walnuts
- 1 teaspoon ground cinnamon
- 1/2 teaspoon ground nutmeg
- 2 cups finely chopped peeled tart apples

ICING:

- 1/2 cup confectioners' sugar
- 2-1/2 teaspoons whole milk

Direction: Serving: 1 dozen. | Prep: 20mins | Cook: 25mins |

✓ On a lightly floured surface, roll out the dough into a 14-inch square.

✓ Top with a buttery coating.

✓ A tiny bowl is all that is needed to coat the apples in the spices and brown sugar.

✓ Sprinkle over dough to within half an inch of the edges.

✓ Press the seam together to seal the roll.

✓ Chopped into a dozen portions

✓ Put the cut side down in an 11x7-inch greased baking dish.

✓ It should take about 40 minutes for the dough to double in bulk.

✓ Bake at 350° for 25 to 30 minutes, or until golden brown.

✓ Frost the warm rolls with the frosting mixture, then serve.

299) Apple Pecan Cinnamon Rolls

Ingredients:

- 1 cup warm milk (70° to 80°)
- 2 large eggs
- 1/3 cup butter, melted
- 1/2 cup sugar
- 1 teaspoon salt
- 4-1/2 cups bread flour
- 2-1/2 teaspoons bread machine yeast
- FILLING:
- 3 tablespoons butter, melted
- 1 cup finely chopped peeled apples
- 3/4 cup packed brown sugar
- 1/3 cup chopped pecans
- 2-1/2 teaspoons ground cinnamon

ICING:

- 1-1/2 cups confectioners' sugar
- 3 ounces' cream cheese, softened
- 1/4 cup butter, softened
- 1/2 teaspoon vanilla extract 1/8 teaspoon salt

Direction: Serving: 12 servings. | Prep: 30mins | Cook: 25mins |

✓ Put the first seven ingredients in the pan of bread machine according to manufacturer's directions.

✓ Set the machine to dough setting (after 5 minutes of mixing, check dough; if needed, add 1-2 tablespoons of flour or water).

✓ Turn dough onto a well-floured surface once the cycle is completed.

✓ Shape into a 21x16-in. rectangle; spread with butter.

✓ Mix the apples, pecans, cinnamon and brown sugar together.

- ✓ Scoop over the dough to within 1/2 in. of edges.
- ✓ From a long side; pinch to seal the seam to shape up jellyroll style.
- ✓ Cut into slices with 1-3/4-in.
- ✓ In a greased 13x9-in. baking dish, put cut side down.
- ✓ Cover and allow to rise about 30 minutes, until it nearly doubles.
- ✓ Bake at 325deg; until golden brown or for 25-30 minutes.
- ✓ Beat the icing ingredients in the small bowl.
- ✓ Spill over warm rolls.

300) *Apricot Breakfast Rolls*

Ingredients:

- 1 package (1/4 ounce) active dry yeast
- 1/2 cup warm water (110° to 115°)
- 2 cups warm fat-free milk (110° to 115°)
- 1 teaspoon salt
- 1 cup whole wheat flour
- 3-1/2 to 4-1/2 cups all-purpose flour
- 1 jar (14-1/2 ounces) apricot spreadable fruit, divided
- 1/2 teaspoon ground cinnamon
- 1 cup confectioners' sugar
- 1/2 teaspoon cold fat-free milk

Direction: Serving: 1 dozen. | Prep: 30mins | Cook: 30mins |

- ✓ In a bowl, mix warm water and yeast.
- ✓ Salt, flour, and warm milk are all that are needed for a smooth mixture.
- ✓ Mix in enough all-purpose flour to create a soft dough.
- ✓ The dough should be malleable and smooth after 6 to 8 minutes of kneading.
- ✓ A bowl that has been sprayed with cooking spray should be used.
- ✓ Allow to rise in a warm environment for about 1-1/4 hours until doubled in size.
- ✓ Remove air from the dough by pressing it down.
- ✓ The dough should be transferred to a floured surface and kneaded for eight cycles.
- ✓ Allow to settle for 5 minutes before removing the cover.
- ✓ Make a square of 18 inches by rolling out the dough.
- ✓ Make sure to distribute a cup of spreadable fruit to within half an inch of the sides, then sprinkle it with cinnamon.
- ✓ Pinch the seam as you go to seal the package.
- ✓ A 13x9-inch baking dish, lightly sprayed with cooking spray, is ideal for this recipe.
- ✓ Put a lid on it and let it rise for 30 minutes, until it's doubled in size.
- ✓ Bake for about 30 to 35 minutes at 350°, or until slightly browned.
- ✓ After 30 minutes on the wire rack, allow to cool.
- ✓ Add confectioners' sugar and cold milk to a bowl to make a glaze.

- ✓ Pour over the rolls.

301) *Asparagus Yeast Rolls*

Ingredients:

- 1 package (1/4 ounce) active dry yeast
- 1 cup plus 2 tablespoons warm water (110° to 115°), divided
- 1 tablespoon mashed potato flakes
- 1/2 cup butter, softened
- 1/4 cup sugar
- 1-1/2 teaspoons salt
- 5-1/4 to 5-3/4 cups all-purpose flour
- 1 cup finely chopped fresh asparagus, cooked and drained

Direction: Serving: 2 dozen. | Prep: 25mins | Cook: 15mins |

- ✓ Melt yeast in 2 tbsp. water in a bowl; stand for 5 minutes.
- ✓ Mix leftover water and potato flakes; add into the yeast mixture.
- ✓ Add 2 cups flour, salt, eggs, sugar and butter; beat till smooth.
- ✓ Add asparagus and enough leftover flour to make a soft dough.
- ✓ Turn onto a floured surface; knead for 6-8 minutes till elastic and smooth.
- ✓ Put into a greased bowl; turn once to grease the top.
- ✓ Cover; refrigerate it for 2 hours – overnight.
- ✓ Shape the dough into 2-in. balls; put into well-greased muffin cups then cover.
- ✓ Rise for 45 minutes' till doubled in a warm place.
- ✓ Bake for 14-16 minutes till golden brown at 400°.Cool for 5 minutes.
- ✓ Run a knife around each roll's outside carefully; remove from the pan then serve warm.

302) *Bacon Cinnamon Buns*

Ingredients:

- 1 package (1/4 ounce) active dry yeast
- 1 cup warm whole milk (110° to 115°)
- 1/4 cup sugar
- 1/4 cup butter, softened
- 1 large egg yolk
- 1-1/2 teaspoons vanilla extract
- 3/4 teaspoon salt
- 1/2 teaspoon ground nutmeg
- 2-3/4 to 3-1/4 cups all-purpose flour

FILLING:

- 5 bacon strips, chopped
- 1/2 cup packed brown sugar
- 1 tablespoon maple syrup
- 2 teaspoons ground cinnamon
- 1/2 teaspoon ground nutmeg

FROSTING:

- 2 cups confectioners' sugar
- 1/2 cup butter, softened
- 2 tablespoons whole milk
- 1 tablespoon maple syrup

Direction: Serving: 1 dozen. | Prep: 50mins | Cook: 20mins |

- ✓ Dissolve the yeast in warm milk in small bowl.
- ✓ Mix 1 cup flour, yeast mixture, nutmeg, salt, vanilla, egg yolk, butter, and sugar in a large bowl; beat for two minutes on medium speed.
- ✓ Mix in plenty leftover flour to make a soft dough (the dough should be sticky).
- ✓ Transfer on a floured surface, then knead for 6 to 8 minutes until elastic and smooth.
- ✓ Put into a greased bowl and flip once to oil top.
- ✓ Cover with plastic wrap and leave to rise for about 1 hour in a warm spot until doubled.
- ✓ Over medium heat, cook the bacon in a small skillet until it is crisp.
- ✓ Take out with slotted spoon and place on paper towels to drain.
- ✓ Get rid of the drippings but save two tablespoons. Mix reserved bacon drippings, nutmeg, cinnamon, syrup and brown sugar in the same skillet; cook while stirring until combined.
- ✓ Let cool to room temperature.
- ✓ Punch down the dough.
- ✓ Roll it into an 18x12- inch rectangle.
- ✓ Drizzle bacon and brown sugar mixture to within half inch of the edges.
- ✓ Roll up beginning with a short side, jellyroll style, then pinch the seams to seal.
- ✓ Split into 12 rolls. Transfer the rolls into a greased 13x9-inch baking dish with the cut side down.
- ✓ Cover the dish and leave to rise for about 45 minutes in a warm spot until doubled.
- ✓ Preheat an oven to 400°. Bake for about 18 to 20 minutes or until it turns golden brown.
- ✓ Let cool for 20 minutes.
- ✓ Beat the frosting ingredients in small bowl until smooth.
- ✓ Pour atop warm rolls.
- ✓ Serve while still warm.

303) *Bacon Onion Crescent Buns*

Ingredients:

- 4-3/4 to 5-1/4 cups all-purpose flour
- 1/2 cup sugar
- 1 package (1/4 ounce) active dry yeast
- 1/2 teaspoon salt
- 1 cup milk
- 1/2 cup butter, cubed
- 1/2 teaspoon caraway seeds
- 3 eggs
- 1 pound sliced bacon, diced
- 1 small onion, finely chopped

- 1/8 teaspoon white pepper
- 2 tablespoons water

Direction: Serving: 4 dozen. | Prep: 40mins | Cook: 15mins |

- ✓ In a large mixing basin, combine the salt, yeast, sugar, and 2 cups flour.
- ✓ In a small saucepan, heat the butter and milk to 120-130 degrees.
- ✓ Combine it with the dry ingredients and beat on medium speed for 2 minutes.
- ✓ Beat in 2 eggs and caraway seeds until smooth. Add enough remaining flour to form a stiff dough.
- ✓ Turn it out onto a floured area and knead for approximately 6 to 8 minutes, or until it becomes smooth and pliable.
- ✓ Place it in a greased bowl and turn it once to coat the top with grease.
- ✓ Cover and allow it to double in size for about an hour in a warm environment.
- ✓ Meanwhile, sauté the bacon in a large frying skillet over medium heat until crisp.
- ✓ Remove it with a slotted spoon and place on paper towels.
- ✓ Sauté the onion in the drippings, then remove it with a slotted spoon and set aside.
- ✓ Once cooled, combine the pepper, onion, and bacon in a bowl and set aside.
- ✓ Punch the dough down.
- ✓ Turn it out onto a lightly floured board and cut it into four pieces.
- ✓ Each one should be rolled into a 12-inch circular and sliced into 12 wedges.
- ✓ Top each wedge with a heaping teaspoon of the bacon mixture.
- ✓ From the wide end, roll it up.
- ✓ Arrange it 2 inches apart on buttered baking trays, pointed end down.
- ✓ Cover and allow to rise for approximately 30 minutes.
- ✓ In a separate bowl, whisk together the remaining egg and water and brush it on top of the rolls.
- ✓ Allow it to bake for 12 to 14 minutes at 350 degrees, or until golden brown.
- ✓ Refrigerate any leftovers.

304) *Bacon Onion Pan Rolls*

Ingredients:

- 1 loaf (1 pound) frozen bread dough, thawed
- 1/4 cup butter, melted, divided
- 1/2 pound sliced bacon, cooked and crumbled
- 1/2 cup chopped onion

Direction: Serving: 1-1/2 dozen. | Prep: 15mins | Cook: 25mins |

- ✓ Roll dough out to 1/4-in. thick on the lightly floured surface.
- ✓ Use the 2-1/2-in. biscuit cutter to cut; brush using 3 tbsp. butter.
- ✓ On half of every roll, put 1 tsp. bacon.

- ✓ Fold over; to seal, pinch.
- ✓ Put into a 9-in. greased square baking pan, pinched edge up, making 3 rows of 6.
- ✓ Use leftover butter to brush the tops.
- ✓ Rise for 30 minutes' till doubled.
- ✓ Bake it at 350° till golden brown for 25-30 minutes.

305) **Banana Pecan Sweet Rolls**

Ingredients:

- 4-3/4 to 5 cups all-purpose flour
- 1/4 cup sugar
- 2 packages (1/4 ounce each) active dry yeast
- 1 teaspoon salt
- 1 cup milk
- 1/4 cup butter, cubed
- 1 cup mashed ripe bananas (about 3 medium)
- 1 egg
- 1 teaspoon vanilla extract

FILLING:

- 3 tablespoons butter, melted
- 1/2 cup chopped pecans
- 1/4 cup sugar
- 1/2 teaspoon ground allspice

ICING:

- 2 cups confectioners' sugar
- 1 tablespoon lemon juice
- 1 to 2 tablespoons milk

Direction: Serving: 32 rolls. | Prep: 50mins | Cook: 15mins |

- ✓ In a large bowl, combine the salt, yeast, sugar, and 2 cups of flour.
- ✓ In a small saucepan, bring the milk and butter to 120-130 degrees Fahrenheit.
- ✓ Incorporate into the dry mixture and mix until barely moistened.
- ✓ Bananas and other ingredients should be added now and beaten well until they are completely smooth.
- ✓ Mix in enough of the remaining flour to form a soft dough (the dough will get sticky).
- ✓ Knead the dough for about 6 to 8 minutes until it's malleable and smooth on a floured surface.
- ✓ Put in a bowl that has been sprayed with cooking spray and then flip it over to coat the other side.
- ✓ Allow the dough to rise for about an hour in a warm environment until it has doubled in size, then remove the cover.
- ✓ The dough should be kneaded.
- ✓ Flip onto a floured surface and cut into two equal halves.
- ✓ Each piece should be rolled into a 16x6-inch rectangle and brushed with a half-inch layer of butter.
- ✓ Then, to within a half-inch of the dough's edges, sprinkle the allspice, sugar, and pecans mixture on top.
- ✓ Starting with a long side, roll jellyroll style, pinching

the seam to seal.

- ✓ Slice each into sixteen equal pieces.
- ✓ Put the cut side up on a prepared baking pan.
- ✓ Put a lid on it and let it rise until it has doubled in size for about 30 minutes in a warm place.
- ✓ To achieve a golden brown color, bake for between 12 and 15 minutes at 400 degrees.
- ✓ Transfer it to wire racks after it's out of the pans.
- ✓ Drizzle heated rolls with a mixture of milk, lemon juice, and confectioner's sugar until it reaches your desired consistency.
- ✓ Serve immediately while hot.

306) **Basil Tomato Rolls**

Ingredients:

- 1 package (1/4 ounce) active dry yeast
- 1-1/3 cups warm water (110° to 115°)
- 1 tablespoon sugar
- 1 tablespoon olive oil
- 1 teaspoon salt
- 3- 1/2 to 4 cups all-purpose flour

FILLING:

- 1 small onion, finely chopped
- 1 tablespoon olive oil
- 1 medium tomato, peeled and chopped
- 1 can (8 ounces) tomato sauce
- 1 garlic clove, minced
- 1-1/4 teaspoons salt
- 1 teaspoon dried basil
- Dash pepper
- 1/4 cup grated Parmesan cheese

Direction: Serving: 1 dozen. | Prep: 30mins | Cook: 25mins |

- ✓ In a large basin, combine yeast and warm water.
- ✓ Combine 2 1/2 cups flour, salt, oil, and sugar in a mixing bowl and whisk until smooth.
- ✓ Then add enough remaining flour to form a stiff dough. Knead for approximately 6-8 minutes on a floured surface, or until elastic and smooth.
- ✓ Place in an oiled bowl, flipping once to coat the top with grease. Cover and let aside in a warm area for approximately 1 hour, or until doubled. Meanwhile, in a skillet, sauté onion in oil until tender.
- ✓ Combine the pepper, basil, salt, garlic, tomato sauce, and tomato in a medium bowl.
- ✓ Bring to a boil and simmer, stirring constantly, until thickened.
- ✓ Allow to cool to approximately 110° - 115°.
- ✓ Following that, punch the dough down.
- ✓ Separate into 12 pieces and transfer to a lightly floured surface. Each should be rolled into a ball.
- ✓ Arrange on a prepared baking sheet 3 in. apart.
- ✓ Make an indentation in the center of each ball and insert 1 spoonful of filling.
- ✓ Sprinkle with grated Parmesan cheese.

- ✓ Allow to rise for approximately 20 minutes, or until doubled, in a warm environment.
- ✓ Bake for 25-30 minutes, or until golden brown, at 375°.
- ✓ Then transfer the pan to a wire rack to cool.
- ✓ Take advantage while the weather is still pleasant.

307) **Best Cinnamon Rolls**

Ingredients:

- 1 package (1/4 ounce) active dry yeast
- 1 cup warm whole milk (110° to 115°)
- 1/2 cup sugar
- 1/3 cup butter, melted
- 2 large eggs
- 1 teaspoon salt
- 4 to 4-1/2 cups all-purpose flour

FILLING:

- 3/4 cup packed brown sugar
- 2 tablespoons ground cinnamon
- 1/4 cup butter, melted, divided

FROSTING:

- 1/2 cup butter, softened
- 1/4 cup cream cheese, softened
- 1/2 teaspoon vanilla extract
- 1/8 teaspoon salt
- 1-1/2 cups confectioners' sugar

Direction: Serving: 16 rolls. | Prep: 40mins | Cook: 20mins |

- ✓ Warm milk can be used to dissolve the yeast.
- ✓ In a separate bowl, use a mixer to blend up the yeast mixture, eggs, butter, and sugar with 2 cups of the flour.
- ✓ Mix in enough of the remaining flour to form a moist, sticky dough.
- ✓ Using a floured surface, roll out the dough and knead it for 6 to 8 minutes, until it's elastic and supple.
- ✓ To grease the top, place in a greased basin and turn to coat.
- ✓ Wrap the area in plastic wrap.
- ✓ Until you've grown two times your original size, spend an hour rising in a warm place before continuing on your journey.
- ✓ Mix brown sugar with cinnamon. Punch down the dough and divide it in half.
- ✓ On a lightly floured board, roll out a portion to an 11x8-inch rectangle.
- ✓ Apply 2 tbsp. of butter on the surface.
- ✓ Sprinkle half of the brown sugar mixture around the sides.
- ✓ Starting from the long side, jellyroll-style, begin rolling. Pinch the seam to seal it.
- ✓ Cut into eight equal-sized pieces.
- ✓ Put the sliced side down in a 13x9-inch pan that has been sprayed with cooking spray.
- ✓ Cover with a kitchen towel.

- ✓ Repeat the process with the remaining filling and dough if necessary.
- ✓ In a warm place, let the dough rest for an hour until it has doubled in size.
- ✓ Set the oven temperature to 350°F.
- ✓ Serve until browned and crispy. Wire racks keep things cool.
- ✓ Salt, vanilla, cream cheese, and butter should be thoroughly mixed together for the frosting.
- ✓ Slowly include confectioners' sugar into the mixture.
- ✓ Put a layer on the top and put the rest in the fridge for later.

308) **Best Ever Crescent Rolls**

Ingredients:

- 3-3/4 to 4-1/4 cups all-purpose flour
- 2 packages (1/4 ounce each) active dry yeast
- 1 teaspoon salt
- 1 cup whole milk
- 1/2 cup butter, cubed
- 1/4 cup honey
- 3 large egg yolks
- 2 tablespoons butter, melted

Direction: Serving: 32 rolls. | Prep: 40mins | Cook: 10mins |

- ✓ Combine 1 1/2 cups flour, yeast, and salt in a large bowl and stir well.
- ✓ In a small saucepan, bring the honey, diced butter, and milk to 120-130°F.
- ✓ Beat on medium speed for 2 minutes after adding the wet components.
- ✓ Add the egg yolks and beat for 2 minutes on high speed.
- ✓ Mix in enough remaining flour to form a soft dough (the dough will get sticky).
- ✓ Turn the dough out onto a floured surface and knead it for 6 to 8 minutes until it is flexible and smooth.
- ✓ Put in a bowl that has been sprayed with cooking spray and flip it over once to coat the top.
- ✓ Using plastic wrap, cover the dough and let it rise for about 45 minutes in a warm place until it has doubled.
- ✓ Put the dough in a resalable plastic bag after it has been pounded out.
- ✓ Close the lid and put it in the fridge overnight to cool down.
- ✓ Dough should be placed on a floured surface and sliced in half before baking.
- ✓ Each piece should be rolled into a 14-inch ring, then cut into 16 wedges.
- ✓ Melted butter can be delicately brushed over the wedges. Seal the ends by pressing the pointed ends together.
- ✓ Place, point side down, on parchment-lined baking pans, spacing them apart by 2 inches.
- ✓ Allow the dough to rise in a warm place for about 45 minutes, until it has doubled.
- ✓ Set the oven temperature to 375°F and begin

preheating.

- ✓ *Bake for about 9 to 11 minutes, or until the bread is golden brown and crispy.*
- ✓ *Serve it warm, straight from the pans.*
- ✓ *Immediately after shaping, freeze rolls on baking sheets lined with parchment paper until they are solid.*
- ✓ *Put it back into the freezer in a resealable plastic bag.*
- ✓ *A maximum of four weeks can be frozen.*
- ✓ *Allow to rise (extend the rise time to 2 1/2 to 3 hours) and bake according to directions before using.*

309) __Bird Rolls__

Ingredients:

- 1 package (1/4 ounce) active dry yeast
- 1 cup warm milk (110° to 115°)
- 1/4 cup butter, melted
- 1/4 cup packed brown sugar
- 2 eggs
- 1 teaspoon salt
- 3-1/2 to 4 cups all-purpose flour

TOPPING:

- 1 egg
- 1 tablespoon water
- 16 whole unblanched almonds

Direction: Serving: 16 rolls. | Prep: 25mins | Cook: 15mins |

- ✓ *Dissolve the yeast in warm milk in a big bowl.*
- ✓ *Add 2 cups of flour, salt, 2 eggs, brown sugar and butter and beat it until it becomes smooth.*
- ✓ *Mix in enough leftover flour until a soft dough forms.*
- ✓ *Flip it onto a floured surface and knead it for about 6 to 8 minutes, until it becomes pliable and smooth.*
- ✓ *Put it in a greased bowl and flip it once to grease the top.*
- ✓ *Put cover and allow it to rise for about an hour in a warm area, until it doubles.*
- ✓ *Punch down the dough.*
- ✓ *Flip it onto a lightly floured surface, then split it into 16 pieces.*
- ✓ *Roll each into a 12- inch rope, then tie each into a knot.*
- ✓ *To shape the birds' head, tuck 1 end back into the knots.*
- ✓ *Cut 2 slits on the opposite end using scissors or a sharp knife to form the tail feathers.*
- ✓ *Put it on the greased baking trays and place it 2 inches apart.*
- ✓ *Put cover and allow it to rise for about 30 minutes, until it doubles.*
- ✓ *Beat the egg with water and brush it on top of the dough.*
- ✓ *Let it bake for 15 to 20 minutes at 350 ° or until it turns golden brown in color.*
- ✓ *Insert an almond into each to make the beak.*
- ✓ *Take it out of the pans, then transfer to wire racks to*

let it cool.

310) __Blender Yeast Rolls__

Ingredients:

- 1 cup warm 2% milk (110° to 115°)
- 1 package (1/4 ounce) active dry yeast
- 1/4 cup sugar
- 2 eggs
- 1/4 cup canola oil
- 3-1/4 cups all-purpose flour
- 1 teaspoon salt

Direction: Serving: about 1 dozen. | Prep: 20mins | Cook: 20mins |

- ✓ *Place all ingredients in a blender with the lid on and blend on low speed for about 30 seconds, until well incorporated.*
- ✓ *In a large basin, combine the salt and flour and stir until a smooth paste forms.*
- ✓ *Add the yeast mixture and stir with a spoon until well-combined.*
- ✓ *Without kneading Bake for about 30 minutes at 350°F until it has doubled in size.*
- ✓ *Reduce the dough's volume by whisking it.*
- ✓ *Half-fill grease-coated muffin cups.*
- ✓ *Bake for about 30 minutes until doubled in size, then remove the lid.*
- ✓ *At 350°F, bake for about 18-20 minutes, or until the bread is golden brown.*
- ✓ *Transfer to wire racks from the pans.*
- ✓ *It's a good time of year to be outside.*
- ✓

311) __Bourbon Soaked Bacon And Ginger Cinnamon Rolls__

Ingredients:

- 8 bacon strips
- 3/4 cup bourbon
- 1 tube (12.4 ounces) refrigerated cinnamon rolls with icing
- 1/2 cup chopped pecans
- 2 tablespoons maple syrup
- 1 teaspoon minced fresh gingerroot

Direction: Serving: 8 rolls. | Prep: 25mins | Cook: 10mins |

- ✓ *Pour the bourbon over the bacon in a shallow dish.*
- ✓ *Refrigerate overnight in an airtight container.*
- ✓ *Remove the bacon and bourbon from the pan, then wipe the pan clean.*
- ✓ *Working in batches, fry the bacon until it is almost crisp but still malleable in a large skillet.*
- ✓ *Drizzle with paper towels as you go.*
- ✓ *All but a teaspoon of drippings should be thrown away.*
- ✓ *Set the oven temperature to 375°F.*
- ✓ *Set aside a frosting package for later use.*
- ✓ *Spiral rolls can be rolled out into long strips or patted out into 6x1-inch pieces.*

- ✓ Every dough strip should have a strip of bacon attached to it, and then the dough should be rolled into a spiral.
- ✓ Close the ends by pressing them together.
- ✓ Repeat the procedure with the remaining dough.
- ✓ Using parchment paper, transfer the dough to a baking sheet and bake for 9 to 11 minutes, or until it's golden brown.
- ✓ Combine maple syrup and pecans in the meantime.
- ✓ In a separate bowl, combine the contents of the icing packet with the ground ginger.
- ✓ In the same skillet, cook the bacon drippings over medium heat.
- ✓ The nuts should be cooked for 2 to 3 minutes, stirring frequently, until they are just toasted.
- ✓ Frost the cinnamon rolls and top them with pecans while they're still warm.

312) **Braided Peppery Cheese Rolls**

Ingredients:

- 4-1/4 to 4-3/4 cups all-purpose flour
- 3 tablespoons sugar
- 2 packages (1/4 ounce each) active dry yeast
- 1-1/2 teaspoons salt
- 1 teaspoon coarsely ground pepper
- 1-1/2 cups 2% milk
- 1/4 cup butter, cubed
- 2 eggs
- 1/2 cup shredded cheddar cheese

Direction: Serving: 1 dozen. | Prep: 30mins | Cook: 15mins |

- ✓ A large bowl should be used to combine the pepper, salt, yeast, sugar, and two cups of flour.
- ✓ 120-130°F is a good target temperature for butter and milk.
- ✓ Beat it for 2 minutes on medium speed with the dry ingredients.
- ✓ Continue beating for an additional 2 minutes after adding 1/2 cup flour and 1 egg.
- ✓ Make a soft dough by adding enough of the remaining flour and cheese.
- ✓ Knead it on a floured board for about six to eight minutes, until it is flexible and smooth.
- ✓ Make sure the top is well-coated by putting it in a greased basin and then flipping it over.
- ✓ Allow it to rise in a warm place for about 30 minutes, or until it has doubled in size.
- ✓ The dough should be kneaded.
- ✓ Allow it to rest for 15 minutes on a floured surface before serving.
- ✓ Split it into 36 equal halves.
- ✓ Each rope should be 6 inches long.
- ✓ Make a braid out of three ropes, then seal the ends by pinching them.
- ✓ Use the remaining dough to repeat the process.
- ✓ Make sure to use oiled baking sheets.
- ✓ For about 30 minutes, cover it and let it rise in a

warm place until it reaches double its original size.
- ✓ Brush the braids with the remaining egg, which has been beaten.
- ✓ Bake at 375° for approximately 15 to 17 minutes, or until golden brown.
- ✓ It's time to remove it from the pan and place it on a cooling rack.

313) **Bran Knot Rolls**

Ingredients:

- 1 cup water (70° to 80°)
- 1/2 cup butter-flavored shortening
- 1 egg
- 1/3 cup sugar
- 3/4 teaspoon salt
- 1/2 cup bran flakes
- 1-1/2 cups bread flour
- 1-1/2 cups whole wheat flour
- 2-1/4 teaspoons active dry yeast
- 1 egg white, lightly beaten

Direction: Serving: 14 rolls. | Prep: 25mins | Cook: 15mins |

- ✓ In a bread machine pan, follow the manufacturer's instructions for putting in the ingredients.
- ✓ Set the dough to the appropriate setting (after 5 minutes of mixing, check the dough, then add 1-2 tbsp of water or flour if necessary).
- ✓ Using a spatula, transfer the dough to a lightly floured work surface.
- ✓ Punch it in the face.
- ✓ Allow it to cool for 10 minutes before putting the cover on.
- ✓ A rope can be made by slicing it into 14 parts, then rolling each piece into the next one.
- ✓ Pinch the ends together and tuck the knot under the sleeve.
- ✓ Make sure to use oiled baking sheets.
- ✓ Then, cover it with a towel and let it rise in a warm place for about 45 minutes until it doubles.
- ✓ Egg white can be used as a brush.
- ✓ Bake it at 375 ° for 15 to 20 minutes, or until it's golden brown.

314) **Bran Rolls**

Ingredients:

- 3/4 cup All-Bran
- 1/2 cup boiling water
- 2 packages (1/4 ounce each) active dry yeast
- 1/2 cup warm water (110° to 115°)
- 1/2 cup butter, softened
- 1/2 cup sugar
- 1-1/2 teaspoons salt
- 1 egg, beaten
- 3-1/2 to 3-3/4 cups all-purpose flour
- 1 tablespoon butter, melted

Direction: Serving: 2 dozen. | Prep: 40mins | Cook: 20mins |

- ✓ In a small bowl, combine boiling water and bran; set aside. In a separate bowl, dissolve yeast in warm water.
- ✓ In a large mixing basin, combine the salt, sugar, and butter.
- ✓ Combine the yeast mixture and egg well. 2 cups flour and bran mixture; beat on low speed for 3 minutes.
- ✓ Add enough remaining flour to form a soft dough.
- ✓ Transfer to a lightly floured surface and knead for 6 to 8 minutes, or until smooth and malleable.
- ✓ Place in an oiled bowl, flipping once to coat the surface with the batter.
- ✓ Cover and allow to double in size in a warm environment.
- ✓ Dough should be deflated.
- ✓ Transfer to a floured surface. Divide dough in half; divide each half into a dozen pieces.
- ✓ Each piece should be formed into a round; place rounds in a greased 13x9-inch baking sheet.
- ✓ Butter should be brushed on.
- ✓ Cover and allow to double in size for an hour.
- ✓ Bake at 375° for approximately 20 to 25 minutes, or until golden brown.
- ✓ Transfer the baked goods from the pan to the wire racks.

315) Breakfast Rolls

Ingredients:

- 1-pound ground beef
- 1 medium onion, chopped
- 2 teaspoons beef bouillon granules
- 1/2 teaspoon pepper
- 1 loaf (1 pound) frozen bread dough, thawed
- 3 slices Swiss cheese, cut into strips

Direction: Serving: 12 servings. | Prep: 25mins | Cook: 20mins |

- ✓ Cook onion and beef in a large skillet over medium heat until no pink color appears in the meat.
- ✓ After that, drain.
- ✓ Combine pepper and bouillon in a separate bowl. Allow 15 minutes for cooling.
- ✓ On a floured board, roll the dough into a 12x8-inch rectangle.
- ✓ Smear the beef mixture up to a half-inch from the short and one-inch from the long sides.
- ✓ Then, jellyroll style, roll up beginning with the long side.
- ✓ Pinch the seam shut.
- ✓ 12 slices Grease a 13x9-inch baking pan.
- ✓ Cover the pan and allow it rise for approximately 30 minutes, or until nearly doubled.
- ✓ Bake at 425° for 15 to 20 minutes, or until golden brown. Each bun should have two cheese strips atop it.
- ✓ Bake for a further five minutes, or until the cheese is melted.

316) Brunch Cinnamon Rolls

Ingredients:

- 3/4 cup 4% small-curd cottage cheese
- 1/3 cup reduced-fat plain yogurt
- 1/4 cup sugar
- 1/4 cup butter, melted
- 1 teaspoon vanilla extract
- 2 cups all-purpose flour
- 2 teaspoons baking powder
- 1/4 teaspoon baking soda
- 1/2 teaspoon salt

FILLING:

- 2 tablespoons butter, melted
- 1 cup chopped pecans
- 2/3 cup packed brown sugar
- 1- 1/2 teaspoons ground cinnamon

MAPLE GLAZE:

- 2/3 cup confectioners' sugar
- 3 tablespoons maple syrup
- 1 teaspoon vanilla extract

Direction: Serving: 1 dozen. | Prep: 30mins | Cook: 20mins |

- ✓ In a food processor, process the first five ingredients until smooth.
- ✓ Pulse in the salt, baking soda, baking powder, and flour until a soft dough forms; cover.
- ✓ Gently knead 4-5 times on a lightly floured surface.
- ✓ Rectangle 15x12 in. Brush butter up to 1/2-inch from the edge.
- ✓ Cinnamon, brown sugar, and pecans should all be combined and sprinkled over dough.
- ✓ Roll in jellyroll fashion, beginning with the long side.
- ✓ Pinch the seam to seal it. 12 slices in total.
- ✓ Place the cut side down in a prepared 9-inch circular baking sheet.
- ✓ At 400 °F, bake for 20-25 minutes, or until golden brown.
- ✓ Allow to cool for 5 minutes before inverting onto serving plate.
- ✓ Drizzle glaze over rolls after combining all of the glaze ingredients.
- ✓ Warm up your serving.

317) Butterfly Rolls

Ingredients:

- 4 cups sliced carrots
- 2 eggs
- 1 cup warm water (110° to 115°), divided
- 2 packages (1/4 ounce each) active dry yeast
- 3/4 cup vegetable oil
- 1/2 cup sugar
- 1 tablespoon molasses
- 2 teaspoons salt

- *8-1/2 to 9 cups all-purpose flour*

EGG WASH:

- *1 egg*
- *1 tablespoon water*
- *Poppy seeds, optional*

Direction: Serving: 2 dozen. | Prep: 30mins | Cook: 15mins |

- ✓ *Place the carrots in a saucepan with enough water to cover them, then bring to a boil.*
- ✓ *Reduce the heat to low, cover, and simmer until the meat is soft.*
- ✓ *Drain the carrots and puree them in a food processor or blender.*
- ✓ *Combine 1/2 cup warm water and the eggs in a food processor and pulse until smooth.*
- ✓ *In a large mixing basin, dissolve the yeast in the remaining warm water.*
- ✓ *Combine 5 cups flour, salt, molasses, sugar, oil, and carrot mixture in a mixing bowl and whisk until smooth.*
- ✓ *Add enough remaining flour to make a soft dough.*
- ✓ *Knead it for about 6 to 8 minutes on a floured surface, until it becomes elastic and smooth.*
- ✓ *Place it in an oiled mixing bowl and turn it once to grease the top.*
- ✓ *Cover and let it rise for approximately an hour in a warm place until it has doubled in size.*
- ✓ *Punch the dough down.*
- ✓ *It should be divided into 48 1 1/2-inch balls, 48 1-inch balls, and 24 3 3/4-inch logs.*
- ✓ *To form the butterflies, arrange the logs 5 inches apart on prepared baking pans.*
- ✓ *To make an antenna, cut a 1/2-inch slit in one end of the log using a sharp knife and separate the cut ends.*
- ✓ *Put two little balls on either side of the cut end, and a huge ball beneath each small ball so they touch.*
- ✓ *Allow it to rise in a warm place for about 45 minutes, or until it has doubled in size.*
- ✓ *Brush the water and egg mixture over the body of the butterflies.*
- ✓ *Sprinkle poppy seeds on top if desired.*
- ✓ *Preheat oven to 350°F and bake for 15 minutes, or until golden brown.*

318) **Buttermilk Pan Rolls**

Ingredients:

- *18 to 23 cups all-purpose flour*
- *1 cup buttermilk blend powder*
- *1/2 cup sugar*
- *2 tablespoons salt*
- *4-1/2 teaspoons active dry yeast*
- *1 teaspoon baking soda*
- *7 cups warm water (120° to 130°)*
- *1 cup vegetable oil*

Direction: Serving: 80 rolls. | Prep: 45mins | Cook: 20mins |

- ✓ *Mix baking soda, yeast, salt, sugar, buttermilk*

powder, and 15 cups flour together in several large mixing bowls.

- ✓ *Oil and water should be added. Until smooth, combine all ingredients.*
- ✓ *To form a soft dough, stir in enough remaining flour.*
- ✓ *Knead for 10 minutes, or until malleable and smooth, on a floured surface.*
- ✓ *Place in a couple large greased basins, tossing once to coat the surface with oil.*
- ✓ *Cover and set aside for 75 minutes to double in size in a warm location. Dough must be deflated.*
- ✓ *Divide the mixture into 80 pieces.*
- ✓ *Make a round out of every piece. 2 15x10x1-inch greased baking pans.*
- ✓ *Allow to rise for 30 minutes or until doubled in size.*
- ✓ *At 375°, bake for 20 minutes to half an hour, or until slightly browned.*
- ✓ *Remove the wire racks from the pans.*
- ✓ *Warm it up and serve it.*

319) **Buttermilk Wheat Rolls**

Ingredients:

- *1-1/2 cups warm buttermilk (70° to 80°)*
- *1/4 cup canola oil*
- *1 teaspoon lemon juice*
- *2 tablespoons sugar*
- *1-1/2 teaspoons salt*
- *1/4 teaspoon baking soda*
- *1/2 cup toasted wheat germ*
- *2 cups whole wheat flour*
- *1-1/4 cups bread flour*
- *2 teaspoons active dry yeast*
- *2 tablespoons butter, melted, optional*

Direction: Serving: 2 dozen. | Prep: 10mins | Cook: 15mins |

- ✓ *In the bread machine pan, layer the first ten ingredients in the sequence indicated by the manufacturer.*
- ✓ *Utilize the dough mode (after five minutes of mixing, check the dough and add one to two tablespoons of flour or water if necessary).*
- ✓ *Once the cycle is complete, turn the dough out onto a lightly floured surface and punch down.*
- ✓ *Divide into 24 equal parts and shape each piece into a ball.*
- ✓ *Distribute evenly across two prepared baking sheets.*
- ✓ *Allow the dough to double in size for around half an hour in a warm environment.*
- ✓ *Brush with butter if desired.*
- ✓ *Bake at 350°F for 12 to 14 minutes, or until golden brown.*
- ✓ *Remove the pans from the oven and cool on wire racks.*

320) **Buttery Crescent Rolls**

Ingredients:

- 1 tablespoon active dry yeast
- 1 teaspoon plus 1/3 cup sugar
- 1/2 cup warm water (110° to 115°)
- 1/2 cup butter, softened
- 1/2 cup warm 2% milk (110° to 115°)
- 1 large egg
- 3/4 teaspoon salt
- 4 cups all-purpose flour

Direction: Serving: 2 dozen. | Prep: 35mins | Cook: 10mins |

- ✓ In a large mixing basin, dissolve the 1 teaspoon sugar and yeast in warm water.
- ✓ 2 cups flour, remaining sugar, salt, egg, milk, and butter; beat until smooth.
- ✓ Add enough remaining flour to form a soft dough.
- ✓ Turn it out onto a floured area and knead for around 6–8 minutes, or until the dough becomes elastic and smooth.
- ✓ Place it in a greased bowl and turn it once to coat the top with grease.
- ✓ Cover and allow it to double in size for about an hour in a warm environment.
- ✓ Punch the dough down. It should be turned out onto a lightly floured surface and then split in half.
- ✓ Each component should be rolled into a 12-inch circle and then sliced into 12 wedges.
- ✓ From the wide end, roll the wedges up and set them on buttered baking pans, point side down, 2 inches apart.
- ✓ Conceal the ends with crescents.
- ✓ Cover and allow it to double in size for around 30 minutes in a warm location.
- ✓ Preheat oven to 350 °.
- ✓ Bake for 10 to 12 minutes, or until golden brown.
- ✓ Remove it from the pans and place on wire racks.

321) **Can't Eat Just One Cinnamon Rolls**

Ingredients:

- 1 package (1/4 ounce) active dry yeast
- 1 tablespoon sugar
- 1/4 cup warm water (110° to 115°)
- 1 cup 2% milk
- 1/3 cup instant vanilla pudding mix (half of a 3.4-ounce package)
- 1 large egg
- 1/4 cup butter, melted
- 1 teaspoon salt
- 3 to 3-1/2 cups all-purpose flour

FILLING:

- 3/4 cup sugar
- 1 tablespoon ground cinnamon

- 1/4 cup butter, melted

FROSTING:

- 1/2 cup butter, softened
- 2 teaspoons vanilla extract
- 1 teaspoon water
- 1-1/2 to 1-3/4 cups confectioners' sugar

Direction: Serving: 2 dozen. | Prep: 60mins | Cook: 20mins |

- ✓ In a small bowl, dissolve 1 tablespoon sugar and yeast in warm water.
- ✓ In a large mixing bowl, beat pudding mix and milk on low speed for 1 minute.
- ✓ Allow to stand for 1 minute or until soft-set.
- ✓ 2 cups flour, yeast mixture, salt, melted butter, and egg; beat on medium speed until smooth.
- ✓ Combine enough remaining flour to form a sticky, soft dough.
- ✓ Turn dough out onto a floured surface and knead for 6-8 minutes, or until smooth and elastic.
- ✓ Place in an oiled bowl and turn once to coat the top with grease.
- ✓ Cover. In a warm environment, rise for 1 hour until doubled.
- ✓ In a small bowl, combine cinnamon and sugar. Punch dough down; divide in half.
- ✓ Turn 1 part of dough onto a lightly floured surface.
- ✓ Roll into a rectangle measuring 18x10 inches.
- ✓ Brush 1/2 melted butter within 1/4-inch of the edges.
- ✓ Sprinkle with 1/2 of the sugar mixture.
- ✓ Roll up beginning with the long side in a jellyroll fashion.
- ✓ Pinch seam to seal.
- ✓ Cut into 12 slices.
- ✓ Rep with the remainder of the filling ingredients and dough.
- ✓ Place all slices, cut side down, in a greased 13x9-inch baking pan.
- ✓ Cover with a kitchen towel.
- ✓ In a warm environment, rise for 45 minutes until nearly doubled.
- ✓ Preheat oven to 350 degrees.
- ✓ Bake for 20-25 minutes, or until golden brown.
- ✓ Cool in pan on a wire rack.
- ✓ Frosting: In a small bowl, beat butter until creamy.
- ✓ Combine the water, vanilla extract, and enough confectioners' sugar to achieve the desired consistency.
- ✓ Spread on heated buns and serve immediately.

322) **Candy Cane Rolls**

Ingredients:

- 1 package (1/4 ounce) active dry yeast
- 1/4 cup warm water (110° to 115°)
- 3/4 cup warm whole milk (110° to 115°)
- 1/4 cup sugar
- 1/4 cup shortening

- 1 large egg
- 1 teaspoon salt
- 3-1/4 to 3-3/4 cups all-purpose flour
- 1 cup red candied cherries, quartered

ICING:
- 1 cup confectioners' sugar
- 1 to 2 tablespoons whole milk

Direction: Serving: 2 dozen. | Prep: 30mins | Cook: 15mins |

- ✓ In a small basin, dissolve yeast in warm water.
- ✓ In a large mixing basin, combine 2 cups flour, yeast mixture, salt, egg, shortening, sugar, and heated milk until blended.
- ✓ Combine cherries and remaining flour to form a soft, sticky dough.
- ✓ Turn out onto a floured surface and knead for 6-8 minutes, or until the dough is elastic and smooth.
- ✓ Place in a greased bowl, turn once to grease the top, and wrap in plastic wrap.
- ✓ In a warm environment, rise for 1 hour until doubled.
- ✓ Dough should be pounded down and allowed to rest for 10 minutes.
- ✓ Turn dough out onto a lightly floured board and divide in half.
- ✓ Each half should be rolled into a 12x7-inch rectangle, then cut into 12 1-inch wide strips and twist each strip.
- ✓ Arrange 2 inches apart on prepared baking pans, bending the end like a cane.
- ✓ Cover with a kitchen towel and allow to double in 45 minutes in a warm place.
- ✓ Preheat oven to 375°, 12-15 minutes till golden brown.
- ✓ Remove from pans and cool on wire racks.
- ✓ In a separate dish, combine confectioners' sugar and enough milk to get the desired consistency; drizzle over rolls.

323) **_Caramel Cinnamon Rolls_**

Ingredients:
- 1 1/2 cups milk
- 1 1/2 teaspoons salt
- 1/2 cup shortening
- 1/2 cup white sugar
- 2 (.25 ounce) packages active dry yeast
- 6 cups all-purpose flour, or more as needed
- 2 eggs, beaten
- 6 tablespoons butter
- 3/4 cup brown sugar
- 2 tablespoons ground cinnamon
- 1 1/2 cups brown sugar
- 3/4 cup butter
- 3/4 cup pecan halves
- 6 tablespoons light corn syrup

Direction: Serving: 27 | Prep: 25mins | Cook: 38mins |
- ✓ In a small saucepan over medium heat, heat milk for

5 minutes, or until it begins to bubble.
- ✓ Combine 1/2 cup sugar, 1/2 cup salt, and 1/2 cup shortening.
- ✓ Allow to cool for a minimum of 10 minutes, or until lukewarm.
- ✓ In a bowl, combine yeast and 1/4 cup warm water.
- ✓ Add to milk mixture together with eggs and flour.
- ✓ Combine thoroughly; cover loosely with a moist towel.
- ✓ 1 hour, or until dough has doubled in volume.
- ✓ Punch down dough.
- ✓ Cover
- ✓ Allow to double in volume for 40 minutes.
- ✓ Place dough on a lightly floured surface.
- ✓ 3 9x15-inch rectangles Each square should include 2 tbsp. butter.
- ✓ In a bowl, combine cinnamon and 3/4 cup brown sugar.
- ✓ Distribute mixture evenly across three rectangles.
- ✓ Roll each rectangle tightly starting with the long side.
- ✓ 27 rolls are obtained by slicing into 9 even pieces.
- ✓ Preheat oven to 190 °C/375 °F.
- ✓ In a bowl, combine corn syrup, pecans, 3/4 cup butter, and 1 1/2 cups brown sugar.
- ✓ Distribute mixture evenly among three baking pans.
- ✓ Bake for 5-10 minutes, or until caramel is bubbling, in a preheated oven.
- ✓ Remove from oven. Place 9 rolls in each pan.
- ✓ Allow to double in volume for 40 minutes.
- ✓ Bake for 30 minutes, or until golden brown, in a hot oven.
- ✓ Invert rolls immediately onto another dish/aluminum foil. Serve immediately.

324) **_Caramel Potato Rolls_**

Ingredients:
- 2-1/2 to 3 cups all-purpose flour
- 1/2 cup sugar
- 1/4 cup mashed potato flakes
- 1/4 cup nonfat dry milk powder
- 1 package (1/4 ounce) active dry yeast
- 1 teaspoon salt
- 1 cup hot water
- 1/4 cup canola oil
- 1 egg, beaten

TOPPING:
- 1 cup packed brown sugar
- 1/4 cup light corn syrup
- 3 tablespoons butter
- 36 pecan halves

FILLING:
- 1/3 cup sugar
- 2 tablespoons ground cinnamon

- 3 tablespoons butter, melted

  Direction: Serving: 1 dozen. | Prep: 20mins | Cook: 25mins |

✓ In a large mixing bowl, combine salt, yeast, milk powder, potato flakes, sugar, and 1 cup flour.

✓ In a small saucepan, heat the oil and water to 120-130 degrees.

✓ Combine with the dry ingredients and beat just until wet.

✓ Beat in the egg until smooth. Add enough remaining flour to form a soft dough (the dough will get sticky).

✓ Turn the dough out onto a floured surface and knead for approximately 6 to 8 minutes, or until malleable and smooth.

✓ Place in a cooking spray-coated bowl, flipping once to oil the top.

✓ Cover and allow to double in size for approximately an hour in a warm area.

✓ Punch the dough down.

✓ In a small saucepan, combine butter, corn syrup, and brown sugar and simmer, stirring constantly, over medium heat until sugar melts.

✓ Pour into a 12x9-inch baking dish that has been well sprayed with cooking spray and sprinkle with pecans.

✓ Turn the dough out onto a lightly dusted floured surface.

✓ Form a 12x15-inch rectangle by rolling. Cinnamon and sugar should be combined.

✓ Brush melted butter all the way to the edge of the pan, then sprinkle sugar mixture on top.

✓ Roll jellyroll manner, beginning with a long side; secure the seam with a pinch. Slice the dough into 12 rolls.

✓ Place the rolls cut side up in the dish.

✓ Cover and allow to double in size for around 15 to 20 minutes in a warm environment.

✓ Meanwhile, preheat the oven to 375 °F.

✓ Bake 25–30 minutes.

✓ Instantly invert onto a serving dish.

325) **Caramel Sweet Rolls**

Ingredients:

- 1/2 cup packed brown sugar
- 1/3 cup heavy whipping cream
- 1/4 cup chopped walnuts
- 1 tube (11 ounces) refrigerated breadsticks
- 2 tablespoons sugar
- 1 teaspoon ground cinnamon

  Direction: Serving: 6 servings. | Prep: 10mins | Cook: 25mins |

✓ In a small bowl, whisk together cream and brown sugar until sugar is melted; distribute in an 8-inch square buttered baking dish.

✓ Add walnuts as a finishing touch.

✓ On a lightly floured surface, unroll the breadstick dough; do not separate.

✓ Cinnamon and sugar should be mixed together and sprinkled over the dough.

✓ Reroll the dough, starting at the short end, and cut into 6 pieces.

✓ Place cut side down in prepared pan.

✓ Bake at 350° for 25-30 minutes, or until golden brown; cool for 1 minute.

✓ Serve heated by inverting onto a serving platter.

326) **Caramel Pecan Sticky Buns**

Ingredients:

- 1 package (1/4 ounce) active dry yeast
- 3/4 cup warm water (110° to 115°)
- 3/4 cup warm milk (110° to 115°)
- 1/4 cup sugar
- 3 tablespoons canola oil
- 2 teaspoons salt
- 3-3/4 to 4-1/4 cups all-purpose flour

FILLING:

- 1/4 cup butter, softened
- 1/4 cup sugar
- 3 teaspoons ground cinnamon
- 3/4 cup packed brown sugar
- 1/2 cup heavy whipping cream
- 1 cup coarsely chopped pecans

  Direction: Serving: 1 dozen. | Prep: 30mins | Cook: 30mins |

✓ In a large mixing basin, dissolve yeast in warm water.

✓ 1-1/4 cup flour, salt, oil, sugar, and milk are combined in a blender.

✓ For 2-3 minutes, beat on medium speed until smooth.

✓ Add enough of the remaining flour to make a soft dough.

✓ Place the dough on a floured board and knead for 6-8 minutes, or until it is elastic and smooth.

✓ Turn once to oil the top of a bowl coated with cooking spray.

✓ Allow to rise in a warm area for about 1 hour, or until doubled.

✓ Knead the dough.

✓ Place the dough on a flour-dusted board.

✓ Form an 18x12-inch rectangle. Butter the edges of the pan to within 1/2 inch of the edge.

✓ Combine the sugar and cinnamon and sprinkle it over the butter.

✓ Beginning with a long side, roll up jellyroll style; crimp seam to close. Cut the pie into 12 wedges.

✓ Combine the cream and brown sugar in a 13x9-inch baking pan sprayed with cooking spray.

✓ Pecans can be sprinkled on top.

✓ Place the sliced side of the rolls on top of the pecans.

✓ Allow to rise for about one hour, or until doubled in size.

✓ Preheat oven to 350°F and bake for 30-35 minutes, or until uniformly browned.

✓ Allow 1 minute to cool before inverting onto a serving dish.

327) Caraway Rolls
Ingredients:

- 2 packages (1/4 ounce each) active dry yeast
- 1/2 cup warm water (110° to 115°)
- 2 tablespoons caraway seeds
- 2 cups (16 ounces) 4% cottage cheese
- 1/2 teaspoon baking soda
- 1/4 cup sugar
- 2-1/2 teaspoons salt
- 2 large eggs, beaten
- 4-1/2 to 5 cups all-purpose flour
- 1 tablespoon butter, melted

Direction: Serving: 2 dozen. | Prep: 15mins | Cook: 20mins |

✓ In a large mixing basin, dissolve the yeast in the water.
✓ Caraway seeds should be added at this point.
✓ In a small saucepan, lukewarm the cottage cheese.
✓ Mix in the baking soda thoroughly.
✓ Incorporate into the yeast mixture.
✓ Combine the eggs, salt, and sugar in a mixing bowl.
✓ Slowly include enough flour to form a soft dough.
✓ Allow the dough to rise in a warm area for about 1 hour, or until doubled.
✓ Reduce the amount of liquid in the mixture.
✓ Divide the dough into 24 pieces on a lightly floured surface.
✓ Fill muffin tins halfway with batter.
✓ Allow for a 35-minute rising time, or until the dough has doubled in size.
✓ Preheat oven to 350°F and bake for 18 to 20 minutes.
✓ Brush with melted butter before transferring to wire racks.

328) Cheddar Pan Rolls
Ingredients:

- 4-1/2 cups all-purpose flour
- 2 tablespoons sugar
- 1 tablespoon salt
- 1 package (1/4 ounces) active dry yeast
- 2 cups milk
- 1 tablespoon butter
- 2 cups shredded cheddar cheese
- 1 egg white, beaten

Direction: Serving: 3 dozen. | Prep: 30mins | Cook: 20mins |

✓ In a large mixing basin, combine the yeast, salt, sugar, and 2 cups flour.
✓ In a saucepan, heat the butter and milk to 120-130 degrees.
✓ Combine it with the dry ingredients and beat until smooth.

✓ To make a soft dough, combine enough remaining flour and cheese. Kneading should be avoided.
✓ Allow it to rise in a warm place for about 45 minutes, or until it doubles in size (the dough will get soft).
✓ Divide the dough into three halves after punching it down.
✓ Make 12 balls out of each section.
✓ Place it in three 9-inch round baking pans that have been buttered.
✓ Allow to rise in a warm place for about 30 minutes, or until almost doubled.
✓ Brush it with egg white and bake it at 350 ° for 20 to 25 minutes, or until golden brown in color.

329) Cheddar/Squash Cloverleaf Rolls
Ingredients:

- 2 tablespoons sugar
- 1/4 cup warm water (110° to 115°)
- 1 package (1/4 ounce) active dry yeast
- 1 cup warm milk (110° to 115°)
- 4 tablespoons butter, melted, divided
- 1 teaspoon salt
- 1 cup mashed cooked winter squash
- 3/4 cup shredded cheddar cheese
- 4 to 4-1/2 cups all-purpose flour
- Sesame seeds, optional

Direction: Serving: 2 dozen. | Prep: 25mins | Cook: 20mins |

✓ With a large mixing basin, dissolve the yeast in water. Sprinkle yeast on top of the water and stir gently.
✓ Rest until the foam is frothy and light.
✓ Combine the cheese, squash, salt, 3 tablespoons of butter, and milk in a mixing bowl.
✓ To get a soft dough, add enough flour.
✓ Transfer dough to a lightly floured surface and knead for 5 minutes, or until it is no longer sticky.
✓ Form into a round and place in an oiled dish, flipping once to coat the surface with oil.
✓ Cover and leave to rise for an hour in a warm place until it has doubled in size.
✓ Meanwhile, lightly grease 2 dozen muffin cups.
✓ Dough should be deflated.
✓ Tear off little pieces and roll into one-inch circles.
✓ Fill each cup with three rounds.
✓ Cover and allow to rise for half an hour in a warm environment until it has doubled in size.
✓ Brush the remaining butter on the tops of the rolls, and sprinkle with sesame seeds if desired.
✓ Bake at 375° for 16 to 18 minutes, or until brown.
✓ Serve when still heated.

330) Cheesy Onion Burger Buns
Ingredients:

- 5-3/4 to 6-3/4 cups all-purpose flour, divided

- 3 tablespoons sugar
- 1- 1/2 teaspoons salt
- 2 packages (1/4 ounce each) active dry yeast
- 2 tablespoons butter, softened
- 2 cups warm water (120° to 130°)
- 1-1/2 cups shredded cheddar cheese
- 1/4 cup dried minced onion

Direction: Serving: 20 hamburger buns. | Prep: 25mins | Cook: 15mins |

✓ In a large mixing basin, combine the butter, yeast, salt, sugar, and 2 cups flour.

✓ Slowly pour in the hot water and beat for 2 minutes on medium speed.

✓ Add 1 cup flour and mix on high speed for 2 minutes.

✓ Combine enough leftover flour, onion, and cheese to form a soft dough.

✓ Turn it out onto a floured area and knead it for 6 to 8 minutes, or until it is smooth and malleable.

✓ Place it in an oiled mixing bowl and turn it once to grease the top.

✓ Cover and let it rise in a warm place for approximately an hour, or until it doubles in size.

✓ Turn the dough out onto a lightly floured surface and punch it down.

✓ Divide the dough into 20 pieces and roll them into smooth balls before placing them on oiled baking sheets.

✓ Allow it to rise in a warm place for about 45 minutes, or until it has doubled in size.

✓ Preheat the oven to 400 ° and bake it for 15 to 20 minutes.

✓ Allow it to cool on wire racks after removing it from the pans.

331) *Cherry Pecan Streusel Rolls*

Ingredients:

- 1/2 cup warm 2% milk (70° to 80°)
- 1/4 cup butter, melted
- 1/4 cup sugar
- 1 large egg
- 1/2 teaspoon salt
- 1-3/4 cups all-purpose flour
- 2/3 cup quick-cooking oats
- 2-1/4 teaspoons bread machine yeast

FILLING:

- 2/3 cup chopped pecans
- 1/2 cup sugar
- 1/3 cup quick- cooking oats
- 1/3 cup butter, melted
- 1-1/2 teaspoons ground cinnamon
- 1/2 cup dried tart cherries, chopped
- 1/3 cup almond paste, finely chopped
- 2 tablespoons all-purpose flour

GLAZE:

- 1 cup confectioners' sugar
- 4 teaspoons 2% milk
- 1/4 teaspoon almond extract

Direction: Serving: 1 dozen. | Prep: 35mins | Cook: 20mins |

✓ In a bread machine pan, combine the first 8 ingredients in the sequence indicated by the manufacturer.

✓ Select a dough setting (after 5 minutes of mixing, check the dough, then add 1-2 tbsp. of water or flour if necessary).

✓ Flip the dough onto a surface covered in a thin layer of flour after the cycle is finished.

✓ Make a 16x8-inch rectangle out of the dough.

✓ In a small mixing bowl, combine the cinnamon, butter, oats, sugar, and pecans. 1/3 cup is set aside for the topping.

✓ Combine the almond paste and cherries with the remaining filling.

✓ To within 1/4-inch of the dough's edges, sprinkle on top.

✓ Begin rolling jellyroll style with a long side, pressing the seam to seal.

✓ Cut each piece into 12 pieces.

✓ Place cut side down in a greased 13x9-inch baking sheet.

✓ Allow to rise for about an hour, or until it has doubled in size.

✓ Preheat the oven to 350 °F.

✓ Combine the flour and reserved topping in a bowl and sprinkle on top of the rolls.

✓ Preheat oven to 200°F and bake for 20–25 minutes, or until golden brown.

✓ In a small bowl, whisk together the extract, milk, and confectioner's sugar until smooth.

✓ Drizzle over warmed rolls.

332) *Chicken Little Cinnamon Rolls*

Ingredients:

- 1 loaf (1 pound) frozen bread dough, thawed
- 3 tablespoons butter, melted
- 1/3 cup sugar
- 2 teaspoons ground cinnamon
- 1 teaspoon grated lemon zest
- 1/2 cup raisins

GLAZE:

- 1/2 cup confectioners' sugar
- 2 tablespoons lemon juice

Direction: Serving: 1 dozen. | Prep: 15mins | Cook: 25mins |

✓ On a lightly floured surface, roll the dough into a 14x10-inch rectangle.

✓ Apply the butter using a brush.

✓ Combine the lemon zest, cinnamon, and sugar in a bowl and evenly sprinkle over the butter.

✓ Toss in some raisins.

✓ Roll up jellyroll manner, starting with the long side.

- ✓ To seal the seam, pinch it together. Cut each roll into 12 pieces.
- ✓ Place cut side down in a greased 11x7-inch baking pan.
- ✓ Cover. Allow 45 minutes for the dough to double in bulk.
- ✓ Preheat oven to 350°F and bake for 25-30 minutes, or until golden brown.
- ✓ Allow 10 minutes for cooling.
- ✓ To make the glaze, combine all of the ingredients and brush it on the rolls.

333) *Chive Garden Rolls*

Ingredients:

- 1 egg 1 cup (8 ounces) fat-free cottage cheese
- 1/4 cup canola oil
- 2 teaspoons honey
- 1 teaspoon salt
- 1 package (1/4 ounce) active dry yeast
- 1/2 cup warm water (110° to 115°)
- 1/4 cup toasted wheat germ
- 2-3/4 to 3-1/4 cups all-purpose flour
- 3 tablespoons minced chives

TOPPING:

- 1 egg, beaten
- 1 small onion, finely chopped

Direction: Serving: about 1 dozen. | Prep: 35mins | Cook: 15mins |

- ✓ In a mixing bowl, combine the salt, honey, oil, cottage cheese, and egg.
- ✓ Add the yeast to the egg mixture after dissolving it in warm water.
- ✓ Combine 1 1/2 cups flour and wheat germ in a mixing bowl. On medium speed, mix for 3 minutes.
- ✓ To make a soft dough, add enough remaining flour and chives.
- ✓ Knead it for about 10 minutes on a floured surface, until it becomes flexible and smooth.
- ✓ Place it in an oiled mixing bowl and turn it once to grease the top.
- ✓ Cover and let it rise for approximately an hour in a warm place until it has doubled in size.
- ✓ Roll out the dough to 3/4-inch thickness after punching it down.
- ✓ Using a 3-inch circle cutter, cut it out.
- ✓ Place it on baking trays that have been buttered.
- ✓ Allow it to rise for about 45 minutes, or until it has doubled in size.
- ✓ Top with an egg wash and a sprinkling of onion.
- ✓ Preheat the oven to 350°F and bake the rolls for 15 to 20 minutes, or until golden brown.

334) *Chocolate Chip Caramel Rolls*

Ingredients:

- 1 package (1/4 ounce) active dry yeast

- 3/4 cup warm water (110° to 115°)
- 3/4 cup warm 2% milk (110° to 115°)
- 3 tablespoons canola oil
- 1/4 cup sugar
- 1-1/2 teaspoons salt
- 3-3/4 to 4-1/2 cups all-purpose flour
- 3/4 cup miniature semisweet chocolate chips

FILLING:

- 1/4 cup butter, softened
- 1/3 cup sugar
- 2 tablespoons ground cinnamon
- 1 cup miniature semisweet chocolate chips

SYRUP:

- 1 cup packed brown sugar
- 3/4 cup heavy whipping cream

Direction: Serving: 1 dozen. | Prep: 40mins | Cook: 30mins |

- ✓ In a large mixing basin, dissolve the yeast in warm water.
- ✓ Add 3 cups flour, salt, sugar, oil, and milk, and beat on medium speed for 3 minutes.
- ✓ To produce a solid dough, add enough of the remaining flour.
- ✓ Turn the dough out onto a floured surface and knead in the chocolate chips for 6 to 8 minutes, or until it is elastic and smooth.
- ✓ Place in an oiled bowl and flip once to coat the top with oil.
- ✓ Cover the dough and let it rest in a warm place for approximately an hour, or until it has doubled in size.
- ✓ The dough should be pressed down and then flipped onto a lightly floured board.
- ✓ To make an 18x12-inch rectangle, roll out the dough. 12 slices of dough, spread with butter to within half an inch of the edges.
- ✓ Combine the cinnamon and sugar, then sprinkle over the butter.
- ✓ Drizzle with chocolate chunks, then carefully press into dough.
- ✓ Roll up the long side first, jellyroll style, and then pinch the seam closed.
- ✓ Cut into slices and place in a greased baking dish.
- ✓ With the cut side up, spread the rolls over the syrup.
- ✓ Cover them and let them rise for about 50 minutes, or until they have doubled in size.
- ✓ Preheat oven to 375°F and bake for 30 to 35 minutes, or until golden brown.
- ✓ Allow 10 minutes for cooling before transferring to a serving plate.
- ✓ Serve while the dish is still warm.

335) *Chocolate Cinnamon Buns*

Ingredients:

- 1 package (1/4 ounce) active dry yeast
- 3/4 cup warm water (110° to 115°)

- 2-1/4 cups all-purpose flour
- 1/2 cup plus 3 tablespoons sugar, divided
- 1/3 cup baking cocoa
- 1/4 cup shortening
- 1 teaspoon salt
- 1 egg
- 1 tablespoon butter, softened
- 1-1/2 teaspoons ground cinnamon

ICING:

- 3/4 cups confectioners' sugar
- 1 to 2 tablespoons milk

Direction: Serving: 15 rolls. | Prep: 25mins | Cook: 20mins |

- ✓ Melt the yeast in warm water and set aside.
- ✓ In a mixing dish, combine the egg, salt, shortening, cocoa, half cup of sugar, and flour.
- ✓ Pour in the yeast mixture to produce a soft dough.
- ✓ Knead for 5 to 10 minutes.
- ✓ Place in an oiled basin, tossing once to coat with oil.
- ✓ Allow to rise for an hour, or until doubled in size.
- ✓ Deflate.
- ✓ Transfer to a floured surface and roll out into a 15x9-inch rectangle.
- ✓ Drizzle the butter on top of the dough.
- ✓ Dust the remaining sugar and cinnamon on top of the butter.
- ✓ Roll up like a jellyroll.
- ✓ Roll the dough into one-inch rolls. Place in an 11x7-inch baking pan that has been greased.
- ✓ Allow to rise for 45 minutes, or until it has doubled in size.
- ✓ Preheat oven to 375°F and bake for 20 to 25 minutes.
- ✓ To make the icing, combine all of the ingredients and sprinkle on top of the warm rolls.
- ✓ Serve immediately.

336) *Chocolate Cinnamon Rolls With Icing*

Ingredients:

- 1 package (1/4 ounce) active dry yeast
- 3/4 cup warm water (110° to 115°)
- 1/4 cup shortening
- 1 teaspoon salt
- 1/4 cup plus 3 tablespoons sugar, divided
- 1 large egg
- 1/3 cup baking cocoa
- 2-1/4 cups all- purpose flour, divided
- 1 tablespoon butter, softened
- 1-1/2 teaspoons ground cinnamon

QUICK WHITE ICING:

- 1 cup confectioners' sugar
- 1/2 teaspoon vanilla extract
- 1-1/2 tablespoons whole milk

Direction: Serving: 1 dozen. | Prep: 30mins | Cook: 25mins |

- ✓ In a large basin, dissolve yeast in warm water; set aside for 5 minutes.
- ✓ Whisk for 2 minutes 1 cup flour, cocoa, egg, 1/4 cup sugar, salt, and shortening.
- ✓ Add remaining flour and stir with a spoon until smooth.
- ✓ Cover and let to double in volume for approximately 1 hour in a warm environment.
- ✓ Then, gently press the dough down and transfer to a well-floured surface (dough will be soft).
- ✓ Extend the rectangle to 12x9 inches.
- ✓ Gently spread butter on top.
- ✓ Combine remaining sugar and cinnamon in a small bowl; sprinkle over butter.
- ✓ Conscientiously roll up, beginning at the wide end.
- ✓ Divide the mixture into 12 equal bits and place in a greased 9-inch square baking pan.
- ✓ Allow to rise in a warm environment for about 45 minutes, then cover and allow to double in volume.
- ✓ Bake for 25 minutes at 375°F.
- ✓ Meanwhile, whisk all ingredients together in a small bowl until the mixture achieves the appropriate spreading consistency.
- ✓ Then, while still warm, frost rolls.

337) *Christmas Cranberry Rolls*

Ingredients:

- 3-3/4 cups all-purpose flour
- 1/4 cup sugar
- 1 package (1/4 ounce) active dry yeast
- 1 teaspoon salt
- 1-1/4 cups milk
- 1/4 cup vegetable oil
- 1 egg
- 3 tablespoons butter
- 3/4 cup packed brown sugar
- 3 tablespoons corn syrup
- 1 cup fresh cranberries, halved
- 1/2 cup chopped citron or mixed candied fruit
- 1/2 cup chopped pecans
- 2 teaspoons grated lemon peel

TOPPING:

- 2/3 cup sugar
- 1 teaspoon ground cinnamon
- 6 tablespoons butter, melted

Direction: Serving: 2-1/2 dozen. | Prep: 40mins | Cook: 25mins |

- ✓ Mix salt, yeast, sugar and 1 3/4 cups flour in a big bowl.
- ✓ Heat oil and milk to 120-130° in a saucepan.
- ✓ Put into dry ingredients; stir well. Add the egg; beat well.
- ✓ To make a soft dough, add enough leftover flour.

- ✓ Turn it onto floured surface; knead for 6-8 minutes till elastic and smooth.
- ✓ Put it into a greased bowl; to grease top, turn once.
- ✓ Cover; rise for 1-hour till doubled.
- ✓ Meanwhile, in a small saucepan, melt butter; mix in corn syrup and brown sugar.
- ✓ Spread it into 2 9-inches.
- ✓ Greased round baking pans; put aside.
- ✓ Mix lemon peel, pecans, citron and cranberries; sprinkle on brown sugar mixture.
- ✓ Punch down dough; turn it onto lightly floured surface.
- ✓ Divide to 30 pieces; roll every piece to 1 1/2-inches ball.
- ✓ Mix cinnamon and sugar in a small bowl.
- ✓ In another bowl, put melted butter.
- ✓ Roll every ball in butter and then roll in cinnamon-sugar.
- ✓ In each pan, put 15 balls.
- ✓ Cover; rise for 1-hour till doubled.
- ✓ Bake it at 375° till golden brown for 22-27 minutes.
- ✓ Cool for 5 minutes.
- ✓ Invert onto serving plates.

338) Christmas Tree Sweet Rolls

Ingredients:

- 2 packages (1/4 ounce each) active dry yeast
- 2-1/2 cups warm water (110° to 115°), divided
- 1/2 cup nonfat dry milk powder
- 1/2 cup canola oil
- 2 tablespoons sugar
- 2 teaspoons salt
- 7 to 8 cups all-purpose flour

FILLING:

- 1 package (8 ounces) cream cheese, softened
- 1/3 cup sugar
- 1 teaspoon vanilla extract
- 1/4 teaspoon ground cinnamon
- 1 can (8 ounces) crushed pineapple, well drained
- 1/2 cup chopped red and green candied cherries
- 1/4 cup chopped pecans

GLAZE:

- 2 cups confectioners' sugar
- 2 tablespoons whole milk
- 1 tablespoon butter, softened
- 1 teaspoon vanilla extract
- Red candied cherries and green colored sugar

Direction: Serving: 2 trees (11 rolls each). | Prep: 25mins | Cook: 20mins |

- ✓ In a large mixing basin, dissolve yeast in 1/2 cup warm water.
- ✓ 2 cups flour, remaining water, salt, sugar, oil, and milk powder; beat on medium speed for 2 minutes.

- ✓ Add enough remaining flour to form a soft dough.
- ✓ Turn out onto a floured surface and knead for approximately an hour, or until flexible and smooth.
- ✓ Meanwhile, in a small bowl, add cinnamon, vanilla, sugar, and cream cheese.
- ✓ Combine the pecans, cherries, and pineapple in a separate bowl and set aside.
- ✓ Punch the dough down.
- ✓ Turn over onto a floured surface and split in two.
- ✓ Each section should be rolled into an 11x9-inch rectangle.
- ✓ Filling should be spread to within a half-inch of the edges.
- ✓ Each rectangle should be rolled jellyroll style, starting with the long side; seal by pinching the seam.
- ✓ To create a tree, cut each log into 1-inch pieces.
- ✓ Cover the two baking sheets with foil and generously grease.
- ✓ Center 1 slice near the top of each foil-lined baking sheet for the treetop.
- ✓ Create a tree by arranging slices with their sides touching in three additional rows, adding one slice for each row.
- ✓ Underneath the tree trunk, center the leftovers slice.
- ✓ Cover and leave to rise for approximately 30 minutes, or until doubled.
- ✓ Bake at 350 degrees for 20 to 25 minutes, or until golden brown.
- ✓ Transfer the foil with the trees to wire racks and let aside for 20 minutes to cool.
- ✓ To make the glaze, in a mixing dish, combine vanilla, butter, milk, and confectioner's sugar until smooth.
- ✓ Transfer to a small plastic or pastry bag and cut a small hole in the bag's corner.
- ✓ Pipe garlands around the trees and decorate with colorful sugar and cherries.

339) Cinnamon Bread Rolls

Ingredients:

- 24 slices soft white sandwich bread, crusts removed
- 2 packages (8 ounces each) cream cheese, softened
- 1-1/2 cups sugar, divided
- 2 large egg yolks
- 2 teaspoons ground cinnamon
- 1 cup butter, melted

Direction: Serving: 2 dozen. | Prep: 20mins | Cook: 20mins |

- ✓ Flatten the bread with a rolling pin.
- ✓ In a large mixing bowl, combine the yolks, 1/2 cup sugar, and cream cheese. Spread the mixture on the bread.
- ✓ As if it were a jellyroll, roll it up.
- ✓ Combine the remaining sugar and cinnamon in a bowl.
- ✓ Rolls are delicately brushed with butter and then dunked in cinnamon-sugar.

- Place on ungreased baking pans and bake at 350°F for 20 minutes.

340) Cinnamon Buns

Ingredients:

- 1/4 cup butter, chilled
- 2 1/2 cups baking mix
- 1/2 cup milk
- 1 egg
- 2 tablespoons margarine, softened
- 3 tablespoons white sugar
- 1 1/2 teaspoons ground cinnamon
- 1 cup confectioners' sugar
- 1 tablespoon milk

Direction: Serving: 12 | Prep: 15mins | Cook: 15mins |

- Preheat oven to 220°C/425°F. Grease an 8-inch square baking pan.
- Cold butter should be cut into quarter-inch cubes. Toss cubes in baking mix until evenly covered.
- Combine egg and half cup milk in a separate bowl; stir into the butter mixture.
- Transfer dough to a cloth-lined board generously dusted with baking mix; turn to coat.
- Ten times fold and knead.
- Flatten into a 15x8-inch rectangle.
- Smear with margarine or butter that has been softened.
- Scatter cinnamon and sugar on top of dough.
- Securely roll up beginning with the 15-inch side.
- Incorporate the edge into the roll.
- Slice into a dozen sections with a sharp knife.
- Place in prepared pan, cut sides down.
- Bake 15 minutes, or until golden.
- Remove from the oven and set aside for 15 minutes to cool.
- 1 tablespoon milk and confectioners' sugar, whisked until smooth.
- Season with salt and pepper and sprinkle on top of cinnamon buns.
- Serve.

341) Cinnamon Cherry Rolls

Ingredients:

- 1/4 cup packed brown sugar
- 1 teaspoon ground cinnamon
- 1 tube (8 ounces) refrigerated crescent rolls
- 2 tablespoons butter, melted, divided
- 1 jar (10 ounces) maraschino cherries, drained and chopped
- 3/4 cup confectioners' sugar
- 4 to 5 teaspoons milk

Direction: Serving: 8 rolls. | Prep: 20mins | Cook: 15mins |

- Preheat oven to 375 °F.

- In a small bowl, combine cinnamon and brown sugar; set aside.
- Receipt dough should be unrolled.
- Divide the rectangle into triangles. 1 tbsp. butter, brush 1 tbsp.
- Sprinkle 1 1/2 teaspoon brown mixture on top; garnish with cherries.
- Roll up from the wide end.
- Arrange point side down on a greased baking sheet.
- Ends with a slight bend.
- Brush remaining butter on.
- Sprinkle any remaining brown sugar mixture on top. 12-15 minutes till golden brown.
- In a small bowl, combine confectioners' sugar and enough milk to achieve a dripping consistency.
- Drizzle over hot rolls.

342) Cinnamon Cream Roll Ups

Ingredients:

- 1 package (8 ounces) cream cheese, softened
- 1 large egg yolk
- 1-1/4 cups sugar, divided
- 1 loaf (1 pound) sandwich bread, crusts removed
- 1 tablespoon ground cinnamon
- 1/4 cup butter, melted

Direction: Serving: 8-10 servings. | Prep: 20mins | Cook: 20mins |

- In a small bowl, whisk together 1/4 cup sugar, egg yolk, and cream cheese.
- Flatten bread pieces with a rolling pin.
- Spread cream cheese mixture on each slice to within 1/2-inch of the edges.
- Roll up diagonally from point to point.
- In a shallow bowl, combine the remaining sugar and cinnamon.
- Rollups should be dipped in melted butter and then in cinnamon-sugar mixture.
- Fill a 15x10x1-inch ungreased baking pan halfway.
- At 350°F, bake for 16-19 minutes, or until gently browned.
- Cool on wire racks.

343) Cinnamon Flat Rolls

Ingredients:

- 1 package (16 ounces) frozen bread dough dinner rolls, thawed
- 5 tablespoons olive oil
- 1/2 cup sugar
- 1 tablespoon ground cinnamon

Direction: Serving: 1 dozen. | Prep: 15mins | Cook: 0 mins |

- On a floured surface, roll each dough into a 5-inch circle.
- Apply oil with a brush.
- Grill, uncovered, for 1 minute per side, or until golden brown.

- ✓ Burst any large bubbles with a fork.
- ✓ Cinnamon and sugar should be combined and sprinkled on rolls.

344) **Cinnamon Mincemeat Buns**

Ingredients:

- 1 package (1/4 ounce) active dry yeast
- 1 cup warm water (110° to 115°)
- 3 tablespoons sugar
- 1-1/2 teaspoons salt
- 1/4 cup canola oil
- 1 egg
- 3-1/2 to 4 cups all-purpose flour

FILLING:

- 1 package (9 ounces) condensed mincemeat
- 1/2 cup unsweetened apple cider or juice
- 1/4 cup packed brown sugar
- 1-1/2 teaspoons ground cinnamon
- 2 tablespoons butter

GLAZE:

- 3/4 cup confectioners' sugar
- 1 tablespoon apple cider or juice
- 1/2 teaspoon ground cinnamon

Direction: Serving: 16 rolls. | Prep: 40mins | Cook: 25mins |

- ✓ Melt yeast in warm water. 1 cup flour, 1 egg, oil, salt, and sugar in a large mixing bowl until smooth.
- ✓ Combine enough remaining flour to form a soft dough.
- ✓ Turn out onto a floured board and knead for 6-8 minutes, or until smooth and elastic.
- ✓ Place in an oiled bowl and turn once to coat the top with grease.
- ✓ Cover. Refrigerate for 4 hours before serving.
- ✓ Crumble mincemeat in a small pot.
- ✓ Add cider and bring to a boil. Cook for 1 minute while stirring.
- ✓ Turn off the heat totally cool.
- ✓ Combine cinnamon and brown sugar in a small bowl; set aside.
- ✓ Punctuate dough.
- ✓ Turn out onto a floured work surface.
- ✓ Roll the dough into a 16x12-inch rectangle.
- ✓ Spread filling to within 1/2-inch of the edges.
- ✓ On top, sprinkle the brown sugar mixture.
- ✓ Make a dot with butter.
- ✓ Roll up starting with the long side in a jellyroll fashion.
- ✓ Pinch the seam together to seal it.
- ✓ Cut into 16 rolls.
- ✓ Greased 9-inch round baking pans, cut side up.
- ✓ Cover and allow to double in size for 1 hour.
- ✓ At 350°F, bake for 25–30 minutes, or until golden brown.

- ✓ Combine glaze ingredients in a small bowl; drizzle over warm rolls.

345) **Cinnamon Roll Biscuits**

Ingredients:

- 2 cups all-purpose flour
- 3 teaspoons baking powder
- 1 teaspoon salt
- 1/4 teaspoon baking soda
- 1 cup buttermilk
- 1/4 cup canola oil
- 1 teaspoon vanilla extract
- 1/2 cup butter, softened
- 1/2 cup sugar
- 3/4 teaspoon ground cinnamon
- 1/4 teaspoon ground cardamom
- 1/2 cup chopped pecans, optional

GLAZE:

- 1 cup confectioners' sugar
- 1 teaspoon vanilla extract
- 3 to 4 teaspoons 2% milk

Direction: Serving: 14 biscuits. | Prep: 25mins | Cook: 20mins |

- ✓ In a large mixing basin, combine baking soda, salt, baking powder, and flour.
- ✓ Combine vanilla extract, oil, and buttermilk in a small bowl; stir into dry ingredients until barely moistened.
- ✓ It's going to be sticky.
- ✓ Knead it 8-10 times on a well-floured surface.
- ✓ Roll out dough to a rectangle measuring 15x9 inches.
- ✓ Spread butter to within 1/2-inch of the edges.
- ✓ Combine pecans (optional), cardamom, cinnamon, and sugar in a small mixing bowl; sprinkle over butter.
- ✓ Roll up beginning with the long side in a jellyroll fashion.
- ✓ Pinch seam to seal 1 1/2-inch slices.
- ✓ Arrange 1 inch apart on a parchment paper-lined baking sheet.
- ✓ Bake at 400° for 20-25 minutes, or until lightly browned.
- ✓ Meanwhile, in a small bowl, combine vanilla, confectioners' sugar, and enough milk to achieve a drizzling consistency.
- ✓ Drizzle warm biscuits with the glaze.
- ✓ Immediately serve.

346) **Cinnamon Roll Cherry Cobbler**

Ingredients:

- 1 can (14-1/2 ounces) pitted tart cherries
- 1/2 cup sugar
- 2 tablespoons cornstarch
- 1/2 cup water

- *3 tablespoons red-hot candies*

CINNAMON ROLL TOPPING:

- *1-1/2 cups all-purpose flour*
- *6 tablespoons brown sugar, divided*
- *2 teaspoons baking powder*
- *1/2 teaspoon salt*
- *1/4 cup shortening*
- *1 large egg, lightly beaten*
- *1/4 cup whole milk*
- *1 tablespoon butter, softened*
- *1/3 cup finely chopped pecans*
- *1/2 teaspoon ground cinnamon*

LEMON GLAZE:

- *1/2 cup confectioners' sugar*
- *1 tablespoon lemon juice*

Direction: Serving: 8 servings. | Prep: 30mins | Cook: 25mins |

- ✓ Drain cherries, reserving juice for later; set cherries aside.
- ✓ In a small saucepan, whisk together the reserved juice, water, cornstarch, and sugar until smooth.
- ✓ Incorporate red-hots; bring to a boil, constantly mixing.
- ✓ Cook until the mixture is bubbling and thick and the red hots have melted, about 1-2 minutes longer.
- ✓ Combine cherries with the sauce and heat thoroughly.
- ✓ Place in a prepared 8-inch square baking dish.
- ✓ In a large mixing basin, combine salt, baking powder, 3 tablespoons brown sugar, and flour.
- ✓ Shortening should be incorporated until crumbly.
- ✓ Combine milk and egg in a separate bowl; stir into crumb mixture until barely combined.
- ✓ Knead 3-4 minutes on a lightly floured surface.
- ✓ Roll into a rectangle measuring 14x10 inches.
- ✓ Butter the surface. Sprinkle pecans on top.
- ✓ Sprinkle remaining brown sugar and cinnamon on top.
- ✓ Roll up beginning with the short side in a jellyroll fashion.
- ✓ Cut into eight slices.
- ✓ Place cut side down over cherry filling.
- ✓ At 400°, bake for 25-30 minutes, or until golden brown.
- ✓ Allow 10 minutes to cool.
- ✓ Combine glaze ingredients in a small bowl; drizzle over cobbler.

347) **Cinnamon Sticky Buns**

Ingredients:

- *1 cup packed brown sugar*
- *1/2 cup corn syrup*
- *1/2 cup butter, cubed*
- *1 cup coarsely chopped pecans*

- *1/2 cup sugar*
- *2 tablespoons ground cinnamon*
- *2 tubes (17.3 ounces each) large refrigerated biscuits*

Direction: Serving: 12-16 servings. | Prep: 25mins | Cook: 25mins |

- ✓ In a saucepan, combine butter, corn syrup, and brown sugar; boil and stir until sugar dissolves.
- ✓ Add pecans.
- ✓ Scoop onto a 13x9-inch greased baking pan.
- ✓ In a small bowl, combine cinnamon and sugar.
- ✓ Each biscuit should be halved and dredged in sugar-cinnamon.
- ✓ Place cut side down on top of brown sugar mixture.
- ✓ Bake at 375° for 25–30 minutes, or until golden brown.
- ✓ Serve immediately after flipping onto a serving plate.

348) **Russian Black Bread**

Ingredients:

- *1 1/4 cups dark rye flour*
- *2 1/2 cups unbleached flour*
- *1 teaspoon instant coffee*
- *2 tablespoons unsweetened cocoa powder*
- *1 tablespoon whole caraway seeds*
- *1/2 teaspoon dried minced onion*
- *1/2 teaspoon fennel seeds*
- *1 teaspoon sea salt*
- *2 teaspoons active dry yeast*
- *1 1/3 cups water, at room temperature*
- *1 teaspoon sugar*
- *1 1/2 tablespoons dark molasses*
- *1 1/2 tablespoons apple cider vinegar*
- *3 tablespoons vegetable oil*

Direction: Servings: 1 Cooking Time: 3 Hours

- ✓ In a mixing bowl, combine all dry ingredients except the yeast.
- ✓ To begin, layer the wet ingredients in the bread pan; then layer the dry ingredients on top.
- ✓ In the center of the dry ingredients, make a well and add the yeast.
- ✓ Press Start and select the Basic bread cycle with a medium crust color.
- ✓ Allow 15 minutes for cooling before slicing.

349) **Chunky Chocolate Loaf**

Ingredients:

- *½ cup coconut flour*
- *¼ cup almond flour*
- *¼ cup protein powder, unsweetened*
- *½ cup no-calorie sweetener of your choice*
- *¼ cup dark chocolate chunks,*
- *70% cocoa solids*
- *¼ cup dark cocoa powder*

- One teaspoon baking soda
- ½ teaspoon salt
- Six eggs
- ½ cup of coconut oil

Direction: Servings: 1 Loaf Cooking Time: 1 Hour And 30 Minutes

✓ In the bread pan, combine the wet ingredients first, followed by the dry components.

✓ Your bread machine's "Quick" or "Cake" setting should be selected.

✓ Allow all cycles to complete.

✓ Take the pan out of the machine.

✓ Ten minutes should pass before removing the loaf from the pan.

✓ Allow the loaf to thoroughly cool before slicing it.

350) __Bread Machine Pizza Dough__

Ingredients:

- Water – 1 ½ cups
- Oil – 1 ½ tbsp.
- Bread flour – 3 ¾ cups
- Sugar – 1 tbsp. plus 1 tsp.
- Salt – 1 ½ tsp.
- Active dry yeast – 1 ½ tsp.

Direction: Servings: 1 Pizza Dough Cooking Time: 1 Hour and 30 Minutes:

✓ Add everything in the bread machine according to bread machine recommendations.

✓ Select the Dough cycle.

✓ Remove the dough when done. Roll it out and bake

351) __Sweet Bread Sugared Doughnuts__

Ingredients:

- 2/3 cup milk
- ¼ cup water
- ¼ cup butter, softened
- 1 egg
- 3 cups bread flour
- ¼ cup sugar
- 1 teaspoon salt
- 2½ teaspoons bread machine or fast-acting dry yeast
- Vegetable oil
- Additional sugar, if desired

Direction: PREP: 30 MINUTES PLUS FERMENTING TIME /MAKES 20 DOUGHNUTS

✓ Preparing the Ingredients. Choose the size of loaf of your preference and then measure the ingredients.

✓ Add all of the ingredients mentioned previously in the list, except for the vegetable oil and additional sugar.

✓ Close the lid after placing the pan in the bread machine.

✓ Make sure the Bake cycle is selected. Select Dough/Manual and avoid using the delay cycle.

✓ To remove the dough from the pan, you'll need to use

floured hands.

✓ Let it rest on a floured surface for 10 minutes before serving.

✓ On a lightly floured surface, roll out the dough to a 3/8-inch thickness. Flour doughnut cutter and cut out doughnuts. Allow 35 to 45 minutes for the board to gradually lift on its own.

✓ In deep fryer or heavy Dutch oven, heat 2 to 3 inches' oil to 375°F.

✓ Fry doughnuts in oil, 2 or 3 at a time, turning as they rise to the surface.

✓ Fry 2 to 3 minutes or until golden brown on both sides.

✓ Transfer to a cooling rack after removing from oil using a slotted spoon.

✓ Roll warm doughnuts in sugar.

352) __Chocolate Cherry Bread__

Ingredients:

- 1 cup milk
- 1 egg
- 3 Tbsp water
- 4 tsp butter
- ½ tsp almond extract
- 4 cups bread flour
- 3 Tbsp sugar
- 1 tsp salt
- 1¼ tsp active dry yeast
- ½ cup dried cherries, snipped
- ½ cup semisweet chocolate pieces, chilled

Direction: PREP: 30 MINUTES PLUS FERMENTING TIME /MAKES 14 SLICES

✓ Preparing the Ingredients In the order and at the temperature specified by the maker of your bread machine, add each ingredient to the bread machine.

✓ Select the Bake Cycle Close the lid, select the sweet loaf, low crust setting on your bread machine, and press start.
Take out the baked bread from the bread machine and allow it to cool on a cooling rack.

353) __Apple Honey Bread__

Ingredients:

- 12 slice bread (1½ pounds)
- 5 tablespoons lukewarm milk
- 3 tablespoons apple cider, at room temperature
- 3 tablespoons sugar
- 2 tablespoons unsalted butter, melted
- 1½ tablespoons honey
- ¼ teaspoon table salt
- 3 cups white bread flour
- 1¼ teaspoons bread machine yeast
- 1 apple, peeled, cored, and finely diced

Direction: PREP: 10 MINUTES PLUS FERMENTING TIME /MAKES 1 LOAF

✓ Preparing the Ingredients. Choose the size of loaf of

your preference and then measure the ingredients.

- ✓ Add all of the ingredients mentioned previously in the list, except for the apples.
- ✓ Close the lid after placing the pan in the bread machine.
- ✓ Make sure the Bake cycle is selected.
- ✓ Then Start the bread machine.
- ✓ For a basic loaf, choose the white option, then the loaf size, and finally the crust color.
- ✓ Begin the process. Immediately after the machine tells you to add ingredients, put the apples into the machine.
- ✓ When the breadmaker cycle is complete, carefully remove the pan from the machine and allow it to cool before serving.
- ✓ Remove the bread from the pan, put in a wire rack to Cool about 5 minutes. Slice

354) Chocolate Chip Peanut Butter Banana Bread

Ingredients:

- 12 to 16 slice bread (1½ to 2 pounds)
- 2 bananas, mashed
- 2 eggs, at room temperature
- ½ cup melted butter, cooled
- 2 tablespoons milk, at room temperature
- 1 teaspoon pure vanilla extract
- 2 cups all-purpose flour
- ½ cup sugar
- 1¼ teaspoons baking powder
- ½ teaspoon baking soda
- ½ teaspoon salt
- ½ cup peanut butter chips
- ½ cup semisweet chocolate chips

Direction: PREP: 10 MINUTES PLUS FERMENTING TIME /MAKES 1 LOAF

- ✓ Preparing the Ingredients. In the bread machine bucket, mix the bananas, eggs, butter, milk, and vanilla extract. Set aside.
- ✓ Toss the flour, sugar, baking powder, baking soda, salt, peanut butter chips, and chocolate chips in a medium basin.
- ✓ To the bucket, add the dry ingredients. Select the Bake Cycle and press Start to program the machine for Quick/Rapid bread.
- ✓ When the bread is finished, insert a knife and check to see if it comes out clean.
- ✓ If the loaf requires an additional few minutes, look for a Bake Only button on the control panel and increase the time by ten minutes.
- ✓ Remove the bucket from the machine once the loaf is finished.
- ✓ Allow 5 minutes for the bread to cool.
- ✓ Shake the bucket gently to extract the loaf, then put it out onto a rack to cool.

355) Easy Apple Coffee Cake

Ingredients:

- 2/3 cup water
- 3 tablespoons butter, softened
- 2 cups bread flour
- 3 tablespoons granulated sugar
- 1 teaspoon salt
- 1½ teaspoons bread machine or fast-acting dry yeast
- 1 cup canned apple pie filling
- Powdered sugar, if desired

Direction: PREP: 10 MINUTES PLUS FERMENTING TIME /MAKES 10 SERVINGS

- ✓ Preparing the Ingredients. Choose the size of loaf of your preference and then measure the ingredients.
- ✓ Add all of the ingredients mentioned previously in the list, except for pie filling and powdered sugar.
- ✓ After placing the pan in the bread maker, close the top.
- ✓ Using lightly floured hands, remove dough from pan.
- ✓ Cover and set aside on a floured surface for 10 minutes.
- ✓ Choose the Bake Cycle Choose between the Dough/Manual cycles. Avoid using the delay cycle.
- ✓ Grease a large cookie sheet with cooking spray.
- ✓ On a lightly floured surface, roll dough into a 128-inch rectangle.
- ✓ Arrange on a cookie sheet. Spoon pie filling lengthwise down the length of the rectangle's center third.
- ✓ On each 13-inch side, using a sharp knife, cut at 1-inch intervals from filling to dough edge. Overfilling ends should be folded up.
- ✓ Overfill strips diagonally, alternating sides and overlapping in the center.
- ✓ Cover and allow to rise for 30 to 45 minutes, or until doubled in size, in a warm area.
- ✓ When touched, the dough is ready if the indentation remains.
- ✓ Preheat oven to 375 degrees Fahrenheit.
- ✓ Bake for 30–35 minutes, or until the top is golden brown.
- ✓ Cool on cooling rack after removing from cookie sheet.
- ✓ Sprinkle with powdered sugar.

356) White Chocolate Bread

Ingredients:

- 12 slice bread (1½ pounds)
- 1 cup lukewarm milk
- 1 egg, at room temperature
- 2 tablespoons unsalted butter, melted
- 1½ teaspoons pure vanilla extract
- 3 tablespoons light brown sugar
- 4 teaspoons cocoa powder, unsweetened
- ¾ teaspoon table salt

- 3 cups white bread flour
- 1¼ teaspoons bread machine yeast
- ⅓ cup semisweet chocolate chips
- ⅓ cup white chocolate chips

Direction: PREP: 10 MINUTES PLUS FERMENTING TIME /MAKES 1 LOAF

✓ Preparing the Ingredients. Choose the size of loaf of your preference and then measure the ingredients.
✓ Add all of the ingredients mentioned previously in the list, except for the chocolate chips. Close the lid after placing the pan in the bread machine.
✓ Select the Bake Cycle Turn on the bread machine.
✓ For a basic loaf, choose the white option, then the loaf size, and finally the crust color.
✓ Reset the loop.
✓ Both chocolate chips should be added when the machine asks for them.
✓ When the breadmaker cycle is complete, carefully remove the pan from the machine and allow it to cool before serving.
✓ Remove the bread from the pan, put in a wire rack to Cool about 5 minutes. Slice

357) Chocolate Sour Cream Bread

Ingredients:

- 12 slice bread (1½ pounds)
- 1 cup sour cream
- 2 eggs, at room temperature
- 1 cup sugar
- ½ cup (1 stick) butter, at room temperature
- ¼ cup plain Greek yogurt
- 1¾ cups all-purpose flour
- ½ cup unsweetened cocoa powder
- ½ teaspoon baking powder
- ½ teaspoon salt
- 1 cup milk chocolate chips

Direction: PREP: 20 MINUTES PLUS FERMENTING TIME /MAKES 1 LOAF

✓ Preparing the Ingredients. Whisk together the sour cream, eggs, sugar, butter, and yogurt in a small bowl until just mixed.
✓ Add the flour, cocoa powder, baking powder, salt, and chocolate chips to the bread machine bucket after the liquid ingredients are added.
✓ Start the machine and program it for Quick/Rapid bread.
✓ When the bread is finished, insert a knife and check to see if it comes out clean.
✓ Choose a Bake Cycle If the loaf requires an additional few minutes, look for a Bake Only button on the control panel and increase the time by ten minutes.
✓
✓ When the loaf is finished, take the bucket from the machine and set aside for 5 minutes to cool.
✓ Shake the bucket gently to extract the loaf, then put it out onto a rack to cool.

358) Chocolate Orange Bread

Ingredients:

- 1⅝ cups strong white bread flour
- 2 tbsp. cocoa
- 1 tsp ground mixed spice
- 1 egg, beaten
- ½ cup water
- ¼ cup orange juice
- 2 tbsp. butter
- 3 tbsp. light muscovado sugar
- 1 tsp salt
- 1½ tsp easy bake yeast
- ¾ cup mixed peel
- ¾ cup chocolate chips

Direction: PREP: 10 MINUTES PLUS FERMENTING TIME /MAKES 14 SLICES

✓ Preparing the Ingredients Sift the flour, cocoa, and spices together in a bowl.
✓ In the order and at the temperature specified by the maker of your bread machine, add each ingredient to the bread machine.
✓ Select the Bake Cycle Close the lid, select the sweet loaf, medium crust setting on your bread machine, and press start.
✓ Add the mixed peel and chocolate chips 5 to 10 minutes before the last kneading cycle ends.
✓ Take out the baked bread from the bread machine and allow it to cool on a cooling rack.

359) Coffee Cake Banana Bread

Ingredients:

- 4 medium bananas, mushed
- 2 tbsp. brown sugar
- 1½ tsp vanilla extract
- ¾ tsp ground cinnamon
- ½ cup butter, softened
- 1 cup sugar
- 2 eggs
- 2 cups all-purpose flour
- 1 tsp baking soda
- ¼ tsp salt
- 2 tbsp. Greek yogurt

Direction: PREP: 10 MINUTES PLUS /MAKES 14 SLICES

✓ Preparing the Ingredients. In the order and at the temperature specified by the maker of your bread machine, add each ingredient to the bread machine.
✓ Select the Bake Cycle Close the lid, select the sweet loaf, low crust setting on your bread machine, and press start.
✓ Take out the baked bread from the bread machine and allow it to cool on a cooling rack.

360) Ginger Spiced Bread

Ingredients:

- 12 slice bread (1½ pounds)
- 1 cup lukewarm buttermilk
- 1 egg, at room temperature
- ¼ cup dark molasses
- 1 tablespoon unsalted butter, melted
- 3 tablespoons sugar
- 1½ teaspoons table salt
- 3½ cups white bread flour
- 1 teaspoon ground cinnamon
- ½ teaspoon ground nutmeg
- ¼ teaspoon ground cloves
- 1½ teaspoons ground ginger
- 2 teaspoons bread machine yeast

Direction: PREP: 10 MINUTES PLUS FERMENTING TIME /MAKES 1 LOAF

- ✓ Preparing the Ingredients. Choose the size of loaf of your preference and then measure the ingredients.
- ✓ Add all of the ingredients mentioned previously in the list. Close the lid after placing the pan in the bread machine.
- ✓ Select the Bake Cycle Turn on the bread machine.
- ✓ Select the Sweet setting, select the loaf size, and the crust color. Press start.
- ✓ When the breadmaker cycle is complete, carefully remove the pan from the machine and allow it to cool before serving.
- ✓ Remove the bread from the pan, put in a wire rack to Cool about 10 minutes.
- ✓ Slice

361) Nectarine Cobbler Bread

Ingredients:

- 12 to 16 slice bread (1½ to 2 pounds)
- ½ cup (1 stick) butter, at room temperature
- 2 eggs, at room temperature
- 1 cup sugar
- ¼ cup milk, at room temperature
- 1 teaspoon pure vanilla extract
- 1 cup diced nectarines
- 1¾ cups all-purpose flour
- 1 teaspoon baking soda
- ½ teaspoon salt
- ½ teaspoon ground nutmeg
- ¼ teaspoon baking powder

Direction: PREP: 10 MINUTES PLUS FERMENTING TIME /MAKES 1 LOAF

- ✓ Preparing the Ingredients. To make the nectarines, put them in the bread machine together with the butter, eggs, sugar, milk, and vanilla extract.
- ✓ To begin baking, select the Quick/Rapid bread bake cycle in the machine's settings and hit the Start button.
- ✓

- ✓ While the wet ingredients are being mixed, in a separate basin, combine the flour, baking soda, salt, nutmeg, and baking powder.
- ✓ The machine will tell you to add the dry ingredients after the initial quick mixing is complete.
- ✓ Before serving, take the bread pan from the breadmaker and allow it to cool down.
- ✓ Remove the bread from the pan, put in a wire rack to Cool about 10 minutes. Slice

362) Almond Chocolate Chip Bread

Ingredients:

- 1 cup plus 2 tbsp. water
- 2 tbsp. softened butter
- ½ tsp vanilla
- 3 cups Gold Medal Better for Bread flour
- ¾ cup semisweet chocolate chips
- 3 tbsp. sugar
- 1 tbsp. dry milk
- ¾ tsp salt
- 1½ tsp quick active dry yeast
- ⅓ cup sliced almonds

Direction: PREP: 10 MINUTES PLUS FERMENTING TIME /MAKES 14 SLICES

- ✓ Preparing the Ingredients Add each ingredient except the almonds to the bread machine in the order and at the temperature recommended by your bread machine manufacturer.
- ✓ Select the Bake Cycle Close the lid, select the sweet loaf, low crust setting on your bread machine, and press start.
  Add almonds 10 minutes before last kneading cycle ends.
- ✓ Take out the baked bread from the bread machine and allow it to cool on a cooling rack.

363) Swedish Coffee Bread

Ingredients:

- 1 cup milk
- ½ tsp salt
- 1 egg yolk
- 2 tbsp. softened butter
- 3 cups all-purpose flour
- ⅓ cup sugar
- 1 envelope active dry yeast
- 3 tsp ground cardamom
- 2 egg whites, slightly beaten

Direction: PREP: 10 MINUTES /MAKES 14 SLICES

- ✓ Preparing the Ingredients In the order and at the temperature specified by the maker of your bread machine, add each ingredient to the bread machine.
- ✓ Select the Bake Cycle Select the dough cycle and press start.
- ✓ Grease your baking sheet. When the dough cycle has finished, divide the dough into three equal parts.
- ✓ Roll each part into a rope 12-14" long. Lay 3 ropes

side by side, and then braid them together.

- ✓ Tuck the ends underneath and put onto the sheet. Next, cover the bread, using kitchen towel, and let it rise until it has doubled in size.
- ✓ Brush your bread with beaten egg white and sprinkle with pearl sugar.
- ✓ Bake until golden brown at 375°F in a preheated oven for 20-25 minutes.
- ✓ When baked, remove the bread and put it on a cooling rack.

364) *Pear Kuchen with Ginger Topping*

Ingredients:

- Bread dough ½ cup milk
- 2 tablespoons butter, softened
- 1 egg
- 2 cups bread flour
- 2 tablespoons sugar
- 1 teaspoon salt
- 1¾ teaspoons bread machine or fast-acting dry yeast

Topping

- 3 cups sliced peeled pears
- 1 cup sugar
- 2 tablespoons butter, softened
- 1 tablespoon chopped crystallized ginger
- ½ cup whipping cream
- 1 egg yolk

Direction: PREP: 20 MINUTES PLUS FERMENTING TIME /MAKES 12 SERVINGS

- ✓ Preparing the Ingredients. Measure carefully, placing all bread dough ingredients in bread machine pan in the order recommended by the manufacturer.
- ✓ Select the Bake Cycle Select Dough/Manual cycle. Do not use delay cycle.
- ✓ With gently floured hands, remove dough from pan; cover and set aside for 10 minutes on a lightly floured surface.
- ✓ Grease 13×9-inch pan with shortening. Press dough evenly in bottom of pan.
- ✓ Arrange pears on dough. In small bowl, mix 1 cup sugar, 2 tablespoons butter and the ginger.
- ✓ Reserve 2 tablespoons of the topping; sprinkle remaining topping over pears.
- ✓ Cover and allow to double in size for 30 to 45 minutes in a warm location. Dough is ready when an indentation remains when touched. Preheat oven to 375°F.
- ✓ Bake 20 minutes.
- ✓ Mix whipping cream and egg yolk; pour over hot kuchen.
- ✓ Bake for a additional 15 minutes, or until the tops are golden.
- ✓ Sprinkle with reserved 2 tablespoons topping. Serve warm.

365) *Walnut Cocoa Bread*

Ingredients:

- ⅔ cup milk
- ⅓ cup water
- 5 tbsp. butter, softened
- ⅓ cup packed brown sugar
- 5 tbsp. baking cocoa
- 1 tsp salt
- 3 cups bread flour
- 2¼ tsp active dry yeast
- ⅔ cup chopped walnuts, toasted

Direction: PREP: 20 MINUTES PLUS FERMENTING TIME /MAKES 14 SERVINGS

- ✓ Preparing the Ingredients Add each ingredient except the walnuts to the bread machine in the order and at the temperature recommended by your bread machine manufacturer.
- ✓ Select the Bake Cycle Close the lid, select the sweet loaf, low crust setting on your bread machine, and press start. Just before the final kneading, add the walnuts.
- ✓ Take out the baked bread from the bread machine and allow it to cool on a cooling rack.

366) *Sweet Applesauce Bread*

Ingredients:

- 12 slice bread (1½ pounds)
- ⅔ cup lukewarm milk
- ¼ cup unsweetened applesauce, at room temperature
- 1 tablespoon unsalted butter, melted
- 1 tablespoon sugar
- 1 teaspoon table salt
- ¼ cup quick oats
- 2¼ cups white bread flour
- ½ teaspoon ground cinnamon
- Pinch ground nutmeg
- 2¼ teaspoons bread machine yeast

Direction: PREP: 10 MINUTES PLUS FERMENTING TIME /MAKES 1 LOAF

- ✓ Preparing the Ingredients. Choose the size of loaf of your preference and then measure the ingredients. Add all of the ingredients mentioned previously in the list.
- ✓ Close the lid after placing the pan in the bread machine.
- ✓ Select the Bake Cycle Turn on the bread machine. Select the Quick/Rapid setting, select the loaf size, and the crust color.
- ✓ Press start.
- ✓ When the breadmaker cycle is complete, carefully remove the pan from the machine and allow it to cool before serving.
- ✓ Remove the bread from the pan, put in a wire rack to Cool about 5 minutes.
- ✓ Slice

367) Mexican Chocolate Bread

Ingredients:

- ½ cup milk
- ½ cup orange juice
- 1 large egg plus 1 egg yolk
- 3 tbsp. unsalted butter cut into pieces
- 2½ cups bread flour
- ¼ cup light brown sugar
- 3 tbsp. unsweetened Dutch-process cocoa powder
- 1 tbsp. gluten
- 1 tsp instant espresso powder
- ¾ tsp ground cinnamon
- ½ cup bittersweet chocolate chips
- 2½ tsp bread machine yeast

Direction: PREP: 10 MINUTES PLUS FERMENTING TIME /MAKES 1 LOAF

✓ Preparing the Ingredients. In the order and at the temperature specified by the maker of your bread machine, add each ingredient to the bread machine.

✓ Select the Bake Cycle Close the lid, select the sweet loaf, low crust setting on your bread machine, and press start.

✓ Take out the baked bread from the bread machine and allow it to cool on a cooling rack.

368) Sour Cream Maple Bread

Ingredients:

- 8 slices bread (1 pound)
- 6 tablespoons water, at 80°F to 90°F
- 6 tablespoons sour cream, at room temperature
- 1½ tablespoons butter, at room temperature
- ¾ tablespoon maple syrup
- ½ teaspoon salt
- 1¾ cups white bread flour
- 1⅛ teaspoons bread machine or instant yeast

Direction: PREP: 10 MINUTES PLUS FERMENTING TIME /MAKES 1 LOAF

✓ Preparing the Ingredients. Choose the size of loaf of your preference and then measure the ingredients. Add all of the ingredients mentioned previously in the list.

✓ Close the lid after placing the pan in the bread machine.

✓ Select the Bake Cycle Turn on the bread machine. Select the Quick/Rapid setting, select the loaf size, and the crust color.

✓ Press start. When the breadmaker cycle is complete, carefully remove the pan from the machine and allow it to cool before serving.

✓ Remove the bread from the pan, put in a wire rack to Cool about 5 minutes.

✓ Slice

369) Chocolate Chip Bread

Ingredients:

- ¼ cup water
- 1 cup milk
- 1 egg 3 cups bread flour
- 3 tbsp. brown sugar
- 2 tbsp. white sugar
- 1 tsp salt 1 tsp ground cinnamon
- 1½ tsp active dry yeast
- 2 tbsp. margarine, softened
- ¾ cup semisweet chocolate chips

Direction: PREP: 10 MINUTES PLUS FERMENTING TIME /MAKES 1 LOAF

✓ Preparing the Ingredients Add each ingredient except the chocolate chips to the bread machine in the order and at the temperature recommended by your bread machine manufacturer.

✓ Select the Bake Cycle Close the lid, select the sweet loaf, low crust setting on your bread machine, and press start.

✓ Add the chocolate chips about 5 minutes before the kneading cycle has finished.

✓ Take out the baked bread from the bread machine and allow it to cool on a cooling rack.

370) Crunchy Wheat-and-Honey Twist

Ingredients:

- Bread dough
- ¾ cup plus 2 tablespoons water
- 2 tablespoons honey
- 1 tablespoon butter, softened
- 1¼ cups whole wheat flour
- 1 cup bread flour
- ⅓ cup slivered almonds, toasted
- 1 teaspoon salt
- 1 teaspoon bread machine or fast-acting dry yeast

Topping

- Butter, melted
- 1 egg, slightly beaten
- 2 tablespoons sugar
- ¼ teaspoon ground cinnamon

Direction: PREP: 10-15 MINUTES PLUS FERMENTING TIME /MAKES 16 slice bread (2 pounds)

✓ Preparing the Ingredients. Choose the size of loaf of your preference and then measure the ingredients. Add all of the ingredients mentioned previously in the list.

✓ Close the lid after placing the pan in the bread machine.

✓ Select the Bake Cycle Turn on the bread machine. Select the Quick/Rapid setting, select the loaf size, and the crust color.

✓ Press start. When the breadmaker cycle is complete, carefully remove the pan from the machine and allow it to cool before serving.

✓ Remove the bread from the pan, put in a wire rack to

Cool about 5 minutes.

✓ *Slice*

371) __Peanut Butter and Jelly Bread__

Ingredients:

- *1 1/2 tablespoons vegetable oil*
- *1 cup of water*
- *½ cup blackberry jelly*
- *½ cup peanut butter*
- *One teaspoon salt*
- *One tablespoon white sugar*
- *2 cups of bread flour*
- *1 cup whole-wheat flour*
- *1 1/2 teaspoons active dry yeast*

Direction: Preparation Time: 2 hours Cooking Time: 1 hour and 10 minutes Servings: 1 loaf

✓ *Place all of the ingredients in the bread machine pan. Select the most basic option.*

✓ *Set the timer for 10 minutes and then remove the pan from the oven.*

372) __Puri Bread__

Ingredients:

- *1 cup almond flour, sifted*
- *½ cup of warm water*
- *2 Tbsp. clarified butter*
- *1 cup olive oil for frying*
- *Salt to taste*

Direction: Preparation Time: 10minutes Cooking Time: 5 minutes Servings: 6

✓ *Salt the water and add the flour.*

✓ *Make some holes in the center of the dough and pour warm clarified butter.*

✓ *Knead the dough and let stand for 15 minutes, covered.*

✓ *Shape into six balls.*

✓ *Flatten the balls into six thin rounds using a rolling pin.*
  Heat enough oil to cover a round frying pan completely.

✓ *Place a puri in it when hot.*

✓ *Fry for 20 seconds on each side.*

✓ *Place on a paper towel.*

✓ *Repeat with the rest of the puri and serve*

373) __Healthy Low Carb Bread__

Ingredients:

- *2/3 cup coconut flour*
- *2/3 cup coconut oil (softened not melted)*
- *Nine eggs*
- *2 tsp. Cream of tartar*
- *¾ tsp. xanthan gum*
- *1 tsp. Baking soda*
- *¼ tsp. salt*

Direction: Preparation Time: 15minutesCooking

Time:35 minutes Servings: 8

✓ *Preheat the oven to 350F. 1 to 2 tsp. butter in a loaf pan*

✓ *Place the melted coconut oil in the freezer to solidify.*

✓ *In a mixing bowl, crack the eggs and whisk them for 2 minutes with a hand mixer.*

✓ *Mix in the coconut oil with the eggs.*

✓ *In a separate bowl, whisk together the dry ingredients until well combined.*

✓ *Mix the dry ingredients into the egg mixture with a hand mixer on low speed until a dough forms and the mixture is fully mixed.*

✓ *Place the dough in the prepared loaf pan and bake for 35 minutes in the preheated oven.*

✓ *Remove the bread pan from the oven and set it aside. Cool, slice, and serve.*

374) __Fluffy Paleo Bread__

Ingredients:

- *One ¼ cup almond flour*
- *Five eggs*
- *1 tsp. lemon juice*
- *1/3 cup avocado oil*
- *One dash black pepper*
- *½ tsp. sea salt*
- *3 to 4 tbsp. tapioca flour*
- *1 to 2 tsp. Poppy seed*
- *¼ cup ground flaxseed*
- *½ tsp. baking soda Top with: Poppy seeds*
- *Pumpkin seeds*

Direction: Preparation Time: 10 minutes Cooking Time: 40 minutes Servings: 15

✓ *Preheat the oven to 350F.*

✓ *Line a baking pan with parchment paper and set aside.*

✓ *In a bowl, add eggs, avocado oil, and lemon juice and whisk until combined.*

✓ *In another bowl, add tapioca flour, almond flour, baking soda, flaxseed, black pepper, and poppy seed. Mix.*

✓ *Add the lemon juice mixture into the flour mixture and mix well.*

✓ *Add the batter into the prepared loaf pan and top with extra pumpkin seeds and poppy seeds.*

✓ *Cover loaf pan and transfer into the prepared oven, and bake for 20 minutes.*

✓ *Remove cover and bake until an inserted knife comes out clean after about 15 to 20 minutes. Remove from oven and cool.*

✓ *Slice and serve.*

375) __Butter Bread Rolls__

Ingredients:

- *1 cup warm milk*
- *½ cup butter or ½ cup margarine, softened*

- ¼ cup sugar
- 2 eggs
- 1 ½ teaspoons salt
- 4 cups bread flour
- 2 ¼ teaspoons active dry yeast

Direction: Preparation Time: 50 minutes Cooking Time: 45 minutes Servings: 24 rolls

- ✓ Place all ingredients in the bread machine pan in the sequence recommended by the manufacturer.
- ✓ Choose a dough setting.
- ✓ Turn dough out onto a lightly floured board when the cycle is finished.
- ✓ Divide the dough into 24 equal pieces.
- ✓ Using your hands, roll the dough into balls.
- ✓ Area in a greased 13-inch-by-9-inch baking pan, cover, and let rise for 30-45 minutes in a warm place.
- ✓ Preheat oven to 350°F and bake for 13-16 minutes, or until golden brown.

376) reakfast Bread

Ingredients:

- ½ tsp. Xanthan gum
- ½ tsp. salt
- 2 Tbsp. coconut oil
- ½ cup butter, melted
- 1 tsp. baking powder
- 2 cups of almond flour
- Seven eggs

Direction: Preparation Time: 15 minutes Cooking Time: 40 minutes Servings: 16 slices

- ✓ Preheat the oven to 355°F and beat the eggs for 2 minutes on high in a mixing bowl.
- ✓ Continue to whisk the eggs with the coconut oil and butter.
- ✓ Using baking paper, line a pan and pour the beaten eggs into it.
- ✓ Pour in the remaining ingredients and stir until the mixture thickens.
- ✓ Bake until a toothpick inserted in the center comes out clean. It takes between 40 and 45 minutes.

377) Low-Carb Bagel

Ingredients:

- 1 cup protein powder, unflavored
- 1/3 cup coconut flour
- 1 tsp. baking powder
- ½ tsp. sea salt
- ¼ cup ground flaxseed
- 1/3 cup sour cream
- 12 eggs Seasoning

topping:

- 1 tsp. dried parsley
- 1 tsp. dried oregano
- 1 tsp. Dried minced onion
- ½ tsp. Garlic powder

- ½ tsp. Dried basil
- ½ tsp. sea salt

Direction: Preparation Time: 15 minutes Cooking Time: 25 minutes Servings: 12

- ✓ Preheat the oven to 350F.
- ✓ Blend sour cream and eggs in a mixer until fully mixed.
- ✓ In a mixing bowl, combine the flaxseed, salt, baking powder, protein powder, and coconut flour.
- ✓ Combine the dry ingredients in a mixing bowl until they become wet components.
- ✓ Ascertain that it is well integrated.
- ✓ In a small bowl, whisk together the topping seasonings.
- ✓ Make a note.
- ✓ Grease two 6-doughnut donut pans.
- ✓ Sprinkle each pan evenly with approximately 1 teaspoon topping seasoning and pour batter into each.
- ✓ Distribute the remaining seasoning mixture evenly over the top of each bagel.
- ✓ Preheat oven to 250°F. Bake for 25 minutes, or until golden brown.

378) Hot Dog Buns

Ingredients:

- One ¼ cups almond flour
- 5 tbsp. psyllium husk powder
- 1 tsp. sea salt
- 2 tsp. baking powder
- One ¼ cups boiling water
- 2 tsp. lemon juice
- Three egg whites

Direction: Preparation Time: 10 minutes Cooking Time: 50 minutes Servings: 10

- ✓ Preheat the oven to 350°F
- ✓ Mix all dry ingredients in a bowl and stir thoroughly.
- ✓ Whisk together the boiling water, lemon juice, and egg whites in the dry mixture until incorporated.
- ✓ Divide the dough into 10 portions and roll each portion into a bun.
- ✓ Transfer to the preheated oven and bake on the lower oven rack for 40 to 50 minutes.
- ✓ Check for doneness and remove it.
- ✓ Top with desired toppings and hot dogs.
- ✓ Serve.

379) Spicy Bread

Ingredients:

- ½ cup coconut flour
- Six eggs
- Three large jalapenos, sliced
- 4 ounces' turkey bacon, sliced
- ½ cup ghee
- ¼ tsp. baking soda
- ¼ tsp. salt

- ¼ cup of water
  Direction: Preparation Time: 6-10 minutes Cooking Time: 40 minutes
- ✓ Preheat the oven to 400F. On a baking sheet, arrange the bacon and jalapenos and roast for 10 minutes.
- ✓ Bake for a further five minutes on the other side.
- ✓ Using a spoon, scrape the seeds off the jalapenos.
- ✓ In a food processor, combine jalapenos and bacon slices and pulse until smooth.
- ✓ In a mixing basin, combine ghee, eggs, and 14 cup water.
- ✓ Then stir in some coconut flour, baking soda, and salt.
- ✓ Add bacon and jalapeno mix.
- ✓ Grease the loaf pan with ghee.
- ✓ Pour batter into the loaf pan. Bake for 40 minutes.
- ✓ Enjoy.

380) **Honey Bread**
Ingredients:

- ½ cup water
- ¾ cup buttermilk
- ¼ cup honey
- 3 Tablespoon butter, softened and cut into pieces
- 3 cups bread flour
- 1½ teaspoon salt
- 2¼ teaspoon yeast (or 1 package)
  Direction: Preparation Time: 5 minutes Cooking Time: 3 hours 45 minutes Servings: 14
- ✓ In the order and at the temperature specified by the maker of your bread machine, add each ingredient to the bread machine.
- ✓ Close the cover and press start. Select the basic bread, medium crust setting on your bread maker.
- ✓ Remove the baked bread from the bread maker and place it on a cooling rack to cool.

381) **Bread Machine Ezekiel Bread**
Ingredients:

- Whole wheat flour
- Bread flour
- Spelled flour
- Honey Millet
- Olive oil
- Wheat germ
- Dry kidney beans
- Barley Dry lentils
- Bread machine yeast
- Dry black beans
- Water at 90°F (320C) Salt
  Direction: Preparation Time: 10 Minutes Cooking Time: 3 Hours Servings: 12 slices
- ✓ In separate bowls, soak all beans and grains overnight.
- ✓ After 1 hour of boiling the black beans and dried

kidney beans, add the lentils, millet, and barley.
- ✓ Boil for a further 15 minutes.
- ✓ In a food processor, combine the boiling ingredients and mash until smooth.
- ✓ Pour 2 tablespoons olive oil and honey into the bread machine pan, then add the flour and wheat germ.
- ✓ START the Dough cycle in one corner by adding salt and yeast in another.
- ✓ Add the mash to the dough when the bread machine sounds, then select the Whole Wheat cycle.
- ✓ Enjoy.

382) **Butter Up Bread**
Ingredients:

- Bread flour Margarine, melted
- Buttermilk at 1100F (450C)
- Sugar
- Active dry yeast
- Egg, at room temperature
- Salt
  Direction: Preparation Time: 10 Minutes Cooking Time: 3 Hours Servings: 12 slices
- ✓ Buttermilk, melted margarine, salt, sugar, flour, and yeast should be added to the bread machine pan in the sequence suggested by your manufacturer.
- ✓ Select the Basic/White Setting and press START. Once baked, cool completely on wire racks before slicing.
- ✓ Enjoy!

383) **Buttermilk Wheat Bread**
Ingredients:

- Buttermilk, at room temperature
- White sugar
- Olive oil
- Salt
- Baking soda
- Unbleached white flour
- Whole wheat flour
- Active dry yeast
  Direction: Preparation Time: 8 Minutes Cooking Time: 4 Hours and 30 Minutes Servings: 16 slices
- ✓ Measure all ingredients in the bread machine pan according to the manufacturer's recommendations.
- ✓ Select the Basic White Bread setting on the machine and push START.
- ✓ After a few minutes, if the ingredients do not form a ball, add additional buttermilk.
- ✓ If it is too loose, add a little of flour.
- ✓ Allow the bread to cool completely on a wire rack before slicing.
- ✓ Enjoy

384) Crunchy Honey Wheat Bread

Ingredients:

- Warm water at 1100F (450C)
- Vegetable oil
- Honey
- Salt
- Bread flour
- Whole wheat flour
- Granola
- Active dry yeast

Direction: Preparation Time: 7 Minutes Cooking Time: 3 Hours and 30 Minutes Servings: 12 slices

- ✓ Following the manufacturer's instructions, add the ingredients to the bread maker in the specified order.
- ✓ Dough cycle on a bread maker can be adjusted to Whole Wheat or Dough mode. Start by pressing the START key.
- ✓ The dough should be formed and placed in a loaf pan that has been sprayed with cooking spray after the bread machine completes its baking cycle.
- ✓ Keep the temperature at a comfortable level and allow it to double in size.
- ✓ For 35-45 minutes, place in a preheated oven set to 350°F (175°C).
- ✓ Enjoy

385) Whole Wheat Yogurt Bread

Ingredients:

- Ground nutmeg (optional)
- Water
- Butter, melted
- Plain yogurt
- Dry milk
- Honey
- Active dry yeast
- Whole wheat flour
- Bread flour
- Ground cinnamon Salt

Direction: Preparation Time: 10 Minutes Cooking Time: 3 Hours and 40 Minutes Servings: 12 slices

- ✓ Pour the ingredients into your bread pan according to the manufacturer's recommended procedure.
- ✓ When it comes to liquids, I always start with them.
- ✓ As a result, I begin by combining the following ingredients in my bread pan: water; yogurt; butter; honey; filtered flour; dry milk; salt; ground cinnamon; and yeast.
- ✓ After selecting the Whole grain setting, press START to begin cooking.
- ✓ Allow it to chill for a few minutes before serving, if desired. Enjoy!

386) Whole Wheat Peanut Butter and Jelly Bread

Ingredients:

- Water at 90°F-100°F (320C-370C)

- Smooth peanut butter
- Strawberry jelly (or any preferable jelly)
- Vital wheat gluten
- Salt
- Baking soda
- Active dry yeast
- Baking powder
- Light brown sugar
- Whole wheat flour

Direction: Preparation Time: 10 Minutes Cooking Time: 3 Hours Servings: 12 slices

- ✓ Add the following in this order to the bread machine pan as you prepare it: water; jelly; peanut butter; brown sugar; baking soda; gluten; whole wheat flour; yeast; and salt.
- ✓ START the machine after selecting 1 12 pound loaf, medium crust, and wheat cycle. Serve it after it has cooled on a cooling rack.

387) Honey-Oat-Wheat Bread

Ingredients:

- Active dry yeast
- Sugar
- Water at 1100F (450C)
- All-purpose flour
- Whole wheat flour
- Rolled oats
- Powdered milk
- Salt
- Honey
- Vegetable oil
- Butter softened
- Cooking spray

Direction: Preparation Time: 10 Minutes Cooking Time: 3 Hours and 45 Minutes Servings: 16 slices

- ✓ In a bread maker, add the following: yeast, sugar, and water.
- ✓ Ten minutes is a good amount of time to allow the yeast to dissolve and foam.
- ✓ Mix together all-purpose flour, whole wheat flour, salt, and oats in a bowl while you prepare the other ingredients.
- ✓ Add the butter, honey, and oil to the yeast mixture, and then the flour mixture on top of that.
- ✓ You'll then press the START button after selecting Dough.
- ✓ Allow the bread machine to finish its work, which takes about an hour and a half. Spray a 9x5-inch loaf pan with cooking spray before placing the dough in it.
- ✓ Allow the bread to rise for one hour in a warm place. Bake for about 35 minutes in a preheated oven, until the top is golden brown and crispy.
- ✓ Enjoy!

388) Butter Honey Wheat Bread

Ingredients:

- Buttermilk Butter, melted
- Honey
- Bread flour
- Whole wheat flour
- Salt
- Baking soda
- Active dry yeast

Direction: Preparation Time: 5 Minutes Cooking Time: 3 Hours and 45 Minutes Servings: 12 slices

✓ Follow the manufacturer's instructions for loading the bread maker with all of the ingredients.
✓ When it comes to liquids, I always start with them.
✓ Run the bread machine on the Whole Wheat setting for a loaf (112 lbs.)
✓ After baking, let the bread rest completely on a wire rack before slicing.
✓ Enjoy!

389) Cracked Fit and Fat Bread

Ingredients:

- Water
- Butter softened
- Brown sugar
- Salt
- Bread flour
- Whole wheat flour
- Cracked wheat
- Active dry yeast

Direction: Preparation Time: 5 Minutes Cooking Time: 3 Hours and 25 Minutes Servings: 16 slices

✓ Measure all ingredients in the bread machine pan in the sequence recommended by the manufacturer.
✓ Before cutting into the bread, let it to cool on a wire rack for a few minutes.
✓ Enjoy!

390) Easy Home Base Wheat Bread

Ingredients:

- Whole wheat flour
- Bread flour
- Butter softened
- Warm water at 900F (320C)
- Warm milk at 900F (320C)
- Active dry yeast
- Egg, at room temperature
- Salt
- Honey

Direction: Preparation Time: 10 Minutes Cooking Time: 3 Hours and 50 Minutes Servings: 12 slices

✓ Add the ingredients to the bread machine pan in accordance with the manufacturer's instructions.
✓ Use the Whole Wheat cycle, select the crust color and weight, then PRESS START!!

✓ After five minutes of kneading, you may need to add either one tablespoon of water or one tablespoon of flour depending on the dough's consistency.
✓ Before slicing, let the bread cool on a wire rack.
✓ Enjoy

391) Lovely Aromatic Lavender Bread

Ingredients:

- ¾ cup milk at 80 degrees F
- 1 tablespoon melted butter, cooled
- 1 tablespoon sugar
- ¾ teaspoon salt
- 1 teaspoon fresh lavender flower, chopped
- ¼ teaspoon lemon zest
- ¼ teaspoon fresh thyme, chopped cups
- white bread flour
- ¾ teaspoon instant yeast

Direction: Preparation Time: 2 hours 10 minutes Cooking Time: 50 minutes Servings: 1 loaf

✓ Set your bread machine on dough cycle and add all of the ingredients.
✓ Set your breadmaker's settings to Basic/White.
✓ Set the crust type to Medium on the bread.
✓ Start by pressing the START button.
✓ Wait for the cycle to complete before moving on to the next one.
✓ Wait for the loaf to cool down for 5 minutes before removing the bucket.
✓ Remove the loaf by squeezing the pail a few times.
✓ Slicing and serving are the final steps.

392) Garlic Bread

Ingredients:

- 1 3/8 cups water
- 2 tablespoons olive oil
- 1 teaspoon minced garlic
- 2 cups bread flour
- 2 tablespoons white sugar
- 3 teaspoons salt
- 1/4 cup grated Parmesan cheese
- 1 teaspoon dried basil
- 1 teaspoon garlic powder
- 2 tablespoons chopped fresh chives
- 1 teaspoon coarsely ground black pepper
- 1/2 teaspoons bread machine yeast

Direction: Preparation Time: 2 hours 30 minutes Cooking Time: 40 minutes Servings: 1 loaf

✓ Make sure you follow the manufacturer's instructions for putting the ingredients in the bread machine pan.
✓ Press the Start button on the machine to begin the process of making bread.

393) Cinnamon Apple Bread

Ingredients:

- 16 slice bread (2 pounds)
- 1⅓ cups lukewarm milk
- 3⅓ tablespoons butter, melted
- 2⅔ tablespoons sugar
- 2 teaspoons table salt
- 1⅓ teaspoons cinnamon, ground
- A pinch ground cloves
- 4 cups white bread flour
- 2¼ teaspoons bread machine yeast
- 1⅓ cups peeled apple, finely diced

Direction: PREP: 10 MINUTES /MAKES 1 LOAF

✓ Preparing the Ingredients. Choose the size of loaf of your preference and then measure the ingredients.

✓ Add all of the ingredients mentioned previously in the list, except for the apples.

✓ Close the lid after placing the pan in the bread machine.

✓ Select the Bake Cycle Turn on the bread machine.

✓ To begin, select the White/Basic or Fruit/Nut (if bread machine has this choice) setting, choose the loaf size, and select the crust color.

✓ Press the start button. Add the apples to the machine when it says to do so.

✓ When the breadmaker cycle is complete, carefully remove the pan from the machine and allow it to cool before serving.

✓ Remove the bread from the pan, put in a wire rack to cool for at least 5 minutes, and slice

394) Cranberry Orange Breakfast Bread

Ingredients:

- ⅛ cup orange juice
- 2 Tbsp vegetable oil
- 2 Tbsp honey
- cups bread flour
- 1 Tbsp dry milk powder
- ½ tsp ground cinnamon
- ½ tsp ground allspice
- 1 tsp salt 1 (.25 ounce) package active dry yeast
- 1 Tbsp grated orange zest
- 1 cup sweetened dried cranberries
- ⅓ cup chopped walnuts

Direction: PREP: 10 MINUTES /MAKES 14 SLICES

✓ Preparing the Ingredients. In the order and at the temperature specified by the maker of your bread machine, add each ingredient to the bread machine.

✓ Select the Bake Cycle Close the lid, select the basic bread, low crust setting on your bread machine, and press start.

✓ Add the cranberries and chopped walnuts 5 to 10 minutes before last kneading cycle ends.

✓ Take out the baked bread from the bread machine and allow it to cool on a cooling rack.

395) Chai-Spiced Bread

Ingredients:

- ¾ cup granulated sugar
- ½ cup butter, softened
- ½ cup cold brewed tea or water
- ⅓ cup milk
- 2 teaspoons vanilla
- 2 eggs
- 2 cups all-purpose flour
- 2 teaspoons baking powder
- ¾ teaspoon ground cardamom
- ½ teaspoon salt
- ¼ teaspoon ground cinnamon
- ⅛ teaspoon ground cloves glaze
- 1 cup powdered sugar
- ¼ teaspoon vanilla
- 3 to 5 teaspoons milk
- Additional ground cinnamon

Direction: PREP: 10 MINUTES /MAKES 1 LOAF

✓ Preparing the Ingredients. Choose the size of loaf of your preference and then measure the ingredients.

✓ Add all of the ingredients mentioned previously in the list.

✓ Close the lid after placing the pan in the bread machine.

✓ Select the Bake Cycle Turn on the bread machine.

✓ Select the White/Basic setting, select the loaf size, and the crust color.

✓ Press start.

✓ When the breadmaker cycle is complete, carefully remove the pan from the machine and allow it to cool before serving.

✓ Remove the bread from the pan, put in a wire rack to cool for at least 2 hours, and slice.

✓ Wrap tightly and store at room temperature up to 4 days, or refrigerate.

396) Raisin Candied Fruit Bread

Ingredients:

- 16 slice bread (2 pounds)
- 1 egg, beaten
- 1½ cups + 1 tablespoon lukewarm water
- ⅔ teaspoon ground cardamom
- 1¼ teaspoons table salt
- 2 tablespoons sugar
- ⅓ cup butter, melted
- 4 cups bread flour
- 1¼ teaspoons bread machine yeast
- ½ cup raisins
- ½ cup mixed candied fruit

Direction: PREP: 10 MINUTES /MAKES 1 LOAF

✓ Preparing the Ingredients. Choose the size of loaf of your preference and then measure the ingredients.

- ✓ Add all of the ingredients mentioned previously in the list, except for the candied fruits and raisins.
- ✓ Close the lid after placing the pan in the bread machine.
- ✓ Select the Bake Cycle Turn on the bread machine. White/Basic or Fruit/Nut (if your machine has this setting) setting, select the loaf size, and the crust color.
- ✓ Press start.
- ✓ When the machine signals to add ingredients, add the candied fruits and raisins.
- ✓ When the breadmaker cycle is complete, carefully remove the pan from the machine and allow it to cool before serving.
- ✓ Remove the bread from the pan, put in a wire rack to cool for at least 10 minutes, and slice.

397) **Strawberry Shortcake Bread**

Ingredients:

- 12 slice bread (1½ pounds)
- 1⅛ cups milk, at 80°F to 90°F
- 3 tablespoons melted butter, cooled
- 3 tablespoons sugar
- 1½ teaspoons salt
- ¾ cup sliced fresh strawberries
- 1 cup quick oats
- 2¼ cups white bread flour
- 1½ teaspoons bread machine or instant yeast.

Direction: PREP: 10 MINUTES /MAKES 1 LOAF

- ✓ Preparing the Ingredients. Choose the size of loaf of your preference and then measure the ingredients.
- ✓ Add all of the ingredients mentioned previously in the list.
- ✓ Close the lid after placing the pan in the bread machine.
- ✓ Select the Bake Cycle Turn on the bread machine.
- ✓ Select the White/Basic setting, select the loaf size, and the crust color.
- ✓ Press start.
- ✓ When the breadmaker cycle is complete, carefully remove the pan from the machine and allow it to cool before serving.
- ✓ Remove the bread from the pan, put in a wire rack to cool for at least 2 hours, and slice.

398) **Chocolate-Pistachio Bread**

Ingredients:

- ⅔ cup granulated sugar
- ½ cup butter, melted
- ¾ cup milk
- 1 egg
- 1½ cups all-purpose flour
- 1 cup chopped pistachio nuts
- ½ cup semisweet chocolate chips
- ⅓ cup unsweetened baking cocoa
- 2 teaspoons baking powder

- ¼ teaspoon salt
- Decorator sugar crystals, if desired

Direction: PREP: 10 MINUTES / MAKES ⅔ CUP (24 SLICES)

- ✓ Preparing the Ingredients. Choose the size of loaf of your preference and then measure the ingredients.
- ✓ Add all of the ingredients mentioned previously in the list.
- ✓ Close the lid after placing the pan in the bread machine.
- ✓ Select the Bake Cycle Turn on the bread machine. Select the White/Basic setting, select the loaf size, and the crust color.
- ✓ Press start.
- ✓ When the breadmaker cycle is complete, carefully remove the pan from the machine and allow it to cool before serving.
- ✓ Remove the bread from the pan, put in a wire rack to cool for at least 2 hours.
- ✓ Wrap tightly and store at room temperature up to 4 days, or refrigerate.

399) **Cinnamon-Raisin Bread**

Ingredients:

- 1 cup water
- 2 Tbsp butter, softened
- 3 cups Gold Medal Better for Bread flour
- 3 Tbsp sugar
- 1½ tsp salt
- 1 tsp ground cinnamon
- 2½ tsp bread machine yeast
- ¾ cup raisins

Direction: PREP: 10 MINUTES / MAKES 14 SLICES

- ✓ Preparing the Ingredients Add each ingredient except the raisins to the bread machine in the order and at the temperature recommended by your bread machine manufacturer.
- ✓ Select the Bake Cycle Close the lid, select the sweet or basic bread, medium crust setting on your bread machine and press start.
  Add raisins 10 minutes before the last kneading cycle ends.
- ✓ Take out the baked bread from the bread machine and allow it to cool on a cooling rack.

400) **Spice Peach Bread**

Ingredients:

- 16 slice bread (2 pounds)
- ½ cup lukewarm heavy whipping cream
- 1 egg, beaten 1
- ½ tablespoons unsalted butter, melted
- 3 tablespoons sugar
- 1½ teaspoons table salt
- ¼ teaspoon nutmeg, ground
- ½ teaspoon cinnamon, ground
- 3½ cups white bread flour
- ½ cup whole-wheat flour

- 1½ teaspoons bread machine yeast
- 1 cup canned peaches, drained and chopped
  Direction: PREP: 10 MINUTES /MAKES 1 LOAF

✓ Preparing the Ingredients. Choose the size of loaf of your preference and then measure the ingredients.

✓ Add all of the ingredients mentioned previously in the list, except for the peach. Close the lid after placing the pan in the bread machine.

✓ Select the Bake Cycle Turn on the bread machine. White/Basic or Fruit/Nut (if your machine has this setting) setting, select the loaf size, and the crust color.

✓ Press start.

✓ When the machine signals to add ingredients, add the peaches.

✓ When the breadmaker cycle is complete, carefully remove the pan from the machine and allow it to cool before serving.

✓ Remove the bread from the pan, put in a wire rack to cool for at least 10 minutes, and slice.

401) *Pineapple Coconut Bread*

Ingredients:

- 6 tablespoons butter, at room temperature
- 2 eggs, at room temperature
- ½ cup coconut milk, at room temperature
- ½ cup pineapple juice, at room temperature
- 1 cup sugar
- 1½ teaspoons coconut extract
- 2 cups all-purpose flour
- ¾ cup shredded sweetened coconut
- 1 teaspoon baking powder
- ½ teaspoon salt
  Direction: PREP: 10 MINUTES /MAKES 1 LOAF

✓ Preparing the Ingredients. Place the butter, eggs, coconut milk, pineapple juice, sugar, and coconut extract in your bread machine.

✓ Program the machine for Quick/Rapid bread and press Start.

✓ While the wet ingredients are mixing, stir together the flour, coconut, baking powder, and salt in a small bowl.

✓ Select the Bake Cycle After the first fast mixing is done and the machine signals, add the dry ingredients.

✓ When the breadmaker cycle is complete, carefully remove the pan from the machine and allow it to cool before serving.

✓ Remove the bread from the pan, put in a wire rack to cool for at least 10 minutes, and slice.

402) *Chocolate-Cherry Bread*

Ingredients:

- 1½ teaspoons baking powder
- ½ teaspoon baking soda
- ¼ teaspoon salt

- ¾ cup sugar
- ½ cup butter, softened
- 2 eggs
- 1 teaspoon almond extract
- 1 teaspoon vanilla
- 1 container (8 oz) sour cream
- ½ cup chopped dried cherries
- ½ cup bittersweet or dark chocolate chips
  Direction: PREP: 10 MINUTES /MAKES 1 LOAF

✓ Preparing the Ingredients. Choose the size of loaf of your preference and then measure the ingredients.

✓ Add all of the ingredients mentioned previously in the list.

✓ Close the lid after placing the pan in the bread machine.

✓ Select the Bake Cycle Turn on the bread machine. Select the White/Basic setting, select the loaf size, and the crust color.

✓ Press start. When the breadmaker cycle is complete, carefully remove the pan from the machine and allow it to cool before serving.

✓ Remove the bread from the pan, put in a wire rack to cool for at least 2 hours.

✓ Wrap tightly and store at room temperature up to 4 days, or refrigerate.

403) *Cocoa Date Bread*

Ingredients:

- 12 slice bread (1½ pounds)
- ¾ cup lukewarm water
- ½ cup lukewarm milk
- 2 tablespoons unsalted butter, melted
- ¼ cup honey
- 3 tablespoons molasses
- 1 tablespoon sugar
- 2 tablespoons skim milk powder
- 1 teaspoon table salt
- 1¼ cups white bread flour
- 2¼ cups whole-wheat flour
- 1 tablespoon cocoa powder, unsweetened
- 1½ teaspoons bread machine yeast
- ¾ cup dates, chopped
  Direction: PREP: 10 MINUTES /MAKES 1 LOAF

✓ Preparing the Ingredients. Choose the size of loaf of your preference and then measure the ingredients.

✓ Add all of the ingredients mentioned previously in the list, except for the dates.

✓ Close the lid after placing the pan in the bread machine.

✓ Select the Bake Cycle Turn on the bread machine. White/Basic or Fruit/Nut (if your machine has this setting) setting, select the loaf size, and the crust color.

✓ Press start.

✓ When the machine signals to add ingredients, add the dates. When the breadmaker cycle is complete, carefully remove the pan from the machine and allow it to cool before serving.

✓ Remove the bread from the pan, put in a wire rack to cool for at least 10 minutes, and slice.

404) *Warm Spiced Pumpkin Bread*

Ingredients:

- 12 to 16 slice bread
- (1½ to 2pounds) Butter for greasing the bucket
- 1½ cups pumpkin purée
- 3 eggs, at room temperature
- ⅓ cup melted butter, cooled
- 1 cup sugar
- 3 cups all-purpose flour
- 1½ teaspoons baking powder
- ¾ teaspoon ground cinnamon
- ½ teaspoon baking soda
- ¼ teaspoon ground nutmeg
- ¼ teaspoon ground ginger
- ¼ teaspoon salt
- Pinch ground cloves

Direction: PREP: 10 MINUTES /MAKES 1 LOAF

✓ Preparing the Ingredients. Lightly grease the bread bucket with butter. Add the pumpkin, eggs, butter, and sugar. Select the Bake cycle.

✓ Program the machine for Quick/Rapid bread and press Start.

✓ Let the wet ingredients be mixed by the paddles until the first fast mixing cycle is finished, about 10 minutes into the cycle.

✓ While the wet ingredients are mixing, stir together the flour, baking powder, cinnamon, baking soda, nutmeg, ginger, salt, and cloves until well blended.

✓ Add the dry ingredients to the bucket when the second fast mixing cycle starts.

✓ Scrape down the sides of the bucket once after the dry ingredients are mixed into the wet.

✓ When the loaf is done, remove the bucket from the machine.

✓ Let the loaf cool for 5 minutes.

✓ Gently shake the bucket to remove the loaf, and turn it out onto a rack to cool.

405) *Ginger-Topped Pumpkin Bread*

Ingredients:

- 1 can (15 oz) pumpkin (not pumpkin pie mix)
- 12/3 cups granulated sugar
- 2/3 cup unsweetened applesauce
- ½ cup milk
- 2 teaspoons vanilla
- 1 cup fat-free egg product or 2 eggs plus 4 egg whites
- 3 cups all-purpose flour
- 2 teaspoons baking soda
- 1 teaspoon salt

- 1 teaspoon ground cinnamon
- ½ teaspoon baking powder
- ½ teaspoon ground cloves glaze and topping
- 2/3 cup powdered sugar
- 2 to 3 teaspoons warm water
- ¼ teaspoon vanilla
- 3 tablespoons finely chopped crystallized ginger

Direction: PREP: 10 MINUTES / MAKES 2 LOAVES (24 SLICES EACH)

✓ Preparing the Ingredients. Choose the size of loaf of your preference and then measure the ingredients.

✓ Add all of the ingredients mentioned previously in the list.

✓ Close the lid after placing the pan in the bread machine.

✓ Select the Bake Cycle Turn on the bread machine.

✓ Select the White/Basic setting, select the loaf size, and the crust color.

✓ Press start.

✓ When the breadmaker cycle is complete, carefully remove the pan from the machine and allow it to cool before serving.

✓ Remove the bread from the pan, put in a wire rack to cool for at least 2 hours.

✓ In small bowl, mix powdered sugar, water and ¼ teaspoon vanilla until thin enough to drizzle. Drizzle over loaves.

✓ Sprinkle with ginger. Wrap tightly and store at room temperature up to 4 days, or refrigerate up to 10 days.

406) *Strawberry Oat Bread*

Ingredients:

- 16 slice bread (2 pounds)
- 1½ cups lukewarm milk
- ¼ cup unsalted butter, melted
- ¼ cup sugar
- 2 teaspoons table salt
- 1½ cups quick oats
- 3 cups white bread flour
- 2 teaspoons bread machine yeast
- 1 cup strawberries, sliced

Direction: PREP: 10 MINUTES /MAKES 1 LOAF

✓ Preparing the Ingredients. Choose the size of loaf of your preference and then measure the ingredients.

✓ Add all of the ingredients mentioned previously in the list, except for the strawberries.

✓ Close the lid after placing the pan in the bread machine.

✓ Select the Bake Cycle Turn on the bread machine. White/Basic or Fruit/Nut (if your machine has this setting) setting, select the loaf size, and the crust color.

✓ Press start.

✓ When the machine signals to add ingredients, add the strawberries.

✓ When the breadmaker cycle is complete, carefully

remove the pan from the machine and allow it to cool before serving.

✓ Remove the bread from the pan, put in a wire rack to cool for at least 10 minutes, and slice.

407) **Black Olive Bread**

Ingredients:

- 12 slices (1½ pounds)
- 1 cup milk, at 80°F to 90°F
- 1½ tablespoons melted butter, cooled
- 1 teaspoon minced garlic
- 1½ tablespoons sugar
- 1 teaspoon salt
- 3 cups white bread flour
- 1 teaspoon bread machine or instant yeast
- ⅓ cup chopped black olives

Direction: PREP: 10 MINUTES /MAKES 1 LOAF

✓ Preparing the Ingredients. Choose the size of loaf of your preference and then measure the ingredients.

✓ Add all of the ingredients mentioned previously in the list.

✓ Close the lid after placing the pan in the bread machine.

✓ Select the Bake Cycle Turn on the bread machine. Select the White/Basic setting, select the loaf size, and the crust color.

✓ Press start.

✓ When the breadmaker cycle is complete, carefully remove the pan from the machine and allow it to cool before serving.

✓ Remove the bread from the pan, put in a wire rack to cool for at least 10 minutes.

408) **Cranberry & Golden Raisin Bread**

Ingredients:

- 1⅓ cups water
- 4 Tbsp. sliced butter
- 3 cups flour
- 1 cup old fashioned oatmeal
- ⅓ cup brown sugar
- 1 tsp salt
- 4 tbsp. dried cranberries
- 4 tbsp. golden raisins
- 2 tsp bread machine yeast

Direction: PREP: 10 MINUTES /MAKES 14 SLICES

✓ Preparing the Ingredients Add each ingredient except cranberries and golden raisins to the bread machine one by one, according to the manufacturer's instructions.

✓ Select the Bake cycle.

✓ Close the lid, select the sweet or basic bread, medium crust setting on your bread machine and press start.

✓ Add the cranberries and golden raisins 5 to 10 minutes before the last kneading cycle ends.

✓ Take out the baked bread from the bread machine and allow it to cool on a cooling rack.

409) **Zucchini Bread**

Ingredients:

- 3 cups shredded zucchini (2 to 3 medium)
- 1⅔ cups sugar
- ⅔ cup vegetable oil
- 2 teaspoons vanilla
- 4 eggs
- 3 cups all-purpose or whole wheat flour
- 2 teaspoons baking soda
- 1 teaspoon salt
- 1 teaspoon ground cinnamon
- ½ teaspoon baking powder
- ½ teaspoon ground cloves
- ½ cup chopped nuts
- ½ cup raisins, if desired

Direction: PREP: 10 MINUTES / MAKES 2 LOAVES

✓ Preparing the Ingredients. Choose the size of loaf of your preference and then measure the ingredients.

✓ Add all of the ingredients mentioned previously in the list.

✓ Close the lid after placing the pan in the bread machine.

✓ Select the Bake Cycle Turn on the bread machine. Select the White/Basic setting, select the loaf size, and the crust color.

✓ Press start.

✓ When the breadmaker cycle is complete, carefully remove the pan from the machine and allow it to cool before serving.

✓ Remove the bread from the pan, put in a wire rack to cool for at least 2 hours before slicing.

✓ Wrap tightly and store at room temperature up to 4 days, or refrigerate up to 10 days.

410) **Cinnamon Figs Bread**

Ingredients:

- 16 slice bread (1½ pounds)
- 1⅛ cups lukewarm water
- 2¼ tablespoons unsalted butter, melted
- 3 tablespoons sugar
- ¾ teaspoon table salt
- ⅓ teaspoon cinnamon, ground
- ¾ teaspoon orange zest Pinch ground nutmeg
- 1⅞ cups whole-wheat flour
- 1⅛ cups white bread flour
- 1½ teaspoons bread machine yeast
- 1 cup chopped plums or sliced figs

Direction: PREP: 10 MINUTES /MAKES 1 LOAF

✓ Preparing the Ingredients. Choose the size of loaf of your preference and then measure the ingredients.

✓ Add all of the ingredients mentioned previously in the list, except for the plums.

✓ Close the lid after placing the pan in the bread machine.

- Select the Bake Cycle Turn on the bread machine. White/Basic or Fruit/Nut (if your machine has this setting) setting, select the loaf size, and the crust color.
- Press start.
- When the machine signals to add ingredients, add the plums.
- When the breadmaker cycle is complete, carefully remove the pan from the machine and allow it to cool before serving.
- Remove the bread from the pan, put in a wire rack to cool for at least 10 minutes, and slice.

411)   *Robust Date Bread*

Ingredients:

- 12 slice bread (1½ pounds)
- ¾ cup water, at 80°F to 90°F
- ½ cup milk, at 80°F
- 2 tablespoons melted butter, cooled
- ¼ cup honey
- 3 tablespoons molasses
- 1 tablespoon sugar
- 2 tablespoons skim milk powder
- 1 teaspoon salt
- 2¼ cups whole-wheat flour
- 1¼ cups white bread flour
- 1 tablespoon unsweetened cocoa powder
- 1½ teaspoons bread machine or instant yeast
- ¾ cup chopped dates

Direction: PREP: 10 MINUTES /MAKES 1 LOAF

- Preparing the Ingredients. Choose the size of loaf of your preference and then measure the ingredients.
- Add all of the ingredients mentioned previously in the list.
- Close the lid after placing the pan in the bread machine Select the Bake Cycle Turn on the bread machine.
- Select the White/Basic setting, select the loaf size, and the crust color.
- Press start.
- When the breadmaker cycle is complete, carefully remove the pan from the machine and allow it to cool before serving.
- Remove the bread from the pan, put in a wire rack to cool for at least 10 minutes before slicing.

412)   *Cranberry Honey Bread*

Ingredients:

- 16 slice bread (2 pounds)
- 1¼ cups + 1 tablespoon lukewarm water
- ¼ cup unsalted butter, melted
- 3 tablespoons honey or molasses
- 4 cups white bread flour
- ½ cup cornmeal
- 2 teaspoons table salt
- 2½ teaspoons bread machine yeast
- ¾ cup cranberries, dried

Direction: PREP: 10 MINUTES /MAKES 1 LOAF

- Preparing the Ingredients. Choose the size of loaf of your preference and then measure the ingredients.
- Add all of the ingredients mentioned previously in the list.
- Close the lid after placing the pan in the bread machine.
- Select the Bake Cycle Turn on the bread maker.
- Select the White/Basic or Fruit/Nut (if your machine has this setting) setting, then the loaf size, and finally the crust color.
- Start the cycle.
- When the machine signals to add ingredients, add the dried cranberries.
- When the cycle is finished and the bread is baked, carefully remove the pan from the machine.
- Use a potholder as the handle will be very hot.
- Let rest for a few minutes.
- Remove the bread from the pan and allow to cool on a wire rack for at least 10 minutes before slicing.

413)   *Apple Spice Bread*

Ingredients:

- 16 slice bread (2 pounds)
- 1⅓ cup milk, at 80°F to 90°F
- 3⅓ tablespoons melted butter, cooled
- 2⅔ tablespoons sugar
- 2 teaspoons salt
- 1⅓ teaspoons ground cinnamon Pinch ground cloves
- 4 cups white bread flour
- 2¼ teaspoons bread machine or active dry yeast
- 1⅓ cups finely diced peeled apple

Direction: PREP: 10 MINUTES /MAKES 1 LOAF

- Preparing the Ingredients. Choose the size of loaf of your preference and then measure the ingredients.
- Add all of the ingredients mentioned previously in the list, except for the apple.
- Close the lid after placing the pan in the bread machine.
- Select the Bake cycle Turn on the bread machine. White/Basic or Fruit/Nut (if your machine has this setting) setting, select the loaf size, and the crust color.
- Press start.
- When the machine signals to add ingredients, add the apple.
- When the breadmaker cycle is complete, carefully remove the pan from the machine and allow it to cool before serving.
- Remove the bread from the pan, put in a wire rack to cool for at least 10 minutes, and slice.

414) Poppy Seed–Lemon Bread

Ingredients:

- 1 cup sugar
- ¼ cup grated lemon peel
- 1 cup milk
- ¾ cup vegetable oil
- 2 tablespoons poppy seed
- 2 teaspoons baking powder
- ½ teaspoon salt
- 2 eggs, slightly beaten

Direction: PREP: 10 MINUTES /MAKES 1 LOAF

- ✓ Preparing the Ingredients. Choose the size of loaf of your preference and then measure the ingredients.
- ✓ Add all of the ingredients mentioned previously in the list.
- ✓ Close the lid after placing the pan in the bread machine.
- ✓ Select the Bake Cycle Turn on the bread machine. Select the White/Basic setting, select the loaf size, and the crust color.
- ✓ Press start.
- ✓ When the breadmaker cycle is complete, carefully remove the pan from the machine and allow it to cool before serving.
- ✓ Remove the bread from the pan, put in a wire rack to cool completely, about 2 hours. Wrap tightly and store at room temperature up to 4 days, or refrigerate.

415) Ginger-Carrot-Nut Bread

Ingredients:

- 2 eggs
- ¾ cup packed brown sugar
- 1/3 cup vegetable oil
- ½ cup milk
- 1 teaspoon vanilla
- 2 cups all-purpose flour
- 2 teaspoons baking powder
- 1 teaspoon ground ginger
- ½ teaspoon salt
- 1 cup shredded carrots (2 medium)
- ½ cup chopped nuts

Direction: PREP: 10 MINUTES /MAKES 1 LOAF

- ✓ Preparing the Ingredients. Choose the size of loaf of your preference and then measure the ingredients.
- ✓ Add all of the ingredients mentioned previously in the list.
- ✓ Close the lid after placing the pan in the bread machine.
- ✓ Select the Bake cycle Turn on the bread machine.
- ✓ Select the White/Basic setting, select the loaf size, and the crust color.
  Press start.
- ✓ When the breadmaker cycle is complete, carefully remove the pan from the machine and allow it to cool before serving.

- ✓ Remove the bread from the pan, put in a wire rack to cool.
- ✓ Cool completely, about 10 minutes.
- ✓ Wrap tightly and store at room temperature up to 4 days, or refrigerate.

416) Orange Bread

Ingredients:

- 16 slice bread (2 pounds)
- 1¼ cups lukewarm milk
- ¼ cup orange juice
- ¼ cup sugar
- 1½ tablespoons unsalted butter, melted
- 1¼ teaspoons table salt
- 4 cups white bread flour
- Zest of 1 orange
- 1¾ teaspoons bread machine yeast

Direction: PREP: 10 MINUTES /MAKES 1 LOAF

- ✓ Preparing the Ingredients. Choose the size of loaf of your preference and then measure the ingredients.
- ✓ Add all of the ingredients mentioned previously in the list.
- ✓ Close the lid after placing the pan in the bread machine.
- ✓ Select the Bake Cycle Turn on the bread machine.
- ✓ Select the White/Basic setting, select the loaf size, and the crust color.
- ✓ Press start.
- ✓ When the breadmaker cycle is complete, carefully remove the pan from the machine and allow it to cool before serving.
- ✓ Remove the bread from the pan, put in a wire rack to cool.
- ✓ Cool completely, about 10 minutes.
- ✓ Slice

417) Lemon-Lime Blueberry Bread

Ingredients:

- 12 slice bread (1½ pounds)
- ¾ cup plain yogurt, at room temperature
- ½ cup water, at 80°F to 90°F
- 3 tablespoons honey
- 1 tablespoon melted butter, cooled
- 1½ teaspoons salt
- 1½ teaspoons salt
- ½ teaspoon lemon extract
- 1 teaspoon lime zest
- 1 cup dried blueberries
- 3 cups white bread flour
- 2¼ teaspoons bread machine or instant yeast

Direction: PREP: 10 MINUTES /MAKES 1 LOAF

- ✓ Preparing the Ingredients. Choose the size of loaf of your preference and then measure the ingredients.
- ✓ Add all of the ingredients mentioned previously in the list.

- ✓ Close the lid after placing the pan in the bread machine.
- ✓ Select the Bake Cycle Turn on the bread machine.
- ✓ Select the White/Basic setting, select the loaf size, and the crust color.
- ✓ Press start.
- ✓ When the breadmaker cycle is complete, carefully remove the pan from the machine and allow it to cool before serving.
- ✓ Remove the bread from the pan, put in a wire rack to cool. Cool completely, about 10 minutes.
- ✓ Slice

418) *Apple-Fig Bread with Honey Glaze*

Ingredients:

- 1½ cups all-purpose flour
- 1½ teaspoons ground cinnamon
- 1 teaspoon baking powder
- ½ teaspoon salt
- ½ teaspoon ground nutmeg
- ¼ teaspoon ground allspice
- 2/3 cup granulated sugar
- ½ cup vegetable oil
- 1 egg
- 1 egg yolk
- 1½ teaspoons vanilla
- ½ cup milk
- 1 cup chopped peeled apples
- ½ cup dried figs, chopped glaze
- 1/3 to ½ cup powdered sugar
- 2 tablespoons honey
- 1 tablespoon butter, softened
- Dash ground allspice

Direction: PREP: 10 MINUTES /MAKES 1 LOAF

- ✓ Preparing the Ingredients. Choose the size of loaf of your preference and then measure the ingredients.
- ✓ Add all of the ingredients mentioned previously in the list.
- ✓ Close the lid after placing the pan in the bread machine Select the Bake Cycle Turn on the bread machine.
- ✓ Select the White/Basic setting, select the loaf size, and the crust color, then press start.
- ✓ When the breadmaker cycle is complete, carefully remove the pan from the machine and allow it to cool before serving.
- ✓ Remove the bread from the pan and let it cool on a wire rack. About two hours later, the food should be totally cooled to room temperature.
- ✓ To make the glaze, combine the honey, butter, and a dash of allspice in a small dish and mix until smooth. Slowly add more powdered sugar to achieve the appropriate consistency.
- ✓ Drizzle the loaf with the glaze.
- ✓ Settling in for the night. For the time being, the glaze

will be a little sticky to the touch.
- ✓ In order to preserve freshness, store in the refrigerator.

419) *Honey Banana Bread*

Ingredients:

- 12 slice bread (1½ pounds)
- ½ cup lukewarm milk
- 1 cup banana, mashed
- 1 egg, beaten
- 1½ tablespoons unsalted butter, melted
- 3 tablespoons honey
- 1 teaspoon pure vanilla extract
- ½ teaspoon table salt
- 1 cup whole-wheat flour
- 1¼ cups white bread flour
- 1½ teaspoons bread machine yeast

Direction: PREP: 10 MINUTES /MAKES 1 LOAF

- ✓ Preparing the Ingredients. Choose the size of loaf of your preference and then measure the ingredients.
- ✓ Add all of the ingredients mentioned previously in the list.
- ✓ Close the lid after placing the pan in the bread machine.
- ✓ Select the Bake Cycle Turn on the bread maker.
- ✓ Choose the Sweet option first, then the loaf size, and then the crust color.
- ✓ Start the cycle, then carefully remove the pan from the machine once the cycle is completed and the bread has baked.
- ✓ Remove the bread from the pan and cool for at least 10 minutes on a wire rack before slicing.

420) *Banana Whole-Wheat Bread*

Ingredients:

- 12 slice bread (1½ pounds)
- ½ cup milk, at 80°F to 90°F
- 1 cup mashed banana
- 1 egg, at room temperature
- 1½ tablespoons melted butter, cooled
- 3 tablespoons honey
- 1 teaspoon pure vanilla extract
- ½ teaspoon salt
- 1 cup whole-wheat flour
- 1¼ cups white bread flour
- 1½ teaspoons bread machine or instant yeast

Direction: PREP: 10 MINUTES /MAKES 1 LOAF

- ✓ Preparing the Ingredients. Choose the size of loaf of your preference and then measure the ingredients.
- ✓ Add all of the ingredients mentioned previously in the list.
- ✓ Close the lid after placing the pan in the bread machine Select the Bake cycle.
- ✓ Turn on the bread machine.

Select the Sweet bread setting, select the loaf size, and the crust color.

✓ Press start.

✓ When the breadmaker cycle is complete, carefully remove the pan from the machine and allow it to cool before serving.

✓ Remove the loaf by shaking the pail and transferring it to a cooling rack.

421) Oatmeal-Streusel Bread

Ingredients:

- Streusel
- ¼ cup packed brown sugar
- ¼ cup chopped walnuts, toasted
- 2 teaspoons ground cinnamon Bread
- 1 cup all-purpose flour
- ½ cup whole wheat flour
- ½ cup old-fashioned oats
- 2 tablespoons ground flaxseed or flaxseed meal
- 1 teaspoon baking powder
- ½ teaspoon salt
- ¼ teaspoon baking soda
- ¾ cup packed brown sugar
- 2/3 cup vegetable oil
- 2 eggs
- ¼ cup sour cream
- 2 teaspoons vanilla
- ½ cup milk Icing
- ¾ to 1 cup powdered sugar
- 1 tablespoon milk
- 2 teaspoons light corn syrup

Direction: PREP: 10 MINUTES /MAKES 1 LOAF

✓ Preparing the Ingredients. Choose the size of loaf of your preference and then measure the ingredients.

✓ Add all of the ingredients mentioned previously in the list.

✓ Close the lid after placing the pan in the bread machine Select the Bake cycle.

✓ Turn on the bread machine.

✓ Select the White/Basic setting, select the loaf size, and the crust color.

✓ Press start.

✓ When the breadmaker cycle is complete, carefully remove the pan from the machine and allow it to cool before serving.

✓ Remove the bread from the pan, put in a wire rack to Cool completely, about 2 hours.

✓ In small bowl, beat all icing ingredients, adding enough of the powdered sugar for desired drizzling consistency.

✓ Drizzle icing over bread.

✓ Let stand until set.

✓ Wrap tightly and store at room temperature up to 4 days, or refrigerate.

✓ To toast walnuts, bake in ungreased shallow pan at

350°F for 7 to 11 minutes, stirring occasionally, until light brown.

422) Garlic Olive Bread

Ingredients:

- 12 slice bread (1½ pounds)
- 1 cup lukewarm milk
- 1½ tablespoons unsalted butter, melted
- 1 teaspoon garlic, minced
- 1½ tablespoons sugar
- 1 teaspoon table salt
- 3 cups white bread flour
- 1 teaspoon bread machine yeast
- ⅓ cup black olives, chopped
- 16 slice bread (2 pounds)
- 1⅓ cups lukewarm milk
- 2 tablespoons unsalted butter, melted
- 1⅓ teaspoons garlic, minced
- 2 tablespoons sugar
- 1⅓ teaspoons table salt
- 4 cups white bread flour
- 1½ teaspoons bread machine yeast
- ½ cup black olives, chopped

Direction: PREP: 10 MINUTES /MAKES 1 LOAF

✓ Preparing the Ingredients Choose the size of loaf of your preference and then measure the ingredients.

✓ Add all of the ingredients mentioned previously in the list, except for the olives.

✓ Close the lid after placing the pan in the bread machine.

✓ Select the Bake Turn on the bread machine. White/Basic or Fruit/Nut (if your machine has this setting) setting, select the loaf size, and the crust color.

✓ Press start.

✓ When the machine signals to add ingredients, add the olives.

✓ When the breadmaker cycle is complete, carefully remove the pan from the machine and allow it to cool before serving.

✓ Remove the bread from the pan, put in a wire rack to cool for at least 10 minutes, and slice.

423) Brown Bread with Raisins

Ingredients:

- 32 slices 1 cup all-purpose flour
- 1 cup whole wheat flour
- 1 cup whole-grain cornmeal
- 1 cup raisins
- 2 cups buttermilk
- ¾ cup molasses
- 2 teaspoons baking soda
- 1 teaspoon salt

Direction: PREP: 10 MINUTES /MAKES 1 LOAF

- ✓ Preparing the Ingredients. Choose the size of loaf of your preference and then measure the ingredients.
- ✓ Add all of the ingredients mentioned previously in the list.
- ✓ Close the lid after placing the pan in the bread machine.
- ✓ Select the Bake cycle Turn on the bread machine. Select the White/Basic setting, select the loaf size, and the crust color.
- ✓ Press start.
- ✓ When the breadmaker cycle is complete, carefully remove the pan from the machine and allow it to cool before serving. Remove the bread from the pan, put in a wire rack to Cool completely, about 30 minutes.

424) Cinnamon Pumpkin Bread

Ingredients:

- 16 slice bread (2 pounds)
- 2 cups pumpkin puree
- 4 eggs, slightly beaten
- ½ cup unsalted butter, melted
- 1¼ cups sugar
- ½ teaspoon table salt
- 4 cups white bread flour
- 1 teaspoon cinnamon, ground
- ¾ teaspoon baking soda
- ½ teaspoon nutmeg, ground
- ½ teaspoon ginger,
- ground Pinch ground cloves
- 2 teaspoons baking powder

Direction: PREP: 10 MINUTES /MAKES 1 LOAF

- ✓ Preparing the Ingredients. Choose the size of loaf of your preference and then measure the ingredients.
- ✓ Add all of the ingredients mentioned previously in the list.
- ✓ Close the lid after placing the pan in the bread machine.
- ✓ Select the Bake Cycle Turn on the bread machine.
- ✓ Select the Quick/Rapid setting, select the loaf size, and the crust color.
- ✓ Press start.
- ✓ When the breadmaker cycle is complete, carefully remove the pan from the machine and allow it to cool before serving.
- ✓ Remove the bread from the pan, put in a wire rack to Cool completely, about 30 minutes.
- ✓ Slice

425) Plum Orange Bread

Ingredients:

- 12 slice bread (1½ pounds)
- 1⅛ cup water, at 80°F to 90°F
- 2¼ tablespoons melted butter, cooled
- 3 tablespoons sugar
- ¾ teaspoon salt

- ¾ teaspoon orange zest
- ⅓ teaspoon ground cinnamon
- Pinch ground nutmeg
- 1¾ cups plus 2 tablespoons whole-wheat flour
- 1⅛ cups white bread flour
- 1½ teaspoons bread machine or instant yeast
- 1 cup chopped fresh plums

Direction: PREP: 10 MINUTES /MAKES 1 LOAF

- ✓ Preparing the Ingredients. Choose the size of loaf of your preference and then measure the ingredients.
- ✓ Add all of the ingredients mentioned previously in the list, except for the plums.
- ✓ Close the lid after placing the pan in the bread machine.
- ✓ Select the Bake Cycle Turn on the bread machine. White/Basic or Fruit/Nut (if your machine has this setting), select the loaf size, and the crust color.
- ✓ Press start.
- ✓ When the machine signals to add ingredients, add the plums.
- ✓ When the breadmaker cycle is complete, carefully remove the pan from the machine and allow it to cool before serving.
- ✓ Remove the bread from the pan, put in a wire rack to cool for at least 10 minutes, and slice.

426) Blueberries 'n Orange Bread

Ingredients:

- 18 slices bread
- 3 cups Original Bisquick mix
- ½ cup granulated sugar
- 1 tablespoon grated orange peel
- ½ cup milk
- 3 tablespoons vegetable oil
- 2 eggs
- 1 cup fresh or frozen (rinsed and drained) blueberries glaze
- ½ cup powdered sugar
- 3 to 4 teaspoons orange juice
- Additional grated orange peel, if desired

Direction: PREP: 10 MINUTES /MAKES 1 LOAF

- ✓ Preparing the Ingredients. Choose the size of loaf of your preference and then measure the ingredients.
- ✓ Add all of the ingredients mentioned previously in the list.
- ✓ Close the lid after placing the pan in the bread machine.
- ✓ Choose the Bake Cycle Set the machine to Basic/White bread, choose between light or medium crust, then push Start.
- ✓ When the loaf is done, remove the bucket from the machine.
- ✓ Let the loaf cool for 5 minutes. Gently shake the bucket to remove the loaf, and turn it out onto a rack to cool.
- ✓ Cool completely, about 45 minutes.

- ✓ In small bowl, mix powdered sugar and orange juice until smooth and thin enough to drizzle.
- ✓ Drizzle glaze over bread; sprinkle with additional orange peel.

427) Peaches and Cream Bread

Ingredients:

- 12 slice bread (1½ pounds)
- ¾ cup canned peaches, drained and chopped
- ⅓ cup heavy whipping cream, at 80°F to 90°F
- 1 egg, at room temperature
- 1 tablespoon melted butter, cooled
- 2¼ tablespoons sugar
- 1⅛ teaspoons salt
- ⅓ teaspoon ground cinnamon
- ⅛ teaspoon ground nutmeg
- ⅓ cup whole-wheat flour
- 2⅔ cups white bread flour
- 1⅛ teaspoons bread machine or instant yeast

Direction: PREP: 10 MINUTES /MAKES 1 LOAF

- ✓ Preparing the Ingredients. Choose the size of loaf of your preference and then measure the ingredients.
- ✓ Add all of the ingredients mentioned previously in the list.
- ✓ Close the lid after placing the pan in the bread machine.
- ✓ Select the Bake Cycle Turn on the bread machine. Select the White/Basic setting, select the loaf size, and the crust color.
- ✓ Press start.
- ✓ When the breadmaker cycle is complete, carefully remove the pan from the machine and allow it to cool before serving.
- ✓ Remove the bread from the pan, put in a wire rack to Cool completely, about 10 minutes.

428) Fresh Blueberry Bread

Ingredients:

- 12 to 16 slices (1½ to 2 pounds)
- 1 cup plain Greek yogurt, at room temperature
- ½ cup milk, at room temperature
- 3 tablespoons butter, at room temperature
- 2 eggs, at room temperature
- ½ cup sugar
- ¼ cup light brown sugar
- 1 teaspoon pure vanilla extract
- ½ teaspoon lemon zest
- 2 cups all-purpose flour
- 1 tablespoon baking powder
- ¾ teaspoon salt
- ¼ teaspoon ground nutmeg
- 1 cup blueberries

Direction: PREP: 10 MINUTES /MAKES 1 LOAF

- ✓ Preparing the Ingredients. Place the yogurt, milk, butter, eggs, sugar, brown sugar, vanilla, and zest in your bread machine.
- ✓ Select the Bake cycle. Program the machine for Quick/Rapid bread and press Start.
- ✓ While the wet ingredients are mixing, stir together the flour, baking powder, salt, and nutmeg in a medium bowl.
- ✓ After the first fast mixing is done and the machine signals, add the dry ingredients.
- ✓ When the second mixing cycle is complete, stir in the blueberries.
- ✓ When the loaf is done, remove the bucket from the machine. Let the loaf cool for 5 minutes.
- ✓ Gently shake the bucket to remove the loaf, and turn it out onto a rack to cool.

429) Blueberry-Basil Loaf

Ingredients:

- 12 slice bread (1½ pounds)
- 1¼ cups fresh blueberries
- 1 tablespoon all-purpose flour
- 2¼ cups all-purpose flour
- 1 cup granulated sugar
- 2 teaspoons baking powder
- 1 teaspoon grated lemon peel
- ½ teaspoon salt
- 1 cup buttermilk
- 6 tablespoons butter, melted
- 1 teaspoon vanilla
- 2 eggs
- ¼ cup coarsely chopped fresh basil leaves Topping
- ½ cup packed brown sugar
- ¼ cup butter, melted
- 2/3 cup all-purpose flour

Direction: PREP: 10 MINUTES /MAKES 1 LOAF

- ✓ Preparing the Ingredients. Choose the size of loaf of your preference and then measure the ingredients.
- ✓ Add all of the ingredients mentioned previously in the list. Close the lid after placing the pan in the bread machine.
- ✓ Select the Bake Cycle Turn on the bread machine.
- ✓ Select the White/Basic setting, select the loaf size, and the crust color.
- ✓ Press start.
- ✓ When the breadmaker cycle is complete, carefully remove the pan from the machine and allow it to cool before serving.
- ✓ Remove the bread from the pan, put in a wire rack to Cool about 1 hour.

430) Savory Sweet Potato Pan Bread

Ingredients:

- 8 wedges
- 1½ cups uncooked shredded dark-orange sweet

potato (about ½ potato)

- ½ cup sugar
- ¼ cup vegetable oil
- 2 eggs
- ¾ cup all-purpose flour
- ¾ cup whole wheat flour
- 2 teaspoons dried minced onion
- 1 teaspoon dried rosemary leaves, crumbled
- 1 teaspoon baking soda
- ½ teaspoon salt
- ¼ teaspoon baking powder
- 2 teaspoons sesame seed

Direction: PREP: 10 MINUTES /MAKES 1 LOAF

✓ Preparing the Ingredients. Choose the size of loaf of your preference and then measure the ingredients.
✓ Add all of the ingredients mentioned previously in the list.
✓ Close the lid after placing the pan in the bread machine.
✓ Select the Bake Cycle Turn on the bread machine.
✓ Select the White/Basic setting, select the loaf size, and the crust color.
✓ Press start.
✓ When the breadmaker cycle is complete, carefully remove the pan from the machine and allow it to cool before serving.
✓ Remove the bread from the pan, put in a wire rack to Cool about 10 minutes.
✓ Serve warm.

431) **_Citrus and Walnut Bread_**

Ingredients:

- ¾ cup lemon yogurt
- ½ cup orange juice
- 5 tsp caster sugar
- 1 tsp salt
- 2.5 tbsp. butter
- 2 cups unbleached white bread flour
- 1½ tsp easy blend dried yeast
- ⅓ cup chopped walnuts
- 2 tsp grated lemon rind
- 2 tsp grated orange rind

Direction: PREP: 10 MINUTES PLUS FERMENTING TIME /MAKES 14 SLICES

✓ Preparing the Ingredients. Choose the size of loaf of your preference and then measure the ingredients.
✓ Add all of the ingredients mentioned previously in the list, except for the walnuts and orange and lemon rind.
✓ Close the lid after placing the pan in the bread machine.
✓ Select the Bake Cycle Close the lid, select the basic bread, medium crust setting on your bread machine, and press start.
✓ Add the walnuts, and orange and lemon rind during

the 2nd kneading cycle: Take out the baked bread from the bread machine and allow it to cool on a cooling rack.

432) **_Almond Milk Bread_**

Ingredients:

- 12 slice bread (1½ pounds)
- ¾ cup lukewarm milk
- 2 eggs, at room temperature
- 2 tablespoons butter, melted and cooled
- ¼ cup sugar
- 1 teaspoon table salt
- 2 teaspoons lemon zest
- 3 cups white bread flour
- 2 teaspoons bread machine yeast
- ⅓ cup slivered almonds, chopped
- ⅓ cup golden raisins, chopped

Direction: PREP: 10 MINUTES /MAKES 1 LOAF

✓ Preparing the Ingredients. Choose the size of loaf of your preference and then measure the ingredients.
✓ Add all of the ingredients mentioned previously in the list, except for the raisins and almonds.
✓ Close the lid after placing the pan in the bread machine.
✓ Select the Bake Cycle Turn on the bread maker. Select the White/Basic or Fruit/Nut (if your machine has this setting) setting, then the loaf size, and finally the crust color.
✓ Start the cycle.
✓ When the machine signals to add ingredients, add the raisins and almonds.
✓ When the breadmaker cycle is complete, carefully remove the pan from the machine and allow it to cool before serving.
✓ Remove the bread from the pan, put in a wire rack to Cool about 10 minutes.

433) **_Slice Rosemary Bread_**

Ingredients:

- 12 slice bread (1½ pounds)
- 1¼ cups water, at 80°F to 90°F
- 2½ tablespoons melted butter, cooled
- 1 tablespoon sugar
- 1½ teaspoons salt
- 1½ tablespoons finely chopped fresh rosemary
- 3 cups white bread flour
- 2 teaspoons bread machine or instant yeast

Direction: PREP: 10 MINUTES /MAKES 1 LOAF

✓ Preparing the Ingredients. Choose the size of loaf of your preference and then measure the ingredients.
✓ Add all of the ingredients mentioned previously in the list.
✓ Close the lid after placing the pan in the bread machine.
✓ Select the Bake Cycle Turn on the bread machine.

Select the White/Basic setting, select the loaf size, and the crust color.

✓ Press start.

✓ When the breadmaker cycle is complete, carefully remove the pan from the machine and allow it to cool before serving.

✓ Remove the bread from the pan, put in a wire rack to Cool about 10 minutes.

✓ Slice

434) Cinnamon Milk Bread

Ingredients:

- 12 slice bread (1½ pounds)
- 1 cup lukewarm milk
- 1 egg, at room temperature
- ¼ cup unsalted butter, melted
- ½ cup sugar
- ½ teaspoon table salt
- 3 cups white bread flour
- 1½ teaspoons ground cinnamon
- 2 teaspoons bread machine yeast

Direction: PREP: 10 MINUTES /MAKES 1 LOAF

✓ Preparing the Ingredients. Choose the size of loaf of your preference and then measure the ingredients.

✓ Add all of the ingredients mentioned previously in the list.

✓ Close the lid after placing the pan in the bread machine.

✓ Select the Bake Cycle Turn on the bread machine. Select the White/Basic setting, select the loaf size, and the crust color.

✓ Press start. When the breadmaker cycle is complete, carefully remove the pan from the machine and allow it to cool before serving.

✓ Remove the bread from the pan, put in a wire rack to Cool about 10 minutes.

✓ Slice

435) Spicy Cajun Bread

Ingredients:

- 12 slice bread (1½ pounds)
- 1⅛ cups water, at 80°F to 90°F
- 1½ tablespoons melted butter, cooled
- 1 tablespoon tomato paste
- 1½ tablespoons sugar
- 1½ teaspoons salt
- 3 tablespoons skim milk powder
- ¾ tablespoon Cajun seasoning
- ¼ teaspoon onion powder
- 3 cups white bread flour
- 1¼ teaspoons bread machine or instant yeast

Direction: PREP: 10 MINUTES /MAKES 1 LOAF

✓ Preparing the Ingredients. Choose the size of loaf of your preference and then measure the ingredients.

✓ Add all of the ingredients mentioned previously in the list.

✓ Close the lid after placing the pan in the bread machine.

✓ Select the Bake Cycle Turn on the bread machine. Select the White/Basic setting, select the loaf size, and the crust color.

✓ Press start.

✓ When the breadmaker cycle is complete, carefully remove the pan from the machine and allow it to cool before serving.

✓ Remove the bread from the pan, put in a wire rack to Cool about 10 minutes.

✓ Slice

436) Oat Nut Bread

Ingredients:

- 1¼ cups water
- ½ cup quick oats
- ¼ cup brown sugar, firmly packed
- 1 tbsp. butter
- 1½ tsp salt
- 3 cups bread flour
- ¾ cup chopped walnuts
- 1 package dry bread yeast

Direction: PREP: 10 MINUTES PLUS FERMENTING TIME /MAKES 1 LOAF

✓ Preparing the Ingredients Choose the size of loaf of your preference and then measure the ingredients.

✓ Add all of the ingredients mentioned previously in the list.

✓ Close the lid after placing the pan in the bread machine.

✓ Select the Bake Cycle Close the lid, select the rapid rise, medium crust setting on your bread machine, and press start.

✓ Take out the baked bread from the bread machine and allow it to cool on a cooling rack.

437) Hazelnut Honey Bread

Ingredients:

- 16 slices bread (2 pounds)
- 1⅓ cups lukewarm milk
- 2 eggs, at room temperature
- 5 tablespoons unsalted butter, melted
- ¼ cup honey
- 1 teaspoon pure vanilla extract
- 1 teaspoon table salt
- 4 cups white bread flour
- 1 cup toasted hazelnuts, finely ground
- 2 teaspoons bread machine yeast

Direction: PREP: 10 MINUTES /MAKES 1 LOAF

✓ Preparing the Ingredients. Choose the size of loaf of your preference and then measure the ingredients.

✓ Add all of the ingredients mentioned previously in the

list.
- ✓ Close the lid after placing the pan in the bread machine.
- ✓ Select the Bake Cycle Turn on the bread machine. Select the White/Basic setting, select the loaf size, and the crust color.
- ✓ Press start.
- ✓ When the breadmaker cycle is complete, carefully remove the pan from the machine and allow it to cool before serving.
- ✓ Remove the bread from the pan, put in a wire rack to Cool about 10 minutes.
- ✓ Slice

438) Aromatic Lavender Bread

Ingredients:

- 16 slices bread (2 pounds)
- 1½ cups milk, at 80°F to 90°F
- 2 tablespoons melted butter, cooled
- 2 tablespoons sugar
- 2 teaspoons salt
- 2 teaspoons chopped fresh lavender flowers
- 1 teaspoon lemon zest
- ½ teaspoon chopped fresh thyme
- 4 cups white bread flour
- 1½ teaspoons bread machine or instant yeast

Direction: PREP: 10 MINUTES /MAKES 1 LOAF

- ✓ Preparing the Ingredients. Choose the size of loaf of your preference and then measure the ingredients.
- ✓ Add all of the ingredients mentioned previously in the list.
- ✓ Close the lid after placing the pan in the bread machine.
- ✓ Select the Bake Cycle Turn on the bread machine.
- ✓ Select the White/Basic setting, select the loaf size, and the crust color.
- ✓ Press start.
- ✓ When the breadmaker cycle is complete, carefully remove the pan from the machine and allow it to cool before serving.
- ✓ Remove the bread from the pan, put in a wire rack to Cool about 10 minutes.
- ✓ Slice

439) Cardamom Honey Bread

Ingredients:

- 16 slices bread (2 pounds)
- 1⅛ cups lukewarm milk
- 1 egg, at room temperature
- 2 teaspoons unsalted butter, melted
- ¼ cup honey
- 1⅓ teaspoons table salt
- 4 cups white bread flour
- 1⅓ teaspoons ground cardamom
- 1⅔ teaspoons bread machine yeast

- ✓ Preparing the Ingredients. Choose the size of loaf of your preference and then measure the ingredients.
- ✓ Add all of the ingredients mentioned previously in the list.
- ✓ Close the lid after placing the pan in the bread machine.
- ✓ Select the Bake Cycle Turn on the bread machine.
- ✓ Select the White/Basic setting, select the loaf size, and the crust color.
- ✓ Press start.
- ✓ When the breadmaker cycle is complete, carefully remove the pan from the machine and allow it to cool before serving.
- ✓ Remove the bread from the pan, put in a wire rack to Cool about 10 minutes.
- ✓ Slice

440) Cracked Black Pepper Bread

Ingredients:

- 12 slice bread (1½ pounds)
- 1⅛ cups water, at 80°F to 90°F
- 1½ tablespoons melted butter, cooled
- 1½ tablespoons sugar
- 1 teaspoon salt
- 3 tablespoons skim milk powder
- 1½ tablespoons minced chives
- ¾ teaspoon garlic powder
- ¾ teaspoon freshly cracked black pepper
- 3 cups white bread flour
- 1¼ teaspoons bread machine or instant yeast

Direction: PREP: 10 MINUTES /MAKES 1 LOAF

- ✓ Preparing the Ingredients. Choose the size of loaf of your preference and then measure the ingredients.
- ✓ Add all of the ingredients mentioned previously in the list.
- ✓ Close the lid after placing the pan in the bread machine.
- ✓ Select the Bake Cycle Turn on the bread machine. Select the White/Basic setting, select the loaf size, and the crust color.
- ✓ Press start.
- ✓ When the breadmaker cycle is complete, carefully remove the pan from the machine and allow it to cool before serving.
- ✓ Remove the bread from the pan, put in a wire rack to Cool about 10 minutes.
- ✓ Slice

441) Pistachio Cherry Bread

Ingredients:

- 16 slices bread (2 pounds)
- 1⅛ cups lukewarm water
- 1 egg, at room temperature
- ¼ cup butter, softened

- ¼ cup packed dark brown sugar
- 1½ teaspoons table salt
- 3¾ cups white bread flour
- ½ teaspoon ground nutmeg
- Dash allspice
- 2 teaspoons bread machine yeast
- 1 cup dried cherries
- ½ cup unsalted pistachios, chopped

Direction: PREP: 10 MINUTES /MAKES 1 LOAF

✓ Preparing the Ingredients. Choose the size of loaf of your preference and then measure the ingredients.

✓ Add all of the ingredients mentioned previously in the list, except the pistachios and cherries.

✓ Close the lid after placing the pan in the bread machine.

✓ Select the Bake Cycle Turn on the bread maker.

✓ If your machine has the option, choose White/Basic or Fruit/Nut as the first option, followed by your preferred loaf size and finally, the color of the crust you like.

✓ To get started, press the start button.

✓ Add the pistachios and cherries when the machine says to do so.

✓ Carefully remove the pan from the machine once the cycle has done and the bread has been baked.

✓ Use a potholder to protect your hands from the hot handle. Allow for a brief period of repose.

✓ At least 10 minutes before slicing, remove the bread from the pan and place it on a cooling rack.

442) **Herb and Garlic Cream Cheese Bread**

Ingredients:

- 12 slices bread (1½ pounds)
- ½ cup water, at 80°F to 90°F
- ½ cup herb and garlic cream cheese, at room temperature
- 1 egg, at room temperature
- 2 tablespoons melted butter, cooled
- 3 tablespoons sugar
- 1 teaspoon salt
- 3 cups white bread flour
- 1½ teaspoons bread machine or instant yeast

Direction: PREP: 10 MINUTES /MAKES 1 LOAF

✓ Preparing the Ingredients. Choose the size of loaf of your preference and then measure the ingredients.

✓ Add all of the ingredients mentioned previously in the list.

✓ Close the lid after placing the pan in the bread machine.

✓ Select the Bake Cycle Turn on the bread machine. Select the White/Basic setting, select the loaf size, and the crust color.

✓ Press start.

✓ When the breadmaker cycle is complete, carefully remove the pan from the machine and allow it to cool

before serving.

✓ Remove the bread from the pan, put in a wire rack to Cool about 10 minutes.

✓ Slice

443) **Mix Seed Raisin Bread**

Ingredients:

- 16 slices bread (2 pounds)
- 1½ cups lukewarm milk
- 2 tablespoons unsalted butter, melted
- 2 tablespoons honey
- 1 teaspoon table salt
- 2½ cups white bread flour
- ¼ cup flaxseed
- ¼ cup sesame seeds
- 1½ cups whole-wheat flour
- 2¼ teaspoons bread machine yeast
- ½ cup raisins

Direction: PREP: 10 MINUTES /MAKES 1 LOAF

✓ Preparing the Ingredients. Choose the size of loaf of your preference and then measure the ingredients.

✓ Add all of the ingredients mentioned previously in the list.

✓ Close the lid after placing the pan in the bread machine.

✓ Select the Bake Cycle Turn on the bread machine.

✓ Select the White/Basic setting, select the loaf size, and the crust color.

✓ Press start.

✓ When the breadmaker cycle is complete, carefully remove the pan from the machine and allow it to cool before serving.

✓ Remove the bread from the pan, put in a wire rack to Cool about 10 minutes.

✓ Slice

444) **Grain, Seed And Nut Bread**

Ingredients:

- ¼ cup water
- 1 egg
- 3 Tbsp honey
- 1½ tsp butter, softened
- 3¼ cups bread flour
- 1 cup milk
- 1 tsp salt
- ¼ tsp baking soda
- 1 tsp ground cinnamon
- 2½ tsp active dry yeast
- ¾ cup dried cranberries
- ½ cup chopped walnuts
- 1 Tbsp white vinegar
- ½ tsp sugar

Direction: PREP: 10 MINUTES /MAKES 1 LOAF

- ✓ *Preparing the Ingredients. Choose the size of loaf of your preference and then measure the ingredients.*
- ✓ *Add all of the ingredients mentioned previously in the list. Close the lid after placing the pan in the bread machine.*
- ✓ *Select the Bake cycle Turn on the bread machine.*
- ✓ *Select the White/Basic setting, select the loaf size, and the crust color.*
- ✓ *Press start.*
- ✓ *When the breadmaker cycle is complete, carefully remove the pan from the machine and allow it to cool before serving.*
- ✓ *Remove the bread from the pan, put in a wire rack to Cool about 10 minutes.*
- ✓ *Slice*

445) **Honey-Spice Egg Bread**

Ingredients:

- 12 slices bread (1½ pounds)
- 1 cup milk, at 80°F to 90°F
- 2 eggs, at room temperature
- 1½ tablespoons melted butter, cooled
- 2 tablespoons honey
- 1 teaspoon salt
- 1 teaspoon ground cinnamon
- ½ teaspoon ground cardamom
- ½ teaspoon ground nutmeg
- 3 cups white bread flour
- 2 teaspoons bread machine or instant yeast

Direction: PREP: 10 MINUTES /MAKES 1 LOAF

- ✓ *Preparing the Ingredients. Choose the size of loaf of your preference and then measure the ingredients.*
- ✓ *Add all of the ingredients mentioned previously in the list.*
- ✓ *Close the lid after placing the pan in the bread machine.*
- ✓ *Select the Bake Cycle Turn on the bread machine. Select the White/Basic setting, select the loaf size, and the crust color.*
- ✓ *Press start.*
- ✓ *When the breadmaker cycle is complete, carefully remove the pan from the machine and allow it to cool before serving.*
- ✓ *Remove the bread from the pan, put in a wire rack to Cool about 10 minutes.*
- ✓ *Slice*

446) **Anise Honey Bread**

Ingredients:

- 16 slices bread (2 pounds)
- 1 cup + 1 tablespoon lukewarm water
- 1 egg, at room temperature
- ⅓ cup butter, melted and cooled
- ⅓ cup honey
- ⅔ teaspoon table salt

- 4 cups white bread flour
- 1⅓ teaspoons anise seed
- 1⅓ teaspoons lemon zest
- 2½ teaspoons bread machine yeast

Direction: PREP: 10 MINUTES /MAKES 1 LOAF

- ✓ *Preparing the Ingredients. Choose the size of loaf of your preference and then measure the ingredients.*
- ✓ *Add all of the ingredients mentioned previously in the list.*
- ✓ *Close the lid after placing the pan in the bread machine.*
- ✓ *Select the Bake Cycle Turn on the bread machine. Select the White/Basic setting, select the loaf size, and the crust color.*
- ✓ *Press start.*
- ✓ *When the breadmaker cycle is complete, carefully remove the pan from the machine and allow it to cool before serving.*
- ✓ *Remove the bread from the pan, put in a wire rack to Cool about 10 minutes.*
- ✓ *Slice*

447) **Cinnamon Bread**

Ingredients:

- 12 slices bread (1½ pounds)
- 1 cup milk, at 80°F to 90°F
- 1 egg, at room temperature
- ¼ cup melted butter, cooled
- ½ cup sugar
- ½ teaspoon salt
- 1½ teaspoons ground cinnamon
- 3 cups white bread flour
- 2 teaspoons bread machine or active dry yeast

Direction: PREP: 10 MINUTES /MAKES 1 LOAF

- ✓ *Preparing the Ingredients. Choose the size of loaf of your preference and then measure the ingredients.*
- ✓ *Add all of the ingredients mentioned previously in the list.*
- ✓ *Close the lid after placing the pan in the bread machine.*
- ✓ *Select the Bake Cycle Turn on the bread machine. Select the White/Basic setting, select the loaf size, and the crust color.*
- ✓ *Press start.*
- ✓ *When the breadmaker cycle is complete, carefully remove the pan from the machine and allow it to cool before serving.*
- ✓ *Remove the bread from the pan, put in a wire rack to Cool about 10 minutes.*
- ✓ *Slice*

448) **Basic Pecan Bread**

Ingredients:

- 16 slices bread (2 pounds)
- 1⅓ cups lukewarm milk
- 2⅔ tablespoons unsalted butter, melted

- 1 egg, at room temperature
- 2⅔ tablespoons sugar1⅓ teaspoons table salt
- 4 cups white bread flour
- 2 teaspoons bread machine yeast
- 1⅓ cups chopped pecans, toasted
Direction: PREP: 10 MINUTES /MAKES 1 LOAF

✓ Preparing the Ingredients. Choose the size of loaf of your preference and then measure the ingredients.

✓ Add all of the ingredients mentioned previously in the list, except the toasted pecans.

✓ Close the lid after placing the pan in the bread machine.

✓ Select the Bake Cycle.

✓ After selecting the White/Basic (if applicable) or Fruit/Nut (if applicable) setting, select the loaf size, and the crust color.

✓ Press start.

✓ When the machine indicates that ingredients should be added, add the toasted pecans.

✓ When the breadmaker cycle is complete, carefully remove the pan from the machine and allow it to cool before serving.

✓ Remove the bread from the pan, put in a wire rack to Cool about 10 minutes.

✓ Slice

449) **Apple Walnut Bread**
Ingredients:

- ¾ cup unsweetened applesauce
- 4 cups apple juice
- 1 tsp salt
- 3 tbsp. butter
- 1 large egg
- 4 cups bread flour
- ¼ cup brown sugar, packed
- 1¼ tsp cinnamon
- ½ tsp baking soda
- 2 tsp active dry yeast
- ½ cup chopped walnuts
- ½ cup chopped dried cranberries
Direction: PREP: 10 MINUTES PLUS FERMENTING TIME /MAKES 1 LOAF

✓ Preparing the Ingredients In the order and at the temperature specified by the maker of your bread machine, add each ingredient to the bread machine..

✓ Select the Bake Cycle Close the lid, select the basic bread, medium crust setting on your bread machine, and press start.

✓ As soon as the bread is done baking, remove and cool on a cooling rack.

450) **Simple Garlic Bread**
Ingredients:

- 12 slices bread (1½ pounds)
- 1 cup milk, at 70°F to 80°F

- 1½ tablespoons melted butter, cooled
- 1 tablespoon sugar
- 1½ teaspoons salt 2 teaspoons garlic powder
- 2 teaspoons chopped fresh parsley
- 3 cups white bread flour
- 1¾ teaspoons bread machine or instant yeast
Direction: PREP: 10 MINUTES /MAKES 1 LOAF

✓ Preparing the Ingredients. Choose the size of loaf of your preference and then measure the ingredients.

✓ Add all of the ingredients mentioned previously in the list.

✓ Close the lid after placing the pan in the bread machine.

✓ Select the Bake Cycle Turn on the bread machine. Select the White/Basic setting, select the loaf size, and the crust color.

✓ Press start. When the breadmaker cycle is complete, carefully remove the pan from the machine and allow it to cool before serving.

✓ Remove the bread from the pan, put in a wire rack to Cool about 10 minutes.

✓ Slice

451) **Herbed Pesto Bread**
Ingredients:

- 12 slices bread (1½ pounds)
- 1 cup water, at 80°F to 90°F
- 2¼ tablespoons melted butter, cooled
- 1½ teaspoons minced garlic
- ¾ tablespoon sugar
- 1 teaspoon salt
- 3 tablespoons chopped fresh parsley
- 1½ tablespoons chopped fresh basil
- ⅓ cup grated Parmesan cheese
- 3 cups white bread flour
- 1¼ teaspoons bread machine or active dry yeast
Direction: PREP: 10 MINUTES /MAKES 1 LOAF

✓ Preparing the Ingredients. Choose the size of loaf of your preference and then measure the ingredients.

✓ Add all of the ingredients mentioned previously in the list.

✓ Close the lid after placing the pan in the bread machine.

✓ Select the Bake Cycle Turn on the bread machine. Select the White/Basic setting, select the loaf size, and the crust color.
Press start.

✓ When the breadmaker cycle is complete, carefully remove the pan from the machine and allow it to cool before serving.

✓ Remove the bread from the pan, put in a wire rack to Cool about 10 minutes.

✓ Slice

452) **Caraway Rye Bread**
Ingredients:

- 12 slice bread (1½ pounds)

- 1⅛ cups water, at 80°F to 90°F
- 1¾ tablespoons melted butter, cooled
- 3 tablespoons dark brown sugar
- 1½ tablespoons dark molasses
- 1⅛ teaspoons salt
- 1½ teaspoons caraway seed
- ¾ cup dark rye flour
- 2 cups white bread flour
- 1⅛ teaspoons bread machine or instant yeast

Direction: PREP: 10 MINUTES /MAKES 1 LOAF

- ✓ Preparing the Ingredients. Choose the size of loaf of your preference and then measure the ingredients.
- ✓ Add all of the ingredients mentioned previously in the list.
- ✓ Close the lid after placing the pan in the bread machine.
- ✓ Select the Bake Cycle Turn on the bread machine.
- ✓ Select the White/Basic setting, select the loaf size, and the crust color.
- ✓ Press start.
- ✓ When the breadmaker cycle is complete, carefully remove the pan from the machine and allow it to cool before serving.
- ✓ Remove the bread from the pan, put in a wire rack to Cool about 10 minutes.
- ✓ Slice

453) *Anise Lemon Bread*

Ingredients:

- 12 slice bread (1½ pounds)
- ¾ cup water, at 80°F to 90°F
- 1 egg, at room temperature
- ¼ cup butter, melted and cooled
- ¼ cup honey
- ½ teaspoon salt
- 1 teaspoon anise seed
- 1 teaspoon lemon zest
- 3 cups white bread flour
- 2 teaspoons bread machine or instant yeast

Direction: PREP: 10 MINUTES /MAKES 1 LOAF

- ✓ Preparing the Ingredients. Choose the size of loaf of your preference and then measure the ingredients.
- ✓ Add all of the ingredients mentioned previously in the list.
- ✓ Close the lid after placing the pan in the bread machine. Select the Bake Cycle Turn on the bread machine.
- ✓ Select the White/Basic setting, select the loaf size, and the crust color.
- ✓ Press start.
- ✓ When the breadmaker cycle is complete, carefully remove the pan from the machine and allow it to cool before serving.
- ✓ Remove the bread from the pan, put in a wire rack to Cool about 10 minutes.
- ✓ Slice

454) *Fragrant Cardamom Bread*

Ingredients:

- 12 slices bread (1½ pounds)
- ¾ cup milk, at 80°F to 90°F
- 1 egg, at room temperature
- 1½ teaspoons melted butter, cooled
- 3 tablespoons honey
- 1 teaspoon salt
- 1 teaspoon ground cardamom
- 3 cups white bread flour
- 1¼ teaspoons bread machine or instant yeast

Direction: PREP: 10 MINUTES /MAKES 1 LOAF

- ✓ Preparing the Ingredients. Choose the size of loaf of your preference and then measure the ingredients.
- ✓ Add all of the ingredients mentioned previously in the list.
- ✓ Close the lid after placing the pan in the bread machine.
- ✓ Select the Bake Cycle Turn on the bread machine.
- ✓ Select the White/Basic setting, select the loaf size, and the crust color.
- ✓ Press start.
- ✓ When the breadmaker cycle is complete, carefully remove the pan from the machine and allow it to cool before serving.
- ✓ Remove the bread from the pan, put in a wire rack to Cool about 10 minutes.
- ✓ Slice

455) *Chocolate Mint Bread*

Ingredients:

- 12 slices bread (1½ pounds)
- 1 cup milk, at 80°F to 90°F
- ⅛ teaspoon mint extract
- 1½ tablespoons butter, melted and cooled
- ¼ cup sugar
- 1 teaspoon salt
- 1½ tablespoons unsweetened cocoa powder
- 3 cups white bread flour
- 1¾ teaspoons bread machine or instant yeast
- ½ cup semisweet chocolate chips

Direction: PREP: 10 MINUTES /MAKES 1 LOAF

- ✓ Preparing the Ingredients. Choose the size of loaf of your preference and then measure the ingredients.
- ✓ Add all of the ingredients mentioned previously in the list.
- ✓ Close the lid after placing the pan in the bread machine.
- ✓ Select the Bake Cycle Turn on the bread machine.
- ✓ Select the White/Basic setting, select the loaf size, and the crust color.
  Press start.
- ✓ When the breadmaker cycle is complete, carefully remove the pan from the machine and allow it to cool before serving.

- ✓ Remove the bread from the pan, put in a wire rack to Cool about 5 minutes.
- ✓ Slice

456) **Molasses Candied-Ginger Bread**

Ingredients:

- 12 slices bread (1½ pounds)
- 1 cup milk, at 80°F to 90°F
- 1 egg, at room temperature
- ¼ cup dark molasses
- 3 tablespoons butter, melted and cooled
- ½ teaspoon salt
- ¼ cup chopped candied ginger
- ½ cup quick oats
- 3 cups white bread flour
- 2 teaspoons bread machine or instant yeast

Direction: PREP: 10 MINUTES /MAKES 1 LOAF

- ✓ Preparing the Ingredients. Choose the size of loaf of your preference and then measure the ingredients.
- ✓ Add all of the ingredients mentioned previously in the list.
- ✓ Close the lid after placing the pan in the bread machine.
- ✓ Select the Bake Cycle Turn on the bread machine.
- ✓ Select the White/Basic setting, select the loaf size, and the crust color.
- ✓ Press start.
- ✓ When the breadmaker cycle is complete, carefully remove the pan from the machine and allow it to cool before serving.
- ✓ Remove the bread from the pan, put in a wire rack to Cool about 5 minutes.
- ✓ Slice

457) **Whole-Wheat Seed Bread**

Ingredients:

- 12 slice bread (1½ pounds)
- 1⅛ cups water, at 80°F to 90°F
- 1½ tablespoons honey
- 1½ tablespoons melted butter, cooled
- ¾ teaspoon salt
- 2½ cups whole-wheat flour
- ¾ cup white bread flour
- 3 tablespoons raw sunflower seeds
- 1 tablespoon sesame seeds
- 1½ teaspoons bread machine or instant yeast

Direction: PREP: 10 MINUTES /MAKES 1 LOAF

- ✓ Preparing the Ingredients. Choose the size of loaf of your preference and then measure the ingredients.
- ✓ Add all of the ingredients mentioned previously in the list.
- ✓ Close the lid after placing the pan in the bread machine. Select the Bake Cycle Turn on the bread machine.
- ✓ Select the Whole-Wheat/Whole-Grain bread, select

the loaf size, and select light or medium crust. Press start.

- ✓ When the breadmaker cycle is complete, carefully remove the pan from the machine and allow it to cool before serving. Remove the bread from the pan, put in a wire rack to Cool about 5 minutes.
- ✓ Slice

458) **Pecan Raisin Bread**

Ingredients:

- 1 cup plus 2 tbsp. water (70°F to 80°F)
- 8 tsp butter
- 1 egg
- 6 tbsp. sugar
- ¼ cup nonfat dry milk powder
- 1 tsp salt
- 4 cups bread flour
- 1 tbsp. active dry yeast
- 1 cup finely chopped pecans
- 1 cup raisins

Direction: PREP: 10 MINUTES /MAKES 1 LOAF

- ✓ Preparing the Ingredients Add each ingredient to the bread machine except the pecans and raisins in the order and at the temperature recommended by your bread machine manufacturer.
- ✓ Select the Bake Cycle Close the lid, select the basic bread, medium crust setting on your bread machine, and press start.
- ✓ Just before the final kneading, add the pecans and raisins.
- ✓ Take out the baked bread from the bread machine and allow it to cool on a cooling rack.

459) **Toasted Pecan Bread**

Ingredients:

- 12 slice bread (1½ pounds)
- 1 cup milk, at 70°F to 80°F
- 2 tablespoons melted butter, cooled
- 1 egg, at room temperature
- 2 tablespoons sugar
- 1 teaspoon salt
- 3 cups white bread flour
- 1½ teaspoons bread machine or instant yeast
- 1 cup chopped pecans, toasted

Direction: PREP: 10 MINUTES /MAKES 1 LOAF

- ✓ Preparing the Ingredients. Add each ingredient to the bread machine except the pecans and raisins in the order and at the temperature recommended by your bread machine manufacturer.
- ✓ Make sure you select the baking cycle you want.
- ✓ Select a light or medium crust for your bread, then click the Start button on your bread maker.
- ✓ When the machine signals, add the pecans, or put them in a nut/raisin hopper and the machine will add them automatically When the breadmaker cycle is complete, carefully remove the pan from the

machine and allow it to cool before serving.

- ✓ Remove the bread from the pan, put in a wire rack to Cool about 5 minutes.
- ✓ Slice

460) **_Market Seed Bread_**

Ingredients:

- 12 slice bread (1½ pounds)
- 1 cup plus 2 tablespoons milk, at 80°F to 90°F
- 1½ tablespoons melted butter, cooled
- 1½ tablespoons honey
- ¾ teaspoon salt
- 3 tablespoons flaxseed
- 3 tablespoons sesame seeds
- 1½ tablespoons poppy seeds
- 1¼ cups whole-wheat flour
- 1¾ cups white bread flour
- 1¾ teaspoons bread machine or instant yeast

Direction: PREP: 10 MINUTES /MAKES 1 LOAF

- ✓ Preparing the Ingredients. Choose the size of loaf of your preference and then measure the ingredients.
- ✓ Add all of the ingredients mentioned previously in the list.
- ✓ Close the lid after placing the pan in the bread machine.
- ✓ Select the Bake Cycle Turn on the bread machine.
- ✓ Select the White/Basic setting, select the loaf size, and the crust color.
- ✓ Press start.
- ✓ When the breadmaker cycle is complete, carefully remove the pan from the machine and allow it to cool before serving.
- ✓ Remove the bread from the pan, put in a wire rack to Cool about 5 minutes.
- ✓ Slice

461) **_Pesto Nut Bread_**

Ingredients:

- 1 cup plus 2 tbsp. water
- 3 cups Gold Medal Better for Bread flour
- 2 tbsp. sugar
- 1 tsp salt
- 1¼ tsp bread machine or quick active dry yeast

For the pesto filling:

- ⅓ cup basil pesto
- 2 tbsp. Gold Medal Better for Bread flour
- ⅓ cup pine nuts

Direction: PREP: 10 MINUTES /MAKES 14 SLICES

- ✓ Preparing the Ingredients In the order and at the temperature specified by the maker of your bread machine, add each ingredient to the bread machine.
- ✓ Select the Bake Cycle Close the lid, select the basic bread, medium crust setting on your bread machine, and press start.
- ✓ In a small bowl, combine pesto and 2 tbsp. of flour

until well blended.

- ✓ Stir in the pine nuts.
- ✓ Add the filling 5 minutes before the last kneading cycle ends.
- ✓ Take out the baked bread from the bread machine and allow it to cool on a cooling rack.

462) **_Double Coconut Bread_**

Ingredients:

- 12 slice bread (1½ pounds)
- 1 cup milk, at 80°F to 90°F
- 1 egg, at room temperature
- 1½ tablespoons melted butter, cooled
- 2 teaspoons pure coconut extract
- 2½ tablespoons sugar
- ¾ teaspoon salt
- ½ cup sweetened shredded coconut
- 3 cups white bread flour
- 1½ teaspoons bread machine or instant yeast

Direction: PREP: 10 MINUTES /MAKES 1 LOAF

- ✓ Preparing the Ingredients. Choose the size of loaf of your preference and then measure the ingredients.
- ✓ Add all of the ingredients mentioned previously in the list.
- ✓ Close the lid after placing the pan in the bread machine.
- ✓ Select the Bake Cycle Program the machine for Sweet bread, select light or medium crust, and press Start.
- ✓ When the breadmaker cycle is complete, carefully remove the pan from the machine and allow it to cool before serving.
- ✓ Remove the bread from the pan, put in a wire rack to Cool about 5 minutes.
- ✓ Slice

463) **_Seed Bread_**

Ingredients:

- 3 tbsp. flax seed
- 1 tbsp. sesame seeds
- 1 tbsp. poppy seeds
- ¾ cup water
- 1 tbsp. honey
- 1 tbsp. canola oil
- ½ tsp salt
- 1½ cups bread flour
- 5 tbsp. whole meal flour
- 1¼ tsp dried active baking yeast

Direction: PREP: 10 MINUTES /MAKES 1 LOAF

- ✓ Preparing the Ingredients In the order and at the temperature specified by the maker of your bread machine, add each ingredient to the bread machine.
- ✓ Select the Bake Cycle Close the lid, select the basic bread, medium crust setting on your bread machine, and press start.
- ✓ Take out the baked bread from the bread machine

and allow it to cool on a cooling rack.

464) __Honeyed Bulgur Bread__

Ingredients:

- 12 slice bread (1½ pounds)
- ¾ cup boiling water
- 3 tablespoons bulgur wheat
- 3 tablespoons quick oats
- 2 eggs, at room temperature
- 1½ tablespoons melted butter, cooled
- 2¼ tablespoons honey
- 1 teaspoon salt
- 2¼ cups white bread flour
- 1½ teaspoons bread machine or instant yeast

Direction: PREP: 10 MINUTES /MAKES 1 LOAF
Direction:

- ✓ Preparing the Ingredients. Place the water, bulgur, and oats in the bucket of your bread machine for 30 minutes or until the liquid is 80°F to 90°F.
- ✓ Place the remaining ingredients in your bread machine as recommended by the manufacturer.
- ✓ Select the Bake Cycle Turn on the bread machine.
- ✓ Select the White/Basic setting, select the loaf size, and the crust color.
- ✓ Press start.
- ✓ When the breadmaker cycle is complete, carefully remove the pan from the machine and allow it to cool before serving. Remove the bread from the pan, put in a wire rack to Cool about 5 minutes.
- ✓ Slice

465) __Chia Seed Bread__

Ingredients:

- ¼ cup chia seeds
- ¾ cup hot water
- 2⅜ cups water
- ¼ cup oil
- ½ lemon, zest and juice
- 1¾ cups white flour
- 1¾ cups whole wheat flour
- 2 tsp baking powder
- 1 tsp salt
- 1 tbsp. sugar
- 2½ tsp quick rise yeast

Direction: PREP: 10 MINUTES /MAKES 14 SLICES

- ✓ Preparing the Ingredients Add the chia seeds to a bowl, cover with hot water, mix well and let them stand until they are soaked and gelatinous, and don't feel warm to touch.
- ✓ In the order and at the temperature specified by the maker of your bread machine, add each ingredient to the bread machine.
- ✓ Select the Bake Cycle Close the lid, select the basic bread, medium crust setting on your bread machine, and press start.

- ✓ When the mixing blade stops moving, open the machine and mix everything by hand with a spatula.
- ✓ Take out the baked bread from the bread machine and allow it to cool on a cooling rack.

466) __Flaxseed Honey Bread__

Ingredients:

- 12 slices bread (1½ pounds)
- 1⅛ cups milk, at 80°F to 90°F
- 1½ tablespoons melted butter, cooled
- 1½ tablespoons honey
- 1 teaspoon salt
- ¼ cup flaxseed
- 3 cups white bread flour
- 1¼ teaspoons bread machine or instant yeast

Direction: PREP: 10 MINUTES /MAKES 1 LOAF

- ✓ Preparing the Ingredients. Choose the size of loaf of your preference and then measure the ingredients.
- ✓ Add all of the ingredients mentioned previously in the list. Close the lid after placing the pan in the bread machine.
- ✓ Select the Bake cycle.
- ✓ Turn on the bread machine.
- ✓ Press start.
- ✓ When the breadmaker cycle is complete, carefully remove the pan from the machine and allow it to cool before serving.
- ✓ Remove the bread from the pan, put in a wire rack to Cool about 5 minutes.
- ✓ Slice

467) __Chia Sesame Bread__

Ingredients:

- 12 slice bread (1½ pounds)
- 1 cup plus 2 tablespoons water, at 80°F to 90°F
- 1½ tablespoons melted butter, cooled
- 1½ tablespoons sugar
- 1⅛ teaspoons salt
- ½ cup ground chia seeds
- 1½ tablespoons sesame seeds
- 2½ cups white bread flour
- 1½ teaspoons bread machine or instant yeast

Direction: PREP: 10 MINUTES /MAKES 1 LOAF
Direction:

- ✓ Preparing the Ingredients. Choose the size of loaf of your preference and then measure the ingredients.
- ✓ Add all of the ingredients mentioned previously in the list.
- ✓ Close the lid after placing the pan in the bread machine.
- ✓ Select the Bake Cycle Turn on the bread machine.
- ✓ Select the White/Basic setting, select the loaf size, and the crust color.
- ✓ Press start.
- ✓ When the breadmaker cycle is complete, carefully remove the pan from the machine and allow it to cool

before serving.

- ✓ *Remove the bread from the pan, put in a wire rack to Cool about 5 minutes.*
- ✓ *Slice*

468) **Sesame French Bread**

Ingredients:

- ⅞ cup water
- 1 Tbsp butter, softened
- 3 cups bread flour
- 2 tsp sugar
- 1 tsp salt
- 2 tsp yeast
- 2 tbsp. sesame seeds toasted

Direction: PREP: 10 MINUTES /MAKES 1 LOAF
Direction:

- ✓ *Preparing the Ingredients In the order and at the temperature specified by the maker of your bread machine, add each ingredient to the bread machine.*
- ✓ *Select the Bake Cycle Close the lid, select the French bread, medium crust setting on your bread machine and press start.*
- ✓ *Take out the baked bread from the bread machine and allow it to cool on a cooling rack.*

469) **Quinoa Whole-Wheat Bread**

Ingredients:

- 12 slice bread (1½ pounds)
- 1 cup milk, at 80°F to 90°F
- ⅔ cup cooked quinoa, cooled
- ¼ cup melted butter, cooled
- 1 tablespoon sugar
- 1 teaspoon salt
- ¼ cup quick oats
- ¾ cup whole-wheat flour
- 1½ cups white bread flour
- 1½ teaspoons bread machine or instant yeast.

Direction: PREP: 10 MINUTES /MAKES 1 LOAF

- ✓ *Preparing the Ingredients. Choose the size of loaf of your preference and then measure the ingredients.*
- ✓ *Add all of the ingredients mentioned previously in the list.*
- ✓ *Close the lid after placing the pan in the bread machine.*
- ✓ *Select the Bake Cycle Turn on the bread machine. Select the White/Basic setting, select the loaf size, and the crust color.*
- ✓ *Press start. When the breadmaker cycle is complete, carefully remove the pan from the machine and allow it to cool before serving.*
- ✓ *Remove the bread from the pan, put in a wire rack to Cool about 5 minutes.*
- ✓ *Slice*

470) **Toasted Hazelnut Bread**

Ingredients:

- 12 slice bread (1½ pounds)
- 1 cup milk, at 70°F to 80°F
- 1 egg, at room temperature
- 3¾ tablespoons melted butter, cooled
- 3 tablespoons honey
- ¾ teaspoon pure vanilla extract
- ¾ teaspoon salt
- ¾ cup finely ground toasted hazelnuts
- 3 cups white bread flour
- 1½ teaspoons bread machine or instant yeast

Direction: PREP: 10 MINUTES /MAKES 1 LOAF

- ✓ *Preparing the Ingredients. Choose the size of loaf of your preference and then measure the ingredients.*
- ✓ *Add all of the ingredients mentioned previously in the list.*
- ✓ *Close the lid after placing the pan in the bread machine.*
- ✓ *Select the Bake Cycle Turn on the bread machine.*
- ✓ *Select the White/Basic setting, select the loaf size, and the crust color.*
- ✓ *Press start.*
- ✓ *When the breadmaker cycle is complete, carefully remove the pan from the machine and allow it to cool before serving.*
- ✓ *Remove the bread from the pan, put in a wire rack to Cool about 5 minutes.*
- ✓ *Slice*

471) **Oatmeal Seed Bread**

Ingredients:

- 12 slice bread (1½ pounds)
- 1⅛ cups water, at 80°F to 90°F
- 3 tablespoons melted butter, cooled
- 3 tablespoons light brown sugar
- 1½ teaspoons salt
- 3 tablespoons raw sunflower seeds
- 3 tablespoons pumpkin seeds
- 2 tablespoons sesame seeds
- 1 teaspoon anise seeds
- 1 cup quick oats
- 2¼ cups white bread flour
- 1½ teaspoons bread machine or instant yeast

Direction: PREP: 10 MINUTES /MAKES 1 LOAF
Direction:

- ✓ *Preparing the Ingredients. Choose the size of loaf of your preference and then measure the ingredients.*
- ✓ *Add all of the ingredients mentioned previously in the list.*
- ✓ *Close the lid after placing the pan in the bread machine.*
- ✓ *Select the Bake Cycle Turn on the bread machine.*
- ✓ *Select the White/Basic setting, select the loaf size, and the crust color.*
- ✓ *Press start.*
- ✓ *When the breadmaker cycle is complete, carefully remove the pan from the machine and allow it to cool before serving. Remove the bread from the pan, put*

in a wire rack to Cool about 5 minutes.

✓ Slice

472) **Nutty Wheat Bread**

Ingredients:

- 12 slice bread (1½ pounds)
- 1½ cups water, at 80°F to 90°F
- 2 tablespoons melted butter, cooled
- 1 tablespoon sugar
- 1½ teaspoons salt
- 1¼ cups whole-wheat flour
- 2 cups white bread flour
- 1¼ teaspoons bread machine or instant yeast
- 2 tablespoons chopped almonds
- 2 tablespoons chopped pecans
- 2 tablespoons sunflower seeds

Direction: PREP: 10 MINUTES /MAKES 1 LO

✓ Preparing the Ingredients. Place the ingredients, except the almonds, pecans, and seeds, in your bread machine as recommended by the manufacturer.

✓ Select the Bake Cycle Turn on the bread machine.

✓ Select the White/Basic setting, select the loaf size, and the crust color.

✓ Press start.

✓ When the breadmaker cycle is complete, carefully remove the pan from the machine and allow it to cool before serving.

✓ Remove the bread from the pan, put in a wire rack to Cool about 5 minutes.

✓ Slice

473) **Sunflower Bread**

Ingredients:

- 12 slice bread (1½ pounds)
- 1 cup water, at 80°F to 90°F
- 1 egg, at room temperature
- 3 tablespoons melted butter, cooled
- 3 tablespoons skim milk powder
- 1½ tablespoons honey
- 1½ teaspoons salt
- ¾ cup raw sunflower seeds
- 3 cups white bread flour
- 1 teaspoon bread machine or instant yeast

Direction: PREP: 10 MINUTES /MAKES 1 LOAF

✓ Preparing the Ingredients. Choose the size of loaf of your preference and then measure the ingredients.

✓ Add all of the ingredients mentioned previously in the list.

✓ Close the lid after placing the pan in the bread machine.

✓ Select the Bake Cycle Turn on the bread machine. Select the White/Basic setting, select the loaf size, and the crust color.

✓ Press start. When the breadmaker cycle is complete, carefully remove the pan from the machine and

allow it to cool before serving.

✓ Remove the bread from the pan, put in a wire rack to Cool about 5 minutes.

✓ Slice

474) **Raisin Seed Bread**

Ingredients:

- 12 slice bread (1½ pounds)
- 1 cup plus 2 tablespoons milk, at 80°F to 90°F
- 1½ tablespoons melted butter, cooled
- 1½ tablespoons honey
- ¾ teaspoon salt
- 3 tablespoons flaxseed
- 3 tablespoons sesame seeds
- 1¼ cups whole-wheat flour
- 1¾ cups white bread flour
- 1¾ teaspoons bread machine or instant yeast
- ⅓ cup raisins

Direction: PREP: 10 MINUTES /MAKES 1 LOAF

✓ Preparing the Ingredients. Choose the size of loaf of your preference and then measure the ingredients.

✓ Add all of the ingredients mentioned previously in the list except the raisins.

✓ Close the lid after placing the pan in the bread machine.

✓ Choose the Bake Cycle Set the machine to Basic/White bread, choose between light or medium crust, then push Start.

✓ Add the raisins when the bread machine signals, or place the raisins in the raisin/nut hopper and let the machine add them.

✓ When the breadmaker cycle is complete, carefully remove the pan from the machine and allow it to cool before serving.

✓ Remove the bread from the pan, put in a wire rack to Cool about 5 minutes.

✓ Slice

475) **Rosemary Bread**

Ingredients:

- 1⅓ cups milk
- 4 tbsp. butter
- 3 cups bread flour
- 1 cup one-minute oatmeal
- 1 tsp salt
- 6 tsp white granulated sugar
- 1 tbsp. onion powder
- 1 tbsp. dried rosemary
- 1½ tsp bread machine yeast

Direction: PREP: 10 MINUTES /MAKES 14 SLICES

✓ Preparing the Ingredients in the order and at the temperature specified by the maker of your bread machine, add each ingredient to the bread machine.

✓ Select the Bake Cycle Close the lid, select the basic bread, medium crust setting on your bread machine and press start.

- ✓ After the bread machine has finished kneading, sprinkle some rosemary on top of the bread dough.
- ✓ Take out the baked bread from the bread machine and allow it to cool on a cooling rack.

476) Cajun Bread

Ingredients:

- ½ cup water
- ¼ cup chopped onion
- ¼ cup chopped green bell pepper
- 2 tsp finely chopped garlic
- 2 tsp soft butter
- 2 cups bread flour
- 1 tbsp. sugar
- 1 tsp Cajun
- ½ tsp salt
- 1 tsp active dry yeast

Direction: PREP: 10 MINUTES /MAKES 14 SLICES

- ✓ Preparing the Ingredients In the order and at the temperature specified by the maker of your bread machine, add each ingredient to the bread machine.
- ✓ Select the Bake Cycle Close the lid, select the basic bread, medium crust setting on your bread machine and press start.
- ✓ Take out the baked bread from the bread machine and allow it to cool on a cooling rack.

477) Turmeric Bread

Ingredients:

- 1 tsp dried yeast
- 4 cups strong white flour
- 1 tsp turmeric powder
- 2 tsp beetroot powder
- 2 tbsp. olive oil
- 1.5 tsp salt
- 1 tsp chili flakes
- 1⅜ water

Direction: PREP: 10 MINUTES /MAKES 14 SLICES

- ✓ Preparing the Ingredients In the order and at the temperature specified by the maker of your bread machine, add each ingredient to the bread machine.
- ✓ Select the Bake Cycle Close the lid, select the basic bread, medium crust setting on your bread machine and press start.
- ✓ Take out the baked bread from the bread machine and allow it to cool on a cooling rack.

478) Pumpkin Coconut Almond Bread

Ingredients:

- 1/3 cup vegetable oil
- 3 large eggs
- 1 1/2 cups canned pumpkin puree
- 1 cup sugar
- 1 1/2 teaspoons baking powder

- 1/2 teaspoon baking soda
- 1/4 teaspoon salt
- 1 tablespoon allspice
- 3 cups all-purpose flour
- 1/2 cup coconut flakes, plus a small handful for the topping
- 2/3 cup slivered almonds, plus a tablespoonful for the topping
- Non-stick cooking spray

Direction: PREP: 5 MINUTES /MAKES 12 SLICES

- ✓ Getting the Ingredients Ready Using nonstick cooking spray, coat the bread maker pan.
- ✓ In a large mixing basin, combine the oil, eggs, and pumpkin.
- ✓ In a separate mixing dish, combine the remaining ingredients.
- ✓ Pour the wet ingredients into the bread maker pan, then sprinkle the dry ingredients on top.
- ✓ Choose the Bake option. Choose the Dough cycle and push the Start button.
- ✓ Open lid and sprinkle saved coconut and almonds on top of bread.
- ✓ Set the timer for 1 hour 30 minutes on Rapid and bake.
- ✓ Before serving, cool for 10 minutes on a wire rack.

479) No Salt Added White Bread

Ingredients: 1 POUND LOAF

- Lukewarm water   ½ cup
- Sugar ¾ tsp
- Instant dry yeast   ¾ tsp
- White all-purpose flour   2 ⅛ cups
- Extra-virgin olive oil ½ tbsp
- Egg white   ½

Direction: Direction: 3 hours and 10 minutes / Prep Time: 10 minutes / Cook Time: 3 hours

- ✓ In a mixing bowl, combine the sugar and water.
- ✓ Stir until the sugar has dissolved then add in the yeast.
- ✓ Add the flour, water mixture, and oil into the bread maker.
- ✓ Select the French loaf setting and medium crust function.
- ✓ Five minutes into the cycle, add in the egg white and allow the bread cycle to continue.
  When ready, turn the bread out onto a drying rack and allow it to cool, then serve.
- ✓ Tip(s): The extra-virgin olive oil can be replaced with vegetable oils such as sunflower or canola.

480) Quinoa Bread

Ingredients: 1 POUND LOAF

- Eggs 1, large
- Olive oil   1 ½ tsp
- Whole wheat flour   1 ½ cups
- Salt ¼ pinch

- *Pumpkin seeds 3 tsp*
- *Sunflower seeds 3 tsp*
- *Flax seeds 3 tsp*
- *Quinoa, cooked   ½ cup*
- *Lukewarm water   ½ cup*
- *Raw sugar 2 tbsp*
- *Active dry yeast   ¾ tsp*

Direction: Direction: 4 hours / Prep Time: 30 minutes / Cook Time: 3 hours and 30 minutes

✓ *Prepare your quinoa the way you'd cook standard rice: for every cup of quinoa, add 2 cups of water into a pot.*

✓ *Bring it to boil, then put the pot lid on and leave to simmer for 15-25 minutes.*

✓ *Give the quinoa time to cool while you perform the rest of this recipe in a separate container, add the lukewarm water, sugar and yeast. Stir, then let it sit as you continue onto step 4.*

✓ *Begin adding the ingredients into your bread machine, either in the order listed, or according to your user manual.*

✓ *In case of conflict or uncertainty, the water/ sugar/ yeast mix should always go in last. Select the whole wheat bread setting.*

✓ *When the bread is finished, turn it out onto a drying rack to cool before serving.*

✓ *Tip(s): Although it's always good practice to check your dough 10 minutes into its cycle, for this recipe you should always check it to see if it needs a little more water.*

481) **Low-Carb Keto Bread**

Ingredients: 1 POUND LOAF

- *Oat fiber   ¼ cup*
- *Flaxseed meal   ⅓ cup*
- *Wheat gluten ½ tsp*
- *Salt ½ tsp*
- *Xylitol ⅛ cup*
- *Xanthan gum ¼ tsp*
- *Lukewarm water ½ cup*
- *Egg 1*
- *Honey ½ tsp*
- *Unsalted butter, softened 1 tbsp*
- *Active dry yeast ½ tbsp*

Direction: 3 hours and 15 minutes / Prep Time: 15 minutes / Cook Time: 3 hours

✓ *In a mixing bowl, combine the oat fiber, meal, gluten, salt, xylitol, and xanthan gum.*

✓ *Add the water, egg, honey, and butter into the bread machine, followed by the oat fiber mixture and yeast.*

✓ *Select the default setting and the soft crust option.*

✓ *When ready, flip the bread out onto a drying rack to cool slightly before serving.*

✓ *Tip(s): Add in a sprinkle of dried herbs when combining the dry ingredients to boost the taste of the bread.*

482) **Paleo and Dairy-Free Bread**

Ingredients: 1 POUND LOAF

- *loaf Flax meal ¼ cup*
- *Chia seeds 2 tbsp*
- *Coconut oil, melted ⅛ cup*
- *Egg 1 ½*
- *Almond milk ¼ cup*
- *Honey ½ tbsp*
- *Almond flour 1 cup*
- *Tapioca flour ⅔ cup*
- *Coconut flour ⅛ cup*
- *Salt ½ tsp*
- *Cream of tartar 1 tsp*
- *Bread machine yeast 1 tsp*

Direction: 3 hours and 20 minutes / Prep Time: 20 minutes / Cook Time: 3 hours

✓ *In a mixing bowl, combine one tablespoon of flax meal with the chia seeds.*

✓ *Stir in the water and set aside.*

✓ *In a separate mixing bowl, pour in the melted coconut oil, eggs, almond milk, and honey.*

✓ *Whisk together.*

✓ *Followed by whisking in the flax meal and chia seed mixture.*

✓ *Pour this into the bread machine.*

✓ *In a mixing bowl, combine the almond, tapioca, and coconut flour.*

✓ *Add the remainder of the flax meal and salt.*

✓ *Add in the cream of tartar and baking soda.*

✓ *Pour the dry ingredients over the wet and finish with the yeast.*

✓ *Select whole wheat as the flour type and the medium crust as the crust type.*

✓ *When ready, flip the bread out onto a drying rack to cool slightly before serving.*

483) **Raisin Bread**

Ingredients: 1 POUND LOAF

- *Lukewarm water ⅙ cup*
- *Unsalted butter, diced 1 ¼ tbsp*
- *Plain bread flour 2 cups*
- *Orange zest 1 pinch*
- *Ground cinnamon 1 ⅓ tsp*
- *Ground clove   1 pinch*
- *Ground nutmeg 1 pinch*
- *Salt 1 pinch*
- *Sugar 1 ¼ tbsp*
- *Active dry yeast 1 ½ tsp*
- *Raisins ½ cup*

Direction: 3 hours and 15 minutes / Prep Time: 15 minutes / Cook Time: 3 hours

✓ *Add the ingredients to the bread machine in the sequence stated above or as directed in the instruction manual for your bread maker.*

- ✓ *Add the raisins last. Select the nut or raisin setting, as well as the medium crust setting.*
- ✓ *Add the raisins when the machine indicates.*
- ✓ *When the bread is finished, flip it out onto a drying rack and allow it to cool slightly before serving.*
- ✓ *TIP(S): For extra taste, add mixed raisins instead of one variety. You can select the basic setting with a medium crust function, and add the raisins in after the first phase of kneading has finished if your machine doesn't give you an "add-in" warning*

484) *Orange Cake Loaf*
Ingredients: 1 POUND LOAF

- Orange juice, room temperature ½ cup
- Butter, softened 2 tbsp
- Large egg, slightly beaten 1 tbsp
- Sugar   ½ cup
- Dry milk powder 1 tbsp
- Corn starch   ½ cup
- All-purpose flour 1 ½ cups
- Baking powder 1 tbsp
- Ingredients for glaze topping
- Orange juice   1 tbsp
- Icing sugar 2 tbsp

Direction: 1 hour and 50 minutes / Prep Time: 5 minutes / Cook Time: 1 hour and 45 minutes

- ✓ *Place all ingredients in the bread machine, except the baking powder and glaze topping components, in the order listed or as directed by your bread machine's instruction manual.*
- ✓ *The cake cycle should be selected.*
- ✓ *After 6 minutes, remove the lid from the machine and scrape the flour from the sides of the bread pan using a spatula.*
- ✓ *As you do this, don't take anything out of the bread machine, including the pan.*
- ✓ *Allow the machine to continue without the lid closed.*
- ✓ *Add the baking powder, as well as any additional flour or orange juice, if necessary, after another 4 minutes (10 minutes after commencing).*
- ✓ *Turn your Loaf out onto a clean tray or cooking surface when it's done.*
- ✓ *Mix your glaze and pour it over the loaf while it's still warm, then set it aside to cool.*
- ✓ *TIP(S): The butter can be swapped out for margarine.*

485) *Fruity Harvest Bread*
Ingredients: 1 POUND LOAF

- Egg ½ cup
- Lukewarm water ½ cup
- Unsalted butter, softened 2 tbsp
- Plain bread flour 2 ½ cups
- Sugar ⅙ cup
- Salt   1 tsp

- Ground allspice   1 pinch
- Ground nutmeg   1 pinch
- Active dry yeast 1 ⅛ cup
- Pecan nuts, diced   ¼ cup
- Mixed dried fruit   ½ cup

Direction: 3 hours and 10 minutes / Prep Time: 10 minutes / Cook Time: 3 hours

- ✓ *Add the ingredients to the bread machine in the sequence stated above or as directed in the instruction manual for your bread maker.*
- ✓ *Add the nuts and fruit last. Select the nut or raisin setting, as well as the medium crust setting.*
- ✓ *When the machine beeps, add the dry fruit and nuts mixture.*
- ✓ *When the bread is finished, flip it out onto a drying rack and allow it to cool slightly before serving.*
- ✓ *TIP(S): You can select the basic setting with a medium crust function, add the dried mixed fruit and nuts after the first phase of kneading has finished*

486) *Eggless Vanilla Loaf*
Ingredients: 1 POUND LOAF

- Lukewarm water   ½ cup
- Olive oil   ⅓ cup
- Vinegar 1 tsp
- Sweetened condensed milk   7 oz
- Vanilla extract   1 tsp
  Sugar 2 tbsp
- Salt 1 pinch
- All-purpose flour 1 ½ cups
- Baking soda ½ tsp
- Baking powder   ½ tsp

Direction: 1 hour and 20 minutes / Prep Time: 5 minutes / Cook Time: 1 hour and 25 minutes

- ✓ *Fill the bread machine with all of the ingredients, either in the order listed or according to the manufacturer's instructions, whichever is preferable.*
- ✓ *Activate the cake cycle.*
- ✓ *Scrape any flour residue on the sides of your machine into the mixture with a spatula about 6 minutes in.*
- ✓ *Poke the Loaf with a knife when the cake cycle is finished.*
- ✓ *Select the bake (typically denoted with a "b") cycle and let it run for 5 minutes if the knife has batter on it.*
- ✓ *Your bread is done when your knife comes out clean.*
- ✓ *After 15-20 minutes of cooling in the machine, tip your Loaf onto a drying rack to cool off further, then serve.*
- ✓ *TIP(S): The oil can be substituted for butter. Any glaze works well with vanilla cake.*

487) *Mardi Gras King Cake*
Ingredients: 1 POUND LOAF

- ¼ cup warm water
- 2 tbsp butter, softened

- 1 large egg, slightly beaten
- 1 cup sour cream
- 3 ½ tbsp white sugar
- ½ tsp salt
- 3 ½ cups all-purpose flour
- 2 ½ tsp active dry yeast Ingredients for spread
- ¼ cup and 1 tbsp white sugar
- 1 tsp cinnamon, ground
- 2 ½ tbsp butter, melted
- ½ cup pecan nuts, chopped Ingredients for glaze
- topping
- 2 cups icing sugar
- 1 ½ tbsp butter, melted
- 12 drops vanilla extract
- 2 tbsp milk
- 1 tbsp sugar, green-colored
- 1 tbsp sugar, sugar, yellow-colored
- 1 tbsp sugar, purple-colored

Direction: SERVING SIZE: 14 servings TIME: 3 hours and 25 minutes / Prep Time: 20 minutes / Cook Time: 3 hours and 5 minutes

- ✓ Place the first eight ingredients in the bread machine in the sequence mentioned or according to the manufacturer's instructions.
- ✓ Activate the dough cycle.
- ✓ Set aside the first three spread ingredients in a bowl.
- ✓ Using cooking spray, grease a baking pan.
- ✓ Remove the dough from the dough cycle, set it on a floured surface, and roll it out into a flat rectangular shape just smaller than 10x28 inches.
- ✓ Apply the spread on the flat dough surface, then evenly sprinkle the pecans on top.
- ✓ Pick up one of the dough's long sides and roll it into a log that's just under 28 inches long.
- ✓ Place the dough log, seam-side down, on a greased baking sheet and shape into a ring. Pinch the ring's ends together to form a ring.
- ✓ This may necessitate moistening the dough.
- ✓ Cover the ring with a cloth and set aside for 30 minutes to allow it to rise.
- ✓ Preheat your oven to 375 degrees Fahrenheit when your loaf has just approximately 15 minutes to rise. Remove the cloth once the cake has risen and bake the cake until the top is golden brown.
- ✓ Combine the first four glaze ingredients in a mixing bowl.
- ✓ To make a smooth, thick consistency, add or subtract milk.
- ✓ Remove the cake from the oven and lay it on a drying rack when it is done.
- ✓ Apply glaze and alternating bands of colored sugar on top of the glazed cake.
- ✓ Allow for complete cooling before serving.

488) **Apple Cake**

Ingredients: 1 POUND LOAF

- ⅔ cup water

- 3 tbsp unsalted butter, softened
- 2 cups plain bread flour
- 3 tbsp granulated sugar
- 1 tsp salt
- 1 ½ tsp active dry yeast
- 1 can apple pie filling

Direction: SERVING SIZE: 10 servings Time: 3 hours and 25 minutes / Prep Time: 25 minutes / Cook Time: 3 hours

- ✓ Add the ingredients to the bread machine in the order listed above, or follow the guidelines in the instruction manual that came with your bread machine.
- ✓ Add the pie filling last. Choose a dough setting.
- ✓ Remove the dough from the bowl and set it on a floured work surface.
- ✓ Cover for 15 minutes with a cotton cloth. The dough should be rolled out into a 13" x 8" rectangle.
- ✓ Place this on a prepared baking sheet.
- ✓ Using a longitudinal motion, fill the dough with the apple filling.
- ✓ Using a sharp knife, cut 1-inch intervals from the filling to the edge of the dough on each 13-inch side.
- ✓ Fold the dough ends up over the filling. Fold the strips over the filling in a diagonal pattern, overlapping in the center and alternating sides.
- ✓ Cover the dough with the towel again and set aside for 30 minutes, or until it has doubled in size.
- ✓ Preheat the oven to 375 degrees Fahrenheit and bake the cake for 40 minutes, or until it has turned a lovely golden color.
- ✓ When the apple cake is done, turn it out onto a cooling rack to cool.
- ✓ Dust with powdered sugar and serve when cool.
- ✓ TIP(S): I added a few cloves to change the flavor of the apple pie filling. This a very versatile recipe, allowing you to add different pie fillings when you feel like it. Instead of folding up the cake to form a pie, you can plait the bread too.

489) **Coffee Cake**

Ingredients: 1 POUND LOAF

- Yolk of one egg
- ¾ cup whole milk
- 1 tbsp unsalted butter, melted
- 2 ¼ cups plain bread flour
- ¼ cup sugar
- 1 tsp salt
- 2 tsp active dry yeast

Ingredients for glaze topping:

- ¼ cup pecan nuts
- ¼ cup walnuts
- 1 tsp ground cinnamon
- ½ cup sugar
- 2 tbsp unsalted butter, melted.

Direction: SERVING SIZE: 1 standard cake Time: 2 hours and 30 minutes / Prep Time: 1 hour / Cook Time: 1

✓ *Add the ingredients to the bread machine in the sequence stated above, or follow the directions on your bread machine's instruction booklet.*

✓ *Choose a dough setting. Grease an 8 × 8" baking pan and set aside.*

✓ *Transfer the cake dough into the oiled baking pan after the dough cycle is complete.*

✓ *Glaze the two tablespoons of melted butter over the top for the topping.*

✓ *Combine the nuts, sugar, and cinnamon in a small mixing dish and sprinkle over the cake dough.*

✓ *Allow the cake dough to rest in a warm room for 30 minutes after covering it with a cloth.*

✓ *Preheat the oven to 375 °F and bake the cake for 20 minutes, or until golden brown.*

✓ *When the bread is done, place it on a drying rack to cool before serving.*

✓ *TIP(S): For an extra kick of decadence combine 1 cup powdered sugar, ½ teaspoon vanilla essence, 1 teaspoon unsalted butter, melted, 2 tablespoons whole milk and 1 cup powdered sugar. Drizzle this over the cake when you remove it from the oven.*

Rolls, Pizza, And Party

490) Po Boy" Rolls from New Orleans

Ingredients:

- 1 cup water
- 1 tbsp granulated sugar
- 1 ½ tsp salt
- 1 tbsp extra-virgin olive oil
- 3 cups plain bread flour
- 1 tbsp instant dry yeast.

Direction: 50 minutes (excluding the rising time of 1 hour and 30 minutes) / Prep Time: 25 minutes / Cook Time: 25 minutes

- ✓ Add the ingredients to the bread machine in the sequence stated above, or follow the directions on your bread machine's instruction booklet.
- ✓ Choose a dough setting. When the dough is ready, divide it into six equal pieces on a floured surface.
- ✓ Then transfer them to a baking tray lined with parchment paper. Turn on the oven for 2 minutes before turning it off.
- ✓ Place the dough in the oven for one hour and 30 minutes, or until it has doubled in size, before removing it.
- ✓ Preheat the oven to 400 degrees Fahrenheit and place an oven-safe dish on the bottom shelf.
- ✓ Make slits in the dough with a sharp knife and spray with water.
- ✓ Place the dough in the oven when the temperature reaches 400 °F and bake for 20 minutes, or until the rolls are golden brown.
- ✓ When the bread is done, place it on a drying rack to cool before serving.
- ✓ TIP(S): If you plan to use the dough the following day, remove the dough the minute the machine has finished its kneading cycle. Place into an oiled bowl and cover tightly with cling wrap, storing in the refrigerator overnight.

491) 100% Whole Wheat Dinner Rolls

Ingredients: 8 ROLLS

- Warm milk   ½ cup
- Butter, melted ¼ cup
- Large egg, lightly beaten 2
- Sugar   2 tbsp
- Salt   ½ tsp
- Whole wheat flour   2 cups
- Instant yeast   1 ½ tsp

Direction: 2 hours and 20 minutes / Prep Time: 5 minutes / Cook Time: 2 hours and 15 minutes

- ✓ Place all ingredients into your bread machine, either in the order listed, or according to your manufacturer.
- ✓ Select the dough setting.
- ✓ When the dough cycle finishes, remove your dough from the bread pan.
- ✓ Split dough into 18/12/8 balls. Place the balls on a prepared baking sheet with 1 inch between them.
- ✓ Cover balls with a cloth and let rise for 45 minutes.

- ✓ Do not put them in the oven yet.
- ✓ When 15 minutes of rising remains, preheat the oven to 350 °F. When fully risen, remove the cloth and place the balls in the oven.
- ✓ Allow them to bake for about 20 minutes, or until they develop a light golden-brown color.
- ✓ Remove from the oven and set aside to cool before serving.
- ✓ TIP(S): Adding a light layer of flour to your ball-rolling surface can prevent residue sticking to countertops.

492) Classic Dinner Rolls Serving

Ingredients:

- 1 egg
- 1 cup water
- 3 ¼ cups plain bread flour
- ¼ cup sugar
- 1 tsp salt
- 3 tsp active dry yeast
- 2 tbsp unsalted butter, softened

Direction: 3 hours / Prep Time: 25 minutes / Cook Time: 2 hours and 35 minutes

- ✓ Add the ingredients to the bread machine in the sequence stated above, or follow the directions on your bread machine's instruction booklet.
- ✓ Do not include the softened butter. Choose a dough setting.
- ✓ Allow for 10 minutes of resting time after transferring the dough to a floured board.
- ✓ The dough should then be evenly divided into 15 balls.
- ✓ Place the dough balls 2" apart on a prepared baking tray. Allow for 30 minutes of resting time in a warm environment, or until the rolls have doubled in size.
- ✓ Preheat the oven to 375°F and bake the rolls for 15 minutes, or until a honeyed color has developed.
- ✓ Brush the softened butter over the tops of the buns before serving.
- ✓ TIP(S): Place the rolls closely together if you enjoy your rolls with softer sides. If you cover the dough rolls with cling wrap, they can keep for two days in the refrigerator

493) Vegan Dinner Rolls

Ingredients: 8 ROLLS

- Lukewarm water   2 ⅔ tbsp
- Almond milk, unsweetened ⅓ tsp
- Vegan butter, softened or melted   1 ⅓ tbsp
- Organic cane sugar   1 ⅓ tbsp
- Salt ⅓ tsp
- Unbleached all-purpose flour 1 ⅓ cups
- Instant yeast 1 ½ tsp

Direction: 2 hours and 20 minutes / Prep Time: 10 minutes / Cook Time: 2 hours and 10 minutes

- ✓ Fill your bread machine with all of the ingredients, either in the order provided or according to your *manufacturer's instructions.*

- ✓ *Choose a dough setting. Remove your dough from the pan when the cycle is finished.*
- ✓ *Using your hands, divide the dough into 18/12/8 balls.*
- ✓ *Place the balls on a prepared baking sheet with 1 inch between them.*
- ✓ *Allow 45 minutes for the balls to rise after being covered with a cloth.*
- ✓ *When the dough has risen for about 15 minutes, preheat the oven to 375 degrees F.*
- ✓ *Place the balls in the oven when the bread has fully risen and bake until they are a bright golden-brown color. It takes roughly 20 minutes to do this task.*
- ✓ *Remove the dish from the oven and set it aside to cool before serving.*
- ✓ *TIP(S): "Earth Balance" brand vegan butter can be purchased from Publix or Kroger. Up to ⅓ of the total flour can be substituted with whole wheat.*

494) **_Buttery Dinner Rolls_**

Ingredients: 8 ROLLS

- Milk, warm   ½ cup
- Butter, softened   ¼ cup
- White sugar   2 tbsp
- Eggs   1, large
- Salt   ⅓ tsp
- Whole wheat flour 1 ⅓ cups
- All-purpose flour   7 tbsp
- Instant yeast   1 tsp

Direction: TIME: 2 hours and 20 minutes / Prep Time: 10 minutes / Cook Time: 2 hours and 10 minutes

- ✓ *Fill your bread maker with all of the ingredients in the precise sequence provided.*
- ✓ *Activate the dough setting.*
- ✓ *Remove the dough from the pan after the cycle has finished.*
- ✓ *Separate the dough into 18/12/8 balls.*
- ✓ *Place them 1 inch apart on a prepared baking sheet.*
- ✓ *Allow 45 minutes for the balls to rise after covering them with a cloth.*
- ✓ *When the dough has risen for about 15 minutes, preheat the oven to 350 °F.*
- ✓ *Place the balls in the oven once the bread has fully risen and baked until they are a light golden-brown color.*
- ✓ *This will take approximately 20 minutes. Remove from the oven and set aside to cool completely before serving.*
- ✓ *TIP(S): 5 minutes into the dough cycle, check for dryness. For this recipe, it's best to err on the wet side, and risk adding too much extra milk rather than too little. Splitting dough into fewer, larger balls is possible, but will increase baking time.*

495) **_Cinnamon Rolls_**

Ingredients:

- INGREDIENTS FOR FILLING:

- 1 cup brown sugar
- ½ cup unsalted butter, softened
- 1 ½ tbsp ground cinnamon Ingredients for icing
- 4 tbsp whole milk
- ½ tsp vanilla essence
- 2 tbsp unsalted butter, melted
- 3 cups powdered sugar

INGREDIENTS FOR DOUGH:

- 1 ⅓ cups lukewarm water
- 1 tbsp unsalted butter, diced
- 5 tbsp sugar
- 1 egg
- 1 tsp salt
- 3 cups white all-purpose flour
- 1 ½ cups plain bread flour
- ¼ cup powdered milk
- 1 tbsp dry active yeast.

Direction: 3 hours and 18 minutes / Prep Time: 3 hours / Cook Time: 18 minutes

- ✓ *Add the dough ingredients to the bread machine in the sequence stated above, or follow the directions in your bread machine's instruction manual.*
- ✓ *Choose a dough setting.*
- ✓ *Place the dough on a floured board and divide it in half.*
- ✓ *Form a rectangle form out of one of the sections.*
- ✓ *Combine the filling ingredients and spread half of it evenly over the rolled-out dough piece.*
- ✓ *Cut the dough into 1" wide strips using a sharp knife.*
- ✓ *Then roll them up into pinwheels.*
- ✓ *Place the pinwheels on a baking tray that has been buttered.*
- ✓ *Repeat with the remaining dough and filling ingredients in the same manner as before.*
- ✓ *Allow the pinwheels to rise for 30 minutes after covering them with a cloth.*
- ✓ *Preheat oven to 375 degrees Fahrenheit and bake cinnamon rolls for 18 minutes.*
- ✓ *To make the icing, combine all of the ingredients and pour it over the heated cinnamon buns before serving.*
- ✓ *TIP(S): When the rolls are baking, you can test if they are ready by tapping your fingers in the middle. If the dough bounces back a little, then they are ready.*

496) **_Pizza Dough Recipe_**

Ingredients:

- 2 cups plain bread flour
- 1 tbsp unsalted butter, softened
- 1 tbsp sugar
- 1 tsp instant dry yeast
- 1 tsp salt
- ½ cup lukewarm water

Direction: 1 hour and 45 minutes / Prep Time: 15

- ✓ Add the ingredients to the bread machine in the sequence stated above, or follow the directions on your bread machine's instruction booklet.
- ✓ Select the dough option and press the start button.
- ✓ Check the dough ten minutes into the bread machine cycle to ensure that the ingredients have blended evenly and that it is not too moist or dry.
- ✓ Preheat the oven to 400 degrees Fahrenheit. When the dough is ready, knead it into a pizza or pan dish form on a floured surface.
- ✓ Bake for 20 to 25 minutes, depending on your desired toppings.
- ✓ TIP(S): For those like me who like a crust that is a tad crunchier, brush the pizza base with a bit of extra-virgin olive oil before placing it into the oven. Double the ingredients to create two standard size pizza bases.

497) Breadsticks

Ingredients: 1 POUND BATCH

- Lukewarm water ⅔ cup
- Butter, softened ½ tbsp
- Sugar ¾ tbsp
- Salt ¾ tsp
- Plain bread flour 2 cups
- Instant yeast 1 tsp

INGREDIENTS FOR DOUGH:

- Water ½ tbsp
- Egg whites 1, small

Direction: 2 hours and 15 minutes / Prep Time: 5 minutes / Cook Time: 2 hours and 10 minutes

- ✓ Add all non-glaze ingredients into your bread machine in the exact order given.
- ✓ Select the dough cycle.
- ✓ When the cycle completes, empty your dough onto a lightly floured countertop.
- ✓ Split dough into 16/12/8 balls.
- ✓ Stretch each ball into a 6-8-inch rope.
- ✓ Place on a baking sheet. No grease required.
- ✓ Preheat the oven to 400 F.
- ✓ Cover with a cloth and allow 20 minutes for the dough ropes to rise.
- ✓ Mix your glaze ingredients together, then brush your ropes after they've risen.
- ✓ After this, remove the cloth and place the balls in the oven to bake until they turn a light golden-brown color.
- ✓ This takes about 10-15 minutes.
- ✓ Remove from the oven, and allow to cool before serving.
- ✓ TIP(S): While glazing, feel free to add coarse salt or fine seeds to the top of your dough ropes for extra crunch and flavor once they're done.

498) Texas Roadhouse-Style Glazed Buns

Ingredients: 1 POUND BATCH

- Lukewarm water ¼ cup
- Lukewarm milk ½ cup
- Salt ½ tsp
- Butter, softened ¾ tbsp
- Egg 1, small
- Sugar 2 tbsp
- Plain bread flour 1 ¾ cup
- Active dry yeast 1 tsp

INGREDIENTS FOR GLAZE TOPPING:

- Salted butter, softened ¼ cup
- Icing sugar 2 ½ tbsp.
- Cinnamon, ground ½ tsp

Direction: TIME: 2 hours and 5 minutes / Prep Time: 5 minutes / Cook Time: 2 hours

- ✓ Place all non-glaze ingredients into the bread machine, either in the order listed, or according to your machine's manufacturer.
- ✓ Select the dough setting. Once finished, place the dough on a lightly floured countertop, and roll it into a rectangle that is half an inch thick.
- ✓ Fold dough in half, cover with a cloth, and let it rest for 15 minutes.
- ✓ Preheat oven to 350 °F.
- ✓ While the oven heats, cut your dough into squares. 18 squares for a 2-pound batch, 12 squares for a 1 ½ pound batch, and 8 squares for a 1-pound batch.
- ✓ On a baking tray, place your dough and put it in the oven until your buns start going golden-brown. This should take 10-15 minutes.
- ✓ While your buns are baking, mix your glaze in a small bowl.
- ✓ Start by beating your butter, then slowly add in the icing sugar, then top it off with cinnamon, mixing well.
- ✓ When your buns are ready, remove them from the oven, apply your glaze over the top of each bun with a spoon or knife while still hot. Can be served warm.
- ✓ TIP(S): You can further glaze your buns with honey for a sweeter flavor.

499) Cranberry and Cardamom Bread

Ingredients: 1 POUND BATCH

- Lukewarm water ½ cup
- Brown sugar 1 tbsp
- Salt ½ tsp
- Coconut oil, melted 1 tbsp
- Plain bread flour 2 cups
- Cinnamon 1 tsp
- Cardamom 1 tsp
- Cranberries, dried ½ cup
- Active dry yeast 1 tsp

Direction: 2 hours and 5 minutes / Prep Time: 5 minutes / Cook Time: 2 hours

- ✓ Place all of the ingredients in your bread machine in

the order stated, and select the sweet bread setting.

✓ When the bread is done, transfer it out onto a drying rack to cool before serving.

✓ TIP(S): Be sure to always check this loaf 10 minutes after the machine begins running. It is prone to needing additional water or flour.

500) *Chocolate Chip Brioche*

Ingredients: 1 POUND BATCH

- Lukewarm water 3 ½ tbsp
- Lukewarm milk 3 ½ tbsp
- Unsalted butter, softened 1 tbsp
- Egg 2, small
- Sugar 1 ⅓ tbsp
- All-purpose flour 1 ⅔ cups
- Salt ⅔ tsp
- Instant yeast ⅔ tsp
- Chocolate chips ⅔ cup

Direction: 2 hours and 45 minutes / Prep Time: 30 minutes / Cook Time: 2 hours and 15 minutes

✓ Place all ingredients, except the chocolate chips, into your bread machine in the order listed.

✓ Select the dough setting.

✓ Add the chocolate chips to the dough about 3 minutes before its final kneading cycle.

✓ When done, place dough on countertop and split into balls.

✓ A 2-pound loaf should have 18 balls, a 1 ½ pound loaf should have 12 balls, and a 1-pound loaf should have 8 balls.

✓ Be gentle when forming them. Cover with a deeply greased plastic wrap and let the balls rise in a warm room for 45 minutes.

✓ Preheat your oven to 400 F.

✓ Once your balls have finished rising, place them on an oven rack until golden brown. This will take about 15 minutes.

✓ Remove from oven and set aside to cool on a drying rack.

✓ Then, serve.

✓ TIP(S): The dough for this recipe will be stickier than most of the others in this book.This is alright. Only add flour if it seems too thin and batter-like. Brioche is best glazed. Apply whichever glaze you prefer between step 4 and 5 under the directions. Traditional brioche uses a glaze made up of beaten egg and pearl sugar. Be sure to give the balls room to breathe before placing them in the oven. Do not be alarmed if they touch as they heat up. This is normal, and means your brioche will form a lovely pull-apart bread when it is done.

501) *Beginner's bread*

Ingredients:

- 1 cup lukewarm water
- 1/3 cup lukewarm milk
- 3 tablespoons butter,
- unsalted 3 3/4 cups unbleached all-purpose flour
- 3 tablespoons sugar
- 1 1/2 teaspoons salt
- 1 1/2 teaspoons active dry yeast

Direction: SERVINGS: 12 | Prep Time: 5 minutes | Cook Time: 3 hours

✓ Into the bread pan, pour the liquid ingredients.

✓ Measure and pour the dry ingredients into the bread pan (excluding the yeast).

✓ In the center of the dry ingredients, make a well and add the yeast.

✓ Close the top and snap the baking pan into the bread maker. Select the Basic option and your favorite crust color before pressing the Start button.

✓ Remove the pan from the machine after the bread is done.

✓ After about 5 minutes, give the pan a gentle shake to free the loaf, then flip it out onto a cooling rack.

✓ Store bread, well-wrapped, on the counter up to 4 days, or freeze for up to 3 months.

502) *Crusty Sourdough Bread*

Ingredients:

- Sourdough Starter:
- 1 ½teaspoons quick active dry yeast
- 4 cups warm water
- 3 cups all-purpose flour
- 4 teaspoons sugar Bread
- ½cup water
- 3 cups bread flour
- 2 tablespoons sugar
- 1 1/2 teaspoons salt
- 1 teaspoon quick active dry yeast.

Direction: SERVINGS :12 | Prep Time: 20 minutes | Cook Time: 3 hours 45 minutes

✓ Dissolve 1 1/2 teaspoons yeast in warm water in a glass bowl at least one week before baking the bread to make the sourdough starter.

✓ 3 cups flour and 4 tablespoons sugar, combined 1 minute on medium speed with an electric mixer, or until smooth.

✓ Cover loosely and set aside for one week at room temperature, or until mixture is bubbling and has a sour scent; when ready, cover tightly and store in the refrigerator until ready to use.

✓ When you're ready to bake the bread, carefully measure out 1 cup of sourdough starter and all of the remaining bread components, placing the wet ingredients in the bread machine pan first, followed by the dry ones.

✓ Press Start after selecting Basic and Medium Crust.

✓ Remove the baked bread from the pan and place it on a wire rack to cool.

503) Basic White Bread(Soft white bakery style)

Ingredients:

- 1 cup warm water
- 2 tablespoons agave nectar
- 1/4 cup applesauce
- 3 cups bread flour
- 1 teaspoon salt
- 2 1/4 teaspoons rapid rise yeast

Direction: SERVINGS: 16 | Prep Time: 10 minutes | Cook Time: 3 hours

- ✓ Fill the bread pan with liquid ingredients.
- ✓ In the bread pan, measure and add the dry ingredients (excluding yeast).
- ✓ Toss the yeast into a well in the center of the dry ingredients.
- ✓ Close the bread maker's cover and snap the baking pan into place.
- ✓ Select the Basic option and your favorite crust color before pressing the Start button.
- ✓ When the cake is done baking, remove it from the oven and let it cool completely on a wire rack before serving.

504) Basic White Bread(Soft white bakery style)

Ingredients:

- 1 ½cups warm water
- 1/2 cup honey
- 1 tablespoon olive oil
- 1 teaspoon sea salt
- 3 cups wheat flour
- 1 cup bread flour, unbleached
- 2 teaspoons active dry yeast

Direction: SERVINGS: 12 | Prep Time: 10 minutes | Cook Time: 2 hours

- ✓ Mix dry ingredients together in a bowl, except for yeast.
- ✓ Add wet ingredients to bread pan first; top with dry ingredients.
- ✓ In the center of the dry ingredients, make a well and pour in the yeast.
- ✓ Select the Wheat Bread setting, your selected crust color, and hit Start.
- ✓ Remove from the oven and cool on a wire rack before serving.

505) Whole Wheat Bread

Ingredients:

- 1 cup warm water
- 2 tablespoons butter
- 1 teaspoon salt
- 3 cups 100% whole wheat flour
- 2 tablespoons dry milk

- 1 tablespoon sugar
- 2 teaspoons active dry yeast.

Direction: SERVINGS: 12 | Prep Time: 10 minutes | Cook Time: 3 hours 30 minutes

- ✓ Fill the bread machine with the liquid ingredients.
- ✓ Except for the yeast, combine the dry ingredients in a mixing bowl.
- ✓ Make a well in the bread flour and pour in the yeast.
- ✓ Place the pan in your bread machine and close the top.
- ✓ Select the Wheat Bread option, then select your favorite crust color before pressing the Start button.
- ✓ Remove the bread from the oven and place it on a wire rack to cool thoroughly before slicing.

506) Honey Wheat Bread Recipe 1

Ingredients:

- 4 1/2 cups 100% whole wheat flour
- 1 1/2 cups warm water
- 1/3 cup olive oil
- 1/3 cup honey
- 2 teaspoons salt
- 1 tablespoon active dry yeast

Direction: SERVINGS: 12 | Prep Time: 10 minutes | Cook Time: 3 hours 30 minutes

- ✓ Fill the bread maker halfway with water, then measure and add the oil, followed by the honey in the same measuring cup: this will help the honey slip out more readily.
- ✓ After that, add salt and flour.
- ✓ Toss the yeast into a shallow well in the flour.
- ✓ Set to Wheat Bread, select a crust color, then push the Start button.
- ✓ Remove from the oven and cool on a wire rack before serving.

507) Rye Bread

Ingredients:

- 1 cup water
- 1 1/2 teaspoons salt
- 2 tablespoons sugar
- 1 tablespoon butter
- 2 teaspoons caraway seed
- 2 cups bread flour
- 1 cup rye flour
- 1 1/2 teaspoons quick active yeast

Direction: SERVINGS: 12 | Prep Time: 5 minutes | Cook Time: 3 hours

- ✓ Place all of the ingredients, except the yeast, in the bread maker pan in the order listed.
- ✓ Make a well in the center of the dry ingredients and pour in the yeast.
- ✓ Use the Basic cycle to make a 1 1/25-pound loaf with a medium crust color.
- ✓ To begin, press the Start button.
- ✓ When the bread is done, take it out of the oven and cool for 10 minutes before slicing with a bread knife.

508) **Potato Bread**

Ingredients:

- 3/4 cup water
- 2/3 cup instant mashed potatoes
- 1 egg,
- 2 tablespoons butter, unsalted
- 2 tablespoons white sugar
- 1/4 cup dry milk powder
- 1 teaspoon salt
- 3 cups bread flour
- 1 1/2 teaspoons active dry yeast

Direction: SERVINGS: 12 | Prep Time: 10 minutes | Cook Time: 3 hours

- ✓ In the sequence listed above, add the ingredients to the bread maker. Save the yeast for the next step.
- ✓ In the center of the dry ingredients, make a well and add the yeast.
- ✓ Select a light to medium crust color and start the Basic bread cycle.
- ✓ Remove the bread from the pan and cool completely on a wire rack before serving.

509) **Multigrain Bread**

Ingredients:

- 2 1/4 cups whole wheat flour
- 3/4 cup ground oatmeal
- 2 tablespoons wheat bran
- 2 tablespoons flaxseed meal
- 2 tablespoons vital wheat gluten
- 1 tablespoon dough enhancer
- 1 teaspoon salt
- 2 2/3 teaspoons active dry yeast
- 2 tablespoons olive oil
- 1 tablespoon agave nectar
- 1 tablespoon brown sugar
- 1 cup warm water (slightly warmer than room temperature

Direction: Serving: 10 | Prep Time: 10 minutes

- ✓ Set aside the yeast, and in a mixing dish, add the remaining dry ingredients.
- ✓ Into the bread maker, pour the liquids first, then the dry ingredients.
- ✓ Toss the yeast into a shallow well in the flour.
- ✓ Start the Whole Wheat cycle with a pale crust color.
- ✓ When the loaf is done, remove it from the oven and place it on a cooling rack until it is cold enough to slice.

510) **Cracked Wheat Bread**

Ingredients

- 1 1/4 cup plus 1 tablespoon water
- 2 tablespoons vegetable oil
- 3 cups bread flour
- 3/4 cup cracked wheat

- 1 1/2 teaspoons salt
- 2 tablespoons sugar
- 2 1/4 teaspoons active dry yeast

Direction: 10 | Prep Time: 15 minutes | Cook Time: 1 hour 20 minutes

- ✓ Bring a pot of water to a boil.
- ✓ Place cracked wheat in a small mixing basin, cover with water, and toss to combine.
- ✓ Allow to cool to 80 degrees Fahrenheit.
- ✓ Place the cracked wheat mixture in the pan first, then all of the other ingredients (excluding the yeast) in the order specified.
- ✓ In the center of the dry ingredients, make a well and add the yeast.
- ✓ Select the Basic Bread cycle with a medium color crust and start the machine.
- ✓ After 5 minutes of kneading, check the dough consistency. It should be a soft, tacky ball of dough. If it's dry and stiff, add 12 teaspoons of water at a time until it's sticky.
- ✓ Add 1 tablespoon of flour at a time if it's too wet and sticky.
- ✓ When the cycle is through, remove the bread and set it aside to cool before serving.

511) **Peasant Bread**

Ingredients:

- 2 tablespoons full rounded yeast
- 2 cups white bread flour
- 1 1/2 tablespoons sugar
- 1 tablespoon salt
- 7/8 cup water

For the topping:

- Olive oil Poppy seeds

Direction: Serving: 12 | Prep Time: 5 minutes | Cook Time: 3 hours

- ✓ Fill the bread machine halfway with water, then halfway with dry ingredients, reserving the yeast.
- ✓ Toss the yeast into a well in the center of the dry ingredients.
- ✓ Select the French cycle and the light crust color before pressing the Start button.
- ✓ Coat the top of the loaf with a little olive oil and a small dusting of poppy seeds after it's done.
- ✓ Allow to cool slightly before serving warm with a drizzle of extra virgin olive oil.

512) **Sweet Dinner Rolls**

Ingredients:

- ½cup warm water
- ½cup warm milk
- 1 egg
- 1/3 cup butter, unsalted and softened
- 1/3 cup sugar
- 1 teaspoon salt
- 3 3/4 cups all-purpose flour

- 1 (1/4 ounce) package active dry yeast
- 1/4 cup butter, softened Flour, for surface

Direction: 16 | Prep Time: 15 minutes | Cook Time: 2 hour 20 minutes

✓ Water, milk, egg, butter, sugar, salt, and flour should be added to the bread pan in this order: water, milk, egg, butter, sugar, salt, and flour. Keep yeast in the fridge.

✓ Toss the yeast into a well in the center of the dry ingredients.

✓ Press Start after selecting Dough cycle.

✓ When the cycle is finished, turn the dough out onto a lightly floured surface.

✓ Roll each half of the dough into a 12-inch circle, then top with 1/4 cup of the softened butter.

✓ Make 8 wedges out of each circle. Starting at the wide end, gently but tightly roll the wedges.

✓ Place on a cookie sheet that hasn't been buttered. Location in a warm place, covered with a clean kitchen towel, for 1 hour to rise.

✓ Preheat the oven to 400 degrees F and bake the rolls for 10 to 15 minutes, or until golden brown.

✓ Serve warm.

513)   Southern Cornbread

Ingredients:

- 2 fresh eggs, at room temperature
- 1 cup milk
- 1/4 cup butter, unsalted, at room temperature
- 3/4 cup sugar
- 1 teaspoon salt
- 2 cups unbleached all-purpose flour
- 1 cup cornmeal
- 1 tablespoon baking powder

Direction: 10 | Prep Time: 5 minutes | Cook Time: 1 hour

✓ In the order stated, add all of the ingredients to your bread machine.

✓ Select the Quick Bread cycle with a light crust color and start the machine.

✓ Allow five minutes to cool on a wire rack before serving warm.

514)   Toasted Almond Whole Wheat Bread

Ingredients:

- 1 cup, plus 2 tablespoons water
- 3 tablespoons agave nectar
- 2 tablespoons butter, unsalted
- 1 1/2 cups bread flour
- 1 ½cups whole wheat flour
- 1/4 cup slivered almonds, toasted
- 1 teaspoon salt
- 1 ½teaspoons quick active dry yeast.

Direction: 12 | Prep Time: 10 minutes | Cook

✓ In a bread machine pan, combine all of the ingredients in the sequence shown above, excluding

the yeast.

✓ In the center of the dry ingredients, make a well and add the yeast.

✓ Press Start after selecting the Basic cycle and a light or medium crust color.

✓ Before slicing, remove the baked bread from the pan and cool on a rack.

515)   Pretzel Rolls Pretzel

Ingredients:

- 1 cup warm water,
- 1 egg white, beaten.
- 2 tablespoons oil,
- 3 cups all-purpose flour
- ½teaspoon salt.
- 1 tablespoon granulated sugar,
- 1 package dry yeast Coarse sea salt, for topping
- 1/3 cup baking soda (for boiling process, *
- DO NOT PUT IN THE PRETZEL DOUGH*) Flour, for surface

Direction: Servings: 4 | Prep Time: 5 minutes | Cook Time: 20 Mins.

✓ In a bread machine pan, layer the ingredients in the sequence stated above, reserving the yeast.

✓ In the center of the dry ingredients, make a well and add the yeast.

✓ Select the Dough cycle and push the Start button.

✓ Divide the dough into four halves and place it on a lightly floured surface.

✓ Using your hands, roll the four sections into balls.

✓ Place on a greased cookie sheet and allow to rise for 20 minutes or until puffy.

✓ 2 quarts water and baking soda, combined in a 3-quart saucepan, bring to a boil. Preheat the oven to 425 degrees Fahrenheit.

✓ 2 pretzels should be placed in the pot and cooked for 10 seconds on each side.

✓ Using a slotted spoon, remove the pretzels from the water and place them on a greased baking sheet; repeat with the remaining pretzels.

✓ Allow to air dry for a few minutes.

✓ Using an egg white, brush the surface and season with coarse salt.

✓ Bake for 20 minutes or until golden brown in a preheated oven.

✓ Allow to cool for a few minutes before serving.

516)   Whole Wheat Rolls

Ingredients:

- 1 tablespoon sugar
- 1 teaspoon salt
- 2 3/4 cups whole wheat flour
- 2 teaspoons dry active yeast
- 1/4 cup water
- 1 egg

- 7/8 cup milk
- 1/4 cup butter

Direction: 12 | Prep Time: 10 minutes | Cook Time: 3 hours

✓ All ingredients should be brought to room temperature before baking.

✓ Add the wet ingredients to the bread maker pan.

✓ Measure and add the dry ingredients (except yeast) to the pan.

✓ Make a well in the center of the dry ingredients and add the yeast.

✓ Carefully place the yeast in the hole. Select the Dough cycle, then press Start.

✓ Divide dough into 12 portions and shape them into balls.

✓ Preheat an oven to 350°F. Place rolls on a greased baking pan.

✓ Bake for 25 to 30 minutes, until golden brown.

✓ Butter and serve warm.

517) *Italian Restaurant Style Breadsticks*

Ingredients:

- 1½ cups warm water
- 2 tablespoons butter, unsalted and melted
- 4 1/4 cups bread flour
- 2 tablespoons sugar
- 1 tablespoon salt
- 1 package active dry yeast

For the topping:

- 1 stick unsalted butter, melted
- 2 teaspoons garlic powder
- 1 teaspoons salt
- 1 teaspoon parsley

Direction: 15 minutes | Cook Time: 3 hours

✓ To your bread maker pan, add the wet ingredients.

✓ Add all of the dry ingredients to the pan except the yeast.

✓ Toss the yeast into a well in the center of the dry ingredients.

✓ Press Start and select the Dough cycle.

✓ When the dough is ready, roll it out and cut it into strips; keep in mind that they will double in size after rising, so roll them out thinner than a standard breadstick to allow for expansion.

✓ Transfer to a baking sheet that has been buttered.

✓ Cover the dough with a light towel and set aside for 45 to an hour in a warm place. Preheat oven to 400 °F (200°C).

✓ 6–7 minutes in the oven

✓ In a small mixing dish, combine the melted butter with the garlic powder, salt, and parsley.

✓ Brush half of the butter mixture over the bread sticks, then return to the oven for another 5–8 minutes.

✓ Remove the breadsticks from the oven and brush the remaining butter mixture all over them.

✓ Before serving, let aside for a few minutes to cool.

Gluten-Free Bread

518) Gluten-Free Simple Sandwich Bread

Ingredients:

- 1 1/2 cups sorghum flour
- 1 cup tapioca starch or potato starch (not potato flour)
- 1/2 cup gluten-free millet flour or gluten-free oat flour
- 2 teaspoons xanthan gum
- 1 1/4 teaspoons fine sea salt
- 2 1/2 teaspoons gluten-free yeast for bread machines
- 1 1/4 cups warm water
- 3 tablespoons extra virgin olive oil 1
- tablespoon honey or raw agave nectar
- 1/2 teaspoon mild rice vinegar or lemon juice
- 2 organic free-range eggs, beaten

Direction: PREP: 10 MINUTES / MAKES 1 LOAF

- ✓ Preparing the Ingredients Set aside the dry ingredients (excluding the yeast) after whisking them together.
- ✓ Pour the liquid ingredients into the bread maker pan first, then slowly pour the combined dry ingredients on
- ✓ top.
- ✓ In the center of the dry ingredients, make a well and add the yeast.
- ✓ Select Rapid 1 hour 20 minutes, medium crust color, then push Start on the Bake Cycle.
- ✓ Place on a wire rack to cool for 15 minutes before slicing to serve.

519) Gluten-Free White Bread

Ingredients:

- 2 eggs
- 1⅓ cups milk
- 6 Tbsp oil
- 1 tsp vinegar
- 3⅝ cups white bread flour
- 1 tsp salt
- 2 Tbsp sugar
- 2 tsp dove farm quick yeast

Direction: PREP: 10 MINUTES OR LESS/ MAKES 1 LOAF

- ✓ Preparing the Ingredients. In the order and at the temperature specified by the maker of your bread machine, add each ingredient to the bread machine..
- ✓ Select the Bake cycle. Close the lid and start the machine on the gluten free bread program, if available.
- ✓ Alternatively use the basic or rapid setting with a dark crust option.
- ✓ Take out the baked bread from the bread machine and allow it to cool on a cooling rack.

520) Gluten-Free Glazed Lemon-Pecan Bread

Ingredients:

- 12 slice bread (1½ pounds)
- ½ cup white rice flour
- ½ cup tapioca flour
- ½ cup potato starch
- ¼ cup sweet white sorghum flour
- ¼ cup garbanzo and fava flour
- 1 teaspoon xanthan gum
- 1 teaspoon gluten-free baking powder
- 1 teaspoon baking soda
- ½ teaspoon salt
- 2 eggs
- ½ cup sunflower or canola oil or melted ghee
- ¼ cup almond milk, soymilk or regular milk
- ½ teaspoon cider vinegar
- 1 tablespoon grated lemon peel
- ¼ cup fresh lemon juice
- 2/3 cup granulated sugar
- ½ cup chopped pecans glaze
- 2 tablespoons fresh lemon juice
- 1 cup gluten-free powdered sugar

Direction: PREP: 10 MINUTES /MAKES 1 LOAF

- ✓ Preparing the Ingredients. Choose the size of loaf of your preference and then measure the ingredients.
- ✓ Add all of the ingredients mentioned previously in the list.
- ✓ Close the lid after placing the pan in the bread machine.
- ✓ Select the Bake cycle. Turn on the bread machine.
- ✓ Select the White/Basic setting, select the loaf size, and the crust color.
- ✓ Press start.
- ✓ When the breadmaker cycle is complete, carefully remove the pan from the machine and allow it to cool before serving.
- ✓ Remove the bread from the pan, put in a wire rack to Cool about 10 minutes.
- ✓ In small bowl, stir all glaze ingredients until smooth.
- ✓ With fork, poke holes in top of loaf; drizzle glaze over loaf. Serve warm.

521) Gluten-Free Brown Bread

Ingredients:

- 2 large eggs, lightly beaten
- 1 3/4 cups warm water
- 3 tablespoons canola oil
- 1 cup brown rice flour
- 3/4 cup oat flour
- 1/4 cup tapioca starch
- 1 1/4 cups potato starch
- 1 1/2 teaspoons salt

- 2 tablespoons brown sugar
- 2 tablespoons gluten-free flaxseed meal
- 1/2 cup nonfat dry milk powder
- 2 1/2 teaspoons xanthan gum
- 3 tablespoons psyllium, whole husks
- 2 1/2 teaspoons gluten-free yeast for bread machines
  Direction: PREP: 5 MINUTES /MAKES 12

✓ Preparing the Ingredients Add the eggs, water and canola oil to the bread maker pan and stir until combined.

✓ Whisk all of the dry ingredients except the yeast together in a large mixing bowl.

✓ Add the dry ingredients on top of the wet ingredients.

✓ Make a well in the center of the dry ingredients and add the yeast.

✓ Select the Bake Cycle Set Gluten-Free cycle, medium crust color, and press Start.

✓ When the bread is done, lay the pan on its side to cool before slicing to serve.

522) *Easy Gluten-Free, Dairy-Free Bread*

Ingredients:

- 1 1/2 cups warm water
- 2 teaspoons active dry yeast
- 2 teaspoons sugar
- 2 eggs, room temperature
- 1 egg white, room temperature
- 1 1/2 tablespoons apple cider vinegar
- 4 1/2 tablespoons olive oil
- 3 1/3 cups multi-purpose gluten-free flour
  Direction: PREP: 15 MINUTES /MAKES 12

✓ Preparing the Ingredients In a large mixing bowl, mix the yeast and sugar with the warm water and stir to combine; let aside until frothy, about 8 to 10 minutes.

✓ In a separate mixing dish, whisk together the 2 eggs and 1 egg white, then pour into the bread maker's baking pan.

✓ In a baking pan, combine apple cider vinegar and oil. In a baking pan, pour the frothy yeast/water mixture. On top, sprinkle the gluten-free multi-purpose flour.

✓ Start by selecting the Bake Cycle Set for Gluten-Free Bread setting.

✓ To take the bread from the baking pan, turn the pan onto a cooling rack and cool completely before slicing to serve.

523) *Basic Honey Bread*

Ingredients:

- 12 slice bread (1½ pounds)
- 1½ cups warm milk
- ¼ cup unsalted butter, melted
- 2 eggs, beaten
- 1 teaspoon apple cider vinegar

- ½ cup honey
- 1 teaspoon table salt
- 3 cups gluten-free flour(s) of your choice
- 1½ teaspoons xanthan gum
- 1¾ teaspoons bread machine yeast
  Direction: PREP: 10 MINUTES /MAKES 1 LOAF

✓ Preparing the Ingredients. Choose the size of loaf of your preference and then measure the ingredients.

✓ Add all of the ingredients mentioned previously in the list, close the lid after placing the pan in the bread machine.

✓ Select the Bake Cycle Turn on the bread machine.

✓ Select the White/Basic or Gluten-Free (if your machine has this setting) setting, select the loaf size, and the crust color.

✓ Press start.

✓ When the bread maker cycle is complete, carefully remove the pan from the machine and allow it to cool before serving.

✓ Remove the bread from the pan, put in a wire rack to cool for at least 10 minutes, and slice.

524) *Onion Buttermilk Bread*

Ingredients:

- 12 slice bread (1½ pounds)
- 1 cup lukewarm water
- 3 tablespoons unsalted butter, melted
- ¾ teaspoon apple cider vinegar
- 3 tablespoons dry buttermilk powder
- chopped 2⅔ teaspoons xanthan gum 1½ teaspoons bread machine yeast
- 3 medium eggs, beaten
- 3 tablespoons sugar
- 1 teaspoon table salt
- ⅓ cup potato flour
- ⅓ cup tapioca flour
- 1½ cups white rice flour
- ¾ tablespoon dill, chopped
- 3 tablespoons green onion,
  Direction: PREP: 10 MINUTES /MAKES 1 LOAF

✓ Preparing the Ingredients. Choose the size of loaf of your preference and then measure the ingredients.

✓ Add all of the ingredients mentioned previously in the list, close the lid after placing the pan in the bread machine.

✓ Select the Bake Cycle Turn on the bread machine.

✓ Select White/Basic or Gluten-Free (if your machine has this setting) setting, select the loaf size, and the crust color.

✓ Press start.

✓ When the bread maker cycle is complete, carefully remove the pan from the machine and allow it to cool before serving.

✓ Remove the bread from the pan, put in a wire rack to cool for at least 10 minutes, and slice.

525) Grain-Free Chia Bread

Ingredients:

- 1 cup warm water
- 3 large organic eggs,
- Room temperature 1/4 cup olive oil
- 1 tablespoon apple cider vinegar
- 1 cup gluten-free chia seeds,
- Ground to flour
- 1 cup almond meal flour
- 1/2 cup potato starch
- 1/4 cup coconut flour
- 3/4 cup millet flour
- 1 tablespoon xanthan gum
- 1 1/2 teaspoons salt
- 2 tablespoons sugar
- 3 tablespoons nonfat dry milk
- 6 teaspoons instant yeast

Direction: PREP: 5 MINUTES /MAKES 12

- ✓ Preparing the Ingredients. Whisk wet ingredients together and add to the bread maker pan.
- ✓ Whisk dry ingredients, except yeast, together and add on top of wet ingredients.
- ✓ Make a well in the dry ingredients and add yeast.
- ✓ Select the Bake Cycle Select Whole Wheat cycle, light crust color, and press Start.
- ✓ Allow to cool completely before serving.

526) Gluten-Free Sourdough Bread

Ingredients:

- 1 cup water
- 3 eggs
- 3/4 cup ricotta cheese
- 1/4 cup honey
- 1/4 cup vegetable oil
- 1 teaspoon cider vinegar
- 3/4 cup gluten-free sourdough starter
- 2 cups white rice flour
- 2/3 cup potato starch
- 1/3 cup tapioca flour
- 1/2 cup dry milk powder
- 3 1/2 teaspoons xanthan gum
- 1 1/2 teaspoons salt

Direction: PREP: 5 MINUTES /MAKES 12

- ✓ Preparing the Ingredients. Combine wet ingredients and pour into bread maker pan.
- ✓ Mix together dry ingredients in a large mixing bowl, and add on top of the wet ingredients.
- ✓ Select the Bake Cycle Select Gluten-Free cycle and press Start.
- ✓ Remove the pan from the machine and allow the bread to remain in the pan for approximately 10 minutes.
- ✓ Transfer to a cooling rack before slicing

527) Fat-Free Whole Wheat Bread

Ingredients:

- Water – 1 7/8 cup
- White whole wheat flour – 4
- 2/3 cups Vital wheat gluten
- 4 tbsp.
- Sugar
- 2 tbsp. Salt
- 1 ½ tsp. Rapid rise yeast
- 2 ½ tsp bread machine

Direction: PREP: 10 MINUTES /MAKES 1 LOAF

- ✓ Preparing the Ingredients. Add the water in the bread machine pan.
- ✓ Add the remaining ingredients according to bread machine recommendation.
- ✓ Select the Bake Cycle Choose Quick-Bake Whole Wheat cycle and press Start.
- ✓ Remove the bread when complete.
- ✓ Cool, slice, and serve.

528) Chocolate Chip Banana Bread

Ingredients:

- Shortening or gluten-free cooking spray, for preparing the pan
- 250 grams All-Purpose Flour Blend
- 1 teaspoon ground cinnamon
- 1 teaspoon xanthan gum
- 1 teaspoon baking powder
- ½ teaspoon baking soda
- ¼ teaspoon salt
- 2 large eggs
- 1 teaspoon vanilla extract
- 90 grams' mini semisweet chocolate chips or nondairy alternative
- 80 grams plain Greek yogurt or nondairy alternative
- 450 grams mashed bananas (about 4 large bananas)
- 8 tablespoons (1 stick) butter or nondairy alternative
- 150 grams' light brown sugar

Direction:

- ✓ Preparing the Ingredients. Measure and add the ingredients to the pan in the order mentioned above.
- ✓ Place the pan in the bread machine and close the lid. Select the Bake Cycle Close the lid, Turn on the bread maker.
- ✓ Select the White / Basic setting, then select the dough size, select light or medium crust.
- ✓ Press start to start the cycle.
- ✓ When this is done, and the bread is baked, remove the pan from the machine.
- ✓ Let the bread cool in the pan for at least 20 minutes, then gently transfer it to a wire rack to cool completely

529) *Gluten-Free Whole Grain Bread*

Ingredients:

- 2/3 cup sorghum flour
- 1/2 cup buckwheat flour 1
- 2 cup millet flour
- 3/4 cup potato starch
- 2 1/4 teaspoons xanthan gum
- 1 1/4 teaspoons salt
- 3/4 cup skim milk
- 1/2 cup water
- 1 tablespoon instant yeast
- 5 teaspoons agave nectar, separated
- 1 large egg, lightly beaten
- 4 tablespoons extra virgin olive oil
- 1/2 teaspoon cider vinegar
- 1 tablespoon poppy seeds

Direction: PREP: 15 MINUTES /MAKES 12 SLICES

✓ Preparing the Ingredients Whisk sorghum, buckwheat,

✓ millet, potato starch, xanthan gum, and sea salt in a bowl and set aside.

✓ Combine milk and water in a glass measuring cup. Heat to between 110°F and 120°F; add 2 teaspoons of agave nectar and yeast and stir to combine.

✓ Cover and set aside for a few minutes.

✓ Combine the egg, olive oil, remaining agave, and vinegar in another mixing bowl; add yeast and milk mixture.

✓ Pour wet ingredients into the bottom of your bread maker.

✓ Top with dry ingredients.

✓ Select the Bake Cycle Select Gluten-Free cycle, light color crust, and press Start.

✓ After second kneading cycle sprinkle with poppy seeds.

✓ Remove pan from bread machine.

✓ Leave the loaf in the pan for about 5 minutes before

✓ cooling on a rack. Enjoy!

530) *Cheese Potato Bread*

Ingredients:

- 12 slice bread (1½ pounds)
- 1 cup lukewarm water
- 2¼ tablespoons vegetable oil
- 2 large eggs, beaten
- ⅓ cup dry skim milk powder
- 3 tablespoons sugar
- ¾ teaspoon apple cider vinegar
- 1⅛ teaspoons table salt
- ⅓ cup cornstarch
- ½ cup cottage cheese
- 3 tablespoons snipped chives
- ⅓ cup instant potato buds

- ⅓ cup potato starch
- ⅓ cup tapioca flour
- 1½ cups white rice flour
- 1½ teaspoons bread machine yeast

Direction: PREP: 10 MINUTES /MAKES 1 LOAF

✓ Preparing the Ingredients. Choose the size of loaf of your preference and then measure the ingredients.

✓ Add all of the ingredients mentioned previously in the list, close the lid after placing the pan in the bread machine.

✓ Select the Bake Cycle Turn on the bread machine. Select the White/ Basic or Gluten-Free (if your machine has this setting) setting, select the loaf size, and the crust color.

✓ Press start.

✓ When the breadmaker cycle is complete, carefully remove the pan from the machine and allow it to cool before serving.

✓ Remove the bread from the pan, put in a wire rack to cool for at least 10 minutes, and slice.

531) *Instant Cocoa Bread*

Ingredients:

- 12 slice bread (1½ pounds)
- 1⅛ cups lukewarm water
- 2 large eggs, beaten
- 2¼ tablespoons molasses
- 1½ tablespoons canola oil
- ¾ teaspoon apple cider vinegar
- 2¼ tablespoons light brown sugar
- 1⅛ teaspoons table salt
- 1½ cups white rice flour
- ½ cup potato starch
- ¼ cup tapioca flour
- 1½ teaspoons xanthan gum
- 1½ teaspoons cocoa powder
- 1½ teaspoons instant coffee granules
- 2 teaspoons bread machine yeast

Direction: PREP: 10 MINUTES /MAKES 1 LOAF

✓ Preparing the Ingredients. Choose the size of loaf of your preference and then measure the ingredients.

✓ Add all of the ingredients mentioned previously in the list, close the lid after placing the pan in the bread machine.

✓ Select the Bake Cycle Turn on the bread machine. Select the White/Basic or Gluten-Free (if your machine has this setting) setting, select the loaf size, select light or medium crust.

✓ Press start.

✓ When the breadmaker cycle is complete, carefully remove the pan from the machine and allow it to cool before serving.

✓ Remove the bread from the pan, put in a wire rack to cool for at least 10 minutes, and slice.

532) **Garlic Parsley Bread**

Ingredients:

- 12 slice bread (1½ pounds)
- 1¼ cups almond or coconut milk
- 3 tablespoons flax meal
- ½ cup + 1 tablespoon warm water
- 3 tablespoons butter
- 2¼ tablespoons maple syrup
- 2¼ teaspoons apple cider vinegar
- 3 tablespoons parsley, loosely chopped
- 8–9 cloves garlic, minced
- ¾ teaspoon table salt
- 6 tablespoons + 2 teaspoons brown rice flour
- ⅓ cup corn starch
- 3 tablespoons potato starch
- 2 teaspoons xanthan gum
- 1½ tablespoons garlic powder
- 1½ tablespoons onion powder
- 1½ teaspoons bread machine yeast

Direction: PREP: 10 MINUTES /MAKES 1 LOAF

- ✓ Preparing the Ingredients. Combine the water and flax meal in a bowl; set aside for 5–10 minutes to mix well.
- ✓ Choose the size of loaf of your preference and then measure the ingredients.
- ✓ Add all of the ingredients mentioned previously in the list, including the flax meal.
- ✓ Close the lid after placing the pan in the bread machine.
- ✓ Select the Bake Cycle Turn on the bread machine.
- ✓ Select the White/Basic or Gluten-Free (if your machine has this setting) setting, select the loaf size, select light or medium crust.
- ✓ Press start.
- ✓ When the breadmaker cycle is complete, carefully remove the pan from the machine and allow it to cool before serving.
- ✓ Remove the bread from the pan, put in a wire rack to cool for at least 10 minutes, and slice.

533) **Italian Herb Bread**

Ingredients:

- 12 slice bread (1½ pounds)
- 1½ cups lukewarm water
- 3 eggs, beaten
- ¼ cup vegetable oil
- 1½ teaspoons table salt
- 3 tablespoons sugar
- 1 cup white bean flour
- 1 tablespoon mixed Italian herbs, dried
- 1 cup white rice flour
- ½ cup tapioca flour
- 1 tablespoon xanthan gum
- 1 cup potato starch

- 2¼ teaspoons bread machine yeast

Direction: PREP: 10 MINUTES /MAKES 1 LOAF

- ✓ Preparing the Ingredients. Choose the size of loaf of your preference and then measure the ingredients.
- ✓ Add all of the ingredients mentioned previously in the list, close the lid after placing the pan in the bread machine Select the Bake Cycle Turn on the bread machine.
- ✓ Select the White/Basic or Gluten-Free (if your machine has this setting) setting, select the loaf size, select light or medium crust.
- ✓ Press start.
- ✓ When the breadmaker cycle is complete, carefully remove the pan from the machine and allow it to cool before serving.
- ✓ Remove the bread from the pan, put in a wire rack to cool for at least 10 minutes, and slice.

534) **Mix Seed Bread**

Ingredients:

- 12 slice bread (1½ pounds)
- 2 cups lukewarm milk
- 6 tablespoons cooking oil
- 1 teaspoon vinegar
- 2 eggs, slightly beaten
- 1 tablespoon sugar
- 1 teaspoon table salt
- 2⅔ cups gluten-free flour(s) of your choice
- 2 tablespoons poppy seeds
- 2 tablespoons pumpkin seeds
- 2 tablespoons sunflower seeds
- 2 teaspoons bread machine yeast

Direction: PREP: 10 MINUTES /MAKES 1 LOAF

- ✓ Preparing the Ingredients. Choose the size of loaf of your preference and then measure the ingredients.
- ✓ Add all of the ingredients mentioned previously in the list, close the lid after placing the pan in the bread machine.
- ✓ Select the Bake Cycle Turn on the bread machine.
- ✓ Select the White/Basic setting, select the loaf size, and the crust color.
- ✓ Press start.
- ✓ When the breadmaker cycle is complete, carefully remove the pan from the machine and allow it to cool before serving.
- ✓ Remove the bread from the pan, put in a wire rack to cool for at least 10 minutes, and slice.

535) **Gluten-Free Pumpkin Pie Bread**

Ingredients:

- 1/4 cup olive oil
- 2 large eggs, beaten
- 1 tablespoon bourbon vanilla extract
- 1 cup canned pumpkin
- 4 tablespoons honey
- 1/4 teaspoon lemon juice

- 1/2 cup buckwheat flour
- 1/4 cup millet flour
- 1/4 cup sorghum flour
- 1/2 cup tapioca starch
- 1 cup light brown sugar
- 2 teaspoons baking powder
- 1 teaspoon baking soda
- 1/2 teaspoon sea salt
- 1 teaspoon xanthan gum
- 1 teaspoon ground cinnamon
- 1 teaspoon allspice
- 1-2 tablespoons peach juice

Direction: PREP: 5 MINUTES /MAKES 12 SLICES

✓ Ingredients Preparation: In a separate bowl, combine the dry ingredients.
✓ In a medium saucepan, combine all wet ingredients except the peach juice.
✓ In a bread maker pan, combine the dry ingredients.
✓ Choose the Sweet bread cycle with a light or medium crust color and push Start.
✓ Utilize a soft silicone spatula to scrape along the sides as the ingredients begin to combine.
✓ If the mixture is too stiff, add 1 tablespoon peach juice at a time until the batter resembles muffin batter in consistency.
✓ Allow to bake, covered with a lid.
✓ 20 minutes before slicing, transfer to a cooling rack.

536)   **Gluten-Free Best-Ever Banana Bread**

Ingredients:

- 16 slices bread
- ½ cup tapioca flour
- ½ cup white rice flour
- ½ cup potato starch
- ¼ cup garbanzo and fava flour
- ¼ cup sweet white sorghum flour
- 1 teaspoon xanthan gum
- ½ teaspoon guar gum
- 1 teaspoon gluten-free baking powder
- 1 teaspoon baking soda
- 1 teaspoon salt
- 1 teaspoon ground cinnamon
- ¾ cup packed brown sugar
- 1 cup mashed very ripe bananas (2 medium)
- ½ cup ghee (measured melted)
- ¼ cup almond milk, soymilk or regular milk 1
- teaspoon gluten-free vanilla
- 2 eggs

Direction: PREP: 10 MINUTES /MAKES 1 LOAF

✓ Preparing the Ingredients. Choose the size of loaf of your preference and then measure the ingredients.
✓ Add all of the ingredients mentioned previously in the

list.

✓ Close the lid after placing the pan in the bread machine.
✓ Select the Bake Cycle Turn on the bread machine. Select the White/Basic setting, select the loaf size, and the crust color.
✓ Press start.
✓ When the breadmaker cycle is complete, carefully remove the pan from the machine and allow it to cool before serving.
✓ Remove the bread from the pan, put in a wire rack to Cool about 1 hour.

537)   **Gluten-Free Oat & Honey Bread**

Ingredients:

- 1 1/4 cups warm water
- 3 tablespoons honey
- 2 eggs
- 3 tablespoons butter, melted
- 1 1/4 cups gluten-free oats
- 1 1/4 cups brown rice flour
- 1/2 cup potato starch
- 2 teaspoons xanthan gum
- 1 1/2 teaspoons sugar
- 3/4 teaspoon salt
- 1 1/2 tablespoons active dry yeast

Direction: PREP: 5 MINUTES /MAKES 12 SLICES

✓ Preparing the Ingredients Add ingredients in the order listed above, except for yeast.
✓ Make a well in the center
✓ Select the Bake Cycle
✓ Press Start after selecting Gluten-Free cycle and light crust color.
✓ Remove bread and cool for 20 minutes on its side on a cooling rack before slicing to serve.

538)   **Gluten-Free Bread**

Ingredients: 1 POUND LOAF

- Lukewarm water 1 ⅛ cups
- Unsalted butter, diced ⅛ cup
- Egg 1 ½
- Apple cider vinegar ¾ tsp
- Honey ⅓cup
- Gluten-free, all-purpose flour   2 ¼ cups
- Salt ¾ tsp
- Xanthan gum 1 ⅛ tsp
- Bread machine yeast 1 ⅛ tsp

Direction: 2 hours and 50 minutes / Prep Time: 15 minutes / Cook Time: 2 hours and 35 minutes

✓ Add the ingredients to the bread machine in the sequence stated above or as directed in the instruction manual for your bread maker.
✓ Choose the default setting and the soft crust option.
✓ When the bread is finished, flip it out onto a drying rack and allow it to cool slightly before serving.

✓ *Tip(s): If your bread maker has a gluten-free cycle, select that function instead of the basic setting. Gluten-free flours differ, so it is important to make this bread using various brands to determine which one produces the best Loaf.*

Classic and Whole-Wheat Breads

539) Country-Styled White Bread

Ingredients:

- 2 Pound loaf
- Lukewarm water 3 cups
- Extra-virgin olive oil 3tbsp
- Baking soda ½ tsp
- Plain bread flour 2 cups
- White all-purpose Flour 5 cups
- Sugar 3 tbs
- Salt ½ tsp
- Bread machine yeast 5 tsp

Direction: 2 hours and 20 minutes / Prep Time: 15 minutes / Cook Time: 2 hours and 5

✓ In a bread machine, add the ingredients in the sequence stated above or according to the instructions in your bread machine's handbook.

✓ Select the medium crust option and the fast setting.

✓ When the bread is done baking, remove it from the oven and let it cool on a cooling rack before serving.

✓ TIP(S): I made this bread using the rapid cycle on my bread machine. Alternatively, you can make this recipe using the regular setting, adding only two teaspoons of yeast instead.

✓ Check your bread machine when kneading. If the dough appears wet, add in a few teaspoons of flour. If the dough is too dense, add a few teaspoons of water

540) Honey and Milk White Bread

Ingredients:

- 2 Pound loaf
- Lukewarm whole milk 1 ¼
- Unsalted butter ½ tbsp
- Honey 1 ½ tbsp
- White all-purpose flour 3 cups
- Salt 1 pinch
- Bread machine yeast 1 ½ tsp

Direction: TIME: 3 hours 10 minutes / Prep Time: 10 minutes / Cook Time: 3 hours

✓ In a bread machine, add the ingredients in the sequence stated above or according to the instructions in your bread machine's handbook.

✓ Select the white bread function and the light crust function.

✓ When ready, turn the bread out onto a drying rack and allow it to cool, then serve.

✓ TIP(S): You are welcome to add another 1 ½ tablespoons of honey to sweeten the bread further as per your taste.

541) Butter Bread

Ingredients: 1 POUND LOAF

- Egg 1
- Lukewarm whole milk 1 ¼ cup
- Unsalted butter, diced ½ cup

- Plain bread flour 2 cups
- Salt 1 pinch
- Sugar 1 pinch
- Instant dry yeast   2 tsp

Direction: 3 hours and 45 minutes / Prep Time: 10 minutes / Cook Time: 3 hours and 35 minutes

✓ Use the ingredients in the bread machine in the sequence listed above, or follow the directions provided with your bread machine.

✓ To get a medium crust, use the French method of baking.

✓ When the bread is done baking, remove it from the oven and let it cool on a cooling rack before serving.

✓ TIP(S): If your bread maker does not have a French setting select the white bread function.

542) Basic White Bread

Ingredients: 1 POUND LOAF

- Lukewarm water   ½ cup
- Lukewarm whole milk ¼ cup
- Unsalted butter, diced 1 ½ tbsp
- White all-purpose Flour 1 ¾ cups
- Sugar 1 ½ tbsp
- Salt ¾ tsp
- Instant dry yeast ¾ tsp

Direction: Time: 3 hours and 10 minutes / Prep Time: 10 minutes / Cook Time: 3 hours

✓ Use the ingredients in the bread machine in the sequence listed above, or follow the directions provided with your bread machine.

✓ To get a medium crust, use the French method of baking.

✓ When the bread is done baking, remove it from the oven and let it cool on a cooling rack before serving.

✓ TIP(S): This bread can store for up to four days if kept in a cloth bag, away from sunlight.

543) Classic French Bread

Ingredients: 1 POUND LOAF

- Lukewarm water 1 cup
- Sugar 2 tsp
- Salt 1 tsp
- Plain bread flour 3 ¼ cups
- Bread machine yeast 1 tsp

Direction: TIME: 3 hours and 15 minutes / Prep Time: 15 minutes / Cook Time: 3 hours

✓ Use the ingredients in the bread machine in the sequence listed above, or follow the directions provided with your bread machine.

✓ To get a medium crust, use the French method of baking.

✓ When the bread is done baking, remove it from the oven and let it cool on a cooling rack before serving.

✓ TIP(S): To flavor the bread, add in half a cup of dried cranberries or raisins for a sweeter flavor. For a savory flavor, add in the leaves from two sprigs of rosemary.

544) Sourdough

Ingredients: 1 POUND LOAF

- Sourdough starter ½ cup
- Lukewarm water ⅓ cup
- Sugar ½ tbsp
- Active dry yeast ½ tbsp
- Plain bread flour 1 ½ cups
- Vegetable oil 1 ½ tbsp
- Salt 1 tsp

INGREDIENTS FOR A SOURDOUGH STARTER:

- white, all-purpose flour 2 cups
- active dry yeast 1 tsp
- lukewarm water 2 cups

Direction: TIME: 3 hours and 20 minutes / Prep Time: 20 minutes for bread, 5 days for sourdough starter / Cook Time: 3 hours

✓ DIRECTIONS FOR A SOURDOUGH STARTER:
✓ Combine the ingredients in a glass or ceramic dish.
✓ Ensure the dish is big enough to allow for expansion.
✓ Cover the dish with cloth, fix the cloth into place using an elastic band.
✓ Allow the starter to rest for five days in a warm area.
✓ Stir the starter once a day. Your starter sourdough is now ready for use.
✓ Refrigerate the remainder and use it when needed.
✓ If you would like to make a few loaves, you can keep the sourdough starter "alive" by feeding it equal amounts of flour and water and allowing it to rest in a warm area and using it when needed.
✓ DIRECTIONS FOR BREAD:
✓ Add the sourdough starter, water, sugar, and yeast into the bread maker.
✓ Using a spatula, combine the ingredients.
✓ Allow it to rest for ten minutes. Add bread flour, oil, and salt.
✓ Select the basic setting and medium crust function.
✓ When ready, turn the bread out onto a drying rack and allow it to cool, then serve.

545) Whole-Wheat Breads

Ingredients: 1 POUND LOAF

- Lukewarm whole milk ½ cup
- Unsalted butter, diced 2 tbsp
- Whole wheat flour 1 cup
- Plain bread flour 1 cup
- Brown sugar 2 ½ tbsp
- Salt ¾ tsp
- Bread machine yeast ¾ tsp

Direction: TIME: 3 hours and 15 minutes / Prep Time: 15 minutes / Cook Time: 3 hours

✓ Fill the bread machine with the ingredients in the sequence stated above, or follow the instructions on your bread machine.
✓ Choose whole wheat and the medium crust option.
✓ When the bread is done, set it aside to cool on a drying rack before serving.
✓ TIP(S): After the bread has kneaded for the first time, sprinkle oats or seeds over the top and then allow the machine to continue baking.

546) Whole Wheat and Honey Bread

Ingredients: 1 POUND LOAF

- Lukewarm water 1 ⅛ cups
- Honey 3 tbsp
- Vegetable oil 2 tbsp
- Plain bread flour 1 ½ cups
- Whole wheat flour 1 ½ cups
- Salt ⅓ tsp
- Instant dry yeast 1 ½ tsp

Direction: TIME: 3 hours and 10 minutes / Prep Time: 10 minutes / Cook Time: 3 hours

✓ Fill the bread machine with the ingredients in the sequence stated above, or follow the instructions on your bread machine.
✓ Choose whole wheat and the medium crust option.
✓ When the bread is done, set it aside to cool on a drying rack before serving.
✓ TIP(S): When the bread is ready, glaze the top with honey and add a few sesame seeds or rolled oats.

547) Whole Wheat Seeds and Syrup Bread

Ingredients: 1 POUND LOAF

- Lukewarm water ⅔ cup
- Olive oil 1 tbsp
- Maple syrup 2 tbsp
- White whole wheat flour 1 ¾ cups
- Salt ¾ tsp
- Instant yeast ¾ tsp

Direction: TIME: 3 hours and 5 minutes / Prep Time: 5 minutes / Cook Time: 3 hours

✓ Fill the bread machine with the ingredients in the sequence stated above, or follow the instructions on your bread machine.
✓ Choose whole wheat and the medium crust option.
✓ When the bread is done, set it aside to cool on a drying rack before serving..
✓ TIP(S): Remember: after your bread machine has kneaded the dough for 10 minutes, quickly examine its consistency. If all is well, your dough should be smooth. If it feels sticky, add some flour. If it feels chunky, add some more water. After that, you should be all set. If you wish for enhanced texture, add one egg for every cup of flour. This should be done after the seeds, but before the salt. To shake things up, you can replace the seeds with muesli.

548) 100% Whole Wheat Bread

Ingredients: 1 POUND LOAF

- Lukewarm water 1 cup
- Milk powder 1 ¼ tbsp

- *Unsalted butter, diced 1 ¼ tbsp*
- *Honey 1 ¼ tbsp*
- *Molasses 1 ¼ tbsp*
- *Salt 1 tsp*
- *Whole wheat flour 2 ¼ cups*
- *Active dry yeast 1 tsp*
  Direction: TIME: 4 hours and 5 minutes / Prep Time: 5 minutes / Cook Time: 4 hours
- ✓ *Fill the bread machine with the ingredients in the sequence stated above, or follow the instructions on your bread machine.*
- ✓ *Choose whole wheat and the medium crust option.*
- ✓ *When the bread is done, set it aside to cool on a drying rack before serving.*
- ✓ *TIP(S): I combine the milk powder and water before adding them to the bread machine.*

549) **Seeded Whole Wheat Bread**

Ingredients: 1 POUND LOAF

- *Lukewarm water ⅔ cups*
- *Milk powder 3 tbsp*
- *Honey 1 tbsp*
- *Unsalted butter, softened 1 tbsp*
- *Plain bread flour 1 cup*
- *Whole wheat flour 1 cup*
- *Poppy seeds 2 tbsp*
- *Sesame seeds 2 tbsp*
- *Sunflower seeds 2 tbsp*
- *Salt ¾ tsp*
- *Instant dry yeast 2 tsp*
  Direction: TIME: 3 hours and 10 minutes / Prep Time: 10 minutes / Cook Time: 3 hours
- ✓ *Fill the bread machine with the ingredients in the sequence stated above, or follow the instructions on your bread machine.*
- ✓ *Choose whole wheat and the medium crust option.*
- ✓ *When the bread is done, set it aside to cool on a drying rack before serving.*
- ✓ *TIP(S): Feel free to make use of any fine seeds, such as pumpkin or sesame seeds.*

550) **Honey and Oatmeal Whole Wheat Bread**

Ingredients: 1 POUND LOAF

- *Lukewarm water ⅔ cup*
- *Olive oil ½ tbsp*
- *Honey 8 tsp*
- *Rolled oats ½ cup*
- *Whole wheat flour ¾ cup*
- *White bread flour ¾ cup*
- *Salt ½ tsp*
- *Instant yeast ½ tsp*
  Direction: TIME: 3 hours and 10 minutes / Prep Time: 10 minutes / Cook Time: 3 hours

- ✓ *Fill the bread machine with the ingredients in the sequence stated above, or follow the instructions on your bread machine.*
- ✓ *Choose whole wheat and the medium crust option.*
- ✓ *When the bread is done, set it aside to cool on a drying rack before serving.*
- ✓ *TIP(S): Feel free to add raisins to sweeten the loaf further. Yeast amount can be doubled to enhance the rise. Oat bran can be used in place of rolled oats. For a 2-pound loaf, having 2 cups of whole wheat flour to one cup of white bread flour can increase the overall density without going overboard.*

551) **Classic White Bread I**

Ingredients:

- *16 slice bread (2 pounds)*
- *1½ cups lukewarm water*
- *1 tablespoon + 1 teaspoon olive oil*
- *1½ teaspoons sugar*
- *1 teaspoon table salt*
- *¼ teaspoon baking soda*
- *2½ cups all-purpose flour*
- *1 cup white bread flour*
- *2½ teaspoons bread machine yeast*
  Direction: PREP: 10 MINUTES/ MAKES 1 LOAF
- ✓ *Preparing the Ingredients Choose the size of bread to prepare.*
- ✓ *Measure and add the ingredients to the pan in the order as indicated in the ingredient listing. Place the pan in the bread machine and close the lid.*
- ✓ *Select the Bake Cycle Close the lid, Turn on the bread maker.*
- ✓ *Select the White / Basic setting, then select the dough size and crust color.*
  Press start to start the cycle.
- ✓ *When this is done, and the bread is baked, remove the pan from the machine.*
- ✓ *Let stand a few minutes.*
- ✓ *Remove the bread from the pan and leave it on a wire rack to cool for at least 10 minutes. After this time, proceed to cut it.*

552) **Everyday White Bread**

Ingredients:

- *8 slice bread (1 pound)*
- *¾ cup water, at 80°F to 90°F*
- *1 tablespoon melted butter, cooled*
- *1 tablespoon sugar*
- *¾ teaspoon salt*
- *2 tablespoons skim milk powder*
- *2 cups white bread flour*
- *¾ teaspoon bread machine or instant yeast*
  Direction: REP: 10 MINUTES/ MAKES 8 – 16 SLICES
- ✓ *Preparing the Ingredients. Put the ingredients in your bread maker according to the manufacturer's instructions.*

- ✓ Select the Bake Cycle Close the lid, Turn on the bread maker.
- ✓ Select the White / Basic setting, then select the dough size and crust color.
- ✓ Press start to start the cycle. When this is done, and the bread is baked, remove the pan from the machine.
- ✓ Gently shake the bucket to remove the loaf, and turn it out onto a rack to cool.

553) **Classic White Bread II**

Ingredients:

- 16 slice bread (2 pounds)
- 1 1/2 cups water, lukewarm between 80 and 90ºF
- 3 tablespoons unsalted butter, melted
- 1 tablespoon sugar
- 2 teaspoons salt
- 3 tablespoons dry milk powder
- 4 cup white bread flour
- 1 1/4 teaspoons bread machine yeast
- 1 1/2 teaspoons bread machine yeast

Direction: PREP: 10 MINUTES/MAKES 1 LOAF

- ✓ Preparing the Ingredients. Choose the size of bread to prepare. Measure and add the ingredients to the pan in the order as indicated in the ingredient listing.
- ✓ Place the pan in the bread machine and close the lid. Select the Bake Cycle Turn on the bread maker.
- ✓ Select the White / Basic setting, then select the dough size and crust color.
- ✓ Press start to start the cycle. When this is done, and the bread is baked, remove the pan from the machine.
- ✓ Gently shake the bucket to remove the loaf, and turn it out onto a rack to cool

554) **Extra Buttery White Bread**

Ingredients:

- ⅛ cups milk
- 4 Tbsp unsalted butter
- 3 cups bread flour
- 1½ Tbsp white granulated sugar
- 1½ tsp salt
- 1½ tsp bread machine yeast

Direction: PREP: 10 MINUTES/MAKES 16 SLICES

- ✓ Preparing the Ingredients Soften the butter in your microwave. In the order and at the temperature specified by the maker of your bread machine, add each ingredient to the bread machine..
- ✓ Select the Bake Cycle Close the lid, select the basic or white bread, medium crust setting on your bread machine, and press start.
- ✓ Take out the baked bread from the bread machine and allow it to cool on a cooling rack.
- ✓ Serve

555) **Wheat Bread**

Ingredients:

- Water - ¾ cup
- Melted butter - 1½ tbsp.,
- cooled Honey - 1½ tbsp.
- Salt - ¾ tsp.
- Whole-wheat bread flour - 2 cups
- Bread machine or instant yeast - 1 tsp.

Direction: PREP: 10 MINUTES / MAKES 1 LOAF

- ✓ Preparing the Ingredients. Choose the size of loaf you would like to make and measure your ingredients.
- ✓ Add the ingredients in the machine according to the manufacturer's instructions.
- ✓ Select the Bake Cycle Press Whole-Wheat/Whole-Grain bread, choose Light or Medium crust, and press Start.
- ✓ When done, remove the bread from the machine and cool. Slice and serve.

556) **Vegan White Bread**

Ingredients:

- 1⅓ cups water
- ⅓ cup plant milk (I use silk soy original)
- 1½ tsp salt
- 2 Tbsp granulated sugar
- 2 Tbsp vegetable oil
- 3½ cups all-purpose flour
- 1¾ tsp bread machine yeast

Direction: PREP: 5 MINUTES / MAKES 14 SILICES

- ✓ Preparing the Ingredients
- ✓ In the order and at the temperature specified by the maker of your bread machine, add each ingredient to the bread machine..
- ✓ Select the Bake Cycle Close the lid, select the basic or white bread, medium crust setting on your bread machine, and press start. When the bread machine has finished baking,
- ✓ Remove the bread and put it on a cooling rack.

557) **Rice Flour , Rice Bread**

Ingredients:

- 3 eggs
- 1½ cups water
- 3 Tbsp vegetable oil
- 1 tsp apple cider vinegar
- 2¼ tsp active dry yeast
- 3¼ cups white rice flour
- 2½ tsp xanthan gum
- 1½ tsp salt
- ½ cup dry milk powder
- 3 Tbsp white sugar

Direction: PREP: 10 MINUTES / MAKES 16 SLICES

- ✓ Preparing the Ingredients In a medium-size bowl, mix the eggs, water, oil, and vinegar.

- ✓ In a large bowl, add the yeast, salt, xanthan gum, dry milk powder, rice flour, and sugar.
- ✓ Mix with a whisk until incorporated.
- ✓ In the order and at the temperature specified by the maker of your bread machine, add each ingredient to the bread machine..
- ✓ Close the lid, select the whole wheat, medium crust setting on your bread machine, and press start.
- ✓ Take out the baked bread from the bread machine and allow it to cool on a cooling rack.

558) Honey Whole-Wheat Bread

Ingredients:

- 12 slice bread (1½ pound)
- 1⅛ cups water, at 80°F to 90°F
- 2 tablespoons honey
- 1½ tablespoons melted butter, cooled
- ¾ teaspoon salt
- 2½ cups whole-wheat flour
- ¾ cup white bread flour
- 1 1/4 teaspoons bread machine yeast
- 1½ teaspoons bread machine or instant yeast
- 1 teaspoon bread machine or instant yeast

Direction: PREP: 10 MINUTES OR LESS/MAKES 1 LOAF

- ✓ Preparing the Ingredients. Choose the size of bread to prepare.
- ✓ Measure and add the ingredients to the pan in the order as indicated in the ingredient listing.
- ✓ Place the pan in the bread machine and close the lid.
- ✓ Select the Bake Cycle Turn on the bread maker.
- ✓ Select the White / Basic setting, then select the dough size and crust color.
- ✓ Press start to start the cycle. When this is done, and the bread is baked, remove the pan from the machine.
- ✓ Let stand a few minutes.
- ✓ Remove the bread from the pan and leave it on a wire rack to cool for at least 10 minutes. Slice and serve

559) French Bread

Ingredients:

- Water - ⅔ cup Olive oil
- 2 tsp. Sugar –
- 1 tbsp. Salt –
- ⅔ tsp. White bread flour –
- 2 cups Bread machine or instant yeast - 1 tsp.

Direction: PREP: 10 MINUTES OR LESS/MAKES 1 LOAF

- ✓ Preparing the Ingredients. Place everything in the bread machine according to machine recommendation.
- ✓ Select the Bake Cycle Press French bread and Light or Medium crust. Press Start.
- ✓ Remove the loaf from the machine and cool. Slice and serve.

560) Classic White Sandwich Bread

Ingredients:

- 12 slice bread (1½ pound)
- 3/4 cup water, lukewarm between 80 and 90⁰F
- 1 1/2 tablespoons unsalted butter, melted
- 1 tablespoon melted butter, cooled
- 1 ½ ounces sugar
- 2 egg whites or 1 egg, beaten
- 2 1/4 cups white bread flour
- 1 1/8 teaspoons bread machine yeast

Direction: PREP: 10 MINUTES OR LESS/ MAKES 1 LOAF

- ✓ Preparing the Ingredients. Choose the size of bread to prepare.
- ✓ Measure and add the ingredients to the pan in the order as indicated in the ingredient listing.
- ✓ Place the pan in the bread machine and close the lid.
- ✓ Select the Bake Cycle Turn on the bread maker.
- ✓ Select the White / Basic setting, then select the dough size and crust color.
- ✓ Press start to start the cycle.
- ✓ When this is done, and the bread is baked, remove the pan from the machine.
- ✓ Let stand a few minutes.
- ✓ Remove the bread from the pan and leave it on a wire rack to cool for at least 10 minutes.
- ✓ Slice and Serve.

561) Oat Bran Molasses Bread

Ingredients:

- Water - ½ cup
- Melted butter - 1½ tbsp., cooled
- Blackstrap molasses - 2 tbsp.
- Salt - ¼ tsp.
- Ground nutmeg - ⅛ tsp.
- Oat bran - ½ cup
- Whole-wheat bread flour - 1½ cups
- Bread machine or instant yeast - 1⅛ tsp.

Direction: PREP: 10 MINUTES / MAKES 1 LOAF

- ✓ Preparing the Ingredients Place the ingredients in the bread machine according to instructions.
- ✓ Select the Bake Cycle Choose Whole-Wheat/Whole-Grain bread, and Light or Medium crust. Press Start.
- ✓ Remove when done and cool. Slice and serve.

562) Molasses Wheat Bread

Ingredients:

- 12 slice bread (1½ pound)
- ¾ cup water, at 80°F to 90°F
- ⅓ cup milk, at 80°F
- 1 tablespoon melted butter, cooled
- 3¾ tablespoons honey
- 2 tablespoons molasses

- 2 teaspoons sugar
- 2 tablespoons skim milk powder
- ¾ teaspoon salt
- 2 teaspoons unsweetened cocoa powder
- 1¾ cups whole-wheat flour
- 1¼ cups white bread flour
- 1⅛ teaspoons bread machine yeast or instant yeast

Direction: PREP: 10 MINUTES OR LESS/MAKES 1 LOAF

- ✓ Preparing the Ingredients. Choose the size of bread to prepare.
- ✓ Measure and add the ingredients to the pan in the order as indicated in the ingredient listing.
- ✓ Place the pan in the bread machine and close the lid.
- ✓ Select the Bake cycle Turn on the bread maker.
- ✓ Select the White / Basic setting, then select the dough size and crust color.
- ✓ Press start to start the cycle.
- ✓ When this is done, and the bread is baked, remove the pan from the machine.
- ✓ Let stand a few minutes.
- ✓ Remove the bread from the pan and leave it on a wire rack to cool for at least 10 minutes. After this time, proceed to cut it.

563) *Baguette Style French Bread*

Ingredients:

- 8 slice bread (1 pound)
- 2 baguettes of 1-pound each
- 1 ⅔cups water, lukewarm between 80 and 90⁰F
- 1 teaspoon table salt
- 4 ⅔ cups white bread flour
- 2 ⅔ teaspoons bread machine yeast or rapid rise yeast
- 2 baguettes of ¾-pound each
- 12 slice bread (1½ pound)
- ¾ cup water, at 80°F to 90°F
- 1 ¼ cups water, lukewarm between 80 and 90⁰F
- ¾ teaspoon table salt
- 3 ½ cups white bread flour
- 2 teaspoons bread machine yeast or rapid rise yeast

Direction: PREP: 10 MINUTES OR LESS/MAKES 1 LOAF

- ✓ Preparing the Ingredients. Choose the size of crusty bread you would like to make and measure your ingredients.
- ✓ Add the ingredients for the bread machine to the bread pan in the order listed above.
- ✓ Place the pan in the bread machine and close the lid.
- ✓ Turn on the bread maker. Select the Bake Cycle Select the dough/manual setting.
- ✓ When the dough cycle is completed, remove the pan and lay the dough on a floured working surface.
- ✓ Knead the dough a few times and add flour if needed so the dough is not too sticky to handle.
- ✓ Cut the dough in half and form a ball with each half.

- ✓ Grease a baking sheet with olive oil.
- ✓ Dust lightly with cornmeal. Preheat the oven to 375⁰ and place the oven rack in the middle position.
- ✓ With a rolling pin dusted with flour, roll one of the dough balls into a 12-inch by 9 -inch rectangle for the 2 pounds' bread size or a 10-inch by 8-inch rectangle for the 1 ½ pound bread size.
- ✓ Starting on the longer side, roll the dough tightly.
- ✓ Pinch the ends and the seam with your fingers to seal.
- ✓ Roll the dough in a back in forth movement to make it into a nice French baguette shape.
- ✓ Repeat the process with the second dough ball.
- ✓ Place loaves of bread onto the baking sheet with the seams down and brush with some olive oil with enough space in between them to rise.
- ✓ Dust top of both loaves with a little bit of cornmeal.
- ✓ Cover with a clean kitchen towel and place in a warm area with any air draught. Let rise for 10 to 15 minutes, or until loaves doubled in size.
- ✓ Mix the egg white and 1 tablespoon of water and lightly brush over both loaves of bread.
- ✓ Place in the oven and bake for 20 minutes.
- ✓ Remove from oven and brush with remaining egg wash on top of both loaves of bread. Place back into the oven taking care of turning around the baking sheet.
- ✓ Bake for another 5 to 10 minutes or until the baguettes are golden brown.
- ✓ Let rest on a wired rack for 5-10 minutes before serving.

564) *Bread Machine Bread*

Ingredients:

- Flour – 2 cups,
- Sifted Warm water – ¾ cup
- Sugar – 1 tsp.
- Active dry yeast – 1.25 tsp.
- Salt – 1 tsp.
- Oil – 1 tsp.

Direction: PREP: 10 MINUTES /MAKES 1 LOAF

- ✓ Preparing the Ingredients Add ingredients according to bread machine recommendation.
- ✓ Select the Bake Cycle Select the Basic setting and press Start.
- ✓ Remove the loaf once it is baked.
- ✓ Cool and slice.

565) *Banana Bread*

Ingredients:

- Eggs – 2
- Butter – 1/3 cup
- Milk – 1/8 cup
- Bananas – 2,
- mashed Bread flour – 1 1/3 cups
- Sugar – 2/3 cup

- Baking powder – 1 ¼ tsp.
- Baking soda – ½ tsp.
- Salt – ½ tsp.
- Chopped nuts – ½ cup, lightly toasted

Direction: PREP: 10 MINUTES /MAKES 1 LOAF

- ✓ Preparing the Ingredients Add the butter, eggs, milk, and bananas to the bread pan and set aside.
- ✓ Combine the remaining dry ingredients in a bowl and add the bread pan.
- ✓ Select the Bake Cycle Use Quick Bread setting to bake the bread. Remove the bread from the pan and leave it on a wire rack to cool for at least 10 minutes.
- ✓ Slice and serve.

566) **Crusty French Bread**

Ingredients:

- 12 slice bread (1½ pound)
- 1 cup water, at 80°F to 90°F
- 1¼ tablespoons olive oil
- 2 tablespoons sugar
- 1¼ teaspoons salt
- 3 cups white bread flour
- 1¼ teaspoons bread machine or instant yeast, or flax seeds (optional)

Direction: PREP: 10 MINUTES /MAKES 1 LOAF

- ✓ Preparing the Ingredients. Put the ingredients in your bread maker according to the manufacturer's instructions.
- ✓ Select the Bake cycle Program the machine for French bread, select light or medium crust, and press Start.
- ✓ When this is done, and the bread is baked, remove the pan from the machine.

567) **Onion Bread**

Ingredients:

- Water – 1 ½ cup
- Butter – 2 tbsp. plus 2 tsp.
- Salt – 1 tsp.
- Sugar – 1 tbsp. plus 1 ½ tsp.
- Bread flour – 4 cups
- Nonfat dry milk – 2 tbsp. plus 2 tsp.
- Active dry yeast – 2 tsp.
- Dry onion soup mix – 4 tbsp.

Direction: PREP: 10 MINUTES /MAKES 1 LOAF

- ✓ Preparing the Ingredients. Place ingredients in the bread pan in the order listed, except the soup.
- ✓ Select the Bake Cycle Select Basic cycle. Add the onion soup mix at the fruit and nut signal.
- ✓ When done, remove and cool. Slice and serve.

568) **Buttermilk Bread**

Ingredients:

- 16 slice bread (2 pounds)

- 1¼ cups lukewarm buttermilk
- 1½ tablespoons unsalted butter, melted
- 1½ tablespoons sugar
- 1⅛ teaspoons table salt
- ⅓ teaspoon baking powder
- 2⅔ cups white bread flour
- 1⅔ teaspoons bread machine yeast

Direction: PREP: 10 MINUTES /MAKES 1 LOAF

- ✓ Preparing the Ingredients. Choose the size of bread to prepare. Measure and add the ingredients to the pan in the order as indicated in the ingredient listing.
- ✓ Place the pan in the bread machine and close the lid.
- ✓ Select the Bake Cycle Close the lid, Turn on the bread maker.
- ✓ Select the White / Basic setting, then select the dough size and crust color.
- ✓ Press start to start the cycle. When this is done, and the bread is baked, remove the pan from the machine.
- ✓ Let stand a few minutes.
- ✓ Remove the bread from the pan and leave it on a wire rack to cool for at least 10 minutes. Slice and serve.

569) **Pumpernickel Bread**

Ingredients:

- 8 slice bread (1½ pounds)
- ½ cup water, at 80°F to 90°F
- ¼ cup brewed coffee, at 80°F to 90°F
- 2 tablespoons dark molasses
- 5 teaspoons sugar
- 4 teaspoons melted butter, cooled
- 1 tablespoon powdered skim milk
- 1 teaspoon salt
- ⅔ cup dark rye flour
- ½ cup whole-wheat bread flour
- 1 teaspoon caraway seeds
- 1 cup white bread flour
- 1½ teaspoons bread machine or active dry yeast

Direction: PREP: 10 MINUTES /MAKES 1 LOAF

- ✓ Preparing the Ingredients. Put the ingredients in your bread maker according to the manufacturer's instructions.
- ✓ Select the Bake Cycle Close the lid, Turn on the bread maker.
- ✓ Select the White / Basic setting, then select the dough size and crust color.
- ✓ Press start to start the cycle. When this is done, and the bread is baked, remove the pan from the machine.
- ✓ Let stand a few minutes.
- ✓ Remove the bread from the pan and leave it on a wire rack to cool for at least 10 minutes. Slice and serve.

570) Oat Molasses Bread

Ingredients:

- 12 slice bread (1½ pounds)
- 1 cup boiling water
- ⅓ cup brewed coffee, at 80°F to 90°F
- 2 tablespoons butter
- 1 large egg, lightly beaten
- Yeast
- 3 cups white bread flour
- 1½ teaspoons table salt
- 3 tablespoons honey
- 1 tablespoon dark molasses
- 3 cups white bread flour
- 2 teaspoons bread machine

Direction: PREP: 10 MINUTES /MAKES 1 LOAF

- ✓ Preparing the Ingredients. Add the boiling water and oats to a mixing bowl.
- ✓ Allow the oats to soak well and cool down completely. Do not drain the water.
- ✓ Choose the size of loaf you would like to make and measure your ingredients Add the soaked oats, along with any remaining water, to the bread pan.
- ✓ Add the remaining ingredients to the bread pan in the order listed above.
- ✓ Select the Bake Cycle Close the lid, Turn on the bread maker.
- ✓ Select the White / Basic setting, then select the dough size and crust color.
- ✓ Press start to start the cycle.
- ✓ When this is done, and the bread is baked, remove the pan from the machine.
- ✓ Let stand a few minutes.
- ✓ Remove the bread from the pan and leave it on a wire rack to cool for at least 10 minutes.
- ✓ Slice and serve.

571) Peanut Butter Bread

Ingredients:

- Water – 1 cup, plus 1 tbsp.
- Peanut butter
- ½ cup Bread flour –
- 3 cups Brown sugar –
- 3 tbsp. Salt –
- 1 tsp. Bread machine
- Yeast – 2 tsp.

Direction: PREP: 10 MINUTES /MAKES 1 LOAF

- ✓ Preparing the Ingredients Place every ingredient in the bread machine according to the manufacturer's recommendation.
- ✓ Select the Bake Cycle Select Basic/White or Sweet and choose Medium or Light crust.
- ✓ Press Start. Remove the bread when finished.
- ✓ Cool, slice, and serve.

572) Whole Wheat Corn Bread

Ingredients:

- 16 slice bread (2 pounds)
- 1⅓ cups lukewarm water
- 2 tablespoons light brown sugar
- 1 large egg, beaten
- 2 tablespoons unsalted butter, melted
- 1½ teaspoons table salt
- ¾ cup whole wheat flour
- ¾ cup cornmeal
- 3 cups whole-wheat bread flour
- 2¾ cups white bread flour
- 2½ teaspoons bread machine yeast

Direction: PREP: 10 MINUTES /MAKES 1 LOAF

- ✓ Preparing the Ingredients. Measure and add the ingredients to the pan in the order mentioned above.
- ✓ Place the pan in the bread machine and close the lid. Select the Bake cycle.
- ✓ Turn on the bread maker. Select the White / Basic setting, then select the dough size and crust color. Press start to start the cycle.
- ✓ When this is done, and the bread is baked, remove the pan from the machine.
- ✓ Let stand a few minutes.
- ✓ Remove the bread from the pan and leave it on a wire rack to cool for at least 10 minutes. After this time, proceed to cut it

573) Quinoa Oatmeal Bread

Ingredients:

- Quinoa flakes – ½ cup
- Buttermilk – 1 cup
- Salt – 1 tsp.
- Sugar – 1 tbsp.
- Honey – 1 tbsp.
- Unsalted butter – 4 tbsp.
- Quick-cooking oats – ½ cup
- Whole wheat flour – ½ cup
- Bread flour – 1 ½ cups
- Yeast – 1 ½ tsp.

Direction: PREP: 10 MINUTES /MAKES 1 LOAF

- ✓ Preparing the Ingredients. Add everything according to the bread machine instructions.
- ✓ Select the Bake Cycle Select Whole Grain and bake.
- ✓ Remove the bread when done. Cool, slice, and serve.

574) Whole-Wheat Buttermilk Bread

Ingredients:

- 12 slice bread (1½ pounds)
- ¾ cup plus 3 tablespoons buttermilk, at 80°F to 90°F
- 1½ tablespoons melted butter, cooled
- 1½ tablespoons honey

- ¾ teaspoon salt
- 1⅛ cups whole-wheat flour
- 1¾ cups plus 1 tablespoon white bread flour
- 1⅔ teaspoons bread machine or instant yeast
  Direction: PREP: 10 MINUTES /MAKES 1 LOAF

✓ Preparing the Ingredients. Put the ingredients in your bread maker according to the manufacturer's instructions.

✓ Select the Bake Cycle Close the lid. Turn on the bread maker.

✓ Select the White / Basic or Whole Wheat setting, then select the dough size and crust color.

✓ Press start to start the cycle. When this is done, and the bread is baked, remove the pan from the machine.

✓ Let stand a few minutes.

✓ Remove the bread from the pan and leave it on a wire rack to cool for at least 10 minutes.

✓ Slice and serve.

575) Wheat Bran Bread

Ingredients:

- 16 slice bread (2 pounds)
- 1½ cups lukewarm milk
- 3 tablespoons unsalted butter, melted
- 2 teaspoons table salt
- ½ cup wheat bran
- 3½ cups white bread flour
- 1½ cups whole-wheat bread flour
- 1 cup oat bran
- 3 cups whole-wheat bread flour
- 2 teaspoons bread machine yeast
  Direction: PREP: 10 MINUTES /MAKES 1 LOAF

✓ Preparing the Ingredients. Measure and add the ingredients to the pan in the order mentioned above.

✓ Place the pan in the bread machine and close the lid.

✓ Place the pan in the bread machine and close the lid.

✓ Select the Bake Cycle Turn on the bread maker. Select the White / Basic or Whole Wheat setting, then select the dough size and crust color.

✓ Press start to start the cycle. When this is done, and the bread is baked, remove the pan from the machine.

✓ Let stand a few minutes.

✓ Remove the bread from the pan and leave it on a wire rack to cool for at least 10 minutes.

✓ Slice and serve.

576) Soft Egg Bread

Ingredients:

- 16 slice bread (2 pounds)
- 1 cup milk, at 80°F to 90°F
- 5 tablespoons melted butter, cooled
- 3 eggs, at room temperature
- ⅓ cup sugar
- 2 teaspoons salt

- 4 cups white bread flour
- 1 cup oat bran
- 3 cups whole-wheat bread flour
- 1½ teaspoons bread machine or instant yeast
  Direction: PREP: 10 MINUTES /MAKES 1 LOAF

✓ Preparing the Ingredients. Put the ingredients in your bread maker according to the manufacturer's instructions.

✓ Select the Bake Cycle Turn on the bread maker.

✓ Select the White / Basic setting, then select the dough size and medium crust.

✓ Press Start.

✓ When this is done, and the bread is baked, remove the pan from the machine. Let stand a few minutes.

✓ Remove the bread from the pan and leave it on a wire rack to cool for at least 10 minutes.

✓ Slice and serve.

577) Date and Nut Bread

Ingredients:

- Water – 1 cup
- Oil – 1 ½ tbsp.
- Honey – 2 tbsp.
- Salt – ½ tsp.
- Rolled oats – ¾ cup
- Whole wheat flour – ¾ cup
- Bread flour – 1 ½ cups
- Active dry yeast – 1 ½ tsp.
- Dates – ½ cups, pitted
- Chopped almonds – ½ cup
  Direction: PREP: 10 MINUTES /MAKES 1 LOAF

✓ Preparing the Ingredients Place everything into the bread pan according to the bread machine recommendation.

✓ Select the Bake Cycle Select Fruit bread/Basic cycle and press Start.

✓ You can add the dates and nuts after the beep or at the very beginning.

578) Multi-Seed Bread

Ingredients:

- Tepid water – 1 cup
- Salt – 1 tsp.
- Olive oil – 2 tbsp.
- Whole wheat bread flour – 1 cup
- White bread flour – 2 cups
- Dried yeast – 1 ½ tsp.
- Mixed seeds – 1/3 cup
- sesame, pumpkin, sunflower, poppy
  Direction: PREP: 10 MINUTES /MAKES 1 LOAF

✓ Preparing the Ingredients. Add the ingredients according to bread machine recommendation.

✓ Select the Bake Cycle Select White bread/Basic cycle and press Start. Remove the bread when done.

✓ Cool, slice, and serve.

✓

579) Healthy Bran Bread

Ingredients:

- 12 slice bread (1½ pounds)
- 1⅛ cups milk, at 80°F to 90°F
- 2¼ tablespoons melted butter, cooled
- 1½ tablespoons unsalted butter, melted
- 3 tablespoons sugar
- 1½ teaspoons salt
- ½ cup wheat bran
- 2⅔ cups white bread flour
- 1½ teaspoon bread machine or instant yeast

Direction: PREP: 10 MINUTES /MAKES 1 LOAF

- ✓ Preparing the Ingredients. Measure and add the ingredients to the pan in the order mentioned above.
- ✓ Place the pan in the bread machine and close the lid.
- ✓ Select the Bake Cycle Turn on the bread maker.
- ✓ Select the White / Basic or Whole Wheat setting, then select the dough size and crust color.
- ✓ Press start to start the cycle.
- ✓ When this is done, and the bread is baked, remove the pan from the machine.
- ✓ Let stand a few minutes.
- ✓ Remove the bread from the pan and leave it on a wire rack to cool for at least 10 minutes.
- ✓ Slice and serve.

580) Classic Whole Wheat Bread

Ingredients:

- 12 slice bread (1½ pounds)
- 1⅛ cups milk, at 80°F to 90°F
- 2¼ tablespoons melted butter, cooled
- 1½ tablespoons unsalted butter, melted
- 3 tablespoons sugar
- 1½ teaspoons salt
- ½ cup wheat bran
- ¾ cup lukewarm water
- ⅓ cup unsalted butter, melted
- 2 eggs, at room temperature
- 1½ teaspoons table salt
- 3 tablespoons sugar
- 1 cup whole-wheat flour
- 2 cups white bread flour
- 1⅔ teaspoons bread machine yeast

Direction: PREP: 10 MINUTES /MAKES 1 LOAF

- ✓ Preparing the Ingredients. Measure and add the ingredients to the pan in the order mentioned above.
- ✓ Place the pan in the bread machine and close the lid.
- ✓ Place the pan in the bread machine and close the lid.
- ✓ Select the Bake Cycle Turn on the bread maker.
- ✓ Select the Whole Wheat setting, then select the dough size and crust color.
- ✓ Press start to start the cycle.
- ✓ When this is done, and the bread is baked, remove the pan from the machine.
- ✓ Let stand a few minutes.
- ✓ Remove the bread from the pan and leave it on a wire rack to cool for at least 10 minutes.
- ✓ Slice and serve.

581) Coffee Rye Bread

Ingredients:

- Lukewarm water – ½ cup
- Brewed coffee – ¼ cup,
- 80°F Dark molasses – 2 tbsp.
- Brown sugar – 5 tsp.
- Unsalted butter – 4 tsp.,
- Softened Powdered skim milk – 1 tbsp
- Kosher salt – 1 tsp.
- Unsweetened cocoa powder – 4 tsp.
- Dark rye flour – 2/3 cup
- Whole-wheat bread machine flour – ½ cup
- Caraway seeds – 1 tsp.
- White bread machine flour – 1 cup
- Bread machine yeast – 1 ½ tsp

Direction: PREP: 10 MINUTES /MAKES 1 LOAF

- ✓ Preparing the Ingredients Place everything in the bread machine pan according to the bread machine recommendation.
- ✓ Select the Bake Cycle Select Basic and Light crust. Press Start.
- ✓ Remove the bread. Cool, slice, and serve.

582) Dark Rye Bread

Ingredients:

- 12 slice bread (1½ pounds)
- 1 cup water, at 80°F to 90°F
- 1½ tablespoons melted butter, cooled
- 1½ tablespoons unsalted butter, melted
- ⅓ cup molasses
- ⅓ teaspoon salt
- 1½ tablespoons unsweetened cocoa powder
- Pinch ground nutmeg
- ¾ cup rye flour
- 2 cups white bread flour
- 1⅔ teaspoons bread machine or instant yeast

Direction: PREP: 10 MINUTES /MAKES 1 LOAF

- ✓ Preparing the Ingredients. Put the ingredients in your bread maker according to the manufacturer's instructions.
- ✓ Select the Bake Cycle Turn on the bread maker.
- ✓ Select the White / Basic setting, then select the dough size and crust color.
- ✓ Press start to start the cycle.
- ✓ When this is done, and the bread is baked, remove the pan from the machine.
- ✓ Let stand a few minutes.

- ✓ Remove the bread from the pan and leave it on a wire rack to cool for at least 10 minutes.
- ✓ Slice and serve.

583) Honey Nut Bread

Ingredients:

- Eggs – 2
- Cottage cheese – 2/3 cup
- Milk – ½ cup
- Butter – ¼ cup
- Honey – 2 tbsp.
- All-purpose flour – 4 cups
- Instant yeast – 1 tbsp
- Salt – 1 tsp.
- Candied nuts – ¾ cups, chopped

Direction: PREP: 10 MINUTES /MAKES 1 LOAF

- ✓ Preparing the Ingredients Add everything, except nuts to your bread machine according to manufacturer recommendation.
- ✓ Select the Bake Cycle Select Basic and choose Light crust type. Press Start. Add the nuts when the machine beeps.
- ✓ Remove the bread when ready.
- ✓ Cool, slice, and serve.

584) Oat Bran Nutmeg Bread

Ingredients:

- 16 slice bread (2 pounds)
- 1 cup lukewarm water
- 3 tablespoons unsalted butter, melted
- ¼ cup blackstrap molasses
- ½ teaspoon table salt
- 3 cups whole-wheat bread flour
- ¼ teaspoon ground nutmeg
- 1 cup oat bran
- 3 cups whole-wheat bread flour
- 2¼ teaspoons bread machine yeast

Direction: PREP: 10 MINUTES /MAKES 1 LOAF

- ✓ Preparing the Ingredients. Choose the size of bread to prepare.
- ✓ Measure and add the ingredients to the pan in the order as indicated in the ingredient listing.
- ✓ Place the pan in the bread machine and close the lid.
- ✓ Select the Bake Cycle Turn on the bread maker.
- ✓ Select the White / Basic setting, then select the dough size and crust color.
- ✓ Press start to start the cycle.
- ✓ When this is done, and the bread is baked, remove the pan from the machine.
- ✓ Let stand a few minutes.
- ✓ Remove the bread from the pan and leave it on a wire rack to cool for at least 10 minutes.
- ✓ Slice and serve.

585) Three-Seed Bread

Ingredients:

- Water – 2/3 cup plus 2 tsp
- Butter – 1 tbsp.,
- Softened Honey – 1 tbsp.
- Sunflower seeds – 2 tbsp.
- Sesame seeds – 2 tbsp.
- Poppy seeds – 2 tbsp.
- Salt – ¾ tsp.
- Whole wheat flour – 1 cup
- Bread flour - 1 cup
- Nonfat dry milk powder – 3 tbsp.
- Active dry yeast – 2 tsp.

Direction: PREP: 10 MINUTES /MAKES 1 LOAF

- ✓ Preparing the Ingredients Put all ingredients in the bread machine pan according to its order.
- ✓ Select the Bake Cycle Select Basic bread and press Start.
- ✓ Remove the bread when done.
- ✓ Cool, slice, and serve.

586) Peasant Bread

Ingredients:

- 2 tablespoons full rounded yeast
- 2 cups white bread flour
- 1 1/2 tablespoons sugar
- 1 tablespoon salt
- 7/8 cup water.

For the topping:

- Olive oil Poppy seeds

Direction: PREP: 10 MINUTES /MAKES 12 SLICES

- ✓ Preparing the Ingredients Add water first, then add the dry ingredients to the bread machine, reserving yeast.
- ✓ Make a well in the center of the dry ingredients and add the yeast.
- ✓ Select the Bake Cycle Choose French cycle, light crust color, and push Start.
- ✓ When bread is finished, coat the top of loaf with a little olive oil and lightly sprinkle with poppy seeds.
- ✓ Allow to cool slightly and serve warm with extra olive oil for dipping.

587) English muffin Bread

Ingredients:

- 12 slice bread (1½ pounds)
- 1¼ cups buttermilk, at 80°F to 90°F
- 1½ tablespoons melted butter, cooled
- 1½ tablespoons sugar
- 1⅛ teaspoons salt
- ⅓ teaspoon baking powder
- 2⅔ cups white bread flour
- 1⅔ teaspoons bread machine or instant yeast

Direction: PREP: 10 MINUTES /MAKES 1 LOAF

- ✓ *Preparing the Ingredients. Put the ingredients in your bread maker according to the manufacturer's instructions.*
- ✓ *Select the Bake Cycle Close the lid, Turn on the bread maker.*
- ✓ *Select the White / Basic setting, then select the dough size, select light or medium crust.*
- ✓ *Press start to start the cycle.*
- ✓ *When this is done, and the bread is baked, remove the pan from the machine.*
- ✓ *Let stand a few minutes.*
- ✓ *Remove the bread from the skillet and leave it on a wire rack to cool for at least 10 minutes.*
- ✓ *Slice and serve.*

588) **Golden Raisin Bread**

Ingredients:

- 8 slice bread (pounds)
- ¾ cup milk, at 80°F to 90°F
- 1 tablespoon melted butter, cooled
- ¼ cup molasses
- 1 tablespoon sugar
- ¾ teaspoon salt
- 2 cups white bread flour
- 1 teaspoon bread machine or instant yeast
- ½ cup golden raisins
- 12 slice bread (1½ pounds)
- 1⅛ cups milk, at 80°F to 90°F
- 1½ tablespoons melted butter, cooled

Direction: PREP: 10 MINUTES /MAKES 1 LOAF

- ✓ *Preparing the Ingredients. Place the ingredients, except the raisins, in your bread machine as recommended by the manufacturer.*
- ✓ *Select the Bake Cycle Program the machine for Basic/White or Sweet bread, select light or medium crust, and press Start.*
- ✓ *Add the raisins at the raisin/nut signal.*
- ✓ *When the loaf is done, remove the bucket from the machine.*
- ✓ *Let the loaf cool for 5 minutes.*
- ✓ *Gently shake the bucket to remove the loaf, and turn it out onto a rack to cool.*

589) **Multigrain Honey Bread**

Ingredients:

- 12 slice bread (1½ pounds)
- 1⅛ cups lukewarm milk
- 2¼ tablespoons unsalted butter, melted
- 3 tablespoons sugar
- 1½ teaspoons table salt
- ⅓ cup wheat bran
- 1½ tablespoons honey
- 1⅛ cups multigrain flour
- 2 cups white bread flour

- 1⅛ cups lukewarm water
- 2 tablespoons unsalted butter, melted

Direction: PREP: 10 MINUTES /MAKES 1 LOAF

- ✓ *Preparing the Ingredients Choose the size of bread to prepare.*
- ✓ *Measure and add the ingredients to the pan in the order as indicated in the ingredient listing.*
- ✓ *Place the pan in the bread machine and close the lid.*
- ✓ *Select the Bake Cycle Close the lid, Turn on the bread maker.*
- ✓ *Select the White / Basic setting, then select the dough size and crust color.*
- ✓ *Press start to start the cycle.*
- ✓ *When this is done, and the bread is baked, remove the pan from the machine.*
- ✓ *Let stand a few minutes.*
- ✓ *Remove the bread from the skillet and leave it on a wire rack to cool for at least 10 minutes.*
- ✓ *Slice and serve.*

590) **Golden Corn Bread**

Ingredients:

- 12 to 16 slices bread (1½ to 2 pounds)
- 1 cup buttermilk, at 80°F to 90°F
- ¼ cup melted butter, cooled
- 2 eggs, at room temperature
- 1⅓ cups all-purpose flour
- 1 cup cornmeal
- ¼ cup sugar
- 2¼ cups whole-wheat bread flour
- 1½ teaspoons bread machine yeast

Direction: PREP: 10 MINUTES /MAKES 1 LOAF

- ✓ *Preparing the Ingredients. Place the buttermilk, butter, and eggs in your bread machine as recommended by the manufacturer.*
- ✓ *Select the Bake Cycle Program the machine for Quick/Rapid bread and press Start.*
- ✓ *While the wet ingredients are mixing, stir together the flour, cornmeal, sugar, baking powder, and salt in a small bowl.*
- ✓ *After the first fast mixing is done and the machine signals, add the dry ingredients.*
- ✓ *When the loaf is done, remove the bucket from the machine.*
- ✓ *Let the loaf cool for 5 minutes.*
- ✓ *Gently shake the bucket to remove the loaf, and turn it out onto a rack to cool.*

591) **Classic Dark Bread**

Ingredients:

- 12 slice bread (1½ pounds)
- 1 cup lukewarm water
- 1½ tablespoons unsalted butter, melted
- ⅓ cup molasses
- ⅓ teaspoon table salt
- ¾ cup rye flour

- 2 cups white bread flour
- 2¼ cups whole-wheat bread flour
- 1½ tablespoons unsweetened cocoa powder
- Pinch ground nutmeg
- 1⅔ teaspoons bread machine yeast
  Direction: PREP: 10 MINUTES /MAKES 1 LOAF

✓ Preparing the Ingredients. Choose the size of bread to prepare.

✓ Measure and add the ingredients to the pan in the order as indicated in the ingredient listing.

✓ Place the pan in the bread machine and close the lid.

✓ Select the Bake Cycle Close the lid, Turn on the bread maker.

✓ Select the White / Basic setting, then select the dough size and crust color.
Press start to start the cycle.

✓ When this is done, and the bread is baked, remove the pan from the machine.

✓ Let stand a few minutes.

✓ Remove the bread from the skillet and leave it on a wire rack to cool for at least 10 minutes.

✓ Slice and serve.

592) **Classic Corn Bread**

Ingredients:

- 12 slice bread (1½ pounds)
- 1 cup lukewarm buttermilk
- ¼ cup unsalted butter, melted
- 2 eggs, at room temperature
- ¼ cup sugar
- 1 teaspoon table salt
- 1⅓ cups all-purpose flour
- 1 cup cornmeal
- 1 tablespoon baking powder
  Direction: PREP: 10 MINUTES /MAKES 1 LOAF

✓ Preparing the Ingredients. Choose the size of bread to prepare.

✓ Measure and add the ingredients to the pan in the order as indicated in the ingredient listing.

✓ Place the pan in the bread machine and close the lid. Select the Bake Cycle Close the lid, Turn on the bread maker.

✓ Select the White / Basic setting, then select the dough size, select light or medium crust.

✓ Press start to start the cycle. When this is done, and the bread is baked, remove the pan from the machine.

✓ Let stand a few minutes.

✓ Remove the bread from the skillet and leave it on a wire rack to cool for at least 10 minutes.

✓ Slice and serve.

593) **Basic Seed Bread**

Ingredients:

- 12 slice bread (1½ pounds)
- 1⅛ cups lukewarm water

- 1½ tablespoons unsalted butter, melted
- 1½ tablespoons sugar
- 1⅛ teaspoons table salt
- 2½ cups white bread flour
- ¾ cup ground chia seeds
- 2 tablespoons sesame seeds
- 1½ teaspoons bread machine yeast
  Direction: PREP: 10 MINUTES /MAKES 1 LOAF

✓ Preparing the Ingredients. Choose the size of bread to prepare.

✓ Measure and add the ingredients to the pan in the order as indicated in the ingredient listing.

✓ Place the pan in the bread machine and close the lid.

✓ Select the Bake Cycle Close the lid, Turn on the bread maker.

✓ Select the White / Basic setting, then select the dough size, select light or medium crust.

✓ Press start to start the cycle.

✓ When this is done, and the bread is baked, remove the pan from the machine.

✓ Let stand a few minutes.

✓ Remove the bread from the skillet and leave it on a wire rack to cool for at least 10 minutes.

✓ Slice and serve.

594) **Double-Chocolate Zucchini Bread**

Ingredients:

- 225 grams grated zucchini
- 125 grams All-Purpose Flour Blend
- 50 grams all-natural unsweetened cocoa powder (not Dutch-process)
- 1 teaspoon xanthan gum
- ¾ teaspoon baking soda
- ¼ teaspoon baking powder
- ¼ teaspoon salt
- ½ teaspoon ground espresso
- 135 grams' chocolate chips or nondairy alternative
- 100 grams' cane sugar or granulated sugar
- 2 large eggs
- ¼ cup avocado oil or canola oil
- 60 grams' vanilla Greek yogurt or nondairy alternative
- 1 teaspoon vanilla extract.
  Direction: PREP: 10 MINUTES /MAKES 1 LOAF

✓ Preparing the Ingredients. Measure and add the ingredients to the pan in the order mentioned above.

✓ Place the pan in the bread machine and close the lid.

✓ Select the Bake Cycle Turn on the bread maker.

✓ Select the White / Basic setting, then select the dough size, select light or medium crust.

✓ Press start to start the cycle.

✓ When this is done, and the bread is baked, remove the pan from the machine.

✓ Let stand a few minutes.

✓ Remove the bread from the skillet and leave it on a

- wire rack to cool for at least 15 minutes.
- ✓ Store leftovers in an airtight container at room temperature for up to 5 days, or freeze to enjoy a slice whenever you desire.
- ✓ Let each slice thaw naturally

595) *Basic Bulgur Bread*

Ingredients:

- 16 slice bread (2 pounds)
- ½ cup lukewarm water
- ½ cup bulgur wheat
- 1⅓ cups lukewarm milk
- 1⅓ tablespoons unsalted butter, melted
- 1⅓ tablespoons sugar
- 1 teaspoon table salt
- 4 cups bread flour
- 3 cups whole-wheat bread flour
- 2 teaspoons bread machine yeast

Direction: PREP: 10 MINUTES /MAKES 1 LOAF

- ✓ Preparing the Ingredients. Measure and add the ingredients to the pan in the order mentioned above.
- ✓ Place the pan in the bread machine and close the lid.
- ✓ Select the Bake Cycle Close the lid, Turn on the bread maker.
- ✓ Select the White / Basic setting, then select the dough size, select light or medium crust.
- ✓ Press start to start the cycle.
- ✓ When this is done, and the bread is baked, remove the pan from the machine.
- ✓ Let stand a few minutes.
- ✓ Remove the bread from the skillet and leave it on a wire rack to cool for at least 10 minutes.
- ✓ Slice and serve.

596) *Oat Quinoa Bread*

Ingredients:

- 12 slice bread (1½ pounds)
- 1 cup lukewarm milk
- ⅔ cup cooked quinoa, cooled
- ¼ cup unsalted butter, melted
- 1 tablespoon sugar
- 1 teaspoon table salt
- 1½ cups white bread flour
- ¼ cup quick oats
- ¾ cup whole-wheat flour
- 1½ teaspoons bread machine yeast

Direction: PREP: 10 MINUTES /MAKES 1 LOAF

- ✓ Preparing the Ingredients. Measure and add the ingredients to the pan in the order mentioned above.
- ✓ Place the pan in the bread machine and close the lid.
- ✓ Select the Bake Cycle Close the lid, Turn on the bread maker.
- ✓ Select the White / Basic setting, then select the dough size, select light or medium crust.

- ✓ Press start to start the cycle.
- ✓ When this is done, and the bread is baked, remove the pan from the machine.
- ✓ Let stand a few minutes.
- ✓ Remove the bread from the skillet and leave it on a wire rack to cool for at least 10 minutes.
- ✓ Slice and serve.

597) *Whole Wheat Sunflower Bread*

Ingredients:

- 12 slice bread (1½ pounds)
- 1 cup lukewarm water
- 1½ tablespoons honey
- 1½ tablespoons unsalted butter, melted
- ¾ teaspoon table salt
- 2½ cups whole-wheat flour
- ¾ cup white bread flour
- 1 tablespoon sesame seeds
- 3 tablespoons raw sunflower seeds
- 1½ teaspoons bread machine yeast

Direction: PREP: 10 MINUTES /MAKES 1 LOAF

- ✓ Preparing the Ingredients. Measure and add the ingredients to the pan in the order mentioned above.
- ✓ Place the pan in the bread machine and close the lid.
- ✓ Select the Bake Cycle Close the lid, Turn on the bread maker.
- ✓ Select the White / Basic setting, then select the dough size, select light or medium crust. Press start to start the cycle.
- ✓ When this is done, and the bread is baked, remove the pan from the machine.
- ✓ Let stand a few minutes.
- ✓ Remove the bread from the pan and leave it on a wire rack to cool for at least 10 minutes.
- ✓ Slice and serve.

598) *Honey Sunflower Bread*

Ingredients:

- 12 slice bread (1½ pounds)
- 1 cup lukewarm water
- 1 egg, at room temperature
- 3 tablespoons unsalted butter, melted
- 3 tablespoons skim milk powder
- 1½ tablespoons honey
- 1½ teaspoons table salt
- 3 cups white bread flour
- 1 teaspoon bread machine yeast
- ¾ cup raw sunflower seeds

Direction: PREP: 10 MINUTES /MAKES 1 LOAF

- ✓ Preparing the Ingredients. Measure and add the ingredients to the pan in the order mentioned above.
- ✓ Place the pan in the bread machine and close the lid.
- ✓ Select the Bake Cycle Close the lid, Turn on the bread maker.

- ✓ Select the White / Basic setting, then select the dough size, select light or medium crust.
- ✓ Press start to start the cycle.
- ✓ When this is done, and the bread is baked, remove the pan from the machine.
- ✓ Let stand a few minutes.
- ✓ Remove the bread from the pan and leave it on a wire rack to cool for at least 10 minutes.
- ✓ Slice and serve.

599)   *Flaxseed Milk Bread*

Ingredients:

- • 16 slice bread (2 pounds)
- • 1½ cups lukewarm milk
- • 2 tablespoons unsalted butter, melted
- • 2 tablespoons honey
- • 2 teaspoons table salt
- • 4 cups white bread flour
- • ½ cup flaxseed
- • 1½ teaspoons bread machine yeast

Direction: PREP: 10 MINUTES /MAKES 1 LOAF

- ✓ Preparing the Ingredients. Measure and add the ingredients to the pan in the order mentioned above.
- ✓ Place the pan in the bread machine and close the lid.
- ✓ Select the Bake Cycle Close the lid, Turn on the bread maker.
- ✓ Select the White / Basic setting, then select the dough size, select light or medium crust. Press start to start the cycle.
- ✓ When this is done, and the bread is baked, remove the pan from the machine.
- ✓ Let stand a few minutes.
- ✓ Remove the bread from the pan and leave it on a wire rack to cool for at least 10 minutes.
- ✓ Slice and serve.

600)   *Honey Wheat Bread Recipe 2*

Ingredients:

- • 16 slice bread (2 pounds)
- • 1⅔ cups boiling water
- • ¼ cup + 4 teaspoons cracked wheat
- • ¼ cup unsalted butter, melted
- • 3 tablespoons honey
- • 1½ teaspoons table salt
- • 1 cup whole-wheat flour
- • 2 cups white bread flour
- • 2 teaspoons bread machine yeast

Direction: Serving: 12 | Prep Time: 50 minutes

- ✓ Preparing the Ingredients. Measure and add the ingredients to the pan in the order mentioned above.
- ✓ Add the boiling water and cracked wheat to the bread pan; set aside for 25–30 minutes for the wheat to soften.
- ✓ Place the pan in the bread machine and close the lid.
- ✓ Select the Bake Cycle Close the lid, Turn on the bread

maker. Select the White / Basic setting, then select the dough size, select light or medium crust.

- ✓ Press start to start the cycle. When this is done, and the bread is baked, remove the pan from the machine.
- ✓ Let stand a few minutes.
- ✓ Remove the bread from the pan and leave it on a wire rack to cool for at least 10 minutes.
- ✓ Slice and serve.

601)   *Bagels*

Ingredients:

- • 1 cup warm water
- • 1 1/2 teaspoons salt
- • 2 tablespoons sugar
- • 3 cups bread flour
- • 2 1/4 teaspoons active dry yeast
- • 3 quarts boiling water
- • 3 tablespoons white sugar
- • 1 tablespoon cornmeal
- • 1 egg white Flour, for surface

Direction: PREP: 10 MINUTES /MAKES 9

- ✓ Preparing the Ingredients Place in the bread machine pan in the following order: warm water, salt, sugar, and flour.
- ✓ Make a well in the center of the dry ingredients and add the yeast.
- ✓ Select the Bake cycle, Select Dough cycle and press Start.
- ✓ When Dough cycle is complete, remove pan and let dough rest on a lightly floured surface.
- ✓ Stir 3 tablespoons of sugar into the boiling water.
- ✓ Cut dough into 9 equal pieces and roll each piece into a small ball.
- ✓ Flatten each ball with the palm of your hand.
- ✓ Poke a hole in the middle of each using your thumb.
- ✓ Twirl the dough on your finger to make the hole bigger, while evening out the dough around the hole. Sprinkle an ungreased baking sheet with 1 teaspoon cornmeal.
  Place the bagel on the baking sheet and repeat until all bagels are formed.
- ✓ Cover the shaped bagels with a clean kitchen towel and let rise for 10 minutes.
- ✓ Preheat an oven to 375°F.
- ✓ Carefully transfer the bagels, one by one, to the boiling water.
- ✓ Boil for 1 minute, turning halfway.
- ✓ Drain on a clean towel. Arrange boiled bagels on the baking sheet.
- ✓ Glaze the tops with egg white and sprinkle any toppings you desire.
- ✓ Bake for 20 to 25 minutes or until golden brown.
- ✓ Let cool on a wire rack before serving.

602) *50/50 Bread*

- *1 Pound loaf*
- *½ cup Lukewarm water*
- *½ tbsp. Honey*
- *1 tbsp. Unsalted butter, diced*
- *¾ cup Plain bread flour*
- *¾ cup Whole wheat flour*
- *¾ tbsp. Brown sugar*
- *¾ tbsp. Powdered milk*
- *¾ tsp Salt*

Direction: PREP: 15 MINUTES /MAKES 12 SLICES

- ✓ *Preparing the Ingredients Add the ingredients into the bread machine as per the order of the ingredients listed above or follow your bread machine's instruction manual.*
- ✓ *Select the Bake cycle Select the whole-wheat setting and medium crust function.*
- ✓ *When ready, turn the bread out onto a drying rack*
- ✓ *and allow it to cool, then serve.*

Sourdough Breads

603) Simple Sourdough Starter

Ingredients:

- 2½ teaspoons active dry yeast
- 2 cups water, at 100°F to 110°F
- 2 cups all-purpose flour

Direction: PREP: 10 MINUTES PLUS FERMENTING TIME MAKES 2 CUPS (32 SERVINGS)

- ✓ Preparing the Ingredients. In a large nonmetallic bowl, stir together the yeast, water, and flour.
- ✓ Cover the bowl loosely and place it in a warm place to ferment for 4 to 8 days, stirring several times per day.
- ✓ Select the Bake Cycle When the starter is bubbly and has a pleasant sour smell, it is ready to use.
- ✓ Store the starter covered in the refrigerator until you wish to use it.

604) No-Yeast Sourdough Starter

Ingredients:

- 2 cups all-purpose flour
- 2 cups chlorine-free bottled water, at room temperature

Direction: PREP: 10 MINUTES PLUS FERMENTING TIME MAKES 4CUPS

- ✓ Preparing the Ingredients. Stir together the flour and water in a large glass bowl with a wooden spoon.
- ✓ Loosely cover the bowl with plastic wrap and place it in a warm area for 3 to 4 days, stirring at least twice a day, or until bubbly.
- ✓ Select the Bake Cycle Store the starter in the refrigerator in a covered glass jar, and stir it before using.
- ✓ Replenish your starter by adding back the same amount you removed, in equal parts flour and water.

605) Classic Sourdough Bread

Ingredients:

- 2 tablespoons lukewarm water
- 2 cups sourdough starter
- 2 tablespoons unsalted butter, melted
- 2 teaspoons sugar
- 1½ teaspoons salt
- 2½ cups white bread flour
- 1½ teaspoons bread machine yeast
- Sourdough Starter
- 2 cups lukewarm water
- 2 cups all- purpose flour
- 2½ teaspoons bread machine yeast

Direction: PREP: 10MINUTES PLUS FERMENTING TIME MAKES 1 LOAF12 SLICE BREAD (1½ pounds)

- ✓ Preparing the Ingredients. Add the water, flour, and yeast to a medium-size nonmetallic bowl.
- ✓ Mix well until no lumps are visible. Cover the bowl loosely and leave it in a warm area of your kitchen for 5–8 days.
- ✓ Do not place in a fridge or under direct sunlight.

- ✓ Stir the mixture several times every day.
- ✓ Always put the cover back on the bowl afterward.
- ✓ The starter is ready to use when it appears bubbly and has a sour smell.
- ✓ Select the Bake Cycle Measure out the ingredients for the loaf size you want to bake.
- ✓ In the sequence stated above, add the ingredients to the bread pan.
- ✓ Closing the bread machine's lid after placing the pan inside is sufficient.
- ✓ Start the bread machine. " Select the White/Basic setting, then the loaf size, and finally the crust color, to get the desired result.
- ✓ Begin the process. Carefully remove the pan from the machine once the cycle has done and the bread has been baked.
- ✓ Use a potholder to protect your hands from the handle's heat.
- ✓ Let it cool down for a while.
- ✓ At least 10 minutes before slicing, remove the bread from the pan and place it on a cooling rack.

606) Potica

Ingredients:

- Bread dough
- ½ cup milk
- ¼ cup cold butter, cut into small pieces
- 1 egg
- 2 cups bread flour
- ¼ cup sugar
- ¼ teaspoon salt
- 1 teaspoon bread machine yeast or fast-acting dry yeast filling
- 2 cups finely chopped or ground walnuts (about 7 oz)
- 1/3 cup honey
- 1/3 cup milk
- 3 tablespoons sugar
- 1 egg white, beaten

Direction: PREP: 20 MINUTES/ MAKES 10 SERVINGS

- ✓ Preparing the Ingredients. Measure carefully, placing all bread dough ingredients in bread machine pan in the order recommended by the manufacturer.
- ✓ Select the Bake Cycle Select Dough/Manual cycle.
- ✓ Do not use delay cycle.
- ✓ Remove dough from pan, using lightly floured hands.
- ✓ Cover and let rest 10 minutes on lightly floured surface.
- ✓ In small saucepan, combine all filling ingredients except egg white.
- ✓ Bring to a boil over medium heat, stirring frequently.
- ✓ Reduce heat; simmer uncovered 5 minutes, stirring occasionally.
- ✓ Spread in shallow dish; cover and refrigerate until chilled.
- ✓ Grease large cookie sheet with shortening.

- ✓ Roll dough into 16×12-inch rectangle on lightly floured surface.
- ✓ Spread filling over dough to within ½ inch of edges.
- ✓ Starting with 16-inch side, roll up tightly; pinch seam to seal.
- ✓ Stretch and shape roll until even. Coil roll of dough to form a snail shape.
- ✓ Place on cookie sheet. Cover and let rise in warm place 30 to 60 minutes or until doubled in size.
- ✓ Dough is ready if indentation remains when touched. Heat oven to 325°F.
- ✓ Brush egg white over dough. Bake 45 to 55 minutes or until golden brown.
- ✓ Remove from cookie sheet to cooling rack.

607) Lemon Sourdough Bread

Ingredients:

- 12 slice bread (1½ pounds)
- ¾ cup Simple Sourdough Starter (here) or No-Yeast Sourdough Starter (here), fed, active, and at room temperature
- ¾ cup water, at 80°F to 90°F
- 1 egg, at room temperature
- 3 tablespoons butter, melted and cooled
- ⅓ cup honey
- 1½ teaspoons salt
- 2 teaspoons lemon zest
- 1½ teaspoons lime zest
- ⅓ cup wheat germ
- 3 cups white bread flour
- 1¾ teaspoons bread machine or instant yeast

Direction: PREP: 10 MINUTES /MAKES 1 LOAF

- ✓ Preparing the Ingredients. Choose the size of loaf of your preference and then measure the ingredients.
- ✓ Add all of the ingredients mentioned previously in the list, close the lid after placing the pan in the bread machine Select the Bake cycle. Turn on the bread machine.
- ✓ Select the Whole-Wheat/Whole-Grain bread setting, select the loaf size, select light or medium crust.
- ✓ Press start.
- ✓ When the breadmaker cycle is complete, carefully remove the pan from the machine and allow it to cool before serving.
- ✓ Remove the bread from the pan, put in a wire rack to cool for at least 10 minutes, and slice.

608) Pecan Apple Spice Bread

Ingredients:

- 12 slice bread (1½ pounds)
- ⅓ cup lukewarm water
- 2¼ tablespoons canola oil
- ¾ teaspoon apple cider vinegar
- 2¼ tablespoons light brown sugar, packed
- ¾ cup Granny Smith apples, grated
- 2 eggs, room temperature, slightly beaten

- ½ cup nonfat dry milk powder
- ½ cup brown rice flour
- ½ cup tapioca flour
- ½ cup millet flour
- ⅓ cup corn starch
- 1½ tablespoons apple pie spice
- ¾ tablespoon xanthan gum
- ¾ teaspoon table salt
- 1¼ teaspoons bread machine yeast
- ⅓ cup pecans, chopped

Direction: PREP: 10 MINUTES /MAKES 1 LOAF

- ✓ Preparing the Ingredients. Choose the size of loaf of your preference and then measure the ingredients.
- ✓ Add all of the ingredients mentioned previously in the list, close the lid after placing the pan in the bread machine.
- ✓ Select the Bake Cycle Turn on the bread machine.
- ✓ Select the White/Basic setting, select the loaf size, and the crust color. Press start.
- ✓ When the cycle is finished, carefully remove the pan from the bread maker and let rest.
- ✓ When the machine signals to add ingredients, add the chopped pecans.
- ✓ Remove the bread from the pan, put in a wire rack to cool for at least 10 minutes, and slice.

609) No-Yeast Whole-Wheat Sourdough Starter

Ingredients:

- 1 cup whole-wheat flour, divided
- ½ teaspoon honey
- 1 cup chlorine-free bottled water, at room temperature, divided

Direction: PREP: 10 MINUTES PLUS FERMENTING TIME MAKES 2 CUPS (32 SERVINGS)

- ✓ Preparing the Ingredients. Stir together ½ cup of flour, ½ cup of water, and the honey in a large glass bowl with a wooden spoon.
- ✓ Loosely cover the bowl with plastic wrap and place it in a warm area for 5 days, stirring at least twice a day.
- ✓ After 5 days, stir in the remaining ½ cup of flour and ½ cup of water.
- ✓ Select the Bake Cycle Cover the bowl loosely again with plastic wrap and place it in a warm area.
- ✓ When the starter has bubbles and foam on top, it is ready to use.
- ✓ Store the starter in the refrigerator in a covered glass jar, and stir it before using.
- ✓ If you use half, replenish the starter with ½ cup flour and ½ cup water

610) Pumpkin Jalapeno Bread

Ingredients:

- 12 slice bread (1½ pounds)
- ½ cup lukewarm water

- *2 medium eggs, beaten*
- *⅓ cup pumpkin puree*
- *2¼ tablespoons honey*
- *1½ tablespoons vegetable oil*
- *¾ teaspoon apple cider vinegar*
- *1½ teaspoons sugar*
- *¾ teaspoon table salt*
- *½ cup brown rice flour*
- *½ cup tapioca flour*
- *⅓ cup corn starch*
- *⅓ cup yellow cornmeal*
- *¾ tablespoon xanthan gum*
- *1 small jalapeno pepper, seeded and deveined*
- *1½ teaspoons crushed red pepper flakes*
- *1¼ teaspoons bread machine yeast*

Direction: PREP: 10 MINUTES /MAKES 1 LOAF

- ✓ *Preparing the Ingredients. Choose the size of loaf of your preference and then measure the ingredients.*
- ✓ *Add all of the ingredients mentioned previously in the list, close the lid after placing the pan in the bread machine.*
- ✓ *Select the Bake Cycle Turn on the bread machine.*
- ✓ *Select the White/Basic setting, select the loaf size, and the crust color.*
- ✓ *Press start. When the cycle is finished, carefully remove the pan from the bread maker and let rest.*
- ✓ *When the machine signals to add ingredients, add the chopped pecans.*
- ✓ *Remove the bread from the pan, put in a wire rack to cool for at least 10 minutes, and slice.*

611) **Basic Sourdough Bread**

Ingredients:

- *12 slice bread (1½ pounds)*
- *2 cups Simple Sourdough Starter (here), fed, active, and at room temperature*
- *2 tablespoons water, at 80°F to 90°F*
- *¾ teaspoon apple cider vinegar*
- *1⅓ teaspoons sugar*
- *1 teaspoon salt*
- *1⅔ cups white bread flour*
- *½ cup nonfat dry milk powder*
- *1 teaspoon bread machine or instant yeast*

Direction: PREP: 10 MINUTES /MAKES 1 LOAF

- ✓ *Preparing the Ingredients. Choose the size of loaf of your preference and then measure the ingredients.*
- ✓ *Add all of the ingredients mentioned previously in the list, close the lid after placing the pan in the bread machine.*
- ✓ *Select the Bake Cycle Turn on the bread machine.*
- ✓ *Select the White/Basic setting, select the loaf size, and the crust color.*
- ✓ *Press start. When the cycle is finished, carefully remove the pan from the bread maker and let rest.*
- ✓ *When the machine signals to add ingredients, add the*

chopped pecans.
- ✓ *Remove the bread from the pan, put in a wire rack to cool for at least 5 minutes, and slice.*

612) **Walnut Banana Bread**

Ingredients:

- *12 slice bread (1½ pounds)*
- *⅓ cup lukewarm water*
- *2 tablespoons canola oil*
- *¾ teaspoon apple cider vinegar*
- *2 eggs, beaten*
- *1½ small bananas, mashed*
- *¾ teaspoon table salt*
- *½ cup brown rice flour*
- *½ cup white rice flour*
- *½ cup amaranth flour*
- *⅓ cup corn starch*
- *¾ tablespoon xanthan gum*
- *¾ teaspoon cinnamon*
- *⅓ teaspoon nutmeg*
- *1½ teaspoons bread machine yeast*
- *¾ cup walnuts, chopped*

Direction: PREP: 10 MINUTES /MAKES 1 LOAF

- ✓ *Preparing the Ingredients. Choose the size of loaf of your preference and then measure the ingredients.*
- ✓ *Add all of the ingredients mentioned previously in the list, close the lid after placing the pan in the bread machine.*
- ✓ *Select the Bake Cycle Turn on the bread machine. Select the Quick/Rapid setting, select the loaf size, and the crust color.*
- ✓ *Press start. When the bread maker cycle is complete, carefully remove the pan from the machine and allow it to cool before serving.*
- ✓ *Remove the bread from the pan, put in a wire rack to cool for at least 10 minutes, and slice.*

613) **Whole-Wheat Sourdough Bread**

Ingredients:

- *12 slice bread (1½ pounds)*
- *¾ cup plus 2 tablespoons water, at 80°F to 90°F*
- *¾ cup plus 2 tablespoons No-Yeast Whole-Wheat Sourdough Starter (here), fed, active, and at room temperature*
- *2 tablespoons melted butter, cooled*
- *2 eggs, beaten*
- *1 tablespoon sugar*
- *1 teaspoon salt*
- *½ cup brown rice flour*
- *1½ teaspoons bread machine yeast*
- *¾ cup walnuts, chopped*

Direction: PREP: 10 MINUTES /MAKES 1 LOAF

- ✓ *Preparing the Ingredients. Choose the size of loaf of your preference and then measure the ingredients.*

- ✓ Add all of the ingredients mentioned previously in the list, close the lid after placing the pan in the bread machine.
- ✓ Select the Bake cycle Turn on the bread machine. Select the Wheat/Whole-Grain bread setting, select the loaf size, and the crust color.
- ✓ Press start.
- ✓ When the loaf is done, remove the bucket from the machine.
- ✓ Let the loaf cool for 5 minutes.
- ✓ Gently shake the bucket to remove the loaf, and turn it out onto a rack to cool.

614) _Multigrain Sourdough Bread_

Ingredients:

- 12 slice bread (1½ pounds)
- ⅔ cup water, at 80°F to 90°F
- ¾ cup Simple Sourdough Starter, fed, active, and at room temperature
- 2 tablespoons melted butter, cooled
- 2½ tablespoons sugar
- ¾ teaspoon salt
- ¾ cup multigrain cereal
- 2⅔ cups white bread flour
- 1½ teaspoons bread machine or instant yeast

Direction: PREP: 10 MINUTES /MAKES 1 LOAF

- ✓ Preparing the Ingredients. Choose the size of loaf of your preference and then measure the ingredients.
- ✓ Add all of the ingredients mentioned previously in the list, close the lid after placing the pan in the bread machine.
- ✓ Select the Bake Cycle Turn on the bread machine.
- ✓ Select the Wheat/Whole-Grain bread setting, select the loaf size, and the crust color.
- ✓ Press start.
- ✓ When the breadmaker cycle is complete, carefully remove the pan from the machine and allow it to cool before serving.
- ✓ Remove the bread from the pan, put in a wire rack to cool for at least 10 minutes, and slice.

615) _Faux Sourdough Bread_

Ingredients:

- 12 slice bread (1½ pounds)
- ¾ cup plus 1 tablespoon water, at 80°F to 90°F
- ⅓ cup sour cream, at room temperature
- 2¼ tablespoons melted butter, cooled
- 1½ tablespoons apple cider vinegar
- ¾ tablespoon sugar
- ¾ teaspoon salt
- 3 cups white bread flour
- 1 teaspoon bread machine or instant yeast

Direction: PREP: 10 MINUTES /MAKES 1 LOAF

- ✓ Preparing the Ingredients. Choose the size of loaf of your preference and then measure the ingredients.
- ✓ Add all of the ingredients mentioned previously in the

list, close the lid after placing the pan in the bread machine.

- ✓ Select the Bake Cycle Turn on the bread machine. Select the Wheat/Whole-Grain bread setting, select the loaf size, select medium crust color.
- ✓ Press start.
- ✓ When the bread maker cycle is complete, carefully remove the pan from the machine and allow it to cool before serving.
- ✓ Remove the bread from the pan, put in a wire rack to cool for at least 10 minutes, and slice.

616) _Sourdough Milk Bread_

Ingredients:

- 12 slice bread (1½ pounds)
- 1½ cups Simple Sourdough Starter (here) or No-Yeast Sourdough Starter (here), fed, active, and at room temperature
- ⅓ cup milk, at 80°F to 90°F
- 3 tablespoons olive oil
- 1½ tablespoons honey
- 1 teaspoon salt
- 3 cups white bread flour
- 1 teaspoon bread machine or instant yeast

Direction: PREP: 10 MINUTES /MAKES 1 LOAF

- ✓ Preparing the Ingredients. Choose the size of loaf of your preference and then measure the ingredients.
- ✓ Add all of the ingredients mentioned previously in the list, close the lid after placing the pan in the bread machine.
- ✓ Select the Bake Cycle Turn on the bread machine.
- ✓ Select the White/Basic setting, select the loaf size, and the crust color.
- ✓ Press start.
- ✓ When the breadmaker cycle is complete, carefully remove the pan from the machine and allow it to cool before serving.
- ✓ Remove the bread from the pan, put in a wire rack to cool for at least 10 minutes, and slice.

617) _Sourdough Beer Bread_

Ingredients:

- 12 slice bread (1½ pounds)
- 1 cup Simple Sourdough Starter (here) or No-Yeast Sourdough Starter (here), fed, active, and at room temperature
- ½ cup plus 1 tablespoon dark beer, at 80°F to 90°F
- 1½ tablespoons melted butter, cooled
- ¾ tablespoon sugar
- 1⅛ teaspoons salt
- 2⅔ cups white bread flour
- 1⅛ teaspoons bread machine or instant yeast

Direction: PREP: 10 MINUTES /MAKES 1 LOAF

- ✓ Preparing the Ingredients. Choose the size of loaf of your preference and then measure the ingredients.
- ✓ Add all of the ingredients mentioned previously in the

list, close the lid after placing the pan in the bread machine.

✓ Select the Bake Cycle Turn on the bread machine. Select the Wheat/Whole-Grain bread setting, select the loaf size, and the crust color.

✓ Press start.

✓ When the breadmaker cycle is complete, carefully remove the pan from the machine and allow it to cool before serving.

✓ Remove the bread from the pan, put in a wire rack to cool for at least 10 minutes, and slice.

618) San Francisco Sourdough Bread

Ingredients:

- 12 slice bread (1½ pounds)
- 1 cup plus 2 tablespoons Simple Sourdough Starter (here) or No-Yeast Sourdough Starter (here), fed, active, and at room temperature
- ½ cup plus 1 tablespoon water, at 80°F to 90°F
- 2¼ tablespoons olive oil
- 1½ teaspoons salt
- 2 tablespoons sugar
- 1½ tablespoons skim milk powder
- ⅓ cup whole-wheat flour
- 2⅔ cups white bread flour
- 1⅓ teaspoons bread machine or instant yeast

Direction: PREP: 10 MINUTES /MAKES 1 LOAF

✓ Preparing the Ingredients. Choose the size of loaf of your preference and then measure the ingredients.

✓ Add all of the ingredients mentioned previously in the list, close the lid after placing the pan in the bread machine.

✓ Select the Bake Cycle Turn on the bread machine. Select the White/Basic setting, select the loaf size, and the crust color.

✓ Press start.

✓ When the breadmaker cycle is complete, carefully remove the pan from the machine and allow it to cool before serving.

✓ Remove the bread from the pan, put in a wire rack to cool for at least 10 minutes, and slice.

619) Sourdough Cheddar Bread

Ingredients:

- 12 slice bread (1½ pounds)
- 1 cup Simple Sourdough Starter or No-Yeast Sourdough Starter, fed, active, and at room temperature
- ⅓ cup water, at 80°F to 90°F
- 4 teaspoons sugar
- 1 teaspoon salt
- ½ cup (2 ounces) grated aged Cheddar cheese
- ⅔ cup whole-wheat flour
- ¼ cup oat bran
- 1⅓ cups white bread flour

- 1½ teaspoons bread machine or instant yeast

Direction: PREP: 10 MINUTES /MAKES 1 LOAF

✓ Preparing the Ingredients. Choose the size of loaf of your preference and then measure the ingredients.

✓ Add all of the ingredients mentioned previously in the list, close the lid after placing the pan in the bread machine.

✓ Select the Bake Cycle Turn on the bread machine. Select the Wheat/Whole-Grain bread setting, select the loaf size, and the crust color.

✓ Press start.

✓ When the breadmaker cycle is complete, carefully remove the pan from the machine and allow it to cool before serving.

✓ Remove the bread from the pan, put in a wire rack to cool for at least 5 minutes, and slice.

620) Herb Sourdough

Ingredients:

- 8 slice bread (1 pound)
- 1⅓ cups No-Yeast Sourdough Starter, fed, active, and at room temperature
- 4 teaspoons water, at 80°F to 90°F
- 4 teaspoons melted butter, cooled
- 1⅓ teaspoons sugar
- 1 teaspoon salt
- 1 teaspoon chopped fresh basil
- 1 teaspoon chopped fresh oregano
- ½ teaspoon chopped fresh thyme
- 1⅔ cups white bread flour
- 1 teaspoon bread machine or instant yeast

Direction: PREP: 10 MINUTES /MAKES 1 LOAF

✓ Preparing the Ingredients. Choose the size of loaf of your preference and then measure the ingredients.

✓ Add all of the ingredients mentioned previously in the list, close the lid after placing the pan in the bread machine.

✓ Select the Bake Cycle Turn on the bread machine.

✓ Select the Wheat/Whole-Grain bread setting, select the loaf size, and the crust color.

✓ Press start.

✓ Remove the bread pan from the bread machine and allow it to cool before slicing.

✓ Remove the bread from the pan, put in a wire rack to cool for at least 5 minutes, and slice.

621) Cranberry Pecan Sourdough

Ingredients:

- 12 slice bread (1½ pounds)
- 2 cups No-Yeast Sourdough Starter (here), fed, active, and at room temperature
- 2 tablespoons water, at 80°F to 90°F
- 2 tablespoons melted butter, cooled
- 2 teaspoons sugar
- 1½ teaspoons salt
- ⅓ teaspoon ground cinnamon

- 2½ cups white bread flour
- 1½ teaspoons bread machine or instant yeast
- ⅓ cup dried cranberries
- ⅓ cup chopped pecans
  Direction: PREP: 10 MINUTES /MAKES 1 LOAF

✓ *Preparing the Ingredients. Choose the size of loaf of your preference and then measure the ingredients.*

✓ *Add all of the ingredients mentioned previously in the list, close the lid after placing the pan in the bread machine.*

✓ *Select the Bake Cycle Turn on the bread machine. Select the Wheat/Whole-Grain bread setting, select the loaf size, and the crust color.*

✓ *Press start.*

✓ *Remove the bread pan from the bread machine and allow it to cool before slicing.*

✓ *Remove the bread from the pan, put in a wire rack to cool for at least 5 minutes, and slice*

622) *Dark Chocolate Sourdough*

Ingredients:

- 12 slice bread (1½ pounds)
- 2 cups No-Yeast Sourdough Starter, fed, active, and at room temperature
- 2 tablespoons water, at 80°F to 90°F
- 2 tablespoons melted butter, cooled
- ¾ teaspoon pure vanilla extract
- 2 teaspoons sugar
- 1½ teaspoons salt
- ⅓ teaspoon ground cinnamon
- ¼ cup unsweetened cocoa powder
- 2½ cups white bread flour
- 1½ teaspoons bread machine or instant yeast
- ½ cup semisweet chocolate chips
- ⅓ cup chopped pistachios
- ⅓ cup raisins
  Direction: PREP: 10 MINUTES /MAKES 1 LOAF

✓ *Preparing the Ingredients. Choose the size of loaf of your preference and then measure the ingredients.*

✓ *Add all of the ingredients mentioned previously in the list, close the lid after placing the pan in the bread machine.*

✓ *Select the Bake Cycle Turn on the bread machine. Select the Wheat/Whole-Grain bread setting, select the loaf size, and the crust color. Press start.*

✓ *When the breadmaker cycle is complete, carefully remove the pan from the machine and allow it to cool before serving.*

✓ *Remove the bread from the pan, put in a wire rack to cool for at least 5 minutes, and slice*

Vegetable Bread

623) Beetroot Bread

Ingredients:

- 16 slice bread (1½ pounds)
- 1 cup lukewarm water
- 1 cup grated raw beetroot
- 2 tablespoons unsalted butter, melted
- 2 tablespoons sugar
- 2 teaspoons table salt
- 4 cups white bread flour
- 1⅔ teaspoons bread machine yeast

Direction: PREP: 10 MINUTES /MAKES 1 LOAF

- ✓ Preparing the Ingredients. Choose the size of loaf of your preference and then measure the ingredients.
- ✓ Add all of the ingredients mentioned previously in the list.
- ✓ Close the lid after placing the pan in the bread machine.
- ✓ Select the Bake Cycle Turn on the bread machine.
- ✓ Select the White/Basic setting, select the loaf size, and the crust color.
- ✓ Press start.
- ✓ When the breadmaker cycle is complete, carefully remove the pan from the machine and allow it to cool before serving.
- ✓ Remove the bread from the pan, put in a wire rack to Cool about 5 minutes.
- ✓ Slice.

624) Yeasted Carrot Bread

Ingredients:

- 12 slice bread (1½ pounds)
- ¾ cup milk, at 80°F to 90°F
- 3 tablespoons melted butter, cooled
- 1 tablespoon honey
- 1½ cups shredded carrot
- ¾ teaspoon ground nutmeg
- ½ teaspoon salt
- 3 cups white bread flour
- 2¼ teaspoons bread machine or active dry yeast

Direction: PREP: 10 MINUTES /MAKES 1 LOAF

- ✓ Preparing the Ingredients. Choose the size of loaf of your preference and then measure the ingredients.
- ✓ Add all of the ingredients mentioned previously in the list.
- ✓ Close the lid after placing the pan in the bread machine.
- ✓ Select the Bake Cycle Turn on the bread machine.
- ✓ Select the Quick/Rapid setting, select the loaf size, and the crust color.
- ✓ Press start.
- ✓ When the breadmaker cycle is complete, carefully remove the pan from the machine and allow it to cool before serving.
- ✓ Remove the bread from the pan, put in a wire rack to Cool about 5 minutes.
- ✓ Slice

625) Sauerkraut Rye Bread

Ingredients:

- 12 slice bread (1½ pounds)
- 1 cup water, at 80°F to 90°F
- 1½ tablespoons melted butter, cooled
- ⅓ cup molasses
- ½ cup drained sauerkraut
- ⅓ teaspoon salt
- 1½ tablespoons unsweetened cocoa powder
- Pinch ground nutmeg
- ¾ cup rye flour
- 2 cups white bread flour
- 1⅔ teaspoons bread machine or instant yeast

Direction: PREP: 10 MINUTES /MAKES 1 LOAF

- ✓ Preparing the Ingredients. Choose the size of loaf of your preference and then measure the ingredients.
- ✓ Add all of the ingredients mentioned previously in the list.
- ✓ Close the lid after placing the pan in the bread machine.
- ✓ Select the Bake Cycle Turn on the bread machine.
- ✓ Select the White/Basic setting, select the loaf size, and the crust color.
- ✓ Press start.
- ✓ When the breadmaker cycle is complete, carefully remove the pan from the machine and allow it to cool before serving.
- ✓ Remove the bread from the pan, put in a wire rack to Cool about 5 minutes.
- ✓ Slice

626) Garden Vegetable Bread

Ingredients:

- ½ cup warm buttermilk (70°F to 80°F)
- 3 tbsp. water (70°F to 80°F)
- 1 tbsp. canola oil
- ⅔ cup shredded zucchini
- ¼ cup chopped red sweet pepper
- 2 tbsp. chopped green onions
- 2 tbsp. grated parmesan cheese
- 2 tbsp. sugar
- 1 tsp salt
- ½ tsp lemon-pepper seasoning
- ½ cup old-fashioned oats
- 2½ cup bread flour
- 1½ tsp active dry yeast Peppercorns

Direction: PREP: 10 MINUTES /MAKES 14 SLICES

- ✓ Preparing the Ingredients. In the order and at the temperature specified by the maker of your bread machine, add each ingredient to the bread machine.
- ✓ Select the Bake Cycle Close the lid, select the basic bread, medium crust setting on your bread machine and press start.
- ✓ Take out the baked bread from the bread machine and allow it to cool on a cooling rack.

627) *Carrot Coriander Bread*

Ingredients:

- 2-3 freshly grated carrots,
- 1⅛ cup lukewarm water
- 2 tbsp. sunflower oil
- 4 tsp freshly chopped coriander
- 2½ cups unbleached white bread flour
- 2 tsp ground coriander
- 1 tsp salt
- 5 tsp sugar
- 4 tsp easy blend dried yeast

Direction: PREP: 10 MINUTES /MAKES 14 SLICES

- ✓ Preparing the Ingredients. In the order and at the temperature specified by the maker of your bread machine, add each ingredient to the bread machine.
- ✓ Select the Bake Cycle Close the lid, select the basic bread, medium crust setting on your bread machine, and press start.
- ✓ Take out the baked bread from the bread machine and allow it to cool on a cooling rack.

628) **Basil Tomato Bread**

Ingredients:

- 12 slice bread (1½ pounds)
- ¾ cup lukewarm tomato sauce
- ¾ tablespoon olive oil
- ¾ tablespoon sugar
- ¾ teaspoon table salt
- 2¼ cups white bread flour
- 1½ tablespoons dried basil
- ¾ tablespoon dried oregano
- 3 tablespoons grated Parmesan cheese
- 2 teaspoons bread machine yeast

Direction: PREP: 10 MINUTES /MAKES 1 LOAF

- ✓ Preparing the Ingredients. Choose the size of loaf of your preference and then measure the ingredients.
- ✓ Add all of the ingredients mentioned previously in the list.
- ✓ Close the lid after placing the pan in the bread machine.
- ✓ Select the Bake Cycle Turn on the bread machine.
- ✓ Select the White/Basic setting, select the loaf size, and the crust color.
- ✓ Press start.
- ✓ When the breadmaker cycle is complete, carefully remove the pan from the machine and allow it to cool before serving.
- ✓ Remove the bread from the pan, put in a wire rack to Cool about 5 minutes.
- ✓ Slice

629) **Savory Onion Bread**

Ingredients:

- 12 slice bread (1½ pounds)

- 1 cup water, at 80°F to 90°F
- 3 tablespoons melted butter, cooled
- 1½ tablespoons sugar
- 1⅛ teaspoons salt
- 3 tablespoons dried minced onion
- 1½ tablespoons chopped fresh chives
- 3 cups plus 2 tablespoons white bread flour
- 1⅔ teaspoons bread machine or instant yeast

Direction: PREP: 10 MINUTES /MAKES 1 LOAF

- ✓ Preparing the Ingredients. Put the ingredients in your bread maker according to the manufacturer's instructions.
- ✓ Select the Bake Cycle Turn on the bread machine.
- ✓ Select the White/Basic setting, select the loaf size, and the crust color.
- ✓ Press start.
- ✓ When the breadmaker cycle is complete, carefully remove the pan from the machine and allow it to cool before serving.
- ✓ Remove the bread from the pan, put in a wire rack to Cool about 5 minutes.
- ✓ Slice

630) **Zucchini Spice Bread**

Ingredients:

- 12 slice bread (1½ pounds)
- 2 eggs, at room temperature
- ½ cup unsalted butter, melted
- ½ teaspoon table salt
- ¾ cup shredded zucchini
- ½ cup light brown sugar
- 2 tablespoons sugar
- 1½ cups all-purpose flour
- ½ teaspoon baking powder
- ½ teaspoon baking soda
- ¼ teaspoon ground allspice
- 1 teaspoon ground cinnamon
- ½ cup chopped pecans

Direction: PREP: 10 MINUTES PLUS FERMENTING TIME /MAKES 1 LOAF

- ✓ Preparing the Ingredients. Choose the size of loaf of your preference and then measure the ingredients.
- ✓ Add all of the ingredients mentioned previously in the list.
- ✓ Close the lid after placing the pan in the bread machine.
- ✓ Select the Bake Cycle Turn on the bread machine.
- ✓ Select the Quick/Rapid setting, select the loaf size, and the crust color.
- ✓ Press start.
- ✓ When the breadmaker cycle is complete, carefully remove the pan from the machine and allow it to cool before serving.
- ✓ Remove the bread from the pan, put in a wire rack to Cool about 5 minutes.
- ✓ Slice

631) *Tomato Herb Bread*

Ingredients:

- 8 slice bread (1 pounds)
- ½ cup tomato sauce, at 80°F to 90°F
- ½ tablespoon olive oil
- ½ tablespoon sugar
- 1 tablespoon dried basil
- ½ tablespoon dried oregano
- ½ teaspoon salt
- 2 tablespoons grated Parmesan cheese
- 1½ cups white bread flour
- 1⅛ teaspoons bread machine or instant yeast

Direction: PREP: 10 MINUTES /MAKES 1 LOAF

✓ Preparing the Ingredients. Choose the size of loaf of your preference and then measure the ingredients.
✓ Add all of the ingredients mentioned previously in the list.
✓ Close the lid after placing the pan in the bread machine. Select the Bake Cycle Turn on the bread machine.
✓ Select the White/Basic setting, select the loaf size, and the crust color.
✓ Press start.
✓ When the breadmaker cycle is complete, carefully remove the pan from the machine and allow it to cool before serving.
✓ Remove the bread from the pan, put in a wire rack to Cool about 5 minutes.
✓ Slice

632) *Potato Honey Bread*

Ingredients:

- 12 slice bread (1½ pounds)
- ¾ cup lukewarm water
- ½ cup finely mashed potatoes, at room temperature
- 1 egg, at room temperature
- ¼ cup unsalted butter, melted
- 2 tablespoons honey
- 1 teaspoon table salt
- 3 cups white bread flour
- 2 teaspoons bread machine yeast

Direction: PREP: 10 MINUTES /MAKES 1 LOAF

✓ Preparing the Ingredients. Choose the size of loaf of your preference and then measure the ingredients.
✓ Add all of the ingredients mentioned previously in the list.
✓ Close the lid after placing the pan in the bread machine.
✓ Select the Bake Cycle Turn on the bread machine.
✓ Select the White/Basic setting, select the loaf size, and the crust color.
✓ Press start.
✓ When the breadmaker cycle is complete, carefully remove the pan from the machine and allow it to cool before serving.

✓ Remove the bread from the pan, put in a wire rack to Cool about 10 minutes. Slice

633) *Mashed Potato Bread*

Ingredients:

- 12 slice bread (1½ pounds)
- ¾ cup water, at 80°F to 90°F
- ½ cup finely mashed potatoes, at room temperature
- 1 egg, at room temperature
- ¼ cup melted butter, cooled
- 2 tablespoons honey
- 1 teaspoon salt
- 3 cups white bread flour
- 2 teaspoons bread machine or instant yeast

Direction: PREP: 10 MINUTES /MAKES 1 LOAF

✓ Preparing the Ingredients. Choose the size of loaf of your preference and then measure the ingredients.
✓ Add all of the ingredients mentioned previously in the list.
✓ Close the lid after placing the pan in the bread machine.
✓ Select the Bake Cycle Turn on the bread machine.
✓ Select the White/Basic setting, select the loaf size, and the crust color.
✓ Press start.
✓ When the breadmaker cycle is complete, carefully remove the pan from the machine and allow it to cool before serving.
✓ Remove the bread from the pan, put in a wire rack to Cool about 10 minutes.
✓ Slice

634) *Dilly Onion Bread*

Ingredients:

- ¾ cup water (70°F to 80°F)
- 1 tbsp. butter, softened
- 2 tbsp. sugar
- 3 tbsp. dried minced onion
- 2 tbsp. dried parsley flakes
- 1 tbsp. dill weed
- 1 tsp salt
- 1 garlic clove, minced
- 2 cups bread flour
- ⅓ cup whole wheat flour
- 1 tbsp. nonfat dry milk powder
- 2 tsp active dry yeast serving

Direction: PREP: 10 MINUTES /MAKES 14 SLICES

✓ Preparing the Ingredients. In the order and at the temperature specified by the maker of your bread machine, add each ingredient to the bread machine..
✓ Select the Bake Cycle Close the lid, select the basic bread, medium crust setting on your bread machine and press start.
✓ Take out the baked bread from the bread machine and allow it to cool on a cooling rack.

635) **_Onion Chive Bread_**

Ingredients:

- 12 slice bread (1½ pounds)
- 1 cup lukewarm water
- 3 tablespoons unsalted butter, melted
- 1½ tablespoons sugar
- 1⅛ teaspoons table salt
- 3⅛ cups white bread flour
- 3 tablespoons dried minced onion
- 1½ tablespoons fresh chives, chopped
- 1⅔ teaspoons bread machine yeast

Direction: PREP: 10 MINUTES /MAKES 1 LOAF

- ✓ Preparing the Ingredients. Choose the size of loaf of your preference and then measure the ingredients.
- ✓ Add all of the ingredients mentioned previously in the list.
- ✓ Close the lid after placing the pan in the bread machine.
- ✓ Select the Bake Cycle Turn on the bread machine.
- ✓ Select the White/Basic setting, select the loaf size, and the crust color.
- ✓ Press start.
- ✓ When the breadmaker cycle is complete, carefully remove the pan from the machine and allow it to cool before serving.
- ✓ Remove the bread from the pan, put in a wire rack to Cool about 10 minutes.
- ✓ Slice

636) **_Confetti Bread_**

Ingredients:

- 8 slice bread (1 pounds)
- ⅓ cup milk, at 80°F to 90°F
- 2 tablespoons water, at 80°F to 90°F
- 2 teaspoons melted butter, cooled
- ⅔ teaspoon white vinegar
- 4 teaspoons sugar
- ⅔ teaspoon salt
- 4 teaspoons grated Parmesan cheese
- ⅓ cup quick oats
- 1⅔ cups white bread flour
- 1 teaspoon bread machine or instant yeast
- ⅓ cup finely chopped zucchini
- ¼ cup finely chopped yellow bell pepper
- ¼ cup finely chopped red bell pepper
- 4 teaspoons chopped chives

Direction: PREP: 10 MINUTES /MAKES 1 LOAF

- ✓ Preparing the Ingredients. In accordance with the manufacturer's instructions, add all of the ingredients except the veggies to your bread machine.
- ✓ Choose the Bake Cycle Set the machine to Basic/White bread, choose between light or medium crust, then push Start.
- ✓ When the machine signals, add the chopped vegetables; if your machine has no signal, add the vegetables just before the second kneading is finished.
- ✓ When the breadmaker cycle is complete, carefully remove the pan from the machine and allow it to cool before serving.
- ✓ Remove the bread from the pan, put in a wire rack to Cool about 10 minutes. Slice

637) **_Honey Potato Flakes Bread_**

Ingredients:

- 12 slice bread (1½ pounds)
- 1¼ cups lukewarm milk
- 2 tablespoons unsalted butter, melted
- 1 tablespoon honey
- 1½ teaspoons table salt
- 3 cups white bread flour
- 1 teaspoon dried thyme
- ½ cup instant potato flakes 2 teaspoons bread machine yeast

Direction: PREP: 10 MINUTES /MAKES 1 LOAF

- ✓ Preparing the Ingredients. Choose the size of loaf of your preference and then measure the ingredients.
- ✓ Add all of the ingredients mentioned previously in the list.
- ✓ Close the lid after placing the pan in the bread machine.
- ✓ Select the Bake Cycle Turn on the bread machine.
- ✓ Select the White/Basic setting, select the loaf size, and the crust color.
- ✓ Press start. When the breadmaker cycle is complete, carefully remove the pan from the machine and allow it to cool before serving.
- ✓ Remove the bread from the pan, put in a wire rack to Cool about 10 minutes. Slice

638) **_Pretty Borscht Bread_**

Ingredients:

- 12 slice bread (1½ pounds)
- ¾ cups water, at 80°F to 90°F
- ¾ cup grated raw beetroot
- 1½ tablespoons melted butter, cooled
- 1½ tablespoons sugar
- 1¼ teaspoons salt
- 3 cups white bread flour
- 1¼ teaspoons bread machine or instant yeast

Direction: PREP: 10 MINUTES /MAKES 1 LOAF

- ✓ Preparing the Ingredients. Put the ingredients in your bread maker according to the manufacturer's instructions.
- ✓ Press Start after setting the machine to Basic/White bread and choose between a light or medium crust.
- ✓ Click on the Bake button. Remove the bucket from the machine after the loaf is done baking.
- ✓ Allow the loaf to cool for five minutes before serving.
- ✓ To remove the loaf, gently shake the bucket, and then turn it out onto a cooling rack.

639) Zucchini Lemon Bread

Ingredients:

- 12 slice bread (1½ pounds)
- ½ cup lukewarm milk
- ¾ cup finely shredded zucchini
- ¼ teaspoon lemon juice, at room temperature
- 1 tablespoon olive oil
- 1 tablespoon sugar
- 1 teaspoon table salt
- ¾ cup whole-wheat flour
- 1½ cups white bread flour
- ¾ cup quick oats
- 2¼ teaspoons bread machine yeast

Direction: PREP: 10 MINUTES /MAKES 1 LOAF

- ✓ Preparing the Ingredients. Choose the size of loaf of your preference and then measure the ingredients.
- ✓ Add all of the ingredients mentioned previously in the list.
- ✓ Close the lid after placing the pan in the bread machine.
- ✓ Select the Bake Cycle Turn on the bread machine.
- ✓ Select the White/Basic setting, select the loaf size, and the crust color.
- ✓ Press start.
- ✓ When the breadmaker cycle is complete, carefully remove the pan from the machine and allow it to cool before serving.
- ✓ Remove the bread from the pan, put in a wire rack to Cool about 10 minutes.
- ✓ Slice

640) Yeasted Pumpkin Bread

Ingredients:

- 8 slice bread (1 pounds)
- ⅓ cup milk, at 80°F to 90°F
- ⅔ cup canned pumpkin
- 2 tablespoons melted butter, cooled
- ⅔ teaspoon grated ginger
- 2¾ tablespoons sugar
- ½ teaspoon salt
- ⅔ teaspoon ground cinnamon
- ¼ teaspoon ground cloves
- 2 cups white bread flour
- 1⅛ teaspoons bread machine or instant yeast

Direction: PREP: 10 MINUTES /MAKES 1 LOAF

- ✓ Preparing the Ingredients. Choose the size of loaf of your preference and then measure the ingredients.
- ✓ Add all of the ingredients mentioned previously in the list.
- ✓ Close the lid after placing the pan in the bread machine.
- ✓ Select the Bake Cycle Turn on the bread machine.
- ✓ Select the White/Basic setting, select the loaf size, and the crust color.

- ✓ Press start.
- ✓ When the breadmaker cycle is complete, carefully remove the pan from the machine and allow it to cool before serving.
- ✓ Remove the bread from the pan, put in a wire rack to Cool about 10 minutes.
- ✓ Slice

641) Oatmeal Zucchini Bread

Ingredients:

- 8 slice bread (1 pounds)
- ⅓ cup milk, at 80°F to 90°F
- ½ cup finely shredded zucchini
- ¼ teaspoon freshly squeezed lemon juice, at room temperature
- 2 teaspoons olive oil
- 2 teaspoons sugar
- ⅔ teaspoon salt
- ½ cup quick oats
- ½ cup whole-wheat flour
- 1 cup white bread flour
- 1½ teaspoons bread machine or instant yeast

Direction: PREP: 10 MINUTES /MAKES 1 LOAF

- ✓ Preparing the Ingredients. Choose the size of loaf of your preference and then measure the ingredients.
- ✓ Add all of the ingredients mentioned previously in the list. Close the lid after placing the pan in the bread machine.
- ✓ Select the Bake Cycle Turn on the bread machine.
- ✓ Select the White/Basic setting, select the loaf size, and the crust color.
  Press start.
- ✓ When the breadmaker cycle is complete, carefully remove the pan from the machine and allow it to cool before serving. Remove the bread from the pan, put in a wire rack to Cool about 10 minutes.
- ✓ Slice

642) Hot Red Pepper Bread

Ingredients:

- 12 slice bread (1½ pounds)
- 1¼ cups milk, at 80°F to 90°F
- ¼ cup red pepper relish
- 2 tablespoons chopped roasted red pepper
- 3 tablespoons melted butter, cooled
- 3 tablespoons light brown sugar
- 1 teaspoon salt
- 3 cups white bread flour
- 1½ teaspoons bread machine or instant yeast

Direction: PREP: 10 MINUTES /MAKES 1 LOAF

- ✓ Preparing the Ingredients. Choose the size of loaf of your preference and then measure the ingredients.
- ✓ Add all of the ingredients mentioned previously in the list.
- ✓ Close the lid after placing the pan in the bread

- machine.
- ✓ Select the Bake Cycle Turn on the bread machine.
- ✓ Select the White/Basic setting, select the loaf size, and the crust color.
- ✓ Press start.
- ✓ When the breadmaker cycle is complete, carefully remove the pan from the machine and allow it to cool before serving.
- ✓ Remove the bread from the pan, put in a wire rack to Cool about 10 minutes.
- ✓ Slice

643) **French Onion Bread**

Ingredients:

- 12 slice bread (1½ pounds)
- 1¼ cups milk, at 80°F to 90°F
- ¼ cup melted butter, cooled
- 3 tablespoons light brown sugar
- 1 teaspoon salt
- 3 tablespoons dehydrated onion flakes
- 2 tablespoons chopped fresh chives
- 1 teaspoon garlic powder
- 3 cups white bread flour
- 1 teaspoon bread machine or instant yeast

Direction: PREP: 10 MINUTES /MAKES 1 LOAF

- ✓ Preparing the Ingredients. Choose the size of loaf of your preference and then measure the ingredients.
- ✓ Add all of the ingredients mentioned previously in the list.
- ✓ Close the lid after placing the pan in the bread machine.
- ✓ Select the Bake Cycle Turn on the bread machine. Select the White/Basic setting, select the loaf size, and the crust color.
- ✓ Press start.
- ✓ When the breadmaker cycle is complete, carefully remove the pan from the machine and allow it to cool before serving.
- ✓ Remove the bread from the pan, put in a wire rack to Cool about 5 minutes. Slice

644) **Golden Butternut Squash Raisin Bread**

Ingredients:

- 16 slice bread (2 pounds)
- 2 cups cooked mashed butternut squash, at room temperature
- 1 cup (2 sticks) butter, at room temperature
- 3 eggs, at room temperature
- 1 teaspoon pure vanilla extract
- 2 cups sugar
- ½ cup light brown sugar
- 3 cups all-purpose flour
- 1 teaspoon baking soda

- 1 teaspoon ground cinnamon
- ½ teaspoon ground cloves
- ½ teaspoon ground nutmeg
- ½ teaspoon salt
- ½ teaspoon baking powder
- ½ cup golden raisins

Direction: PREP: 10 MINUTES /MAKES 1 LOAF

- ✓ Preparing the Ingredients. In your bread machine, add the butternut squash, butter, eggs, vanilla, sugar, and brown sugar.
- ✓ Select the Bake Cycle and press Start to program the machine for Quick/Rapid bread.
- ✓ In a small bowl, whisk together the flour, baking soda, cinnamon, cloves, nutmeg, salt, and baking powder while the wet ingredients are combining. Add the dry ingredients and raisins when the initial quick mixing is complete and the machine signals.
- ✓ When the breadmaker cycle is complete, carefully remove the pan from the machine and allow it to cool before serving.
- ✓ Remove the bread from the pan, put in a wire rack to Cool about 5 minutes.
- ✓ Slice

645) **Sweet Potato Bread**

Ingredients:

- 12 to 16 slices (1½ to 2 pounds)
- 1½ cups mashed cooked sweet potato, at room temperature
- ¾ cup buttermilk, at room temperature
- ½ cup sugar
- ¼ cup melted butter, cooled
- 1 egg, at room temperature
- 1½ cups all-purpose flour
- 1 teaspoon ground cinnamon
- ½ teaspoon baking powder
- ½ teaspoon baking soda
- ¼ teaspoon ground cloves
- ¼ teaspoon salt

Direction: PREP: 10 MINUTES /MAKES 1 LOAF

- ✓ Preparing the Ingredients. Fill your bread machine halfway with sweet potato, buttermilk, sugar, butter, and egg.
- ✓ Select the Bake Cycle and press Start to program the machine to make Quick/Rapid bread.
- ✓ Combine the flour, cinnamon, baking powder, baking soda, cloves, and salt in a small basin while the liquid ingredients are mixing. Add the dry ingredients when the initial rapid mixing is complete and the machine signals.
- ✓ When the breadmaker cycle is complete, carefully remove the pan from the machine and allow it to cool before serving.
- ✓ Remove the bread from the pan, put in a wire rack to Cool about 5 minutes.
- ✓ Slice

646) ***Potato Thyme Bread***

Ingredients:

- 12 slice bread (1½ pounds)
- 1¼ cups milk, at 80°F to 90°F
- 2 tablespoons melted butter, cooled
- 1 tablespoon honey
- 1½ teaspoons salt
- 1 teaspoon dried thyme
- ½ cup instant potato flakes
- 3 cups white bread flour
- 2 teaspoons bread machine or instant yeast

Direction: PREP: 10 MINUTES /MAKES 1 LOAF

- ✓ Preparing the Ingredients. Choose the size of loaf of your preference and then measure the ingredients.
- ✓ Add all of the ingredients mentioned previously in the list.
- ✓ Close the lid after placing the pan in the bread machine.
- ✓ Select the Bake cycle Turn on the bread machine.
- ✓ Select the White/Basic setting, select the loaf size, and the crust color.
- ✓ Press start.
- ✓ When the breadmaker cycle is complete, carefully remove the pan from the machine and allow it to cool before serving.
- ✓ Remove the bread from the pan, put in a wire rack to Cool about 5 minutes.
- ✓ Slice

647) ***Caramelized Onion Bread***

Ingredients:

- ½ Tbsp butter
- ½ cup onions, sliced
- 1 cup water
- 1 Tbsp olive oil
- 3 cups Gold Medal Better for Bread flour
- 2 Tbsp sugar
- 1 tsp salt
- 1¼ tsp bread machine or quick active dry yeast

Direction: PREP: 10 MINUTES /MAKES 14 SLICES

- ✓ Preparing the Ingredients Melt the butter over medium-low heat in a skillet.
- ✓ Cook the onions in the butter for 10 to 15 minutes until they are brown and caramelized - then remove from the heat.
- ✓ Add each ingredient except the onions to the bread machine in the order and at the temperature recommended by your bread machine manufacturer.
- ✓ Select the Bake Cycle Close the lid, select the basic bread, medium crust setting on your bread machine and press start.
- ✓ Add ½ cup of onions 5 to 10 minutes before the last kneading cycle ends.
- ✓ Take out the baked bread from the bread machine and allow it to cool on a cooling rack.

648) ***Light Corn Bread***

Ingredients:

- 12 slice bread (1½ pounds)
- ¾ cup milk, at 80°F to 90°F
- 1 egg, at room temperature
- 2¼ tablespoons butter, melted and cooled
- 2¼ tablespoons honey
- ¾ teaspoon salt
- ⅓ cup cornmeal
- 2⅔ cups white bread flour
- 1¾ teaspoons bread machine or instant yeast

Direction: PREP: 10 MINUTES /MAKES 1 LOAF

- ✓ Preparing the Ingredients. Choose the size of loaf of your preference and then measure the ingredients.
- ✓ Add all of the ingredients mentioned previously in the list.
- ✓ Close the lid after placing the pan in the bread machine.
- ✓ Select the Bake cycle Turn on the bread machine. Select the White/Basic setting, select the loaf size, and the crust color.
  Press start.
- ✓ When the breadmaker cycle is complete, carefully remove the pan from the machine and allow it to cool before serving.
- ✓ Remove the bread from the pan, put in a wire rack to Cool about 5 minutes. Slice

649) ***Chive Bread***

Ingredients:

- ⅔ cup milk (70°F to 80°F)
- ¼ cup water (70°F to 80°F)
- ¼ cup sour cream
- 2 Tbsp butter
- 1½ tsp sugar
- 1½ tsp salt
- 3 cups bread flour
- ⅛ tsp baking soda
- ¼ cup minced chives
- 2¼ tsp active dry yeast leaves

Direction: PREP: 10 MINUTES /MAKES 14 SLICES

- ✓ Preparing the Ingredients In the order and at the temperature specified by the maker of your bread machine, add each ingredient to the bread machine.
- ✓ Select the Bake cycle Close the lid, select the basic bread, medium crust setting on your bread machine and press start.
- ✓ Take out the baked bread from the bread machine and allow it to cool on a cooling rack.

650) ***Caramelized Onion Focaccia Bread***

Ingredients:

- 3/4 cup water

- 2 tablespoons olive oil
- 1 tablespoon sugar
- 1 teaspoon salt
- 2 cups flour
- 1 1/2 teaspoons yeast
- 3/4 cup mozzarella cheese, shredded
- 2 tablespoons parmesan cheese, shredded

Onion topping:
- 3 tablespoons butter
- 2 medium onions
- 2 cloves garlic, minced

Direction: PREP: 10 MINUTES /MAKES 4

- ✓ Preparing the Ingredients Place all ingredients, except cheese and onion topping, in your bread maker in the order listed above.
- ✓ Grease a large baking sheet.
- ✓ After 30 minutes in a warm place, shape the dough into a 12-inch circle on the pan.
- ✓ Melt butter in large frying pan over medium-low heat.
- ✓ Cook onions and garlic in butter 15 minutes, stirring often, until onions are caramelized. Preheat an oven to 400°F.
- ✓ Make deep depressions across the dough at 1-inch intervals with the handle of a wooden spoon.
- ✓ Spread the onion topping over dough and sprinkle with cheeses.
- ✓ Bake for 15–20 minutes, or until the tops are golden brown.
- ✓ Cut into wedges and serve warm.

651)   *Pumpkin Cinnamon Bread*

Ingredients:
- 1 cup sugar
- 1 cup canned pumpkin
- ⅓ cup vegetable oil
- 1 tsp vanilla
- 2 eggs
- 1½ cups all-purpose bread flour
- 2 tsp baking powder
- ¼ tsp salt
- 1 tsp ground cinnamon
- ¼ tsp ground nutmeg
- ⅛ tsp ground cloves

Direction:
- ✓ Preparing the Ingredients In the order and at the temperature specified by the maker of your bread machine, add each ingredient to the bread machine.
- ✓ Select the Bake Cycle Close the lid, select the quick, medium crust setting on your bread machine and press start.
- ✓ Take out the baked bread from the bread machine and allow it to cool on a cooling rack.

652)   *Potato Dill Bread*

Ingredients:
- 1 (.25 oz) package active dry yeast
- ½ cup water
- 1 Tbsp sugar
- 1 tsp salt
- 2 Tbsp melted butter
- 1 package or bunch fresh dill
- ¾ cup room temperature mashed potatoes
- 2¼ cups bread flour

Direction: PREP: 10 MINUTES /MAKES 14 SLICES

- ✓ Preparing the Ingredients In the order and at the temperature specified by the maker of your bread machine, add each ingredient to the bread machine.
- ✓ Select the Bake Cycle Close the lid, select the basic bread, medium crust setting on your bread machine, and press start.
- ✓ Take out the baked bread from the bread machine and allow it to cool on a cooling rack.

653)   *Tomato Basil Bread*

Ingredients:
- 3/4 cup warm water
- 1/4 cup fresh basil, minced
- 1/4 cup parmesan cheese, grated
- 3 tablespoons tomato paste
- 1 tablespoon sugar
- 1 tablespoon olive oil
- 1 teaspoon salt
- 1/4 teaspoon crushed red pepper flakes
- 2 1/2 cups bread flour
- 1 package active dry yeast Flour, for surface.

Direction: PREP: 10 MINUTES /MAKES 16 SLICES

- ✓ Preparing the Ingredients Add ingredients, except yeast, to bread maker pan in above listed order.
- ✓ Form a well in the flour and pour the yeast into it.
- ✓ Activate the Bake Cycle. Choose the Dough cycle and push the Start button.
- ✓ Knead the dough for 3 to 5 minutes, or until smooth and elastic, on a floured surface.
- ✓ Place in an oiled mixing bowl and turn once to grease the surface. Allow to rise in a warm area until doubled in size, about 1 hour.
- ✓ Knead dough for 1 minute after punching it down.
- ✓ Form the dough into a circular loaf.
- ✓ Spread out on a greased baking sheet. Allow 1 hour for the dough to double in size.
- ✓ With a sharp knife, cut a large "X" in top of loaf. Bake at 375°F for 35-40 minutes or until golden brown.
- ✓ Remove from pan and cool on a cooling rack before serving.

Conclusion

When you are ready to enjoy fresh bread and get your hands flurry, this bread machine book serves up the perfect instructions and suggests the perfect recipes to satisfy your bread cravings without the guilt or failing your diet. This book includes tried and tested instructions about the best bread machine there is on the market.

Appendix Index

Made in the USA
Las Vegas, NV
11 January 2024